A Thorn in the Rosebush

A Thorn in the Rosebush

The American Bartók Estate and Archives During the Cold War, 1946–67

Carl S. Leafstedt

Copyright © Carl S. Leafstedt 2021
All rights reserved

ISBN 978-1-943596-23-2

KKL Publications LLC, Helena History Press
Reno, Nevada USA

Publishing scholarship about and from Central and East Europe
www.helenahistorypress.com

Distributed by IngramSpark and available through all major e-retail sites
info@helenahistorypress.com

Contents

Introduction. Francis. 1

Chapter 1

From Budapest to New York: Béla Bartók, Victor Bator,
and the Creation of an American Manuscript Collection 17

Victor Bator: My Experiences with Béla Bartók in the United States, 1940–45 45

Chapter 2

"Reasons for Bartók's Confidence in Me" 53

Battles in Philadelphia, I. The Third Piano Concerto, 1945–46 91

*Battles in Philadelphia, II. The Philadelphia Orchestra
and Bluebeard's Castle, 1951–52* 101

Chapter 3

One Will or Three? The Wills of 1940, 1943, and 1945 111

Correspondence: Estate Management, 1957–59 151

Chapter 4

Old Ties Bind 173

Correspondence: Estate Correspondence with the Bartók Heirs, 1957–63 195

Chapter 5

The Early Years of the American Bartók Estate, 1945–53 209

Correspondence: The Litigation of 1959–61 233

Chapter 6

A Thorn in the Rosebush 245

Chapter 7

Per Finire 313

Acknowledgements 331

Works Cited 335

Appendix A

*Victor Bator: Memorial Speech On the 15th Anniversary
of Bartók's Death (1960)* 341

Appendix B

*Victor Bator: "The Hungarian Problem, from Memorandum
on the History of the Bartók Estate (1959–60)* 349

Appendix C

Victor Bator: Affidavit in the Litigation Proceedings of 1959–61 (1960) 385

Appendix D

Victor Bator: Bartók, Politics, and "Dollar Imperialism" (ca. 1952–53) 395

For Francis Bator and Benjamin Suchoff, in gratitude

Introduction. Francis.

> "I've been waiting thirty years for someone to call me about this. So, yes, I'm glad to talk with you."
>
> —Francis Bator, 2010

When I wrote to Francis Bator in 2010 to inquire about his father's involvement with the Estate of Béla Bartók, I had no idea what I'd hear back, or even if I'd hear back. Francis was then retired from Harvard University, where he was Littauer Professor of Political Economy emeritus at the Kennedy School of Government. His email address was listed online. Whether he was still alive, or in a position where his health would allow him to remember events of a half century ago, I could not predict. Clearly, I didn't yet know Francis. He replied politely within 24 hours. We set up a time to talk by phone.

In our first conversation he was encouraging and helpful, but also somewhat wary. No wonder. The American Bartók Estate had been in his father's care from 1945 to 1967, during the post-war period when Bartók's music attained considerable popularity around the globe, driven by musicians' interest in performing and recording works like the Concerto for Orchestra, the Third Piano Concerto, the six string quartets, and the *Mikrokosmos*. Francis and his two brothers had been children when their parents found themselves in the position of helping the Bartók family in New York City. Bator family vacations from time to time absorbed Béla and Ditta Bartók into the flow of guests at their summer home on the coast of Massachusetts. Victor Bator managed the Bartók Estate on behalf of the heirs. Sadly, over time his relationship with the Bartók family broke down, aggravated by the determined manipulation of the heirs by the communist government in Hungary, as well as suspicions and jealousies caused by the large amount of money the Estate was earning by the 1950s. All three Bator boys when older found themselves reluctantly pulled into the swamp of legal squabbles that engulfed the Bartók Estate.

"What can you tell me about your father?" I asked. And off we went. After several long phone conversations about his father's life and ties to the Bartók world, Francis became increasingly supportive of my inquiries. He took me into his confidence, remembering long dormant stories and bits of information in his mind about his family's history of involvement with the Bartóks. ("My two brothers took piano lessons from Ditta in 1944 or so. There in our home. It was done by my parents more out of charity, I think, a way they could help her earn money and gain some independence.") He spoke candidly about the inner

Introduction. Francis

workings of the Bartók Estate, and about all the Hungarians in his parents' social circle. He spoke freely about Peter Bartók, who he felt had turned unjustly against his father. I transcribed our phone interviews, then followed up with further questions, more and more intrigued by what I was learning. One day he wrote back, "Since we last spoke, I found a box of old Victor Bator/Bartók files and papers in my basement storage area here. It contains a treasure trove of stuff that will interest you." Perhaps if I could arrange my schedule, he suggested, I could come up to see these papers in person.

Who can refuse an offer like that? I flew up to Massachusetts. I spent two days in October 2010 visiting with Francis at his home near Boston. In his study he showed me the shelves holding his father's many books, and one by one he took me through their contents. He shared with me his family photo albums from pre-war Hungary, showing the Bator family at home, with friends, and on vacation. He showed me Zoltán Kodály's condolence card written after the death of his mother in 1962, and letters Harry Truman had written his father from the White House. Finally, he pulled out for me a stack of about 300 typed pages of business correspondence that his father had kept as a record of his involvement with the Bartók Estate. All were onionskin copies or photostats retained for reference; the originals had gone out in the mail in the 1950s and 60s, and most likely were lost by now, or, at best, saved haphazardly by their recipients. For two days Francis walked me through these photographs and letters, remembering names, court cases, personalities, and telling me what he knew.

Warming to the project, over the next few months he made introductions for me with old friends of his, still alive, who knew his father personally or by reputation. I conducted phone interviews with some. From others I received letters and emails. With Lajos Vékás, former Rector of the Law School at Eötvös Loránd University, I enjoyed a long lunch at a restaurant tucked away in a courtyard on the Buda hill, where he spoke to me at length about Victor Bator's reputation as a legal scholar in Hungary. Learning about the Bator family and the decades of litigation the Estate went through became an ongoing series of revelations, especially when Francis's version of events meshed so well with court records and correspondence he had preserved. The scales fell from my eyes. I realized that most of what I had heard over the years about Bator and the Estate was wrong. His side of the story had never been told. At a 2011 Bartók conference in Hungary I presented my initial discoveries in a talk titled "Rediscovering Victor Bator, Founder of the New York Bartók Archives." For *Studia Musicologica* I wrote up my findings as part of the conference proceedings.[1]

---

[1] Carl Leafstedt, "Rediscovering Victor Bator, Founder of the New York Bartók Archives," *Studia Musicologica* 53/1–3 (2012): 349–72.

Francis, I discovered to my pleasure, was an uncommonly gifted conversationalist. As former Deputy National Security advisor for the White House in the mid-1960s, he possessed an inexhaustible supply of stories about Lyndon Johnson and the US presidency. He established, as founding chairman, the public policy program at Harvard University, now known as the Kennedy School of Government. He had been professionally involved in economics and government his entire life, and even in his 80s his memories were crisp and specific. His recall was exceptional. An amateur downhill ski racer in his youth, skilled enough to warrant a feature profile and cover photo in an American ski magazine, he still retained the bearing of a former athlete: light on his feet, active, fit in body and mind. His eyes sparkled with amiable intelligence. With the habits of a lifelong professor, he would ease into his favorite topics and talk in well-formed paragraphs about Hungarian politics in the 1930s, or about U.S. involvement in Vietnam. Wit he savored. "You know what they say about the perils of writing history," he said with an economist's smile and a slight pause before delivering the punch line. "It's just inference from a data set of one."

His father had worked alongside numerous high-level figures in Hungarian politics and business prior to emigration in 1939, including the Weiss and Chorin families. Béla Imrédy, a former classmate, had been an upstairs neighbor. Tibor Eckhardt was a friend in Hungary and later in the US, when he and Bator and several others conspired to form a Hungarian government in exile. The Bators counted people like Allen Dulles, Bauldwin Maull, and Candler Cobb as family friends here in the US, their friendships sometimes dating back to business work together in Europe in the 1920s and 30s. Paul Kempner, director of Mendelssohn Bank in the 1930s prior to its Nazification, remained a close friend later in the U.S., as did another old acquaintance from Budapest, Marc McNitzky, who later became a prominent New York investment banker. (In Budapest McNitzky had been a staff writer for the leading business newspaper, *Pester Lloyd*.) As time went on musicians like Arthur Schnabel, Yehudi Menuhin, Wilhelm Backhaus, and Joseph Szigeti became familiar figures to the Bator children. Francis warmly reminisced about taking walks with Schnabel and his wife at the Waldhaus resort in Switzerland in 1947. The more we talked, the more a lost world began to reappear, all of it valuable context for a study of the Bartók Estate.

Victor Bator's papers, I felt, seemed worthy of publication on their own. With Francis's encouragement I began to mull ideas for a book. "You'd better get moving on that," he cautioned. "I'm not going to be around forever." Had I reached him even a few years earlier, he might have lived to see this project

Introduction. Francis

through completion. As it turns out, our last conversation took place in January 2018, just two months before his death.[2]

* * *

At its peak the Béla Bartók Archives was one of the largest archives in the world devoted to the legacy of a single artistic figure. Launched at the height of the Cold War, the same year as John F. Kennedy's "Ich bin ein Berliner" speech in West Berlin, the archives contained approximately 90% of the world's Bartók materials.[3] The core of its holdings was the comprehensive collection of autograph manuscripts and folk song materials Bartók carefully assembled in the late 1930s with the intent of preserving them intact in the coming war. The archives also contained an extraordinary collection of correspondence—over 3,000 letters—dating from Bartók's entire career; carefully ordered binders containing originals and copies of most known photographs of Bartók; personal copies of concert programs he had played; dozens of publisher's contracts; household business documents, including individual items such as passports, Social Security Cards, U.S. visa paperwork, even complete runs of his U.S. bank statements and cancelled checks. Also in the collection were extensive holdings from his career as a folk music researcher, including drafts, field recordings, and preparatory materials for the studies of Rumanian, Turkish, and Serbo-Croatian folk music that remained unpublished at the time of his death. The archive even boasted a collection of Bartók-themed art: busts, bronzes, medallions, and, most notably, the Róbert Berény oil portrait that came to the archive in 1957. For research purposes the archive staff accumulated a comprehensive clippings file of articles and reviews from around the globe, all carefully arranged in binders. Microfilms and high-quality copies were made of all the scores to facilitate scholarly study. What had been saved of Bartók's own U.S. personal library after his death—the foreign language dictionaries and other books on his shelves—could also be examined.

Acting on behalf of Bartók's widow, and guided by memories of his own conversations with the composer about his goals for his legacy, for over two decades Victor Bator negotiated with publishers, recording company executives, musicologists, musicians, and anyone interested in the performance or propa-

---

2 Highlights from Francis Bator's career can be found in his obituary in *The New York Times* ("Francis Bator, 92, White House Economist," *The New York Times*, Wednesday, March 21, 2018). His passing also received notice in *The Wall Street Journal* and *The Boston Globe*.

3 Percentage figures such as this one, of course, can only be approximations. In the international community of Bartók scholars the 90% figure was commonly used when I first entered the field in the 1990s. It no longer holds.

Introduction. Francis

Fig. 1.1. The Béla Bartók Archives, 28 E. 72nd Street, New York. Photograph (1963) of the original vaults, showing Benjamin Suchoff (left) and Victor Bator (right) in consultation.
Source: Bator, *The Béla Bartók Archives*. Photographer: uncredited.

gation of Bartók's music. He played a vital role in the reception history of Bartók's music in the U.S. and internationally. He ensured the Bartók family's financial wellbeing, and generally looked out for their interests. He used his extensive network of contacts, for example, to help Ditta Bartók return to Hungary in 1946. Among his many achievements was the publication of Bartók's monumental *Rumanian Folk Music* beginning in 1967. In the late 1940s he began to collect souvenirs and mementos of Bartók's career. The idea of establishing an archive came to him over time. Bator's firm, business-like manner and positional authority as trustee gave him the upper hand in most negotiations. Many people owning Bartók memorabilia were quite content to buy into his vision of a Bartók archive. Others resisted, requiring more direct methods of persuasion, which he deployed as needed. Universal Edition and Boosey & Hawkes finally yielded to his negotiating, turning over to him their extensive holdings of Bartók correspondence for safekeeping in the Archives. The battle royale between Bator and Paul Sacher over the Stefi Geyer violin concerto manuscript is perhaps the best-known episode from these collection-building days. (More about this history can be found below, in Chapter 6.)

5

Introduction. Francis

When it opened its doors to the public in 1963 the Béla Bartók Archives was housed in an attractive office suite on New York City's Upper East Side (Fig. 1.1). It welcomed serious researchers and had an on-site staff of part-time musicologists ready to provide help. A handsomely produced booklet, published in 1963, announced its opening to the world.[4] Putting to rest any doubts about its ambitions and financial strength, on its board of directors could be found Joseph Szigeti and Yehudi Menuhin, renowned musicians with long records of advocating for Bartók's music, and Paul Henry Lang of Columbia University, one of the most prominent musicologists of the mid-20th century. Also on the board were Victor Bator, Francis Bator, and Charles Szladits. By 1966 they had been joined by Antal Doráti and Eugene Ormandy, even Leslie Boosey. An elegant little pamphlet was produced for inclusion in the many brochure racks found near the entrances of museums, theaters, and concert halls around New York City (Fig. 1.2). Behind the scenes, conversations were underway to place the Archives at Lincoln Center, Columbia University, NYU, or some other center of learning in the United States. Funding, most important, was plentiful.

What could possibly go wrong?

* * *

On September 26, 1945, Béla Bartók died in a New York City hospital. He was buried in Ferncliff Cemetery in Westchester County, some 25 miles north of Manhattan. He had lived in the shadow of chronic illness for most of his final years in the United States. After his hospitalization for exhaustion and symptoms of leukemia in early 1943, and in light of the ongoing war, he prepared a Last Will and Testament in case he should die abroad. In that will he named Victor Bator and Gyula Báron as executors, and co-trustees of a trust that would form upon his death. The named beneficiary of the trust was to be his wife Ditta. His two sons, Béla Jr. and Peter, were assigned subsidiary roles. Béla Jr. still lived in Hungary, at the time an enemy country officially at war with United States. Peter was 19 years old.

This Last Will and Testament cast the die for what was to come. Fair and reasonable in its disposition of assets (it had been drafted by a well regarded attorney in New York City), it gave considerable authority to Bator and Báron as trustees, empowering them with managing the Estate's business affairs on behalf of Ditta Bartók. Trusteeship, in American law, carried then, as it still does today, firm expectations of fiduciary responsibility. Trustees are required

---

4 Victor Bator, *The Béla Bartók Archives: History and Catalogue* (New York: Bartók Archives Publication, 1963).

Fig. 1.2. Tri-fold pamphlet produced in late 1966 for distribution around New York City. Source: BSCB Tampa. Photographer: G.D. Hackett.

to responsibly administer the material property of the trust for the benefit of the beneficiaries. High standards for "duty of care" and "duty of loyalty" also apply.

Several early bumps notwithstanding, relationships between Bator and the Bartók heirs unfolded smoothly in the late 1940s as they all grew into their new roles. Conflict arose only later. In Bartók's last days a revised Last Will and Testament had been drafted and prepared for his signature. It stipulated different terms for his wife and two sons. Death came too suddenly, not just for the Viola Concerto's completion, but also for the new will, which never got signed. For Peter Bartók the unsigned deathbed will was further proof of the mistreatment his father experienced in his last days at the hands of those supposed to be caring for him.[5] Later the Hungarian communist government, not unexpectedly, refused to acknowledge the 1943 American will's legitimacy. Using imaginative lawyering and bully tactics, it pressed courts to nullify it in favor of the Hungarian will Bartók had reviewed and signed in 1940 in Hungary. Even though only one was legally valid at the time of his death, Bartók's three known wills (1940, 1943, 1945) went on to become legal fodder during the Cold War era. I tell this

---

5 Peter Bartók, *My Father* (Homosassa, FL: Bartók Records, 2002), 137.

Introduction. Francis

story below. As recently as 2017 the Hungarian government—under Viktor Orbán now tilting strongly in the opposite political direction—was making quiet inquiries about Bartók's Will through its US embassy in Washington. Francis Bator called me one day out of the blue. "Carl, I've just been contacted by the Hungarian legation in Washington. They're asking to come see me about Bartók's Will. Why?! What could they possibly have in mind that I can help them with? I don't even have a copy of it." His veteran political mind engaged, and more than a little irritated with the intrusion, Francis decided to stonewall the inquiry. Conversation with him would be of little use, he warned the Hungarians. He reported back to me several weeks later that "this had stopped them." His father, I thought, would have been proud.

Before its doors even opened, the Béla Bartók Archives became enmeshed in litigation now infamous for its epic length. By the early 1950s the American Bartók Estate had drawn the attention of the Hungarian communist government, which began to manipulate the situation through Bartók's two sons and his widow, a process which would accelerate in intensity over the next ten years. Ditta Bartók, now back in Hungary, emotionally frail, and locked away without a passport behind the Iron Curtain, had no choice. She had to accede to the government's position. A feud began, or, more properly: feuds. Control of Bartók's legacy became a matter of deep importance for many parties. Its income stream was considerable: over $100,000 a year by the early 1960s—all in hard currency.

In 1959 the Estate was subjected to its first legal action from a Bartók heir. Peter Bartók filed a claim in New York Surrogate's Court that year to challenge certain aspects of an accounting report Victor Bator had prepared. He was encouraged in this action by his step-brother and mother, both of whom were hostage to the wishes of the communist regime. Suddenly, removing Bator as trustee became the goal. Peter's fateful step marked the beginning of his life's work litigating against the Estate. In a 1961 judgment the Surrogate's Court denied his complaints in all respects. The Hungarian People's Republic pushed for control of the Estate through courts in New York, Vienna, and Budapest. These and other claims occupied court systems throughout the 1960s and 70s. When he died in 1967, Victor Bator could not have predicted that the Bartók Archives he created and announced to the world would have its doorway darkened by the shadow of continuous litigation for another 18 years.

Physical access to the Archives became difficult in the late 1960s. Minus the manuscripts, which were kept in a bank vault in Manhattan, the entire collection was moved out to Long Island at the direction of successor trustee Benjamin Suchoff. Armed with lawyers, and with the support of Bator's three sons (now reluctantly involved as co-executors of their father's own Estate), Suchoff directed the Bartók Archive's activities for many years, continuing its practice of producing edited volumes that enhanced the availability of Bartók's life work. Eventually he renamed it the New York Bartók Archive.[6] He handled the burden of litigation—evidence hearings, correspondence, affidavits, meetings with lawyers, court appearances, letters from Peter filled with demands—while managing the ongoing business affairs. He edited two volumes of Bartók's early piano music for Dover Editions and produced the landmark English-language reference collection of Bartók's writings, *Bartók Essays*, in 1976. Over bitter opposition from Peter Bartók he saw into print one of the Archive's landmark achievements, the 5-volume posthumous edition of Béla Bartók's Rumanian folk music studies (1969–75).

Litigation over the American Bartók Estate lasted 36 years, from 1959 to 1985. It ended only with the death of Ditta Bartók in Budapest in December 1982 and the reversion of her legal rights as beneficiary to her son Peter, then living in Florida. An extra two and a half years were required for probate and to clear up residual plaintiffs' and third party complaints.

Once the Archives collection was legally his, in 1985 Peter transferred it from New York to Florida—thus taking the "New York" out of its name, an action as symbolic as it was practical. He physically moved the entire collection over 1,000 miles south. (He had lived in Florida since 1973.) According to legend he rented a truck, drove straight to the bank vault and loaded everything in. He stopped in Long Island long enough to collect everything else from storage. In June of 1985 the manuscripts for the three piano concertos, most of the quartets, *Miraculous Mandarin*, *Bluebeard's Castle*, and thousands of other autograph pages lumbered down Interstate 95 in a rental truck to Florida—past all the rest stops, past the ubiquitous Roy Rogers and McDonald's restaurants, past one Sunoco station after another, all headed to a quiet residential area on the gulf coast, Homosassa, known internationally as a wintertime haven for Florida's most charismatic endangered species, the manatee, and, in East Coast cultural circles, as the inspiration a century earlier for Winslow Homer's idyllic watercolors of fly fishermen pursuing tarpon in mangrove-lined inlets. To this quiet setting on Florida's gulf coast the vast holdings of the New York Bartók Archive were transferred. There they remained intact for many years. Until his death very recently, in December of 2020, Peter carefully preserved the Archives

---

6   As he explained to me, "I never really understood why Victor called it an Archive*s*—using the plural. Maybe it was because it was both the Estate and an Archive? In any event, I just called it what it was. The Hungarians had their own Bartók Archive in Budapest by then, and I thought it would be helpful to put 'New York' back in the name" (Suchoff, interview with the author, June 19, 2002). In the musicology profession any permutation or minor variant of these names refers to the same collection.

Introduction. Francis

as a personal collection known formally as Bartók Records, the sound recording business he established in New York City in 1950. He hired staff to help him produce new editions of his father's music. He took over right where Bator and Suchoff left off. He handled permissions and all other business stemming from his father's remaining copyrights. It was, and still is, a not inconsiderable volume of work.

***

Like the editor in Vladimir Nabokov's *Pale Fire*, who, when beholding the underweave of a topic sees his self intercoiling "with the fate of an innocent author," my own life became entwined with this saga long ago. After completing my Ph.D. dissertation on *Duke Bluebeard's Castle*, when I moved to Texas in the mid-1990s I realized it was time to start studying the *other* end of Bartók's career. I had written enough, and spoken enough, on *Bluebeard*. (It took Bartók one year to write the opera. It took me seven years to write the dissertation and follow-up book. Time to move on.) I started teaching at Trinity University in the fall of 2001. A National Endowment for the Humanities summer research stipend encouraged me to conduct interviews with older musicians I could find who knew Bartók in their younger days. David Diamond, Storm Bull, Arthur Berger . . . through the lens of oral history my work on Bartók's years in America was launched. I sought out Suchoff at his office in Palm Beach, recording many hours of interviews about his experiences as trustee.

Any musicologist living in the state of Texas in those days knew Elliott Antokoletz as an important figure in North American Bartók studies. Antokoletz, then in the middle of his long teaching career at the University of Texas, had published his monumental study of Bartók's compositional language in 1984, changing the complexion of the field overnight. His fascination with the inner coherence and substance of Bartók's music produced numerous articles and one famous book so mindbogglingly rich it reshaped the field of Bartók studies around the world. Thirty-plus years of students in his Bartók seminars at UT-Austin read excerpts from his *The Music of Béla Bartók: A Study of Tonality and Progression in Twentieth-Century Music*. Most of them, to hear them talk, understood little beyond the opening chapters. But his intellectual fascination with Bartók's music captivated them. They became Bartók enthusiasts. They learned to recognize "z cells" and "x cells," and they learned through his clear, detailed prose how Bartók's basic language owed itself to folk sources and styles. Stories of Antokoletz's dazzling photographic memory were legion. "I covered that on page 83 of my book, footnote 4," he'd recall from memory with a quick grin and a little chuckle, as if to say I know it's unusual, but my brain just works like this. Antokoletz's intellectual energy and great personal charm as a human being made him a valuable mentor to many students and scholars around the United States.

I had gotten to know Antokoletz in the fall of 1989. For personal reasons I decided that year to take a leave of absence from my doctoral work at Harvard University. My future wife Ann was a law student at the University of Texas, and in order to put our lives together it made sense to put my studies on hold, move to Texas, and then resume the Ph.D. later on. Reassuring the skeptical Harvard music faculty of the soundness of my plan took some work. No, I wasn't abandoning the Ph.D. program; I actually planned to return. Christoph Wolff made a point of mentioning Elliott Antokoletz's name. "He's a very good violinist, Juilliard trained. He taught my daughter. Maybe you can take a course with him while you're down there. That will keep you involved in musicology." Several months later, newly settled in Austin, I contacted Elliott by phone, asking if I could come by to introduce myself. With a generosity I later came to see as entirely typical, he immediately suggested that I should sit in on a graduate Bartók seminar that started the following January. "Don't worry if you're not formally enrolled at the university. It'll be nice to have you in the class. You can just sit in."

And that's how it began. During that course Elliott shared with us the printer's proofs of an article he had just written on *Bluebeard's Castle* for *College Music Symposium*. That article, and the course material that semester, opened new horizons for me. I began to imagine possibilities for a doctoral dissertation topic. With his support I submitted to Harvard, one year later, a formal proposal to write my dissertation on *Bluebeard*. He agreed to serve as mentor from afar.

Through Elliott Antokoletz I was introduced to the dark underworld of Cold War and personal animosities that clouded the field of Bartók studies from the 1950s onward. Antokoletz's graduate students at the University of Texas all knew that he had been appointed Successor Trustee of the New York Bartók Archives. The stories were amazing. "What this means in legal terms," he liked to wrap up with, "is that basically Peter was suing his mother all those years." Elliott played an offstage role in the drama beginning in the 1980s, when Suchoff tapped the young Antokoletz to be his successor trustee should the need arise. Antokoletz never stepped into that role. He made that clear. He did become Suchoff's confidant, however, gaining inside access into the causes of the Bartók Estate's unrest. He later became the Estate's first public chronicler, pulling aside the veil of secrecy to review some of its later history.[7]

---

7   Elliott Antokoletz, "The New York Bartók Archives: Genesis and History," *Studia Musicologica* 53/1–3 (2012): 341–48.

Introduction. Francis

The imploding of the New York Bartók Archives in the 1960s–80s, and its subsequent removal to cloistered quarters, irreversibly harmed the serious study of Bartók's music for two generations of musicians. It seemed a tragic tale when we first heard it from Elliott. That he had also been directly involved in the University of Texas's effort to land both the Stravinsky and Bartók Estate materials in the 1980s for the Humanities Research Center, an effort which did not succeed, only added to the lore he passed on to students eager to learn from a man so intimately connected to the task of finding a safe resting place for the Estates of two giants of 20th-century music.[8]

Back in Boston two years later I began my doctoral work on Bartók with Reinhold Brinkmann as my advisor. Brinkmann, a German native and Schoenberg scholar, freely admitted that his record of research on Bartók was not extensive. In his younger days, he told me, he had closely studied at one time the structure of the first movement in *Music for Strings, Percussion, and Celesta*. Neither of us were worried. I felt eager to work with someone whose knowledge of 20th-century music seemed limitless to me. Any concerns about my choice of topic were eased for us both knowing that Antokoletz was on board. Early on we recognized that I would have to learn Hungarian if I had any hope of carrying out this study competently. Harvard like most North American schools being no place to study the Hungarian language through regular coursework, I arranged with the department's support to study Hungarian privately with tutors. (Adam Tolnay, Erika Kiss: thank you.) Gregory Nagy of the Classics Department two years later administered my Hungarian language exam. I wrote Peter Bartók with my first inquiry about *Bluebeard* sources in 1991. Large envelopes from Florida began to arrive by return mail, each filled with color photocopies of autograph scores.

In preparations for this book I chanced upon a letter Brinkmann had written as a young scholar in Germany to the New York Bartók Archives. On July 14, 1981, he wrote to Suchoff inquiring about the manuscript sources for *Music for Strings, Percussion, and Celesta*. "In my opinion it is a critical point in Bartók analyses that nobody refers to the autographs and that we know very little about the creative process of Bartók's composing," he explained. "I'm sure that I could pay for a microfilm if you send it to me." Suchoff's reply to this letter survives. His answer? No. "It is with regret," he explained, "that I must inform you of my inability to furnish you with a microfilm." "You will be most welcome to visit

---

8   Extensive correspondence documenting the Stravinsky and Bartók Estate negotiations is preserved in Antokoletz's private papers. The Humanities Research Center, now named after Harry Ransom, had recently obtained the massive Durand archive of autograph manuscripts and publication correspondence for the music of Ravel, Duparc, Fauré, Roussel, Debussy, and other French musicians.

with me at the New York Bartók Archive," he added by way of softening the news, "if at some future time you visit this country." He encouraged Brinkmann to correspond further with "Professor Dr. Elliott Antokoletz" at the University of Texas. "His work on Bartók is in my opinion primary, that is, it will supersede the (mostly unsupported) findings of various theorists here and abroad."[9]

Thus turned away, Brinkmann never returned to Bartók studies until he helped me with my dissertation. Many scholars of his generation had the door to Bartók studies closed on them just like this, through no fault of their own—and, to be perfectly fair, through no fault of Suchoff, whose hands were tied by litigation in ways he was reluctant to explain to outsiders. In 1982 László Somfai described as "rather hopeless" the state of serious musicological research into Bartók's music for scholars at the Budapest Bartók Archive, with "two separate groups" on opposite sides of the Atlantic and "growing frustration" among the entities charged with preservation of Bartók's musical legacy.[10] Somfai himself encountered vexing barriers to his research while at the Archives in 1968. Tibor Serly flew into regular rages when dealing with the Estate. What Eugene Ormandy thought when Bator refused his request to record *Bluebeard's Castle* in 1951 can well be imagined. (See below.)

Significant improvements became possible after 1985, particularly through the generous sharing program put in place between Peter Bartók and the Budapest Bartók Archive which resulted in high quality photocopies of the music manuscripts in the Florida collection being sent to Budapest. You couldn't consult the actual scores in Florida, but you could see high quality photocopies of those same scores in Budapest. (And later, exquisitely crisp *color* photocopies, also furnished by Peter.)[11] Peter freely shared photocopies of scores with young scholars like me. Many of us remember receiving packages in the mail from him, always accompanied by a cover letter he had typed himself on his distinctive, unchanging, cream-colored Bartók Records stationery. In 1996 Peter began the important, and to him, final process of physically transferring actual manuscripts to the Sacher Foundation in Basel, Switzerland, for safekeeping. That year there was an exhibition in Basel to honor Paul Sacher's 90th birthday. Peter arranged to have the autograph of *Music for Strings, Percussion, and Celesta* brought to Basel for inclusion in the exhibition. Two years later, in 1998, he

---

9 Benjamin Suchoff, letter to Reinhold Brinkmann, 25 July 1981. Copy preserved in private collection of Elliott Antokoletz, where a copy of Brinkmann's letter is also found.
10 László Somfai, "The Budapest Bartók Archives," proceedings of the IAML Annual Conference in Budapest, *Fontes Artis Musicae* 29/1–2 (Jan–June 1982): 62 and passim.
11 Using a high-end camera and a professional work station at his home in Florida, Peter Bartók produced four complete sets of color copies of the main music manuscripts in his collection. Of these four sets, one was sent to Budapest, one was sent after 2000 to Basel, and two were kept at his Bartók Records office in Florida, where they remain at the time of this writing.

delivered that same score to the Sacher Foundation for longterm safekeeping. In 2000 a more formal arrangement was concluded by which Peter Bartók would deliver to the foundation all the important manuscripts and letters in his possession, leaving them on deposit.

Today the Budapest Bartók Archívum and the Sacher Foundation both welcome visitors and maintain staffs with deep expertise in musicology. Working on premises at those locations is a joy, especially when surrounded by kindred spirits for whom musicological research is a primary expression of their love for music. Scholars learn early on, however, that access for publication purposes is still tightly controlled, and that some requests, particularly for autograph materials, simply can't be honored. Witness Brinkmann's perfectly reasonable inquiry from 1981. It's one reason there aren't more Bartók books out there. Or Bartók scholars.

I've often wondered how things got to this point.

Although the genesis of the Béla Bartók Archives has been described elsewhere, notably by Bator himself, after decades of litigation its inner dramas and turbulent existence completely obscured the nobility of its original purpose—certainly for today's observers. *So little* is known about what really went on. Bator never wrote publicly about the turmoil the Estate went through. Nor did Suchoff. Nor did the heirs. Their views were not secret, but little was said in print: the battles took place, for the most part, behind palace walls. Many musicians and scholars bore witness to the effects of constant litigation. The purpose of this book is to offer a different perspective on the history of the Bartók Estate. By recording its history from Victor Bator's point of view we gain crucial insight into the shaping of Bartók's post-war legacy. "The Estate *is* the history of Bartók's music after World War II," Francis Bator emphasized to me, exaggerating slightly to make his point. The correspondence included below shows plainly the role of the trustee in deciding how Bartók was written about, by whom, and in what languages. Trustees' influence can also be discerned in the outlines of Bartók's legacy in recorded sound. All of Peter Bartók's many recordings of his father's music in the 1950s, to take only one example, were funded by disbursements from the Estate; their production costs could be staggeringly high. (See Chapter 5.) Victor Bator gave Béla Bartók's son every advantage he needed to launch his career.

Correspondence from Victor Bator's desk is reproduced for the first time in aggregate below, together with a selection of longer documents from the years when the estate was mired in Cold War politics. In them we see the issues developing clearly, before the veil of litigation forced the estate into a fraught position in the eyes of the international musicological community, publishers, and record companies. From the letters Francis Bator preserved at his home in

Massachusetts I have chosen a representative selection. To those letters I have added several primary documents (Appendix) that reveal how Hungarian communist government agencies tried to wrest the Estate and Archives from Bator. Throughout the book I draw liberally on Victor Bator's 310-page Memorandum on the History of the Bartók Estate, which survives in a single copy in the Benjamin Suchoff Collection of Bartókiana at the University of South Florida. None of this material has been published before. Its publication is made possible by permission of Francis Bator, who before he died gave me his principled blessing to develop this material into a book.[12] In Chapter 6 I explain the title of the book.

To avoid excess explication, I arrange the book in two parallel streams, alternating my own writing with groupings of Bator's letters, allowing the necessary interpretive background to flow around and across the primary documents which tell their own tales. Bator's firm authorial voice is bracing to read. He spoke with authority. I see no reason to relegate his voice to the end, which would be the customary practice for a documentary study.[13]

---

12 In the wake of Francis's death, his son Christopher Bator kindly granted permission to publish the documents in this book. I am grateful to the Bators for their ongoing support of this project.
13 See, by way of example, the approach Donald Maurice uses in his outstanding documentary study of the Viola Concerto (*Bartók's Viola Concerto: The Remarkable Story of His Swansong* [New York: Oxford University Press, 2004]).

Chapter 1

From Budapest to New York: Béla Bartók, Victor Bator, and the Creation of an American Manuscript Collection[1]

Among scholars and archivists who work with Bartók's autograph materials the story of how the bulk of his manuscript collection came to the United States has long been familiar in its general outlines. By the mid-1930s Bartók had grown increasingly worried about his future. His concern extended to his autograph scores, and even more important, to his ongoing folksong research, which he sensed might soon be interrupted. Hungary, he lamented, was "the home of uncertainty" after 1935. Events in Europe darkened his mood, feeding a pessimism he gave full expression to in letters from the time. After the Anschluss he wrote to Sándor Albrecht:

> The political events of the recent past will shortly put me into a critical position: a major part of my works has fallen into the hands of gangs of robbers, similarly the handling of all performance fees. If I do not succeed in some manner in escaping from their clutches, then evil days will follow for me... There is the imminent danger that Hungary will surrender to this regime of thieves and murderers. The only question is—when and how? And how can I go on living in such a country or—which means the same thing—working, I simply cannot conceive. As a matter of fact, I would feel it my duty to emigrate, so long as that were possible.[2]

When Universal Edition yielded to the inevitable and fell under Nazi control, he sought another publisher. Boosey & Hawkes stepped in. Imagining a time soon when he'd need to leave Hungary, he sifted through his personal collection of scores. He began to sort the manuscripts with the idea of assembling

---

1 Portions of this chapter were published previously in "Rediscovering Victor Bator, Founder of the New York Bartók Archives," *Studia Musicologica* 53/1–3 (September 2012): 349–72. Reproduced by permission.
2 Béla Bartók, letter to Sándor Albrecht, April 12, 1938. As translated by Tibor Tallián in *Béla Bartók: The Man and His Work* (Budapest: Corvina, 1981), 198.

them into a mobile collection.³ He decided to leave in Budapest some of his juvenilia and student works—scores which later served as inspiration for the establishment of the Budapest Bartók Archívum. The body of work he wished to preserve, from *Kossuth* on, he assembled into folders numbered 1-51A, pulling together for each work any sketches, drafts, completed autographs, and manuscript copies he had in his possession. Always thorough by nature, he also made a list of missing and lost manuscripts at this time.

Letters to his closer acquaintances abundantly document the importance he placed in getting these manuscripts out of Hungary to safe harbor. To Szigeti in December 1938 he confessed,

> As I have written to you before, I've conceived a loathing for all of Europe. I would like to get away for good, for the rest of my life. The trouble is that I am already 57 years old. To put down roots at a new place somewhere in a foreign land is a dangerous adventure. I have already taken my manuscripts into Switzerland, but even there I don't think that they are safe. Have you anybody in the U.S. or an institution who would be willing to take these mementos on deposit? It would be even better if I found a purchaser: I need the money for the publication of my scholarly works (collections), much money...⁴

Stefi Geyer, he hoped, could courier the manuscripts to safety in Switzerland. When that became difficult—the Anschluss forestalled her planned visit to Budapest—he sent them by mail instead to Annie Müller-Widmann in Basel, whom he knew and trusted as a friend of Paul Sacher. Geyer, one of his oldest friends from their conservatory days together, was married to Walther Schulthess, owner of a concert promotion business and music store in Zürich. She and her husband heard from Bartók again in March 1939. Their help was still needed. Could they collect the manuscripts from Ms. Müller-Widmann and send them along to London? Parallel instructions were sent to Müller-Widmann. In a moving passage he revealed to his Basel supporter his state of mind, explaining what he would like her to do:

> These last events (you must know by now what I mean—the overrunning and incorporation of Czechoslovakia) appear to me alarming and

---

3   László Somfai records the chronology of what he calls Bartók's "general sorting" of manuscripts in 1938–39 in *Béla Bartók: Composition, Concepts, and Autograph Sources* (Berkeley, CA: University of California Press, 1996), 26-27.
4   Béla Bartók, letter to József Szigeti, December 1, 1938. Working translation prepared by the New York Bartók Archives staff (BSCB Tampa). Punctuation and syntax corrected by the author.

dangerous. (I am convinced that you are over there concerned yourselves also.) I felt I ought to take, though with very heavy heart, precautionary measures. This is the reason that I request you to send to my new publishers, Boosey & Hawkes, 295 Regent Street, London, my manuscripts, accompanied by their list. Please do not send them all together, and not on the same day, but divided as to time also… After all, London is somewhat further away from the land of horror. This is a sad step for me, but, on the other hand, I find a little consolation in the fact that this relieves you of a certain responsibility… God only knows what else is going to happen and… you understand what I mean. Really, these manuscripts should go to America, but I do not as yet have anyone there. I am full of anxiety. I wish I could leave this place today, but perhaps nothing matters much more.[5]

Through Schulthess's Zürich office, five packages containing manuscript folders 1-51A were mailed to London on April 15.[6] They were received at Boosey & Hawkes offices two days later. A copy of the accompanying inventory's first page (Fig. 1.1) shows how Bartók had assembled and numbered his collection. The process now well underway, he rounded up more manuscripts in Budapest, and when he embarked on his last European concert tour in June, he brought the remainder with him to Basel, again depositing them with Mrs. Müller-Widmann for safekeeping. She forwarded this latest batch to London on his behalf. Receipt of those manuscripts completed a sequential deposit process that had started almost a year earlier, in May 1938, when Bartók sent three earlier manuscripts to his new publisher, including the Second Piano Concerto, asking him to hold onto them as a favor.[7] Bator, who knew this facet of the composer's mind as well as anyone, writes that the preservation of these autograph manuscripts had become a "solemn and insistent concern" for the composer by the late 1930s.[8]

During this entire time he was preoccupied with composing. In an extraordinary burst of productivity he drafted the Divertimento and Sixth Quartet, assembled the *Mikrokosmos* into their final form, and put the finishing touches on all new works he had composed since 1936, including the Violin Concerto,

---

5   Béla Bartók, letter to Annie Müller-Widmann, April 8, 1939. As translated in Victor Bator, *The Béla Bartók Archives: History and Catalogue*, 13.
6   Walther Schulthess, letter to Boosey & Hawkes, April 15, 1939. Schulthess's letter was accompanied by a 3-page typed inventory that itemizes the manuscript folders and their placement in the five packages being sent to London that day. A copy of the letter and inventory is preserved in BSCB Tampa.
7   Bartók, letter to Ralph Hawkes, May 8, 1938 (BBC-PSS Basel).
8   Bator, *The Béla Bartók Archives*, 13.

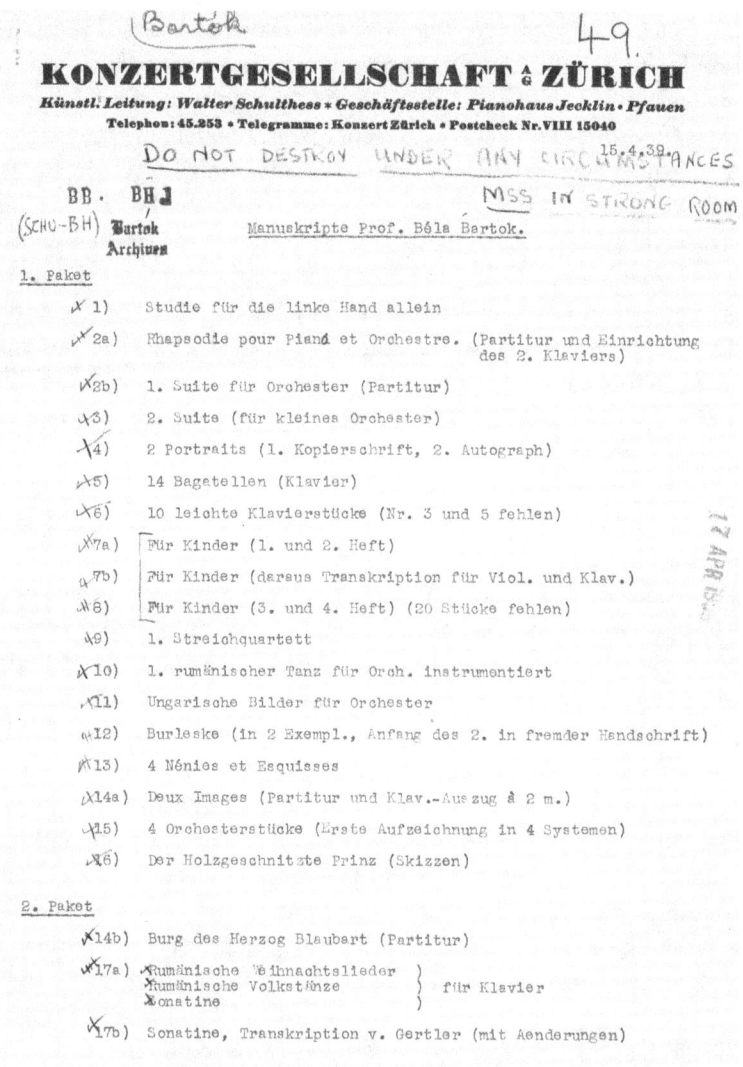

Fig. 1.1. Page 1 of the inventory prepared by Walther Schulthess's firm to accompany Bartók's manuscripts when mailed from Switzerland to London on April 15, 1939. Source: BBC-PSS Basel.

Contrasts, and the Sonata for Two Pianos and Percussion, the last of which had received a flurry of additional performances since its premiere in Basel on January 16, 1938. Some of these most recent manuscript scores were still in his possession, evidently, when he left Hungary in early 1940 for his exploratory tour of the United States. The next steps became apparent to him. London was "further away from the land of horror." But New York was even further. Once Columbia University announced its awarding of an honorary degree and gave him specific promise of working on the Parry collection, Bartók knew he had found a viable path forward.

Before he left New York he took one extra step that left his luggage a little lighter going home. On May 15, 1940, just days before his scheduled departure, he created a new legal trust that authorized two trustees to care for and, if necessary, sell certain manuscripts on his behalf. Schulhof and Heinsheimer, his managers at the time, must have helped him implement this idea as security for his future in the United States. Into the trust Bartók placed seven of his recent manuscripts; these scores had travelled with him to New York and were ready to convey into safe hands. They are listed on the trust document as follows:

MIKROKOSMOS	153 Piano Pieces
DIVERTIMENTO	String Orchestra (Rough copy and final copy)
VIOLIN CONCERTO	Orchestral Score (Final copy)
6TH STRING QUARTET	
3 PIECES FOR CLARINET – VIOLIN and PIANO	(Rough and final copies)[9]

Two trustees were identified: George Herzog and Ralph Hawkes. According to the document's language they were given "power to sell the manuscripts, and to collect and receive the proceeds therefrom." Any funds received from the sale were to be used 1) "to pay for the Grantor's collection of Romanian and Slovakian folk music until the entire costs of production and publication of the said collection shall have been paid in full;" 2) any remaining funds were "to be paid to the Grantor during his lifetime;" and 3) in the event of his death, the income was "to be paid to and divided equally share and share alike among Edith Bartok, his widow, and his sons, Bela Bartok, Jr. and Peter Bartok, or the survivors of them, such payments to be made semi-annually." In accordance with New York state law the trustees were given broad powers to sell or retain these specific manuscripts. They "shall only be required to act according to their best judgment," the signed document read. The manuscripts had already been

---

9   A copy of this 3-page, typed trust agreement is found in BBC-PSS Basel, in the Ralph Hawkes correspondence. Who drafted the trust agreement for Bartók cannot be reconstructed; probably it was an attorney or law firm familiar to Boosey & Hawkes staff. In the spring of 1940 Victor Bator was not yet involved in Bartók's business matters.

received for safekeeping at Boosey & Hawkes's New York offices.[10] Three days later, on May 18, Béla Bartók was back on board a ship, returning to Europe.

On its surface obviously a wartime document, conceived in difficult circumstances, this 1940 trust agreement reveals the desperate measures Bartók was willing to contemplate in order to avoid the risk that his folk music research might die with him, unfinished and unpublished. Selling manuscripts? He had always found this notion distasteful. Now, apparently, he would condone such a sacrifice if it helped him achieve larger goals.[11] Without Herzog the plan could not have been conceived. Any actions or decisions while Bartók was abroad would depend on Herzog's familiarity with the academic world of folk song research and publication. Now, at the very least, some of his most recent autograph manuscripts were secure. These seven autographs became the first installment of manuscripts to find their way to America, a vanguard, a beachhead, as it were, for the larger collection soon to arrive.[12]

As a first step in end-of-life planning, the trust agreement initiated trains of thought that would lead Bartók later that fall, back in Budapest, to prepare his Last Will and Testament. This new Hungarian Will would specifically reference the American trust. (See Chapter 3.) The significance of the 1940 American trust becomes clearer when viewed in the larger context of Bartók's final years. For the first time he had created a wall of legal protection around his autograph manuscripts. They were no longer just stored on the proverbial shelf. The trust offered protections for the manuscripts under American law, and provided guardians in the form of trustees who could carry out his expressed wishes. Importantly, it specified co-trustees, not just a single trustee; his later American will would do the same. He had little time to absorb the conse-

---

[10] A statement was prepared by Ralph Hawkes on May 13, 1940, acknowledging receipt of these manuscripts and indicating they had been "put in vault." A copy of this statement showing Bartók's later annotations is preserved in BSCB Tampa.

[11] From his parents' generation and years of working for Victor Bator at the Archives, Iván Waldbauer retained a rich lore of stories. He spoke with me about the way Bartók's manuscripts arrived in the US. "Now, a little known fact. Bartók did bring with him all his manuscripts. He thought he could sell them. On his earlier trip to America he saw that libraries had musical scores in their possession, valued at various amounts of dollars, and he thought he could sell his own manuscripts and publish his Romanian folk music collection on little sheets. He didn't know these were tax dodgers. Rodgers and Hammerstein, after having a successful round of their latest musical, would donate their manuscript to the library in the value of a certain amount of money. This was essentially for tax purposes. No actual dollars transferred hands. When Bartók found this out, he had his manuscripts in a suitcase, and he went to Victor Bator and said, 'here it is, this is for you to take care of, help me to do something with them if you can.' This is the beginning of what would turn into the Bartók Archives" (Interview with the author, Nov. 29, 2010).

[12] The autograph manuscript of the Third Quartet had been housed in Philadelphia since 1928, when it was brought over by Bartók on his first American tour.

quences of its creation, but Bartók had just passed through an important conceptual barrier, drawing his collection forward into a different future.

When he returned to the United States in October 1940 he instructed his London publishers to forward the main manuscript collection to their New York offices.[13] They complied. There these manuscripts (1–51A) joined the seven more recent autographs to enlarge the corpus of the overall collection—physically joined, but also walled off from the first seven in legal terms: the trust still governed disposition of the earlier arrivals. (The new arrivals weren't part of the trust.) Eventually, much later, Bartók's attention circled around to this custodial discrepancy. In 1942, his own circumstances now somewhat more settled, at least in terms of whether he would stay in the United States, he decided to dissolve the trust. He was beginning to sense that the folk song collections might not be published once the US got dragged into the war. Rising levels of irritation with his representation by Boosey & Hawkes, especially its concert management division, weakened his faith in the firm. He instructed Ralph Hawkes to resign as trustee:

> You remember you signed as a co-trustee (with Dr. G. Herzog) a kind of agreement (or what it is called) concerning my manuscripts. Now, that I see how conditions here are, I realize that the purpose I wanted to attain with these manuscripts, can never be attained. Therefore, I ask you to agree with the cessation of this "agreement" and to send me a statement with your declaration of consent.[14]

Hawkes's reply is dated September 4, 1942. He agrees to the termination of the agreement. Herzog's response has not been preserved, but he had no reason not to agree, either. The trust formally terminated upon receipt of both their consent letters. Thus dissolved, its physical holdings now could join the larger collection—without moving an inch.

As of yet Bartók had no reason to change where the manuscripts were being stored. Whether or not he felt charitably towards his publisher, Boosey & Hawkes's offices on W. 23rd Street promised more security than his apartments. The arrangement made sense. For almost two years the manuscripts stayed at his publishers' offices, free of charge. During this time Victor Bator entered his

---

13 Suchoff, *Béla Bartók: Life and Work* (Lanham, MD: Scarecrow Press, 2001), 134. Victor Bator's preface to the Bartók Archives Catalogue (p. 13–14) gives the impression, likely inaccurate, that the manuscripts were forwarded to New York in 1939.
14 Béla Bartók, letter to Ralph Hawkes, August 3, 1942 (BBC-PSS Basel). Spelling and punctuation shown here as in the original. This excerpt is also reproduced in Bator, *The Béla Bartók Archives*, 14.

Chapter 1

life. They had met before, in Budapest, through common friends and acquaintances, but had no particularly strong basis for personal friendship. By 1942, though, Bartók was spending more time with Victor Bator than anyone else in the Hungarian expatriate community. That contact, and the relationship that followed, would affect the course of both men's lives. The manuscript collection soon changed homes, entering into the care of the man who would look after it for the next 34 years.

* * *

Well known to the field of Bartók studies in its early, formative stages, Victor Bator's name since the 1980s has slipped into that liminal state time forces on all of us. When I began my inquiries with his son in 2010, I knew little about him other than the stories I had heard while drinking coffee at conferences with older scholars. Years of listening to Elliott Antokeletz and Ben Suchoff talk about the Bartók Estate's messy history had given me what I thought were the general outlines. Imagination filled in the rest. My conversations with Francis Bator forced me to realize that the field of Bartók studies—all of us, it seemed—had lost sight of who Victor Bator had been before he entered Bartók's life in 1940. All we knew was *late* Bator, if you will, not early- and mid-Bator. Bartók placed extraordinary faith in Victor Bator when they found themselves together in New York. Why? Bartók, never one for casual decisions, or casual friendships, clearly felt comfortable placing his worldly affairs in Bator's hands. No parallels for this relationship can be found in his earlier life. His recent experiences with Paul Sacher may have lowered his habitual guard. With Sacher, as with Bator, and to a large degree with Annie Müller-Widmann, too, Bartók shed his resolute independence ever so little. He allowed into his life patrons whose support and commanding social position eased the stresses he felt when trying to escape the growing war.

Unlike the leaders of the Budapest Bartók Archive, Viktor Bátor (1891–1967) did not come to his role through musicology. "I really do not know much about music," he demurred in a public lecture about Bartók he gave in the early 1950s.[15] "He wasn't especially musical," his son affirmed.[16] Bátor, who anglicized his name to Victor Bator, was careful never to present himself as an expert on Bartók's music. Like many educated men and women of his generation in Hungary he placed high value on music, literature, theater, and art as ingredients in a life well-lived. His role in Bartók's Estate management thrust him into

---

15 Victor Bator, Lecture on Bartók and "Dollar Imperialism" (Appendix).
16 Francis Bator, Email communication with the author, October 3, 2012.

the world of professional musicians. He was no stranger there, however. He enjoyed a lifelong friendship with one of Hungary's leading violinists, Imre Waldbauer, and followed his career closely, attending concerts as a supporter. Public modesty about his ability in music was perhaps his natural response to being linked through historical circumstance to Béla Bartók.

His own professional achievements lay in other areas, as Bartók well knew. Victor Bator was born in Komárom, a small border city on the Danube River across from Slovakia. His father was a municipal lawyer. In an autobiographical sketch Bator mentions attending a Catholic school in Komárom, the San Benedikt Gymnasium, for part of his childhood.[17] He moved to Budapest in time for the 1904–5 school year. He continued his schooling at the 5th district's Állami Főgimnázium on Markó utca, where he graduated with distinction in 1909. He decided to attend the law program at Eötvös Loránd University. In 1911 he attended the summer session of the London School of Economics. Evidence of distinction in his academic studies became apparent when a paper he wrote on "The Role of Free Competition in National Economic Life" won a state prize in the 1910–11 school year. The following year he took the prize in the university's civil law area. His professors at law school included Béni Grosschmid (d. 1938), the great scholar of Hungarian civil law and its English common law antecedents; and Károly Szladits (d. 1956), whose six-volume *Magyar Magánjog* [Hungarian civil law, 1938–42], a project co-authored with two dozen legal scholars, including Bator and Miksa Teller, the father of physicist Edward Teller, would remain an important reference—"the Bible of Hungarian Civil Law"—until well into the 1990s.[18] Bator would later contribute essays to Festschrifts for both men, and serve on the editorial boards for those volumes.

Contemporaries of his at the university included Lóránt Nyevicsky, later a prominent lawyer; Tihamér Fabinyi, who would go on to become a renowned bank manager and Minister of Finance; and Béla Imrédy, whose political ambitions led him to the Presidency of the Hungarian National Bank in the 1930s, followed by a brief term as a notoriously right-wing Prime Minister from 1938–39.[19] Imrédy's name will reappear elsewhere in this book.

---

17 Dr. Viktor Bátor, application letter for a position with the Pesti Magyar Kereskedelmi Bank, R.T., October 24, 1918. Unpublished typescript with handwritten annotations, 4 p. Magyar Országos Levéltár, file number XXIX-L-1-g. This is the most authoritative source of information we have about Bator's early career. I draw freely from it in these paragraphs to establish the events of his life before 1920. Personal collection of Francis Bator.
18 Lajos Vékás, interview with the author, Budapest, July 15, 2011.
19 In the early 1990s Francis Bator commissioned Dr. János Botos, eminent historian of Hungarian banking, to research the life of his father in Hungarian archives. Botos's report, sent to Francis in 1995, and later shared with me, forms the basis for some of the information and perspectives in these paragraphs and in Chapter 2. I acknowledge his work with gratitude.

Chapter 1

After graduating in 1913 Victor Bator went to work at the law office of Dr. Arthur Szilágyi doing general business law for clients such as Skoda-Werke A.G., Dynamit-Nobel R.T., and Deutsche Bank. In World War I he served on the Italian and Russian fronts as an artillery officer. He spent approximately four years in the Hungarian army, receiving multiple decorations for meritorious service. He was wounded in the knee by a grenade. A portion of the thumb on one hand was blown off. That wounded thumb, his grandson Christopher Bator told me, would fascinate his grandchildren, whom he liked to tease with it. Family legend had it that Victor walked out of the country, on foot, to Austria during the troubles of 1919–20. "My father established his anti-communist credentials very early," Francis assured me.[20] After the war he began working as a lawyer for one of Budapest's leading banks, the Pesti Magyar Kereskedelmi Bank, in 1919, following a stint at the offices of Magyar-Cseh Iparbank. He was already capable of writing in four languages, including English. (He learned English in college, a somewhat unusual decision in those days; he put it to use immediately in his business career.) When Hungary went through the rounds of post-war negotiations that preceded the Treaty of Trianon, Bator was sent to Vienna as part of a delegation from the Hungarian government. From August 8 to December 20, 1919, he took part in international negotiations aimed at settling the outstanding business contracts and liabilities from suppliers to the Hungarian army.

This experience marked him in many ways, deepening an already strong interest in foreign affairs and economics. After 1921 he became known as a specialist in the financial repercussions of the Versailles treaty. The Commercial Bank, his employer, promoted him to the position of Deputy General Counsel in May 1921. Less than two years later the bank elevated him to General Counsel—one of the more powerful positions in the Hungarian banking world. He was only 32 years old. In 1924 he married Franciska Sichermann (1898–1962), from a family of lawyers and landowners in the village of Mád, in the Tokaj region. Sichermann and her older brother, István, had been orphaned at an early age. They were raised by a paternal uncle, Bernard Sichermann.[21] Francis

---

20 Francis Bator, interview with the author, October 11, 2010.
21 István (later Stephen) Sichermann also served in the Hungarian army in World War I. Captured by the Russians on the eastern front, he spent three years as a prisoner-of-war. He escaped by walking out through Siberia. He went into manufacturing, working first for the famous Weiss-Manfréd industrial works and, later, after emigrating to the U.S., as President of Natvar. Among other pursuits he was a gifted competitor in the game of bridge. Francis Bator remembered with pleasure the stories about his uncle playing high-stakes contract bridge with other passengers on ships crossing the Atlantic and earning enough winnings to pay for his first-class ticket. Stephen and his sister retained ownership of the family vineyard in Mád through the late 1940s, when it was nationalized by the communist government. The Bators often visited the vineyard during grape harvest season in September, bringing their three young boys with them to stay in the family house.

Fig. 1.1. Victor and Franciska Bator. Studio photographs, Budapest, ca. 1930.
Source: personal collection of Francis Bator.

remembered his mother with fondness as a "warm, graceful, bright woman, beloved by all who knew her. She was a highly cultivated woman." János Zwack, scion of the famous Hungarian distilling and manufacturing family, once told the Bator sons that their mother "was known as the most beautiful and charming woman in Budapest"—a story Francis happily passed along to me many years later.[22] With her husband Victor she had three sons: Francis, born August 10, 1925, and four years later two twins, Peter and Paul, both born on July 2, 1929. The children were raised in the Catholic faith, per their mother's preference. Victor Bator himself was born Jewish; he converted to the Evangelical Lutheran faith in 1918, then Catholicism for his marriage.

Two studio photographs of Victor and Franciska Bator taken in Budapest around 1930 capture their image as elegantly dressed, prosperous young Hungarians (Fig. 1.1)

During the 1920s and 30s Victor Bator lectured on financial law at the university. At his bank he rapidly accumulated connections to the broader Euro-

---

22 Francis Bator, interview with the author, November 8, 2012.

Chapter 1

Fig. 1.2. The Bator family home in Budapest, 19 Somlói utca, District 11, shown shortly after its completion in 1936. Photographer: Victor Bator.
Source: personal collection of Francis Bator.

pean finance world. He was appointed counsel to both the American and French legations in Budapest. By the late 1920s the government granted him the honorary title of senior advisor to the Hungarian cabinet, "magyar királyi kormányfőtanácsos," a distinguished title, especially noteworthy for someone who, as his son remembers, came from a "provincial family with Jewish antecedents."²³ He represented the American investment bank Lee, Higginson & Co., of Boston, Massachusetts, for over ten years, helping them manage their European bond investments. Growing personal prosperity made possible, in 1936, the construction of a beautiful Bauhaus-style home for his family dramatically situated on the Gellért Hill (Fig. 1.2).²⁴

As he practiced law Bator translated his experiences into academic writing, an impulse that further distinguished him from the majority of his peers in the

---

23 Francis Bator, interview with the author, October 8, 2012.
24 The Bátor home was distinctive enough to warrant recognition in András Ferkai's architectural study of great homes in Budapest, *Buda építészete a két világháború között: muvészeti emlékek* (Budapest: Magyar Tudományos Akadémiai Muvészettörténeti Kutató Intézet, 1995). Damaged during the siege of Budapest in 1944–5, it was later despoiled by the communist government, which added a third floor of rooms on the house and constructed an apartment building in the garden. Its original Italian marble exterior panels were removed for re-use in a movie house elsewhere in Budapest, a theater, Francis told me with an ironic smile, called the "Béla Bartók Theater."

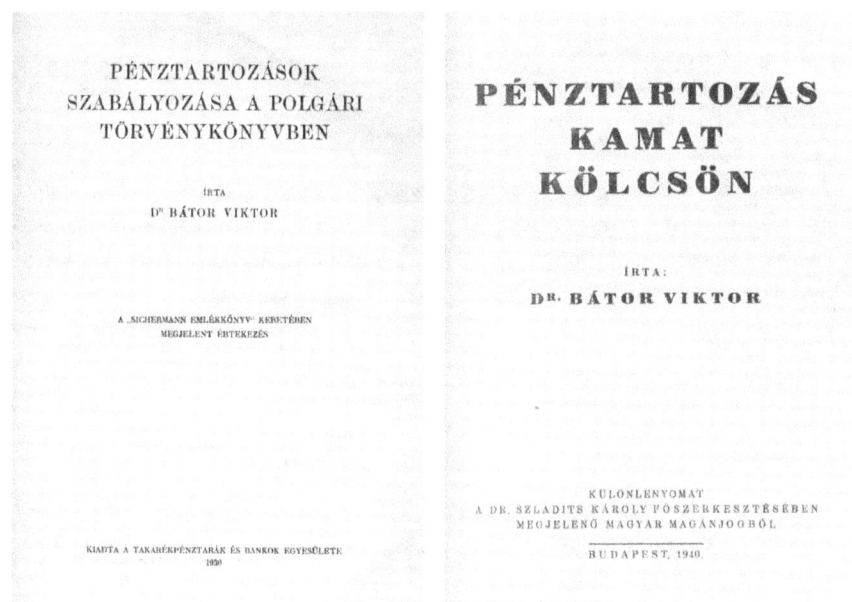

Fig. 1.3. Victor Bator as legal scholar in pre-World War II Hungary. Title pages for two of the books that established his reputation as a banking lawyer. Left) *The Regulation of Debts in Civil Law*. Right) *Debt, Interest, Loans*, special printing from the forthcoming Károly Szladits, ed., *Hungarian Civil Law*. Source: personal library of Francis Bator.

Hungarian legal profession. A number of book-length studies of international banking law resulted (Fig. 1.3) He published two books on the movement of dollar-based assets through the world finance and regulatory system. International debt was his specialty. In his work for the Commercial Bank, he routinely brought government and commercial bond offerings to the international market and served as a point of contact for foreign entities moving capital to invest in Hungary. Together with other leading Hungarian banks, the Commercial Bank negotiated with North American, British, and German banks to arrange long-term loans that funded the expansion of the economy in the 1920s.[25] In total he wrote or contributed chapters to almost a dozen books published in Hungary after 1921 (Table 1.1). Many of these books were brought out under the imprimatur of various Hungarian banking societies and institutes, including the Association of Savings Banks and Banks (Takarékpénztárak és bankok egyesülete), Hungary's main post-World War I banking trade group.

---

25 János Botos, "The Hungarian Banking System from the Trauma of Trianon to Nationalization," http://bankszovetseg.hu/Public/gep/2017/175-194%20Botos%20Janos.pdf.

Chapter 1

Table 1.1. Selected publications by Victor Bator, 1921-67, listing the majority of his Hungarian-language studies in the fields of banking law and civil law. List assembled with the help of Francis Bator and Lajos Vékás.

A békeszerződés clearing-rendszére (A takarékpénztárak és bankok egyesületében 1921. Április 7-dikén tartott előadás.) [The clearing arrangements of the Peace Treaty: A lecture given on April 7, 1921] Budapest: A takarékpénztárak és bankok egyesülete és a Pénzintézeten országos egyesülete kiadása, 1921.

Pénztartozások szabályozása a polgári törvénykönyvben [The regulation of debts in civil law] Budapest: A takarékpénztárak és bankok egyesülete, 1930. 61 p.

A pénztartozások jogszabályai [The laws of credit and debt]. Budapest: Grill Károly Könyvkiadóvállalata, 1932. 2nd edition published in 1939. 248 p.

A kölcsönszerződés jogszabályi és a dollárbetétek értékelése [The laws governing contract and debt and the valuation of dollar-based assets]. Budapest: Grill Károly Könyvkiadóvállalata, 1932.

A dollárbetétek felértékelése [The valuation of dollar deposits]. Budapest: A Tébe Kiadóvállalata, 1938. 65 p.

A keretbiztosítéki jelzálogjog átruházása [The transfer of insurance on liens]. Budapest: A Tébe Kiadóvállalata, 1939. 29 p.

Pénztartozás, kamat, kölcsön [Debt, interest, loans]. Budapest: Grill Károly Könyvkiadóvállalata, 1940. 187 p.

"Pénztartozás, Kamat" [Debt, interest.] In Károly Szladits, ed., *Magyar Magánjog*, Budapest: Grill Károly Könyvkiadóvállalata, 1941. 130 p.

The Béla Bartok Archives: History and Catalogue. New York: Bartók Archives Publication, 1963.

Foreword to Béla Bartók, *Rumanian Folk Music*, ed. Benjamin Suchoff. The Hague: Martinus Nijhoff, 1967.

Vietnam: A Diplomatic Tragedy. The Origins of the United States Involvement. Dobbs Ferry, New York: Oceana, 1965. Reprint. New York: Faber and Faber, 1967.

From volumes like these it is easy to see how Bator earned his reputation as one of Hungary's major intellectual figures in law. György Tallós, the distinguished historian of Hungarian banking, estimates Bator to have been one of the three great bank lawyers in Hungarian history.²⁶ Lajos Vékás, a specialist in estate law, Rector of the Law School at Eötvös Lóránd University, and member of the Hungarian Academy of Sciences, described Bator to me as "the leading expert in banking law in Hungary between the two World Wars."²⁷ In Hungarian academic law circles his name was still remembered into the early 21ˢᵗ century; his contribution to one of the standard legal references used in the country, the so-called "Nagy Szladits," meant that all Hungarian law students after 1942 came across his work during their training.²⁸ (Fig. 1.3, at right, in a separate special printing.) Connections with the law school were a defining feature of his career in Budapest. Long relationships with eminent members of the Hungarian law professoriate testify to the esteem they held for their former student. Károly Szladits, in particular, became a close personal and family friend.²⁹ Szladits had two sons, one of whom, Charles Szladits, also a lawyer, left Hungary after World War II and found employment teaching at the Parker School of Foreign and Comparative Law at Columbia University. Bartók scholars know the younger Szladits's name as a trustee for the Béla Bartók Archives, a position he accepted in 1963 at Bator's invitation.

His last publication in Hungary appeared in 1941, a 130-page chapter on banking law written for the massive reference assembled by the senior Szladits. That same year, on October 8, the Nazified government in Budapest revoked his Hungarian citizenship in response to his prominent political activity in the United States. As reported in *The New York Times*, Victor Bator was one of five Hungarians thus targeted, all of whom were known to be engaged in an effort to establish a provisional Hungarian government in exile in North America. In an unusual twist, after the war Bator was again declared a non-citizen, in 1948, by yet another Hungarian government, this time the communists. Two different governments took away Victor Bator's Hungarian citizenship between 1941 and 1948. "That didn't happen to many people," Francis Bator noted appreciatively. "My father was a committed anti-Nazi and a committed anti-communist. He didn't like totalitarian regimes. He was stripped of his Hungarian citizenship by the communist *and* the Nazi government. There were very few people who could boast of *that* being done to them."³⁰

---

26 Dr. János Botos, personal conversation with Tallós. As communicated in a letter to Francis Bator, November 2, 1995.
27 Lajos Vékás, Email communication with the author, October 10, 2012.
28 Lajos Vékás, interview with the author, Budapest, July 18, 2011.
29 Francis Bator remembers Szladits as one of his father's very closest friends. He told me that Szladits was known to have said on more than one occasion that Victor Bator was his favorite student.
30 Francis Bator, interview with the author, October 27, 2012.

Chapter 1

Fig. 1.4. The Hungarian Commercial Bank headquarters in downtown Budapest. Victor Bator's office was here in this building. Source: Commercial postcard, ca. 1924.

A family story sums up Bator's views on politics. "Sometime during the mid-1930s," Francis remembered, "when I was around ten years old, my father was talking to me about politics, with Hitler ensconced in Berlin and Stalin in Moscow. He said to me, 'If you ever have a choice of becoming a cabinet minister in Berlin or Moscow, or a street cleaner in London… go to London!'"[31]

* * *

Bator, then, was a lawyer. A bank lawyer. But his was no ordinary bank. The Pesti Magyar Kereskedelmi Bank was the leading and largest of Hungary's banks. Its headquarters stood in a prominent location in the heart of downtown Pest, overlooking Szechényi tér and the Chain Bridge, adjacent to the Gresham Palace; the building, which survived the war, is currently occupied by the Ministry of the Interior (Fig. 1.4). Affiliate banks were located all over Hungary. Some measure of its prominence in the Hungarian economy can be seen from an advertisement found on the back of a telegram delivered to Bartók in September 1940 (Fig. 1.5)

---

31   Francis Bator, interview with the author, October 8, 2012.

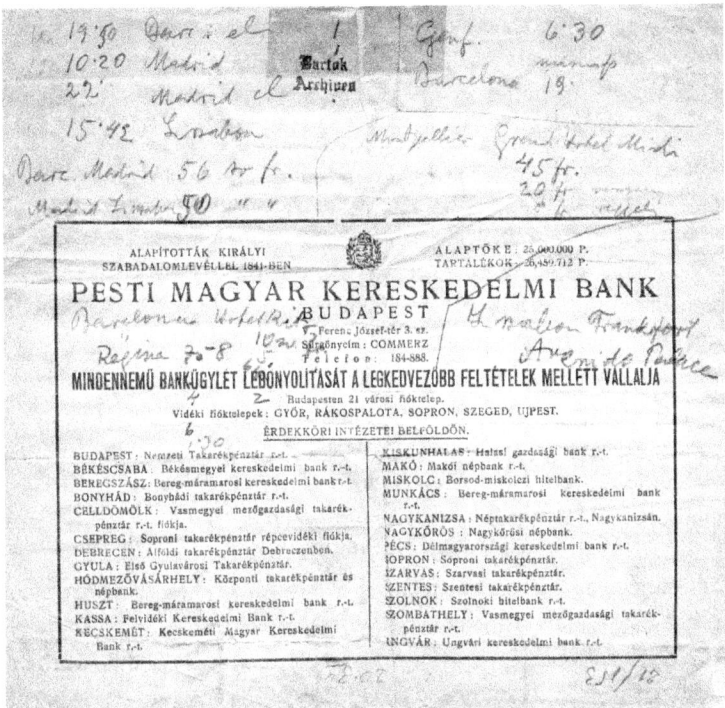

Fig. 1.5. Advertisement for Pesti Magyar Kereskedelmi Bank found on the back side of a telegram delivered to Béla Bartók in September 1940. This telegram confirmed his ship passage across the Atlantic to New York. The pencil jottings, in Bartók's own hand, are travel notes he made en route to Lisbon in October. Source: CPB Homosassa.

In the early 20th century, together with the Hungarian General Credit Bank, the Commercial Bank controlled a full third of Hungary's credit market—the bonds and loans necessary for economic growth. These two banks, notes historian György Ránki, were intimately associated with the conglomerates that controlled around 50 percent of Hungarian industry. Much of the capital that financed Hungary's recovery after World War I flowed through their doors, including bonds backed by American interests concerned about stabilizing Europe to ward off the threat of communism. The Commercial Bank was tied into a sprawling business group centered around the steel and engineering works of the Weiss Manfréd Company, the Rimamurányi Iron Works, and the Salgótárjan Coal Mining Company. This corporate entity controlled 83 other important industrial enterprises, including National Paper Mill, for which Bator served as a director.[32]

---

32 György Ránki, "The Hungarian Economy in the Interwar Years," in Peter Sugar, Péter Hanák, Tibor Frank, eds., *A History of Hungary* (Bloomington, IN: Indiana University Press, 1990), 364–65.

Victor Bator represented the bank in its business affairs, working with lawyers and bankers around Europe on finance and credit transactions. As General Counsel he ensured compliance with statutes and regulatory practices that shifted unpredictably across the European and American markets. Called to testify in 1941 before the New York Supreme Court as an expert witness for a related matter, he summarized his role in the 1930s as representing "some of the largest creditors of Hungary or of Hungarian debtors, as Hungarian counsel."[33]

Inevitably this activity drew him into what we today would call global investment banking. "The American equivalent of my father's position in Hungary would be something like General Counsel of Morgan Chase bank," Francis Bator explained to me. "He was once asked if he would become President of the bank. He said no. He wanted to maintain his independence as a lawyer." In 1930 Bator was one of the Hungarian lawyers who participated in an International Law Association meeting held in New York City.[34] He was in the U.S. again in 1934 for business. His position at the Commercial Bank brought him to the attention of the Wall Street law firm Sullivan and Cromwell, specialists in international finance who were already, by then, a well-known American firm. He helped that firm's New York lawyers with their bankruptcy work in Central Europe.[35] His relationship with John Foster Dulles and Allan Dulles dates to those early days working alongside each other on large-scale financial transactions. In the 1920s massive bond offerings were issued by the Hungarian government and industries to help rebuild the national economy. Some of those bonds were brought to the American market for sale through Lee, Higginson of Boston, who repackaged them as "European Mortgage and Investment Corporation" bond offerings for sale at handsome return rates of 7% or 7 1/2%.[36] Bator's bank originated and structured many of these deals, requiring senior bank officers to work routinely with investment banking partners outside Hungary.

---

33 Gersten and Finn vs. Schroder Trust Co, New York State Supreme Court, Appellate Division, Second Department (September 1941), 212.
34 "World Law Session to Bring Notables," *The New York Times*, July 27, 1930. Bator is listed in this article as one of approximately 150 foreign representatives to attend the meeting. U.S. immigration records also show that he visited the U.S. in 1934 and, again, in February 1939.
35 Many of Bator's acquaintances in the American investment banking community suffered catastrophic losses in one of that era's most sensational bankruptcies, the collapse of Swedish Match and its American affiliate, International Match Corporation, after founder Ivar Kreuger's notorious suicide in Paris in 1932. Ripple effects from these financial events were felt around Europe. Bator was directly involved with some of Kreuger and Toll's bond issues; he represented Hungary's interests in the bankruptcy proceedings.
36 A detailed account of the bank's activities since its founding was prepared by its board of directors in a suitably impressive book published for its centenary celebrations in 1941: *A Pesti Magyar Kereskedelmi Bank: Százéves Története, 1841–1941* (Budapest: Pesti Magyar Kereskedelmi Bank, 1941). It details individual bond placements and the bank's role in stabilizing the Hungarian economy after World War I.

Other friendships developed that read like a Who's Who of American and European finance leaders in the 1930s. The Bator family attended the 1936 Olympics in Berlin as guests of Paul Kempner, director of the Mendelssohn & Co. bank and a leading German financier. ("My father refused to stand when Hitler's motorcade came into view," Francis assured me.) In August 1936 the Bator family continued their vacation by attending a tennis tournament in Sweden, where they made the acquaintance of the royal family. With them for part of that summer were Baldwin Maull and his family. Maull was a young lawyer at Sullivan and Cromwell who would go on many years later to become President and CEO of The Marine Midland Trust Co. in New York. "A lot of my father's contacts were with contemporaries who were lawyers in New York," Francis recollected. Many of these lawyers specialized in investment banking and finance. Their presence in New York would ease the Bator family's transition to life in North America, so much so that the eldest son, Francis, could still remember 70 years later that "I never *really* felt like an immigrant."[37]

Financial gymnastics of the sort needed to keep German industrial giant Robert Bosch operating freely after 1933 exemplify the type of corporate restructurings that took place in this era. Bator was peripherally involved with this cautionary tale of global finance. The diesel engine company Robert Bosch Co. of Germany sold itself in 1934 to a group of international investors anchored by the Mendelssohn Bank. Majority ownership was transferred to Amsterdam in the offices of the famously ostentatious German financier Fritz Mannheimer (1890–1939), head of Mendelssohn & Co.'s Dutch affiliate. Lawyers from Sullivan and Cromwell helped arrange the sale, working on behalf of Bosch's exclusive American licensee, the American Bosch Company. As recounted in the published history of Sullivan and Cromwell, when American Bosch sent executives to Germany in 1938 to negotiate new terms, they somehow spilled information about the American industrial process, a breach of national security. Mannheimer died on August 9, 1939. The timing of his death precipitated the final collapse of the Mendelssohn Bank. The German ownership of Bosch now had to find a new owner for American Bosch "that would remain subservient to the German parent company." Political calculations led the Germans to sell American Bosch to a Swedish banking entity, Enskilda Bank, headed by the Wallenbergs, Sweden's richest family. Half of American Bosch, in turn, was subsequently sold back to American investors to keep the company qualified to do business in the United States—a politically charged maneuver. Lawyers from Sullivan & Cromwell advised on this tangled nest of transactions, including John Foster Dulles, managing partner,

---

37   Francis Bator, interview with the author, October 8, 2012.

Chapter 1

with his recent history of compromise with the Germans hanging in a cloud over his head.[38]

In 1939 Bator emigrated to the US with his wife and three sons. The family had planned a summer vacation on the East Coast. They started in Rumson, New Jersey, visiting family friends from the Sullivan and Cromwell world. The oldest son, Francis, was 13 years old at the time, about to turn 14. He had been in school in England. Telling the story many years later he remembered it as "an accident" that the family ended up staying in America. "We stayed because the war broke out some three weeks after our arrival." He continued, "A senior partner in a Dutch investment bank had shot himself, so my father had to go back to Holland—he flew on a Pan Am Clipper. My mother and brothers and I were left in Rumson. We listened to Chamberlain's speech on September 1 at the Rumson Inn. My father came back a few days later and said we're going to stay. He set about getting us into schools. I landed at Groton." Francis remembers he and his brothers asking their parents, "When are we going home?" Their father answered, "We're not going home, we're staying. And I've got to find schools for you boys."

Fritz Mannheimer was that "senior partner in a Dutch investment bank." He had died under mysterious circumstances, rumored to be a suicide. At the time his death was a public sensation, drawing news coverage around Europe and the US, including *The New York Times* and *Time* magazine. That Bator was linked to at least one of Mannheimer's investors, probably the Commercial Bank, and to Mendelssohn et Cie. itself, is proven by his emergency flight back to Amsterdam that August. Margaret Kempner, née Mendelssohn, was close friends with Franciska Bator. What capital assets he could salvage for investors ended up in America, at least in part, where they were immediately pledged to new use or re-securitized. Unfortunately, association with any of the sixty or so lawyers of Sullivan and Cromwell in that difficult era brought with it an unwanted whiff of complicity; the firm's historic working relationship with German banks and large industrial companies like Bosch pulled it into politically fraught territory after 1933. Many of the firm's younger associates were deeply uncomfortable with John Foster Dulles's early support of Hitler in the mid-1930s, some of which spilled out into public view in the United States, notably in an article, "Road to Peace," that appeared in *The Atlantic Monthly* in October 1935.[39] Allan Dulles, his brother, took a more oppositional view based on his recent European experiences. The firm's partners closed its Berlin office in 1935.

---

38 The story of Dulles, Fritz Mannheimer, and Mendelssohn & Cie of Amsterdam is told in the pages of the firm's unofficial history, *A Law Unto Itself: The Untold Story of the Law Firm Sullivan and Cromwell*, by Nancy Lisigor and Frank Lipsius (New York: William Morrow, 1988), 146–51.
39 Lisigor and Lipsius, *A Law Unto Itself*, 144–45.

***

Like many Hungarian émigrés the Bators remained in New York City. After renting an apartment on Park Avenue, by 1941 they purchased a home occupying the 16th floor of an apartment building located at 30 E. 72nd Street, on New York's upper east side. This would be the family's home until Victor's death in 1967. They summered with their three boys in Nonquitt, Massachusetts, in 1940 at the recommendation of family friend Candler Cobb, the suave young Sullivan and Cromwell lawyer who spent much of the 1930s in European capitals renegotiating American-financed bonds to ensure payment continuity. By 1941 they had purchased a second home in Nonquitt to use for vacations.

Financial prosperity afforded Victor Bator a more rapid integration into American life than most Hungarian émigrés were able to enjoy. From his career in banking he had made "a modest fortune," his son remembers. His position as General Counsel gave him an ownership interest in the bank; a small portion of the bank's profits every year went to him. This portion was less than 1%, but it still allowed him to accumulate considerable wealth by the mid-1930s. The nature of his work, which often included foreign clients, meant that some money stayed abroad in different currencies as it was earned, an arrangement unusual for a Hungarian lawyer at the time. A story told to me by his son illustrates the situation:

> Béla Imrédy was a law school classmate of my father's. The Imrédys were neighbors of ours and became family acquaintances. When he became head of the National Bank in Hungary, in the mid-1930s, my father said, "finally, we have someone in that position with brains." Imrédy would soon thereafter turn pro-Nazi on misplaced Hungarian patriotic grounds, out of the belief that the only way to secure revision of the Treaty of Trianon was through Berlin. I asked my father what went wrong in 2 ½ years to make Imrédy turn toward the Nazis. His response at the time I still remember: "brains are not enough." While President of the National Bank Imrédy once said to my father, "Victor, you have these special arrangements to leave your foreign earnings overseas. We're going to have to stop that." My father told him, "If you do that, I will leave Hungary the next day." My father was allowed to keep his earnings overseas that way.

After the war, in 1946–47, the bank paid out substantial suspended honoraria to him. "At *no* time did I ever have the sense that he found himself financially pressed," Francis told me.

Since Bator is sometimes described as "Bartók's lawyer," it is important to recognize that he never practiced law in the United States. When he arrived stateside in late 1939 he was still employed by the Hungarian Commercial Bank. Friends at Sullivan and Cromwell lent him the use of an office at their firm. To practice law in the US, and be licensed, he would have to go back to law school to learn the American legal system. As Francis told me, "he decided that putting himself through American law school at age 50, spending 2–3 years becoming an American common law lawyer, made no sense."[40] Ben Suchoff affirmed that Bator didn't practice law in New York. "He had the respect of all these law firms," though, he stated in a 2002 interview, and "he had a great understanding of the law. I learned a lot from him about the law."[41] Later on, in the 50s and 60s, Bator became an expert in international copyright law through self-study. When he would visit his son Francis in Cambridge, Massachusetts, Francis remembers that "he would go off to meet professors at the law school to talk about copyright law."[42]

Specific problems for international banking lawyers in the World War II years included the nationalization of assets by the Nazi government across Europe, bank closures, the seizure of innumerable assets by foreign governments, and desperate efforts by investors and businesses of all sizes—including American companies—to recover or protect threatened property. How much of this work Bator stayed involved with once he had relocated to New York is impossible to determine. He continued to work for the Commercial Bank until 1941, representing its interests from afar. In America, however, he soon branched into other pursuits. "My father was involved in a range of things," remembered Francis. "He had an entrepreneurial side." In 1941 Bator helped purchase a New Jersey-based company that manufactured electrical insulation. The business, known as Natvar, grew rapidly.[43] It prospered, in part by helping with the U.S. war effort. Bator was Chairman of its board of directors. Stephen

---

40 Francis Bator, interview with the author, October 5, 2012.
41 Benjamin Suchoff, interview with the author, June 20, 2002.
42 Francis Bator, interview with the author, October 22, 2012.
43 Natvar's factory and corporate offices were located at 239 Randolph Avenue, Woodbridge, New Jersey, approximately 20 miles southwest of Manhattan, in northern New Jersey's industrial region. It was formerly The National Varnished Products Corporation. Its products included varnished papers, insulation, electrical tapes and tubing. For the US Navy it produced insulation for cables. Paper trails no longer exist for the purchase of Natvar, but given the US Treasury Department regulations governing transfer of assets from abroad in wartime, I suspect that its purchase was motivated by the need for its new owners to quickly reinvest assets in the United States. Kempner's involvement suggests that remainders of the Mendelssohn Bank fortune may also have been part of the transaction. If true, the decision to redirect the factory's output to support the American war effort would have represented a particularly satisfying form of quiet vengeance.

Sichermann, his wife's brother, was President. Paul Kempner, his friend from the Mendelssohn Bank, helped them purchase the company, and also ran it as a director until his own death in 1956. Bator's sons, later board members themselves, agreed to sell the firm in the late 1960s, after their father's death. He invested in real estate. In 1942 he arranged to purchase one-half of the 30 East 72nd Street apartment building, the 16th floor of which comprised the apartment where they lived. The other half was owned by the real estate company Webb and Knapp.[44] The adjoining 28 East 72nd Street annex would soon house the growing Bartók Archive and its operations.

An activity of a more public sort was his purchase, in 1945, of America's oldest Hungarian newspaper, the New York-based *Amerikai Magyar Népszava*. He became publisher of this important source of news and opinion about Hungary. In this role, he and his business partners met with President Harry Truman several times in 1948 as part of the President's efforts to enlist media support for the battle against communism (Figure 1.6). Bator was described in *Time* magazine's June 21, 1948, issue as a "blue eyed New Jersey manufacturer" who had been involved in the purchase of *Népszava*, a transaction that cost its new owners $100,000. Ownership of the newspaper was not an economic opportunity, however. Far from it. "I'm quite sure it *lost* money," Francis emphasized in conversations with me. "I think my father must have subsidized it for a long time. He did it pro bono, *not* to make money."[45] His work in this area led to the removal of his Hungarian citizenship a second time in 1948 by the communists.

As publisher and businessman, with real estate and other ventures on the side, Bator lived the rest of his life in New York, summering in Nonquitt. He became a naturalized American citizen on September 6, 1945. He served on the board of directors for the American Ballet Theatre, serving for a while as its President. His wife Franci died in 1962 of a stroke suffered after returning from a chamber music event at the Metropolitan Museum of Art. With Zoltán Kodály she had enjoyed a warm friendship going to their Budapest years. When Kodály learned of her death he sent a hand-drawn memorial note to Victor that has stayed in the family (Fig. 1.7). Bator would die five years later; he suffered a fatal cerebral hemorrhage during the second act of *La Traviata* at the Metropolitan Opera while in the company of his guest that evening, the famous Hun-

---

44 A partner in the firm Webb and Knapp was William Zeckendorf, one of New York City's most prominent real estate developers. Zeckendorf, owner of the Hotel Astor, the Chrysler Building, and other properties, was known to New Yorkers for his role in assembling the property on which the United Nations was built. He lived in the penthouse apartment directly above the Bators. (Francis Bator, conversation with the author, October 10, 2012).

45 Francis Bator, phone interview with the author, October 27, 2012.

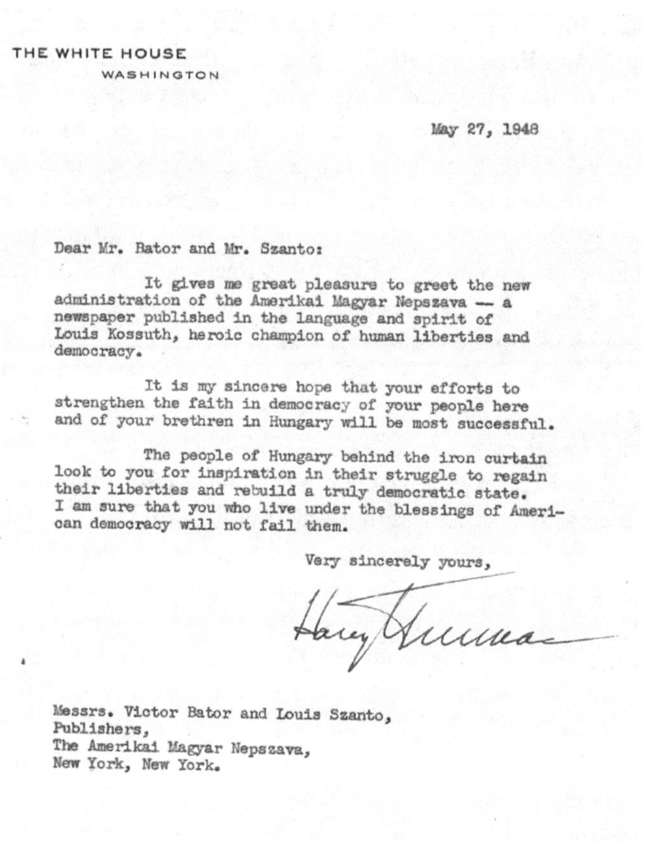

Chapter 1

> THE WHITE HOUSE
> WASHINGTON
>
> May 27, 1948
>
> Dear Mr. Bator and Mr. Szanto:
>
> It gives me great pleasure to greet the new administration of the Amerikai Magyar Nepszava — a newspaper published in the language and spirit of Louis Kossuth, heroic champion of human liberties and democracy.
>
> It is my sincere hope that your efforts to strengthen the faith in democracy of your people here and of your brethren in Hungary will be most successful.
>
> The people of Hungary behind the iron curtain look to you for inspiration in their struggle to regain their liberties and rebuild a truly democratic state. I am sure that you who live under the blessings of American democracy will not fail them.
>
> Very sincerely yours,
>
> Harry Truman
>
> Messrs. Victor Bator and Louis Szanto,
> Publishers,
> The Amerikai Magyar Nepszava,
> New York, New York.

Fig. 1.6. President Harry Truman, letter to Victor Bator and Louis Szanto, May 27, 1948. Source: personal collection of Francis Bator.

garian actress Lili Darvas, widow of Ferenc Molnár. A generously proportioned obituary appeared in *The New York Times* several days later. Late in life he wrote a substantial and still respected book on the Vietnam War, in English, for American audiences. Bator had a lifelong serious and deeply informed concern with international politics, and public policy in general. His Vietnam book "was driven in part by his feeling that the US had gotten itself enmeshed in a terrible mess, without having a first order national interest."[46]

Managing Bartók's Estate was only one of many pursuits in a varied and productive career that spanned two continents. Prompted to summarize his activities in the United States many years later, Victor Bator pointed to his leadership of Natvar as one of his most personally satisfying activities. He also

---

46 Francis Bator, Email communication to the author, October 3, 2012.

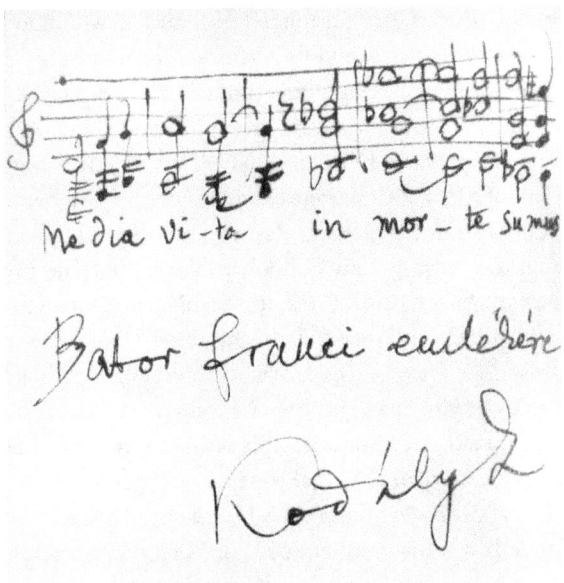

Fig. 1.7. Zoltán Kodály's memorial note to the Bator family after learning of Franciska Bator's death in 1962. The music quotation comes from his choral motet "Media vita in morte sumus," written as a memorial for Mátyás Seiber in 1960. After her death, framed copies of this note were prepared by Victor Bator for distribution to her three sons, allowing each of them to keep in their own homes this souvenir of the family's cherished connections to Hungary.
Source: personal collection of Francis Bator.

expressed pride for his involvement in a global news source, Deadline Data on World Affairs, which charged $250/year for subscription in the late 1950s and was read by the Senate Foreign Relations Committee, the CIA, the State Department, the US Air Force, and the United Nations, in addition to The New York Times, Newsweek, and many university libraries around the country.[47] For Deadline Data he was a director and Chairman of the Board, and owned 50% of the shares.

Victor Bator's intellectual acumen and international outlook were traits he passed down to his three sons. It is useful to consider their achievements here. All three sons would later become involved, directly or indirectly, with the long trail of Bartók Estate litigation they inherited as part of their father's legacy. Francis, Peter, and Paul Bator each attended Groton in Massachusetts for preparatory school. Peter Bator did his undergraduate work at Harvard University, where he wrote his senior honors thesis on the Treaty of Trianon. Interested in

---

47 Victor Bator, Memorandum on the History of the Bartók Estate, 272-73 (BSCB Tampa).

Chapter 1

politics and law like his father, he attended Harvard Law School, became editor of the *Harvard Law Review*, and finished tied for first in his class. He went on to become a senior partner at the prestigious law firm Davis, Polk, in New York City, where he was head of their mergers and acquisitions department. His twin brother Paul Bator was a Princeton University valedictorian who became a graduate student of history at Harvard as a Wilson Fellow. Seeing his brother already at law school a few hundred yards away, across the Harvard campus, he decided to switch to Harvard Law School, where he became President of the *Law Review* and graduated, also at the top of his class, two years after Peter. He clerked for Justice Harlan on the U.S. Supreme Court. He was later a law professor and Associate Dean at the Harvard Law School, a law faculty member at the University of Chicago, and Deputy Solicitor General during the Reagan administration. Paul Bator inherited his father's interest in the business side of art, becoming an expert in the legal aspects of the international art trade.[48] He made multiple appearances before the U.S. Supreme Court.

Francis, who outlived his two younger brothers, was a distinguished economist whose 1960 book, *The Question of Government Spending*, was described by Arthur Schlesinger, Jr., as "an indispensable book for all Americans who care about the direction their country is heading." In childhood he sang in the famed Cisztercien Gimnasium choir in Budapest; growing up he possessed what he described to me as "a pretty classy boy soprano voice," his face breaking into a smile at the memories. As a young man he spent three years in the U.S. Army during World War II, rising to the rank of First Lieutenant. He attended M.I.T. as an undergraduate, continuing on at the same institution to received his Ph.D. in economics in 1956. His doctoral work was completed under the supervision of the celebrated American Nobel laureate economists Paul Samuelson and Robert Solow. Joining the M.I.T. economics faculty after graduation, he taught there until 1963, when he joined the U.S. government, ending up at the White House as Deputy National Security Advisor to President Lyndon Johnson, with responsibilities for U.S./European relations and for foreign economic policy worldwide. Beginning in 1967 he taught at Harvard University's Kennedy School of Government, where he was founding chairman of the school's public policy program. From the U.S. Treasury Department he received the Distinguished Service Award. Francis and Paul Bator—two of the three sons—were elected Fellows of the American Academy of Arts and Sciences during their lifetimes.

* * *

---

48 See Paul M. Bator's *The International Trade in Art* (Chicago: University of Chicago Press, 1983).

Victor Bator's recollection of how he first crossed paths with Béla Bartók is worth citing in full. "It is impossible or difficult to see in proper perspective the circumstances preceding my appointment as Trustee and the authority vested in me by the Last Will of Béla Bartók," he begins his Memorandum on the History of the Bartók Estate, "without giving the history of my association with the testator."

> My connection with Béla Bartók dates back to 1919. At that time I was living in Vienna (Austria) in voluntary exile, refugee from the short-lived communist regime of Béla Kun that controlled Hungary for four months. Communism and the "White Terror" that followed it were not to Bartók's taste, and [he] began correspondence to find a position outside of Hungary where freedom and independence were respected. Mutual friends intervened with me and I helped him in his correspondence in that connection. I made it possible for him to send and receive letters that he did not want to pass through censorship. Sometime in 1920 he gave up his plans. Afterwards we continued to see each other occasionally at rehearsals of his works, and concertising mostly in the house of our next-door neighbor who was a mutual friend, but our acquaintance did not develop into friendship or intimacy.[49]

Surviving evidence on Bartók's side also points to the limited nature of their relationship early on. In September 1919 Bartók requested a six-month leave of absence from the Academy of Music. "It is indeed possible to live here," he wrote to his mother in October 1919, "but to work—that is, to do the work I want to do (folk music study), will not be possible for at least ten years."[50] The following month he wrote to Emil Hertzka inquiring about moving to Vienna and making a new living there. At the end of the letter he indicates that Hertzka should communicate to him through two intermediaries, Viktor Bátor in Vienna or Imre Waldbauer in Budapest, and lists their addresses.[51] No other references to Bator are found in Bartók's letters until the early 1940s, when both men encountered each other again, now across the ocean in New York City.

---

49 Victor Bator, Memorandum on the History of the Bartók Estate, Chapter B, 6 (BSCB Tampa).
50 Bartók, letter to his mother, October 23, 1919. Quoted in Halsey Stevens, *The Life and Music of Béla Bartók*, Rev. Ed. (New York: Oxford University Press, 1964): 57.
51 Bartók, letter to Emil Hertzka, September 22, 1919 (BBC-PSS Basel).

Victor Bator: My Experiences with Béla Bartók in the United States, 1940–45

Under pressure from litigation to document his activities as trustee of the Bartók Estate, in late 1959 and early 1960 Bator drafted a lengthy, 310-page memorandum to establish a written record of its history. It is by far the most accurate single source for understanding the estate's activities during the Cold War. It has never been published before, in whole or in part. Its purpose was to serve as a guide for lawyers involved in the litigation brought by Peter Bartók. It was never intended for the public eye, although now, in view of its historical importance, it amply deserves to be better known. Originally it was accompanied by an assemblage of letters from the trust's business correspondence. In the memorandum's text Bator identifies those supplemental letters as "enclosures," numbering them sequentially throughout the entire document, i.e., "Enclosure A_5." (The memorandum is organized into chapters by topic, identified alphabetically, A–L. The chapter found below is Chapter B, the second of twelve.) In his methodical style Bator organizes the enclosures chronologically, building his narrative from the documentation he has assembled. The memorandum is very much a document prepared by a trained lawyer for use by other trained lawyers and judges: it relies on the careful presentation of facts and dated documents to persuade.

Bator's memorandum survives in a single typed copy preserved in the Benjamin Suchoff collection at University of South Florida.[1] It has long since been separated from the letters it once accompanied.[2] In the text reproduced below all references to supporting documents are retained for reference; this will allow future scholars to identify where an item once existed, even if it no longer survives. In this book I include por-

---

1 Bator intended this copy to be preserved with the Béla Bartók Archives materials; its pages are numbered sequentially 1-277 in the upper corners of each page, using the same ink stamp we see on other documents processed by archive staff in the 1950s and 60s. Benjamin Suchoff kept the Memorandum out of the materials he transferred to Peter in 1985, no doubt fearing for its preservation. The entire document is typed, double space, on onionskin paper, with numerous ink and pencil corrections in Bator's hand.
2 Sharp-eyed musicologists will notice Bator's handwritten enclosure numbers on certain items of estate correspondence, contracts, and legal documents, most dating from 1951-59, preserved in BSCB Tampa and CPB Homosassa. They look like this: "C_3," "F_{12}," or G_{17}." By 1963 these enclosures had been re-integrated into the Archives collection. A full reconstruction of the original Memorandum, with all enclosures, is no longer possible: most of the Estate's business correspondence has not survived.

Victor Bator: My Experiences with Béla Bartók

tions from Chapters B, C, and I. A short prologue (Chapter A, p. 1-5, not included) expresses the same spirit of his Introduction to the Béla Bartók Archives catalogue, published three years later. The portion reproduced below comprises all of Chapter B (p. 6-19), with the exception of its two introductory paragraphs, which I detached to form the closing page of Chapter 1 of this book, immediately preceding. Bator's Chapter B bears no title in the original: just the typed heading seen below. The title above is my own.

Here Victor Bator revisits how he began to assist Béla Bartók during World War II, eventually becoming his friend.

Background and Origin of Appointment as Trustee

When Bartók arrived in the U.S.A. in October 1940 we met in the home of another mutual friend soon after his arrival, and from that day on our friendship has developed into an intimate relationship granting me the privilege of his friendship, sharing many of his worries, problems, and pleasures. More and more often he came to my house as guest. In 1942 he spent the summer as our guest in our Massachusetts country home. In 1941 he joined a Committee of Independent Hungary formed by four Hungarians supported by the U.S. Government to head the struggle for liberation of Hungary from Nazi rule. At the time when the Committee of which I was one of the members was formed, he insisted that this be kept secret until his son Peter could get out of Hungary. Thereupon I engineered the emigration of Peter Bartók and his admittance into the U.S. Under-Secretary of State Mr. Sumner Welles upon the request of the Committee instructed the U.S. Consulate in Budapest to grant to Peter Bartók a U.S. visa. As soon as this was achieved, my secretary in Hungary, Miss Brem, and a friend of Béla Bartók, Dr. Hajnal, financed out of funds I left behind in Hungary the campaign to get Peter Bartók out of Hungary, and with pull, trick, and money they helped him through to Switzerland. There, friends of Béla Bartók took him over and arranged his trip to Lisbon. Even though he had the U.S. visa he could not sail because he was a Hungarian alien-enemy for the British. Dozens of cables were sent to Boosey & Hawkes, London, British friends of mine to persuade the British Foreign Office to instruct the Lisbon Consulate to let him board a boat. No shipping company would dare to transport an enemy subject without prior clearance by the British Foreign Office. Even the British Consul, Mr. Hart, had not the authority to grant a sailing permit without clearance from London. Finally Peter Bartók got the sailing permit, arrived to the U.S.A., and was reunited with his family.

Soon afterwards Peter Bartok reached the age of Draft. He as alien had the right to object—with the consequence that he could never be a citizen. It had taken six months until I persuaded him to withdraw his objection, let himself be drafted in the Navy and after 6 months service was naturalized as a citizen.

Between his arrival in this country on April 29th, 1942, and the date he became a sailor in the U.S. Navy in 1944, almost two years, Peter Bartók had to be taken care of. He spoke very little English. His high-school education was not as good as that of most Hungarian youth, he changed schools in Hungary where it is an unusual and odd occurrence, several times, he spoke Hungarian only, not even German that is a natural part of Hungarian education. I obtained a job for him in a poultry farm owned by friends of mine who promised to let him share their family life with their son and two daughters, all three of about the same age. At the beginning he could not understand as much as the questions "how are you" or "how old are you" as he related this in a letter, but he got salary or rather pocket money and spent the summer 1942 in the healthy climate of a farm and acquired the speaking knowledge of English; he could visit during weekends his father who spent the summer at our country-home, equally in Massachusetts. His schooling problem had to be solved. I succeeded to secure him a place in the technical school of the Radio Corporation of America where gratis education of three years was given to promising future engineers. Another possibility was the Pratt Institute also with tuition-free engineering education. Ultimately, he chose the Pratt Institute, learned audio engineering there, but dropped out before graduation for reasons I do not remember.

Meanwhile Béla Bartók, an exile-refugee from Nazi-Hungary, experienced the sad fate of many other celebrities of science and art who had come to this country with invitations from the State Department, from Universities—people of best intentions and found themselves unappreciated, neglected. The basic problem that was at the core of the hardships and difficulties Bartók experiences I shall describe presently was a misunderstanding. On the European continent and specifically in Hungarian institutes of higher learning, a university is by definition a national institution, maintained out of taxes, whose professors have always tenure and are employees of the State. There is no exception to this rule in France, Germany, Switzerland, the Scandinavian countries, Italy, and of course Hungary, either. For a Hungarian like Bartók an invitation by a university of world renown like Columbia meant "university tenure," security for life and respectable income. Bartók disliked the Nazi-influenced atmosphere of Hungary, but there he was professor of the National Academy of Music, an institute of high learning specializing in music, his salary paid by the Academy was by itself a respectable yearly income. His authority there was so high that in order to enable him to use as much time as possible for his scholarly work on folk-music he was relieved of teaching duty (like the professors of the Princeton Institute of Advanced Studies or the College of France in Paris). Thus, without the offer of Columbia University he would not have left Hungary. On the contrary, when the news of declaration of war reached him in Switzerland in September 1939 at the mountain-retreat of a Swiss friend, he interrupted his composing work begun there and hurried home. But with the invitation of Columbia he was willing to emigrate. A farewell concert of Bartók works was arranged. His dearest friend Kodály, a great composer and musician himself, wrote to him a letter of censure. He left behind his two sons, yet he emigrated, under the impression that the academic and musical world of American will embrace him. The letdown was tremendous.

The fact of the situation was that Columbia had never intended to appoint him as professor. Columbia appointed him as research fellow, not out of the budget of the university but out of the money of a fund, the Ditson Fund, that was to be used by Columbia for aiding American musicians with the restriction that no scholarship or contribution could be repeated and extended. Those who arranged the appointment believed that escaping from a Nazi-controlled country was preferable to any arm-chair comfort in Hungary that could not be but temporary, unsafe, oppressive if not intolerable. This general belief in the U.S.A. was fostered by the long line of famous scholars who had come from Germany and Austria who were either racially of Jewish ancestry or Jews or members of leftist political groups who were in mortal danger of being exposed to degradation and humiliation. To those hundreds any escape was welcome. In the case of Bartok this was not true, but the people of academic life here who worked hard to get visas and minute salaries for such Germans assumed that this was true in Hungary also, and transferred this spirit of charitable help and urge to save the most valuable members of their scientific and scholarly field to some like Bartók where it was unwarranted and misplaced.

Bartók's difficulties began right away. The salary of Columbia was $3,000 a year. That sounds nice expressed in Hungarian currency, but this was even then not much for a man without house, home, or office. His luggage got lost in Portugal. A large number of his manuscripts, all the folk music scholarly writings, folk-song collections not replaceable ever, many of his musical manuscripts and clothing. He played in a New York concert in the dinner jacket borrowed from a friend. He soon discovered that he was not a member of the faculty, that he had no teaching duties at Columbia though he was given the choice to do whatever he wanted. The Dean of the Music Department, as I heard it from him years later, meant to show his deep respect toward Bartók by not requiring any routine work from him, while he took that as an offense. He never liked to teach composition, in fact had refused positions where that would have been his job.

He hated to teach piano because second-class music making was an unbearable nervous strain on a genius of his caliber. So he chose to study, digest, and write up the musical content of an important Serbian folk music collection by a Harvard professor, Perry, recorded by phonograph mainly as a linguistic study of Slavic dialects. This work was his only consolation and ultimately the book he wrote and Columbia undertook to publish was published, but not earlier than in 1949, four years after his death. Whether this would have happened if some prodding, urging, had not been done by me, it is difficult to say.

But in every other respect he was sorely tried. The U.S. was engaged in the war effort. Millions left their home to join the armed forces and do unusual jobs. Little attention, time, and money was left for art. Colleges were empty. Concerts were few, and he became afflicted by a mysterious illness causing never ceasing temperatures preventing or at least hampering him in regular work. The predicament of Bartok was truthfully described in the N.Y. Sun in an article by Irvin Kolodin (Encl. B1).

While Bartók was in the Mount Sinai Hospital in the spring of 1943, ASCAP—even though he was not member of this American Society of Authors, Composes, and Publishers paid—as a gesture of recognition—the expense of the capital, doctors, drugs. The little income he had from the royalties of his musical creations was used for keeping his wife, paying the rent of the modest apartment. But by June 1943 the Columbia fellowship was to expire with no hope of renewal with the soaring prospect of no appointment, no job, no concerts. As a result of a conference I had with Joseph Szigeti, the great violinist, friend of Bartók to whom two of his violin concertos were dedicated, I began a campaign to collect funds to be donated to Columbia University out of which his Research Fellowship would be renewed. I drew up a memorandum (Encl. B_2) to explain the scientific purpose of the donations. Since Bartók would have never agreed to a charity-campaign collecting funds even for "scientific" purposes but connected with him would have been an unpardonable insult in his eyes. Thus Bartók has not had the slightest inkling about the campaign but just in case it would have become known to him only the last sentence did disclose that by helping the scholarly work "this would also assure to Béla Bartók a modest income to live on." Using mostly Szigeti's name I sent out the memo in about 50 copies to persons, institutions known to be patrons of music.

Meanwhile I negotiated with Columbia University to create a cover up for the charity. On April 5th, 1943, I had a conference with the Provost of the University, Frank D. Fackenthal, and with the help of two professors of the Music Department, Douglas Moore and Paul Lang, a Bartók Research Fund was established that would accept the donations out of the proceeds of which

Columbia would reappoint Bartók as Research Fellow without disclosing the origin of the funds.

Meanwhile some money was needed for the immediate living expenses of Mrs. Bartók and Peter Bartók. Professor Moore succeeded to obtain a loan of 500 dollars from the Artists' and Writers' Relief Fund of the National Institute of Art and Letters (633 West 155th Street, New York). It was supposed to be a loan, yet Bartók would have not accepted it. So it was agreed between the President, Secretary-Treasurer of the Institute and me that I shall execute as Attorney in Fact the Note, representing the debt that I shall deposit the check in Bartók's bank account without his seeing the "Artists' and Writers' Fund" printed on the check, and he would believe our story that this was a prize awarded for his excellence and merits (Letter of the National Institute dated March 30, 1943, Encl. B3).

To describe the campaign and the efforts which were thought to be necessary to reach the goal, i.e., enough to assure a one-year extension of the Columbia appointment, would be voluminous. I purchased many copies of the Sun carrying Kolodin's feature article. I wrote letters on my own behalf on behalf of Szigeti. I sent my original Memo as an enclosure in my letter. At the time I myself had much less income than usual, was struggling with keeping my family, surviving the war-crisis to keep my children in schools. I went to work daily in New Jersey in my little factory to save it from liquidation. The costs of secretaries doing this work were heavy. In order to document the kind of campaign that was set on foot I enclose a copy of a letter to the nationally known music patron, Mrs. Elizabeth S. Coolidge, dated April 21, 1943 (Encl. B4).

The response to the request was devastating. The letter of Mrs. Coolidge here-enclosed is typical (B5). Even those who contributed gave so little that it was humiliating to accept it. The letter of the American Composers Alliance announcing 13 (*thirteen*) dollars donated by five (5) composers, among them Goddard Lieberson, now Executive Vice President of CBS, is enclosed (B6). The donations reaching $200.00 numbered 2 (two): $200.00 from Benny Goodman and $250 from the members of the Philadelphia Orchestra. The total donated altogether was $1067.04, *not enough for even one term of a half year*. I added out of my own funds $500.00 (five hundred dollars). Thus I deposited at Columbia $1567.00, and Bartók's pride and minimum subsistence equaling the salary of $250.00 a month were made possible. As a sad epilogue a sum of $67.04 excess over $1500.00 was unexpectedly remitted to me in 1948.

A letter summarizing the connection of Béla Bartók with Columbia University was written to me by the head of the Department of Music on Nov. 30, 1949 (Encl. B7). There is one error in this letter. There never were royalties due or paid on the Yougoslav Folk Music work. Proceeds of sale have and are still being retained to cover the printing expenses which by 1949 were much higher than $2500.00 contributed by the Ditson Fund.

From the spring of 1942 Bartók was seriously ill. Whether the doctors did not know what caused continuous high temperatures or just pretended not to know is not clear. In March 1942 he dissolved his agency contract with his concert-management because they could not get one single concert engagement for him [B8]. But it was just as well because in May 1942 he wrote to his publisher that while he was able to continue his non-musical folk music work he was absolutely unable to do composing, a creative activity for which health, inspiration, and proper living conditions are sine qua non [B9]. Then came a surprising recovery from summer 1943 until summer 1945 during which period he created some of his greatest compositions. During all that time our friendship grew into intimacy. It was in 1943 that he took almost all his valuable musical manuscripts from his publishers Boosey & Hawkes, who had kept them since 1939 in fireproof vaults, in safety, and deposited them with me.

Enclosures B10- give the facts of this operation. He dissolved a Trust-agreement that made Boosey & Hawkes and Dr. George Herzog Trustees with broad powers to sell some of the manuscripts and use the proceeds for the printing and publication of his Roumanian Folk Music work. After this had been achieved, consent of the Trustees given, he instructed Boosey & Hawkes to deliver all manuscripts held by them to Victor Bator. First I took over all but 4, then the remaining four. I stored them in a metal cabinet in my home—a not very satisfactory arrangement. Once or twice he added some more manuscripts. Once he took out one. Once he asked me to take out one and make a note about the gift he used it for. But by and large until his death they were in my house. (After his death I put them immediately into a bank safe. I wanted to do that before, but he kept on saying that some he may need once a while, and the bank safe would be cumbersome.) The list of the manuscripts taken over from Boosey & Hawkes is on Enclosure A.

It is difficult or hardly possible to give tangible reasons for Bartók's confidence in me as evidenced in the manuscript incident, the appointment as Trustee, and his reliance on my judgment in all his private and professional affairs. He was a diffident man, very reserved. In my opinion he developed this confidence because I and my family had never used this friendship for prestige; we have not let ourselves be photographed with him, we let him enjoy our home family-life and did never make him become conscious that he was "Bartók." He offered me a less important manuscript as gift. I refused, saying that a collection is infinitely more important than the personal pleasure that such a gift would give me. But whatever the reasons, the facts are self-explanatory. His older son whom he valued highly was prisoner of a Nazi-controlled political situation, followed by communist dictatorship. Ever since he came to the U.S.A. he tried to live separately from Mrs. Bartók. They lived together only when lack of money forced them together, and even then he fled the apartment whenever she practiced her piano. His younger son was of age, but it seems that Béla Bartók did not trust his steadfastness, his psychological balance, and judgment. It would be embarrassing to relate and publicize family relationship problems on which my advice and help was requested by Mr. and Mrs. Bartók alike which would support the above hypothesis. But the facts of the entire relationship may suffice and make the disclosing other facets unnecessary. After all, I engineered the escape of Peter Bartók, his reuniting with his parents, I helped Bartók in his most humiliating financial situation. I helped him in making secure his treasured manuscripts. He knew that my hand was involved in obtaining the "prize money" of the National Institute of Arts and Letters. He could spend a summer on the Massachusetts seashore before the much publicized ASCAP support made his life tolerable working quietly on his Folklore writings (assisted by Dr. Báron and myself in the translation job as he mentioned it in a letter to his publishers). We took care of Mrs. Bartók by having her in our country home while Bartók was in Saranac Lake. He was a welcome guest at our home whenever he felt like longing for congenial company, and we had at such occasions with us other friends, writers, musicians, his friends. We took him to the concerts (very few) where his works were performed. To make the long story short, we were intimate friends with no disturbing incident or elements. He disliked people who intruded on his privacy. We never did this but were available when he needed us. In the last year of his life, in 1944-45, he needed me less. He was seemingly in better health, he worked on his three last great compositions, the support of ASCAP gave him a feeling of confidence in recovery that lasted until September 1945 when suddenly the pernicious anemia overcame the forces of natural resistance, and when telegraphed to New York, I arrived at his death-bed only 48 hours before the end.

Chapter 2

"Reasons for Bartók's Confidence in Me"

Later on, as he managed the Bartók estate for the heirs, Victor Bator drew moral sustenance for his work from the many conversations he had with Béla Bartók during World War II about the care and future disposition of his materials. As the preceding pages reveal, he interacted often with Bartók after 1940, in a broad variety of situations that led naturally to acquaintance with his wife and son, who also benefited directly from his support. With his influential contacts he helped drive the process of getting Peter Bartók out of Europe. Surviving correspondence for that event, much of it still unpublished, shows him to have been a savvy navigator of officialdom across Europe and in the US, a skill he had already deployed to the Bartóks' advantage in other areas. Worldly annoyances forced year after year on the Bartóks by US immigration authorities persisted through 1945 and (for Ditta) 1946. Their regular requests to extend visas, or to change their visa status, triggered cascades of critically important instructions that could not be ignored. Bator was always on hand to facilitate this immigration paperwork—to ask questions, to confirm appropriate responses, to remove obstacles. His network of well-placed friends in Washington and New York came in handy. He had no hesitation in tapping them to ease the Bartóks' path.

Entry into Bartók's orbit happened quickly in the United States. The subsequent unfolding and deepening of their relationship in 1941–43 warrants further exploration, however, if we are to place Bator back on the shelf as one of Bartók's closer, if not closest, friends in America. Why Bator? What trains of thought led Béla Bartók to entrust a Hungarian lawyer and businessman with his life's work, his physical possessions, and with the care and safety of his family? How did it all start? These are reasonable question to ask. Until recently Bator has been airbrushed out of many accounts of Bartók's American years, an unconscious act for most writers, I suspect, attributable to the estate's contentious history during the Cold War and the distinctive archival impediments that resulted. Many names need to be brought out from the shadows like this—the Kecskemétis, Serly, Sándor, Reiner, Herzog, Lang, Creel, Schulhof, even Ditta Bartók herself—before we can claim for our era a more rounded portrayal of Bartók's American experience.

Chapter 2

Scholars writing about this period in Bartók's life will find Bator's reminiscences in the Memorandum useful when developing fresh narrative lines. Even the details hold promise for future investigation, as in, for example, his description of Bartók as an "exile-refugee," a coinage that adds an intriguingly accurate, hyphenated construction to the list of terms by which Bartók's time in the US has previously been described. Of particular value are his well-informed recollections of Bartók's time at Columbia University. How a sequence of appointments to one of the most eminent universities in the world could lead to disappointment is rarely expressed as sympathetically as Bator does here. Challenge after challenge came to the Bartóks during the war. To help Peter get established in the United States Bator coordinated Peter's summer spent working on a farm in Concord, Massachusetts, in 1942; he offered specific guidance and action for Peter's next steps in education in New York City; he counseled the entire Bartók family on the merits of military registration for Peter as a path towards American citizenship.[1]

No small part of Bator's attraction for many Hungarians in New York City was the hospitality of his wife Franci, herself clearly an appealing social presence for the Bartóks, too. Tellingly his account slips into a plural voice at times:

> We took care of Mrs. Bartók by having her in our country home while Bartók was in Saranac Lake. He was a welcome guest at our home whenever he felt like longing for congenial company, and we had at such occasions with us other friends, writers, musicians, his friends. We took him to the concerts (very few) where his works were performed. **To make the long story short, we were intimate friends with no disturbing incident or elements.**

Franci Bator played a large (and to this day, uncredited) role in providing "congenial company" anytime the Bartóks visited.[2] Béla's notoriously insular behavior in social settings mustn't keep us from appreciating the value to the rest of

---

[1] In New York City Bator knew personally the head of US Selective Service, Candler Cobb, from Sullivan and Cromwell and their earlier work together in global finance. No correspondence survives, to my knowledge, that documents interaction between them on the subject of Peter Bartók's draft decision, or of Bator's own son Francis, who was drafted into the Army in 1943. Knowing Bator's ways of working it seems unlikely that he would have left untouched this opportunity to solicit advice about the wisest paths into wartime service.

[2] "My parents were warmly disposed to Ditta," Francis recalled. "To what degree if at all this was reciprocated, I cannot say. I'm not sure Ditta was capable of that sort of reaction." Francis Bator, interview with the author, October 25, 2010. Elsewhere, Francis suggested that while Béla, Ditta, and Peter visited Nonquitt on multiple occasions, he was not sure that they ever—all three of them—were guests there at the same time.

his family of routine social interactions like this. Periodic visits to the Bator homes in New York and Nonquitt offered Peter a chance to talk to other Hungarian boys his own age, and to observe how they interacted and talked with a mother and father so different from his own. The "we" used in the last sentence of this quotation—"we were intimate friends" —allows an ambiguity to surface in Bator's account that is perfectly fitting. (The bold emphasis here is my own.) At first glance this declaration reads as Bator's summary description of his relationship with Béla Bartók—his stated purpose, after all, in writing this part of the Memorandum. It also seems to reflect the two families' relationships as a whole, in which case his choice of the word "intimate" suggests something broader: that each members of the Bator and Bartók families, parents and children, came to feel ease and comfort with each other as their interactions multiplied. "No disturbing incident or elements" is how Bator remembered this time together. Supporting the Bartóks was a *family* endeavor for the Bators. Victor Bator, the family photographer, sometimes took out his camera to capture informal moments (Fig. 2.1). We need only remember that the Bators hired Ditta Bartók as piano instructor for the twins as much for Ditta's benefit as for their two sons' advancement in the art of playing piano. Those lessons took place in the welcoming comfort of the Bators' home on E. 72nd Street, allowing further layers of familiarity to develop.

Visa and Immigration Stress Accumulates for the Bartóks

Peter Bartók's serendipitous reunion with his father on the streets of New York City in April 1942 has long been a cornerstone in accounts of the composer's American years. Deservedly so. His published retellings have kept the story alive through the years.[3] Less familiar to us—and probably unrecoverable at this point—is the cumulative psychological burden Béla and Ditta must have carried during their first year-and-a-half in the United States knowing that their son remained at risk back in Budapest.[4] Emigration, with its many hurdles, has always broken up families. Deciding to leave children or a spouse behind, and sending for them later once money or travel circumstances permit, is nothing new. Among the Bartóks' circle of acquaintances in New York, the Hollós, too, had to leave one child behind. Ágnes Holló, a 24-year-old mathe-

---

3   Peter Bartok, *My Father*, 84–87. See also Éva Árokszállási, "Peter Bartók in Budapest," translated by Peter Laki from an original Hungarian source. Unpublished photocopy preserved in the Elliott Antokoletz papers.
4   A fictionalized but probably accurate representation of the fear Ditta felt for Peter is found in Agatha Fassett, *The Naked Face of Genius*, 227–35.

Chapter 2

Fig. 2.1. Waterfront gathering, Nonquitt, Massachusetts, Summer 1944. From left, Francis Bator, Franci Bator, Béla Bartók, and Gyula Báron. Photographer: Victor Bator. Source: CPB Homosassa.

matician, arrived in New York in September 1941, nearly two years after her parents.[5] Their son, older, already had emigrated to Palestine. Following the war the Waldbauers emigrated in sequence out of necessity: Imre first in late 1946, to take his teaching position at The University of Iowa, then Isabella and Ivan, separately, the following fall. Fortunately, some documentation of Peter Bartók's escape from Hungary was preserved in the New York Bartók Archives, reminding us what a huge undertaking this was for Peter and his parents.

Bator's Memorandum materially advances our knowledge of this episode. Peter Bartók acknowledges in *My Father* that Bator had been "of substantial help" in connection with the visa process.[6] But the details have been lost with time. Once all the surviving documents for Peter's epic journey can be considered as a whole, this critical episode in their lives can take its proper place as a defining experience of the war years for the Bartóks. It was a massive undertaking for them all, with many helping hands. And it was very, *very* expensive.

---

5 Gyula and Elsa Holló arriving singly in New York in October and December 1939, respectively. Before she left Budapest in 1941 Ági (Agnes) Holló tutored Iván Waldbauer in math. He fondly remembered the experience and what her teaching meant to him as a teenage boy. "I think of her in 1941 as a guardian angel, and as a burning torch who opened for me the road to the wondrously beautiful world of math." Waldbauer, letter to the author, July 12, 2004.

6 Peter Bartók, *My Father*, 239.

Already by February 1941 Bator was helping the Bartóks with their visa renewals. They all had re-encountered each other "in the home of a mutual friend" in New York three months earlier, shortly after the Bartóks arrived. (Possibly the Laxes or the Hollós.) Now, a few months into their time in the United States, Béla was about to head out on a month-long tour across the United States, to California and back, accompanied by Ditta. Their absence threatened to stall their visa renewal paperwork's routine progress through official channels. Bator offered to take care of its Hungarian documentation requirements. He could claim no special expertise in American visa regulations: he was newly arrived himself. He possessed skilled legal instincts, though, and a lifetime of experience threading his way through bureaucratic processes. Back in Budapest, furthermore, his personal secretary remained on standby, ready to help on any matters, only a telegram away.

Through this mundane task of visa renewal a relationship was rekindled. At its core, at first, the relationship was based on service: Bator took pleasure in being able to help Bartók. Tibor Serly observed that many Hungarians were similarly inclined. "Here in New York the situation was just as it was at home," Serly commented many years later. "Everyone regarded him as a Prince and sought to serve him."[7] Twenty years earlier Bator had proven himself as a reliable go-between for Bartók's personal mail in Vienna. And while no reason to interact further arose as their respective careers unfolded in the 1920s and 30s, through common friends in Budapest's artistic and intellectual world they remained conscious of each other's presence. An occasional casual encounter took place. We can safely surmise that Bator, because he cultivated personal interests in Hungarian art, literature, and music, was more aware of Bartók than vice versa. Bartók knew him as one of Imre Waldbauer's friends.

Victor Bator's personal secretary, Lujza Brem, worked for him at his house in Budapest; during the 1930s she became a trusted member of the family's inner circle (Fig. 2.2). When Bator was stripped of his Hungarian citizenship on October 8, 1941, that ruling by the Cabinet of Ministers meant he could no longer legally own property in the country. Brem was granted custody of his personal property, including his financial holdings and the Gellért Hill home on Somlói út, with its magnificent terrace view over the city below.[8] During the war she watched over the home and generally looked out for the family's interests. (A driver and housekeeper also remained at the house, their salaries, like hers, covered as long as possible.) A familiar figure to the Bator children, loyal

---

7   Serly, as Interviewee "E," in Vilmos Juhasz, *Bartók's Years in America* (New York: Occidental Press, 1981), 65.
8   János Botos, "The Stages of Viktor Bátor's Career," unpublished document, personal collection of Francis Bator.

Fig. 2.2. Lujza Brem, personal secretary for Victor Bator and his family in Budapest. Studio photograph, Budapest, ca. 1935. Photographer: unidentified.
Source: personal collection of Francis Bator.

to them all, fluent in English, German, and her native Hungarian, "Miss Brem" kept working for the Bators into late 1944, only to be killed in the war's final months, during the siege, as a civilian casualty.⁹ Because more correspondence and telegrams from her may surface in archives in decades ahead, and because she played a supporting role in getting Peter Bartók out of Hungary, I preserve this image of her here in order to give her name tangible presence. Her facility in languages would be deeply missed by Bator later on, as would the stability she represented to them all.

On February 13, 1941, Victor cabled Miss Brem to help him obtain several required items for the Bartóks: morality certificates for Béla and Ditta from the Budapest police, attesting to their good character, and a formal certificate from the Academy of Music confirming Bartók's record of employment.¹⁰ He also asked her to get the process started for a visitor visa for Peter Bartók. Thus began Bator's direct involvement in Béla Bartók's personal affairs. His financial involvement began now, too, in a fashion so typical for Bator, whose prosperity allowed him to wave away any costs, small or large, incurred in the name of friendship.¹¹

---

9   Francis Bator remembered her to me with great affection. "She was a saint and a remarkable human being." Her death shocked and horrified the family. She died in captivity in Budapest in January 1945, having been imprisoned by the Nazi occupiers for remaining active in the resistance. Béla Bartók, in a letter to Peter written on June 22, 1945, relates the story of her death, as well as other news of the Bators' household (in Peter Bartók, *My Father*, 319). The Bators learned the news only after the war had ended.
10 Victor Bator, cable to Lujza Brem, in English. Copy. February 13, 1941. CPB Homosassa. The resulting police morality certificates and other visa documents have been preserved. Their English-language translations, neatly typed and notarized, are the work of Claire (Klára) Roth, born in Győr in 1915 and emigrated to the US as a child in 1921. Roth made a living in New York as a translator. Who paid her for them in 1941 cannot be determined, but I would suggest they represent exactly the sort of required official paperwork that Bator handled on behalf of the Bartóks.
11 In a letter to Béla Jr., Bartók reminds his son that he had requested his help with these documents in late 1940, but now that Bator was involved the matter had been quickly resolved. He absolves his son of further responsibility. Béla Bartók, letter to Béla Bartók Jr., 19 March 1941 (BBA).

"I engineered the emigration of Peter Bartók and his admittance to the U.S.," Bator writes in the Memorandum. A statement this bold could be dismissed were it not for its author's record of arranging many such extractions. (See Chapter 4.) Ralph Hawkes's intervention in the Lisbon phase, when Peter was help up for months waiting for travel clearance by British authorities, is already known to scholars. Once we begin to draw lines among the many names found in the correspondence that survives in Florida, Bator's presence becomes more apparent. Marc McNitzky, a close friend of his from the Budapest business world, managed all the financial transactions from his office on Wall Street—wire transfers, deposits, purchase of tickets, international confirmation cables—for almost a full year, starting in April 1941. McNitzky fronted costs as needed, knowing that Bator, behind the scenes, guaranteed payment. From his accounting we learn that the total cost of bringing Peter to the US was $1,452.41—an amount equal to almost half of his Columbia University salary that year. Bartók paid the entire amount in installments.[12]

In his Memorandum Bator specifically credits Miss Brem and Tibor Hajnal for managing the Budapest side of Peter's emigration. They worked "with pull, trick, and money" to get him as far as Zürich, via Croatia and Italy, at which point Stefi Geyer and her husband Walther Schulthess stepped in. Hajnal, the Bartóks' family doctor, was a trusted figure in their family; he had recently been given testamentary authority for Peter as a minor.

In October 1941 Bator awoke one day to find his name identified in *The New York Times* as one of five Hungarian businessmen and politicians whose citizenship had just been stripped from them by their own government back in Budapest.[13] For several months that fall his business correspondence for the Commercial Bank had been covertly monitored by Hungarian counter-espionage examiners. The German-leaning government had grown concerned over his collaboration with Tibor Eckhardt and other prominent Hungarians abroad who opposed Nazi accommodation. On October 6, 1941, the far-right newspa-

---

12 In family financial papers preserved in CPB Homosassa can be found a handwritten tally of the McNitzky costs, ca. mid 1942, bearing Bartók's annotation, "pay to Bator." Bator likely arranged the hiring of James Oliver Murdock in 1941 to help represent the Bartóks in Washington, D.C., with miscellaneous visa and income tax issues. (Several references to Murdock are found in Béla Bartók's correspondence that year.) Murdock, a graduate of the University of Chicago and of Harvard Law School, worked at the State Department and in private practice until joining the law faculty of George Washington University in 1945. An appreciation of his career can be found online at https://scholar.smu.edu/cgi/viewcontent.cgi?article=3559&context=til.

13 "Hungary Disowns Five," *The New York Times*, Oct. 9, 1941. In this brief notice, the Associated Press reported that five individuals were identified on Hungarian radio as having their citizenship deprived due to their involvement in the Free Hungary movement abroad. They were identified by the Hungarian National Broadcasting Company as Tibor Eckhardt, Victor Bator, John Pelényi, Anto Balaz, and Anton Zsilinsky.

Chapter 2

per *Virradat* published an article spuriously accusing Bator of acting as "director of emigration affairs" in the United States; his temper on important political issues, the article reported, was further evident from his association with *Amerikai Magyar Népszava*. In the article Bator was called a Jew. Two days later the Cabinet of Ministers passed Resolution No. 7210/1941 declaring the interests of the Hungarian nation endangered by Bator and four other prominent Hungarians abroad who recently committed to leading an opposition movement. The Budapest Bar Association promptly suspended him as a member. In response the Executive Committee of his bank ordered its President, Károly Lamotte, to take actions that would ensure Victor Bator no longer acted on behalf of the bank in any capacity, especially overseas. On October 30, 1941, the Board of Directors of the bank submitted Bator's employment agreement to an internal disciplinary committee. The Board met on November 18 to discuss the committee's recommendations, and on November 19, 1941, the Pesti Magyar Kereskedelmi Bank formally terminated his employment. His right to receive his pension was likewise ended.[14]

Ferenc Chorin, Vice President of the bank (1932–41), had been forced out earlier in 1941 due to his Jewish heritage. Francis Bator remembered Chorin as "a very close family friend" and also one of Regent Horthy's closest personal friends. He told me a wry little story to illustrate how tightly interwoven the business and political elite could be in Budapest:

> Imrédy was the most strident pro-Nazi in Budapest. He was a brilliant lawyer and former upstairs neighbor of ours before we moved into our house on Gellért Hill. He was a close acquaintance of my father's. I used to pal around with his son. Before he became prime minister, Imrédy's politics would have been sharply right of center, but very much on the white collar side. Then he becomes prime minister, and all of a sudden he's a virulent Nazi. You know, the only thing wrong with Nikolaus Horthy is that he was not very smart. He was no more a fascist . . . he was an English gentleman. With a gorgeous wife. And he loved playing bridge. One of his favorite bridge partners was Ferenc Chorin, who was a very close family friend of ours, and who married into the Weiss family. His grandfather had been one of the grand rabbis. So when the Imrédy crowd started, and the Germans came in, Horthy stopped the deportation of the Budapest Jewish community. He put an absolute stop to it. But before he did that he said, 'Oh, and please don't touch my dear

---

14 The processes and decisions outlined in this paragraph are taken from János Botos, research report on Victor Bator (1994–5). Transl. Etelka Nyilasi.

friend Chorin Ferenc.' 'Feri bácsi,' he called him. So it was a very mixed up kind of business.[15]

Bator still had friends at the Commercial Bank after the war. They interceded on his behalf to grant him access to his pension account from August 1, 1946, to June 30, 1947, the first year of the new forint currency.

The Movement for Independent Hungary, 1941–42

Until Nándor Dreisziger published his study of Bartók's wartime political engagement in 2005, the Bartók studies field, its attention trained in other directions, had paid scant attention to the topic.[16] Dreisziger assembled evidence that tied Bartók to a government-in-exile plan known as the Movement for Independent Hungary that flourished in the United States from mid-1941 to late 1942. He measured this information against Bartók's evolving political inclinations across his lifetime, from the overt nationalism of his youth to the nuanced views of his later years, when he held "negative views of left-wing radicalism" as well as chronic "disappointment with Hungarian right-wing politics." His findings were, and are, convincing. A number of adjacent studies of Hungarian wartime politics also appeared in the early 2000s. For historians the passage of time had allowed the topic's intrinsic political charge to dissipate, making way for balanced, critical perspectives. Várdy, Kádár Lynn, Cornelius, Dreisziger, Puskás, and other excellent scholars drew on archival holdings and personal memoirs to decode the proper interplay of events. Many of their studies were written in English for an international audience.[17]

15　Francis Bator, interview with the author, Oct. 27, 2012.
16　Nándor F. Dreisziger, "A Hungarian Patriot in American Exile: Béla Bartók and Émigré Politics," *Journal of the Royal Musical Association* 130/2 (2005): 283–301. In condensed form his research also appeared in "Spying on 'Mr. Bartók' in Wartime America," *The Hungarian Quarterly* 46, No. 179 (Autumn 2005), available online at www.hungarianquarterly.com/no179/17.shtml.
17　A crucial early source on this topic is John Pelényi, "The Secret Plan for a Hungarian Government in the West at the Outbreak of World War II," *The Journal of Modern History* 36/2 (June 1964): 170–77. Research from outside the field of musicology includes Julianna Puskás, *Ties That Bind, Ties That Divide: 100 Years of Hungarian Experience in the United States* (New York and London: Holmes & Meier, 2000); Stephen Béla Várdy, "Hungarian Americans During World War II: Their Role in Defending Hungary's Interests," in M.B.B. Biskupski, ed., *Ideology, Politics and Diplomacy in East Central Europe* (Rochester, NY: Rochester University Press, 2003): 120–46; and Katalin Kádár Lynn, *Tibor Eckhardt: His American Years, 1941–1972* (Boulder, CO: East European Monographs, distr. Columbia University Press, 2007). Anne Applebaum's *Iron Curtain: The Crushing of Eastern Europe, 1944-1956* (New York: Doubleday, 2012) documents the unrelenting cruelty and violence that accompanied the Soviet takeover in Eastern Europe.

Chapter 2

When Bator and his staff began systematically organizing the New York Bartók Archives in the 1950s they came across materials Bartók had saved from his work for the Movement for Independent Hungary. They gathered these documents into a binder for preservation, labelling them "Political: Cultural Committee / 1941–42." Within its pages can be found multiple typed copies, in different versions, of the "Principles of Organization of the Cultural Group of the Movement for Independent Hungary in the U.S.A." and dozens of replies from prominent Hungarians to the invitation letters sent out over Bartók's name in 1942. A typed letter from Bartók to Eckhardt dated December 31, 1941, is one of many items that show Bartók advancing the group's goals.

Dreisziger appears not to have had access to these documents when he conducted his research, and their promise to musicologists, as a tightly focused collection, is high. I will touch on some highlights here to emphasize the role that politics played in bring Bator and Bartók closer together. What interests us, for our purposes, is what the Florida documents reveal about Bator and Bartók's joint involvement, so clearly memorialized in this small aggregation of papers. All are stamped "1941" or "1942" by Archives staff. To augment the items Bartók saved, Bator added memorabilia from his own files, including, for example, drafts of a long letter he wrote to Tibor Eckhardt in 1942. Marked-up working drafts of the Organizing Principles, and the many return letters sent to Bartók at his Columbia University address, all probably came to the Archives many years later through Paul Henry Lang as a record of his own involvement as Secretary of the Cultural Group, and, later, board member for the New York Bartók Archives. Lists of prospective members also probably came from Lang. At least three different styles of handwriting can be discerned on these various documents, most of which are typed and therefore did not originate with Bartók himself. At best these documents preserve a fragmented, incoherent view of the Cultural Group through its charter documents. But at least they were saved. Incidentally, and not unimportantly, they reveal many details about Bartók's activities for the organization.

The factors that compelled the Movement for Independent Hungary into existence, with Tibor Eckhardt as its primary spokesman, all have roots in the messy political dramas that rippled through Hungary in the buildup to the war. By 1939 Prime Minister Pál Teleki, together with Regent Horthy, had become deeply worried that pressure groups within their country would drive Hungary into the arms of Germany after the Anschluss. Internal agitation by the Arrow Cross movement and other pro-German constituencies increased pressure on the Hungarian government to adopt revisionist positions that would return the country to its pre-Trianon boundaries. The possibility that events might force their capitulation led Teleki, in early 1940, to order the National Bank to secretly wire $5,000,000 to the United States. Should it be needed, this money could be tapped to support a government-in-exile committed to longstanding Hungarian democratic ideals. Hungarian Ambassador to the US John Pelényi was charged with helping US officials recognize that Horthy, already compromised by his willingness to accommodate right-wing elements sympathetic to Hitler, did not necessarily speak for the country as a whole, and that Hungary wished to retain the benevolence of Western powers.[18]

Within Hungary a tense standoff ensued as certain political factions tacked right, pushing relentlessly for alignment with fascist ideology. Teleki's suicide on April 3, 1941, stunned the nation, leaving Horthy with one less voice of moderation to hold the line. A ferocious German attack on Belgrade gave opportunistic Hungarian politicians the permission they needed to allow a military push south into Yugoslavia, reclaiming former Hungarian territory. In response Britain immediately broke off diplomatic relations. Within three months the country was drawn into war against Soviet Russia, a decision that would soon hold tragic consequences for its Second Army. Allied diplomatic relations grew frostier when Hungary declared support for the Berlin–Tokyo–Rome Tripartite Pact. Japan's bombing of Pearl Harbor forced Hungary, on account of its treaty obligations, to declare war on the United States. In January 1942 the Hungarian military and gendarmes slaughtered 3,000 residents in a Serbian city in the name of suppressing partisan attacks. The Novi Sad massacre, as this horrific action was soon called, blackened Hungary's eye in the international press.

When Tibor Eckhardt arrived in New York in late summer 1941 Hungary was still not at war with the US. Eckhardt landed with an immediate goal: to rally patriotic Hungarians into creating a political movement that would remind the world that Hungary was not a pro-Nazi country. In so doing he hoped to lay the base for a possible government-in-exile that would advance Hungary's diplomatic interests among the Western Allies. He went into exile, Victor Bator would later write, "in order to represent, outside the country—if necessary, alone—the true spirit of democratic, anti-Nazi Hungary and her people."[19]

Eckhardt had been serving in Hungarian politics for two decades. He carried prestige as leader (1932–41) of the politically moderate Independent Smallholders' Party. In 1929-30 he had visited the United States for an extended lec-

---

18   Pelényi, "The Secret Plan," 172.
19   Victor Bator, "Tibor Eckhardt: Portrait of a Statesman," *Amerikai Magyar Népszava* (January 28, 1945): 3. Bator's detailed account of Eckhardt's political career in Hungary appeared in the monthly English-language section of *Amerikai Magyar Népszava*. His article is noteworthy for its reliance on copies of Eckhardt's speeches in Hungarian Parliament as a foundation for its narrative.

ture tour, five months long, sponsored by the Carnegie Endowment for International Peace. He served as Executive Vice President (1928–41) for The Hungarian League for Revision, an irredentist organization that sought political solutions for the return of Hungary's lost territory. Prime Minister Gömbös appointed him Hungary's Chief Delegate to the League of Nations in 1934-35. This work increased his familiarity with the changing political environment in Germany. He was an early and outspoken opponent of Hitler's ambitions, identified in newspapers abroad as an "anti-fascist" actively working in Hungary to mute Hitler's rising influence. Antal Ullein-Reviczky, Press Chief for the Hungarian government in the early years of World War II, appreciated Eckhardt's Smallholder's Party for never abandoning its motto: "Liberty Inside, Independence Outside," which meant fighting off attempts to subjugate its own people, while staving off foreign pressures that would lead to loss of freedom.[20] In his non-parliamentary life Eckhardt served as Executive Vice President for *The Hungarian Quarterly* for five years between the wars, and as vice president of the Anglo-Hungarian Cultural Association.

Like Bartók, Eckhardt had made an exploratory tour of the United States in early 1940, ostensibly for personal reasons, but in reality a concerted effort to build political goodwill and connections for his later return. A luncheon was given in his honor by the Chairman of Chase Bank, Winthrop Aldrich, that was attended by Victor Bator, László Medgyessy, consul general of Hungary in New York, John Pelényi, and others. He also made the rounds of political offices in Washington, D.C., where he was honored at a lunch event by the board of directors of the Federal Reserve. Other stops included Denver, Des Moines, Minneapolis and St. Paul, and Portland, Oregon. In Washington he met with President Roosevelt at the White House.[21] "It is little wonder," concludes Kádár Lynn as she surveys Eckhardt's many activities and the people he met on this short American tour, "that the Hungarian government had high hopes for his success when he undertook his last and most important journey on its behalf."[22]

When he returned to the United States in the late summer of 1941, a path had been prepared for him by the American Hungarian Federation. Later recollections of one Federation participant identify the names of individuals who greeted Eckhardt at the Movement's organizing convocation in Pittsburgh that September:

---

20 Antal Ullein-Revitczky, *German War, Russian Peace: The Hungarian Tragedy*, transl. Lovice Mária Ullein-Revitczky (Reno, NV: Helena History Press, 2014): 29.
21 Eckhardt's many official appointments and professional activities up to 1941 are outlined in Kádár Lynn, *Tibor Eckhardt's American Years*, Ch. 1: 27–53, where his 1940 exploratory tour of the US is also described.
22 Kádár Lynn, *Tibor Eckhardt's American Years*, 49.

Eckhardt announced that, as a Hungarian politician who had fled from Nazism, he intends to establish a general movement embracing all Hungarians living in various countries of the world so as to defend the Hungarian people from the charge of Nazism... At the Federation's and the Independence Movement's joint meeting in September 1941 in Pittsburgh... Dr. Eckhardt was accompanied by the ambassadorial counselor Antal Balássy and the industrialist Viktor Bátor. They announced that the leadership of their movement counts among its members Ambassador János Pelényi and the noted diplomat Antal Zsilinszky, who resided in London.[23]

(The description of Bator as an "industrialist" suggests that his association with the Chorin and Weiss families defined him in Hungarian business circles as much as his banking background.) A Proclamation on September 27 announced the establishment of the Movement, with Tibor Eckhardt at its head. The Proclamation denounced the Nazis, claiming that Hungary's government was an unwilling hostage to German interests, and further declared that it was every Hungarian's "sacred duty" to fight Nazi rule.[24]

The Movement's idealism was enshrined in its Proclamation, whose language spoke in lofty tones of human rights, national determination, and historical justification, clearly inspired by the "We the People" style of the French Declaration of the Rights of Man and the American Declaration of Independence. St. Stephen, Rákóczi, Petőfi, and Kossuth had shown Hungarians the path to a country founded on principles of liberty and freedom. Those principles were now under threat.

> In this intolerable situation, we Hungarians living outside of Hungary, fortunate in being able to express our views freely, have not only the right but also the sacred duty to give voice to the genuine convictions of the Hungarian people and to take up the fight against Nazi domination. The fate of our nation depends wholly on the outcome of this fight for independence. The magnitude of the task, the supreme values at stake, demand the united effort of all Hungarians wherever they may be. No

---

23   Reverend György Borshy-Kerekes, as cited in Várdy, "Hungarian Americans During World War II," 130-31.
24   Dreisziger, "A Hungarian Patriot in Exile," 291-92, summarizes the Movement's manifesto in words I paraphrase here. See also Paul Nadányi, *Hungary at the Crossroads of Invasions* (New York: The Amerikai Magyar Népszava, 1942), and Nadányi, *The Free Hungary Movement* (New York: The Amerikai Magyar Népszava, [April] 1942), which offer historical justification for the new movement for American audiences.

difference in party or religious affiliations, or of racial origin, no class distinction shall be allowed to separate us.

Let us join hands to dedicate ourselves once more to the service of our traditions of true Christian ideals, respect of human rights and national independence. In fighting for these high ideals, we are inspired by eternal aspirations of free men everywhere, as expressed in the American Declaration of Independence and the Bill of Rights, as well as in the third point of the joint declaration of President Roosevelt and Prime Minister Churchill, wishing to "see sovereign rights and self-government restored to those who have been forcibly deprived of them."

We solemnly declare that the Hungarian nation is not responsible for the policies and acts of its present government whose decisions are obviously subject to Nazi pressure.[25]

It's hard to imagine the composer of *Cantata Profana* not being deeply moved by these words. Bartók was not present at the birth of the Movement—he had little interest in professional politics, per se—but it didn't take him long. Within a matter of days he was on board, unable to resist the call to action this Movement presented.[26] Bator, Eckhardt, and other Hungarians prevailed upon him to lend his name to the new Movement, if not right away, then as soon as the timing might be auspicious. What remained was figuring out how he could help.

A long letter by Candler Cobb to *The New York Times* on October 15, 1941, testifies to the integrity of the men who founded the Movement. Cobb had spent much of "the past seven or eight years" working in Hungary. He knew the Executive Committee members well from his time in Budapest. Dr. Eckhardt, he writes, "stands high among Hungarians who in the last seven years fought an untiring battle against nazism and its political agents in Hungary." Pelényi and Balassy "are former Hungarian diplomats of unchallenged integrity who resigned their positions the moment the present Hungarian Government under Nazi pressure signed the Axis treaty." Victor Bator, he explains to *Times* readers, "is one of the leading lawyers in Hungary and is known to every business man who came in touch with matters in Hungary." All of them are "first-class

---

25 The entire Proclamation is reproduced in facsimile in Kádár Lynn, *Tibor Eckhardt in America*, 208. The original is one page long in broadsheet format, presented over the typed signature of Tibor Eckhardt on behalf of the Executive Committee, and dated "New York, N.Y., on the 27th day of September in the year of our Lord Nineteen Hundred and Forty-One."
26 Béla Bartók, letter to Tibor Eckhardt, December 31, 1941 (CPB Homosassa).

Fig. 2.3. Franci Bator and Tibor Eckhardt outside the Bator summer home, Nonquitt, Mass., 1944. Photographer: Victor Bator. Source: personal collection of Francis Bator.

associates."[27] Tibor Kerekes, President of the American Hungarian Federation, vouched for the character of Eckardt in a letter published October 4 in *The Washington Post*.[28] In an editorial titled "New Hungary" *The Washington Post* quickly threw its voice into the battle, too. Eckhardt, it explained, was a "new Kossuth" fighting for "the sacred flame of liberty . . . which continues to burn in all occupied countries" in Europe.[29]

The Movement surged in popularity that fall, quickly drawing the support of not only the American Hungarian Federation, but also the majority of the several hundred Hungarian fraternal and religions organizations in the United States. Once reports of its existence filtered back to Budapest, however, each of the men on its Executive Committee had his Hungarian citizenship publicly revoked in retaliation. Their public commitment to opposition made them personae non gratae to a Hungarian government in thrall to baser motives.

Bator served as the main conduit for Bartók's introduction to the Movement. Credit for encouraging Bator to get involved in the first place may have belonged to Gyula Báron—another invisible link to explain Bartók's later

---

27 Candler Cobb, letter to the Editor, "Dr. Eckhardt Upheld," *The New York Times*, Oct. 21, 1941.
28 Tibor Kerekes, letter to the Editor, "New Hungary," *The Washington Post*, Oct. 7, 1941.
29 "New Hungary," *The Washington Post*, Sept. 28, 1941.

Chapter 2

choice of these two men as co-executors of his estate.³⁰ From the beginning of his time in the United States Tibor Eckhardt was a regular guest at the Bator family homes in New York and Massachusetts. A many-layered personal friendship with Victor and Franci developed (Fig. 2.3). "He and my father didn't become friends until World War II in New York," Francis explained. "My father wasn't active in political circles in Budapest. They certainly knew each other in Budapest, then became more involved with each other later." Never short of anecdotes when the conversation turned to politics, Francis even remembered playing tennis with Eckhardt in New York and in Nonquitt.³¹ He didn't say who won.

For recent Hungarian émigrés, public involvement in politics always came with some risks, even though the US State Department did not place Hungary at the top of its list of concerns. A document found among the pages of Archives visa correspondence shows plainly how immigration matters troubled Bartók during this time. An affidavit written for US immigration processes in October 1941 concludes:

> As soon as Bartok will immigrate, his son Peter, 16 years old, shall be entitled to a non-quota immigration visa. It has to be feared however that if Bartok's association with the "Movement for Independent Hungary" becomes public, his son will never get permission to leave Hungary.
>
> It is requested that a visitors visa shall be granted to Peter Bartok enabling him to join his father and enabling the "Movement for Independent Hungary" to obtain the name and cooperation of Bartok[,] the importance of which is very great.³²

Evidently Bartók's willingness to declare association with the Movement correlated directly with the status of Peter's emigration. Once Peter arrived in the US, a primary source for his hesitation was removed. He could now become more active and no longer fear for his son. Until that time he requested that his involvement remain secret.³³ He agreed to serve on a committee of prominent Hungarian artists and scientists who would lend their names to the Movement's

---

30 Francis Bator proudly acknowledged his father as one of the organizers of the Movement. Victor Bator played "a key role in getting Béla Bartók to accept this position," he remarked. "It was Gyula Báron who asked my father if he'd be willing to take this on, and my father said yes." Francis Bator, interview with the author, July 10, 2011.
31 Francis Bator, interview with the author, October 27, 2012.
32 Typed affidavit, 1 p., undated (CPB Homosassa).
33 Dreisziger, "Spying on Mr. Bartók," online at www.hungarianquarterly.com/no179/17.shtml.

goals. Soon he became President of this committee. Paul Henry Lang consented to act as Executive Vice President, with László Stenger as Executive Secretary.

Over the winter of 1941–42 Eckhardt's leadership of the Movement came under increasing fire from left-leaning Hungarians in the United States, who found him an unacceptable choice to represent their interests despite their common distaste for Nazism. Dreisziger, Várdy, and Kádár Lynn show their strengths as historians when accounting for the collapse of Eckhardt's presidency by mid-1942. Eckhardt had "too many skeletons in his closet," Dreisziger explains, particularly from early in his political career when he espoused ardent right-wing political views, which some Hungarian émigrés had not forgotten, and were unwilling to forgive, despite abundant evidence that his views had shifted since then.[34] (Francis Bator: "Tibor Eckhardt was a complicated figure. After World War I he was part of the extreme right wing. Then he became a supporter of the liberal Bethlen, and part of the Smallholders Party: a centrist, democratic.") Within the Hungarian community in the US the traditional distrust among many fraternal groups for anything they perceived as representing the interests of the Hungarian elite further destabilized the Movement. Várdy identifies two main orientations within what he calls "the colorful spectrum of Hungarian American political life" during the war: the so-called "conservative-nationalists," which included the Movement for Independent Hungary, and the "liberal-internationalists." Each of these possessed an extreme fringe, the chauvinists and the communists, respectively. Both groups spent much of the war trying to undermine each other's credibility.[35] Most Hungarian Americans and Canadians were strongly anti-communist and strongly anti-Nazi, mirroring sentiments at home.

Conservative-nationalist groups like the Movement for Independent Hungary defined their identity by renouncing fascism. They felt equally strong antipathy for leftist ideology. In exchange they drew heavy fire from partisans on both sides. Soviet and Nazi propaganda from overseas stirred up clouds of dubious information. Russian disinformation, for example, spread the opinion that Eckhardt was in actuality a fascist hiding among more the more true democrats Rusztem Vámbéry, Oszkár Jászi, and Mátyás Rákosi. Communist ideologues issued fusillades of denunciations, private and public. The communist press in the United States enthusiastically threw itself into battle. Chief agents of the anti-Eckhardt campaign were those whose loyalties lay with what Paul Nadányi at the time called "a certain coterie of imperialist Czech politicians or

---

34 Dreisziger, "A Hungarian Patriot in American Exile," 292–93.
35 Várdy, "Hungarian Americans During World War II," 124–25.

with the Soviet regime."[36] The Czechs, for strategic territorial reasons, sought to keep Hungary from gaining a stronger voice around the table of Western democracies. Czech and Russian interests conspired to undermine Eckhardt even before he arrived, working at times directly with his opponents in the global Hungarian émigré community, including Vámbéry, whose articulate voice in the academic community amplified doubts among many liberal-minded Hungarians abroad.[37]

Béla Bartók Appointed President of the Movement for Independent Hungary

Eckhardt became a casualty of these conflicts. In July 1942 he agreed to step aside, painfully aware that his leadership had lost its viability due to the barrage of personal attacks. The Movement's Executive Committee met in New York on July 9, 1942, during the course of which meeting they decided to elevate Bartók to the presidency, assuming—and hoping—he would accept. He did. Archival sources consulted by Dreisziger reveal that Bartók was Eckhardt's first choice; he represented "a sort of Paderewski" who could unite Hungarians. With a musician's ascendancy to the role came a fundamental reconfiguration of the Movement's goals. No longer a "lobby of émigré politicians and diplomats," in Dreisziger's felicitous phrasing, it now became a group of concerned Hungarian-American intellectuals, scientists, and artists. Or, in other words, a group where Bartók's example carried real weight. From July 1942 onward date the majority of the letters he wrote to Hungarians around the US, inviting them to pledge their names to the Movement. His activity as a correspondent was characteristically industrious. But dozens and dozens of letters sent out over a name even as prominent as his could not hold together a Movement that had exhausted its ability to unite fractious Hungarians in a time of war.[38] Its individual participants would continue on their own paths after December 1942.

For about 15 months, then, from September 1941 to December 1942, Béla Bartók gave expression to his Hungarian patriotism through involvement in

---

36 Paul Nadányi, letter to John Montgomery, Jan. 22, 1942. Reproduced in facsimile in Kádár Lynn, *Tibor Eckhardt's American Years*, 209–210.
37 Kádár Lynn's analysis of Rusztem Vámbéry's role in undermining Eckhardt demonstrates his active collusion with Czech propagandists during the war. See Kádár Lynn, "The Vámbéry Faction," in *Tibor Eckhardt's American Years*, 121–27.
38 Bartók's mixed success at epistolary solicitation can be seen in a letter he wrote to Bator on November 27, 1942, where he communicates news of his recent appeals to other Hungarians. The letter he sent to Leo Kapp was returned to him in the mail, he reports, its recipient no longer present at the address. Tóth, meanwhile, declined involvement in the Movement. Bartók would try once more with Térbessy, who wants to join, but can't. "I was adamant with him" (BBC-PSS Basel).

this most well-known of Hungary's government-in-exile efforts. His involvement was sporadic at first, cautious even. The Movement's ideals stirred his patriotism to life, offering him, as it did for thousands of others, at home and abroad, a flickering flame of hope in the midst of bleakness. Regular contact with Bator, who was publicly engaged from the beginning, accelerated the pace of his involvement. They discovered common ground in wartime politics. Later, in the summer of 1945, he and Bator again fell into their familiar collaborative mode on behalf of Hungary. At Bator's prompting Bartók agreed to publicize and write letters for the American Hungarian Relief, Inc., an International Red-Cross affiliated organization whose goal was to send material aid to Hungary in the closing days of the war.[39]

Even if, as it has been suggested, Bartók agreed to engage in these projects out of gratitude for Bator's help, it was an honest gratitude—unforced and authentic. Paul Kecskeméti remembered Bartók being drawn to the Movement for Independent Hungary because he was furious at the turn of events that allowed "Hitlerites" to take over the country. Even though the Movement had little real power to create change back in Hungary, Kecskeméti observed, it gave Bartók and other freedom-loving Hungarian patriots and diplomats a way to publicly register their protest. Bartók "willingly endorsed" the group.[40] Kecskeméti knew Bartók's mind well during these years. His recollections have the ring of truth. Bartók himself went further: in a letter to Eckhardt in 1941 he expressed his willingness to join the Movement, and closed by affirming that he was a "true believer."[41]

In light of what was to come with the Bartók estate in the 1950s and 60s, it's important for us to recognize that one of the deepest tap roots sustaining Victor Bator in his fierce defense of the estate from communist encroachment lay in his absolute certainty of Bartók's personal political orientation. This knowledge had its birth in their work together on the Movement for Independent Hungary, where it was reinforced and affirmed. While opposition to Nazism was the Movement's hallmark, its members also felt sharp suspicions for communism because of their narrow escape in 1919–20. The bitter fruits of more recent experience only sharpened this antipathy. Their patriotism was of the Solzhenitsyn type, a "healing, salutary, moderate patriotism" grounded in pres-

---

39 A cluster of 20 documents and letters on this topic is preserved in CPB Homosassa.
40 Paul Kecskeméti, conversation with Tibor Serly, as reproduced in Serly's unpublished typescript for a book on Bartók (Tibor Serly papers, Rare Books Room, Butler Library, Columbia University).
41 Béla Bartók, letter to Tibor Eckhardt, December 31, 1941 (CPB Homosassa). Transl. Etelka Nyilasi.

Chapter 2

ervation of the people rather than demands for territorial return.[42] Occasionally their distrust for Russian imperialism broke into the open: the many invitation letters Bartók sent out in late 1942 for the Movement framed the "fatalistic struggle between nations" as "between the democracies and the dictatorships," before inviting recipients to declare their support.[43] (Which countries suffered under dictatorships needed no explanation.) "Not surprisingly," Dreisziger writes, "during his American exile he refused to have anything to do with the organizations of communist or even socialist émigrés."[44] Bator—more routinely engaged with politicians and diplomats—helped reinforce this stance. A letter he wrote to Bartók in the summer of 1945 urges that they continue to keep their distance from Vámbéry on account of his leftist orientation. I'm sure you'll remember, he comments at one point in the letter, that Vámbéry's "usual approach to Hungarian problems" is something "you would not approve of."[45] Years later, Bator remembered that Bartók always said "no" to Vámbéry's efforts to seduce him away from the Movement for Independent Hungary; those refusals originated in Bartók's disapproval of "Russia-friendly, Benešian, half-Bolshevik Hungarians." (See Appendix A.) Nadányi wondered aloud in 1942 if Soviet agitation lay in the background of the personal attacks on Eckhardt. Perhaps these denunciations were coming from local press, the editor of *Amerikai Magyar Népszava* mused. Or perhaps were they part of the policy of the Soviet government that was using Beneš for its own purposes in Central Europe, laying the groundwork for Bolshevist revolution? He cautions readers not to leap from the frying pan into the fire. "Let's not make any mistake. We are not fighting against the Nazis to let another totalitarian system take its place."[46]

For convenience and privacy a number of the Movement's Executive Committee meetings were held in Victor Bator's home. Peter Bartók remembers being present when his father attended one of these.

> Later there was a meeting at Victor Bátor's residence, where Tibor Eckhardt and his associates retired after dinner with my father in a separate

---

42 The concept of "moderate" or "reasonable" patriotism has been the subject of numerous books and essays. It bears further investigation with regard to Béla Bartók. An appealing introduction to Alexander Solzhenitsyn's embrace of its principles can be found in a recent editorial by his son Ignat, at https://www.wsj.com/articles/russia-and-the-soviet-union-solzhenitsyn-knew-the-difference-11603477436, whose formulation I borrow in this sentence.
43 In a letter dated Oct. 28, 1942, Bartók invited Serly to join the group. Serly reproduces the letter in his unpublished typescript for a book on Bartók (Tibor Serly papers, Rare Book Room, Butler Library, Columbia University).
44 Dreisziger, "A Hungarian Patriot in American Exile," 288.
45 Victor Bator, letter to Béla Bartók, June 29, 1945, in English (CPB Homosassa).
46 Paul Nadányi, *The "Free Hungary" Movement*, 59-60.

room. After a long while they re-emerged, my father looking distinctly tired. Afterwards he told my mother and me that the talk was, as expected, on the subject of his joining the group that he did not wish to do; as he felt obligated to Victor Bátor, however, he finally agreed to a compromise, where he would be associated with a cultural department of the organization.[47]

It's certainly possible that Bartók felt heavy in spirit after leaving a meeting, and that his son noticed. Shouldering large responsibilities when ill will wring a sigh out of most people. The specific information this recollection purports to convey, however, cannot be accurate. Bartók had joined the Movement long before Peter arrived in the United States. Peter could not have actually witnessed the evening he describes here. Dreisziger, too, grapples with this passage's apparent contradictions. In the end he interprets it as charitably as possible by suggesting that "oral tradition in the Bartók family" preserved some memory of Béla being pressured to join the Movement.[48] The problem with that explanation is that no oral tradition in the Bartók family existed after 1946. While it's reasonable to believe that Peter may have remembered meeting Eckhardt as a boy one evening at Bator's home—Eckhardt was a famous politician, after all—it's hard to trust his gloss on that evening's events.

Visa Renewals Unbalanced by Wartime Politics

Seen against this background, the political risks of the Bartók family's various visa renewals come into proper focus. After mid-1941, especially, due to Peter Bartók's planned emigration and Bartók's growing involvement as a figurehead in the American resistance, any increased scrutiny by US or Hungarian immigration officials risked collateral damage to others. Béla's prominence within the Hungarian émigré community did not necessarily help him. It cut both ways. His renown in cultural circles assured him closer scrutiny by State Department officials charged with sifting for political perils. That same visibility assured him internal advocates at high levels, including, if needed, John Montgomery and George Creel, both Roosevelt political appointees who were now back in the US, as well as John Pelényi. All of these concerns—Peter's emigration, visa renewals, the Movement for Independent Hungary—grew thickly intertwined. A type of cautious equilibrium existed among them: any actions or movement in one area might set off a corresponding reaction in another.

---

47 Peter Bartók, *My Father*, 239.
48 Dreisziger, "A Hungarian Patriot in American Exile," 297.

His most exposed moment with US immigration officials came in the summer of 1942. On June 5, 1942, Congress voted, unanimously, to declare war with Hungary, Bulgaria, and Romania. Bartók learned in mid-June—during hospitalizations and testing for his mysterious illness—that "a preliminary examination" of his most recent visa application "has not resulted in a favorable recommendation to the American consular officer involved."[49] The US Department of State was not recommending Bartók's visa for renewal. If he wished to argue the ruling, or give them further information, the letter indicated, either he or his appointed representatives needed to appear in person before the Interdepartmental Visa Review Committee in Washington, DC. Two Applications for Appearance were enclosed with this letter. Receipt of the completed applications would allow a date to be set for a hearing.

Though expressed euphemistically, the message was clear. All their plans to stay in the United States could come undone. More than his own personal safety was at stake. Since April he had become openly associated with the Movement for Independent Hungary. Keeping him in the United States to lead this exile group was critical. Nothing less than Hungary's future hung in the balance, or so it seemed to the Movement's leaders, who were painfully aware of the political crosscurrents engulfing Eckhardt that in a matter of weeks would result in his stepping down. Hungary's declaration of war on the United States on December 13, 1941, threw a wrench into any interactions between Hungarian nationals and the US State Department or Justice Department. Officially an "alien" when he landed in 1940, required to carry an alien registration card with him at all times, Bartók was now an "enemy alien"—even with his proper immigration papers.

A letter Victor Bator wrote to the US Secretary of State on behalf of the Bartók family on June 26, 1942, survives. In the letter Bator offers to attend the meeting in Washington next month instead of Bartók. He would be accompanied in this quest by Francis Deák, who, like him, was "interested as friends of [the] applicant."[50] Deák, a professor at Columbia University's law school, could speak with authority on any Hungarian political issue. He had recently co-edited for publication a massive collection of Hungarian foreign policy documents pertaining to the aftermath of World War I.[51] His 1942 book *Hungary at the Paris Peace Conference: The Diplomatic History of the Treaty of Trianon*, pub-

---

49 Eliot Coulter, Acting Chief, Visa Division, US Department of State, letter to Bartók, June 12, 1941 (CPB Homosassa).
50 Victor Bator, letter to the US Secretary of State, June 26, 1942 (CPB Homosassa).
51 Francis Deák and Dezső Ujváry, ed., *Papers and Documents Relating to the Foreign Relations of Hungary*, Vol. 1, 1919–20 (Budapest: Royal Hungarian Ministry for Foreign Affairs; New York: Columbia University Press, 1939).

lished by Columbia University Press, solidified his standing as an eminent foreign policy intellectual. His presence would add substance to their reassurances about Bartók's recent activities. Perhaps more important, as far as the US State Department was concerned, he had recently been elected to join the directorate of the American Hungarian Federation, by many orders of magnitude the largest organized group of expatriate Hungarians in the United States. Among its leaders were many individuals known to the US State Department and appreciated by its senior staff as reasonable, intelligent, well informed voices.

One month later, on July 27, 1942, Bator reversed course. He wrote back to the Visa Division to withdraw his name. He would no longer represent Bartók at the upcoming hearing. He tersely cited his "former Hungarian citizenship," and his "status in connection therewith" as reasons.[52] Washington was no longer confident in its assessment of Eckhardt. Lobbying by the Hungarian left and Little Entente states had sown doubts that could not be easily put to rest.[53] Bator sensed that his close association with Eckhardt might be a liability now, or, at the very least, might raise uncomfortable questions. Instead, he indicated, Deák would appear alone, with all the necessary forms. Apparently Deák lent just the right diplomatic touch: the Interdepartmental Visa Review Committee hearing went well, or well enough, and Béla Bartók's visa would soon be approved for another year.[54]

Orchestrating the Campaign to Aid Bartók in Spring 1943

More than any other episode during these years, the collapse of Béla's health in early 1943 cemented the growing bond between the Bator and the Bartóks. This catastrophic turning point in his career precipitated many changes for Bartók, professional and personal, as any crisis in health must do. Pertinent to our discussion here are two specific actions he took during his hospitalization: the signing of a new Last Will and Testament, and his decision to commend his manuscript collection to Victor Bator's home for safekeeping. Five weeks in the hospital in March and April 1943—an anxious shuffle of blood draws and X-rays, consulting doctors, and conflicting opinions about the underlying cause

---

52 Victor Bator, letter to H.K. Travers, July 27, 1942 (CPB Homosassa).
53 Várdy, "Hungarian Americans During World War II," 132-33.
54 Deák himself had been in Washington in June to visit the State Department on a separate diplomatic mission for the Movement. See his letter to John von Neumann, Princeton University, June 30, 1942 (CPB Homosassa). The appearance of his name on lists for the Movement for Independent Hungary, exact date uncertain, suggests that no later than the summer of 1942 he was also involved on the Arts and Sciences Committee of that organization.

Chapter 2

of his collapse—had certainly given him time to think and reflect.[55] He now saw, as he hadn't before, the need to prepare for a time when he might no longer be alive to provide for Ditta and Peter, or to see into print his recently completed folksong studies. In his hospital bed on March 28, 1943, witnessed by Dr. Gyula Holló and one of the attending nurses, Bartók signed his new Will. The document named Bator and Gyula Báron co-executors of his estate, and co-trustees of the trust that would form after his probate.

Bartók had just launched his lectureship at Harvard University. The Harvard appointment required his presence in Boston, of course, and in February he began to commute by train to South Station, and from there into Cambridge, where he had been given a room at Eliot House to stay in as needed. The exertion cost him dearly. Gaunt and still recovering from his 1942 hospitalizations for the early stages of leukemia, unable to shake off the night sweats and persistent low grade fevers that arose as the disease progressed, he weakened precipitously. By February he weighed less than 90 pounds. He was able to give his first lectures (or "conferences," his preferred term) for Harvard students in mid-February. Exhausted by the strain on his body, he returned to his apartment in New York. On March 4 he wrote to Tillman Merritt, Chairman of the Music Department, to cancel the upcoming lecture on March 11, and to warn that he probably wouldn't be able to make the next one either on March 18. "The sad fact is that my state of health which was not very good since last April (as I explained to you at our first meeting) deteriorated rapidly during Febr.," he explained. The following day, March 5, he entered Mt. Sinai Hospital in New York on the advice of his hematologist, Dr. Nathan Rosenthal, for further testing and monitoring. Merritt's telegram to Bartók on March 6 acknowledged the bad news, reassuring him to not worry about the lecture or other conferences. "They can be given later."[56]

For most of March 1943 Bartók would be in and out of the hospital. He was readmitted in April, too. Dr. Holló looked after him there and at home, making house calls to his famous patient when necessary. On one occasion he arrived at Bartók's apartment with another physician that Harvard had brought in to consult: Dr. Bernard Oppenheimer, a leading New York cardiologist. That little money was available to carry the Bartóks through this time of trial

---

55 Estimates for the amount of time Bartók spent in the hospital in early 1943 show little agreement in the literature. Here I take the amount of five weeks from Bartók himself, who calculated that total on his 1943 US Income Tax form when prompted to list medical expenses for the year (CPB Homosassa). See also Suchoff, *Béla Bartók: Life and Work*, 153.
56 The history of Bartók's Harvard lectures in 1943 and the subsequent illness is given comprehensive treatment in Vera Lampert's "Bartók at Harvard University as Witnessed in Unpublished Archival Documents," *Studia Musicologica Academiae Scientiarum Hungaricae* 35/1-3 (1993–94): 113-54.

was painfully clear to those who knew him. Merritt, to his lasting credit, quietly covered all of Oppenheimer's costs that spring without mentioning it to the Bartóks. The hospital's costs were less flexible. On March 20 Ditta Bartók received in the mail a gift of money from "Harvard friends" via money order, with the note, "More following in honor of your distinguished and beloved husband." Elizabeth Sprague Coolidge contributed to that purse. Joseph Szigeti sprang into action once he learned the situation, encouraging Koussevitzky to program *Music for Strings, Percussion, and Celesta* on an upcoming concert "as an act of healing."[57] Koussevitzky's solution, instead, famously, was to commission in May a new orchestral work that became the Concerto for Orchestra, whose creation later that summer quickened Bartók's "retour à la vie." ASCAP even rose to the occasion by agreeing to take on the costs of Bartók's convalescence going forward, their generosity spurred by the intervention of Ernő Balogh.

All of these efforts to help Bartók have been generously covered in biographies and specialized studies.[58] The first four months of 1943, for health and professional reasons, brought Bartók to his lowest ebb. Yves Lenoir characterizes the start of 1943 as "a great void" in Bartók's professional activity.[59] Tallián expresses the financial and medical woes of early 1943 as an "intolerable position," and finds in the subsequent writing of the Concerto for Orchestra "the dividing line between the two halves of the American period."[60] Oppenheimer, at the time, noticed how Bartók's outlook had changed from March to April. "I have not seen Mr. Bartok since he left the hospital," he wrote to Merritt later in April, "but have heard from Dr. Hollo that he has taken a new lease on life, is now anxious to live and is co-operating—whereas previously he thought 'his number was up' and it was not worth the effort even to eat."[61]

For the Bartóks, the beginning of 1943 marked a sharp turn in their fortunes. Caring for Béla during and after his hospitalizations brought Ditta inordinate stress; her world, and any aspirations she may have had for herself, grew suddenly smaller as she was reduced to caring for a profoundly weakened, anxious, workaholic husband. She never fully recovered. From this time forward Bartók would race against the illness that stalked him, newly conscious of its

---

57 Szigeti, letter to Koussevitzky, April 8, 1943 (Koussevitzky Collection, Library of Congress).
58 See, among others, Klára Móricz's excellent scholarly introduction to the Complete Critical Edition of the Concerto for Orchestra (Budapest: Editio Musica Budapest, 2017); Peter Bartók's *My Father;* Vera Lampert's "Bartók at Harvard University;" Gillies, "Bartók in America;" and Suchoff, "Bartók in America."
59 Lenoir, *Folklore et transcendance,* 109.
60 Tallián, *Béla Bartók: The Man and His Work,* 225.
61 Bernard Oppenheimer, letter to Tillman Merritt, April 26, 1943. In Vera Lampert, "Bartók at Harvard University," 147–48.

formidable power. His performing career, faltering since 1942, came to a firmer end. His university affiliation was cast into doubt, too, deeply demoralizing him. The current contract with Columbia University had ended on December 31, 1942, suspending progress on the Serbo-Croatian transcription work. Harvard's timely offer promised a single semester of employment. Beyond, the future appeared darker than ever, uncertain, with vanishingly few prospects for sustained employment, and only sporadic radio and concert performances of his music to generate income. For Ditta and Peter their toehold in America became overnight more fragile.

In published accounts of this episode in Bartók's life we typically find Victor Bator's name either ignored, minimized by relegation to footnotes, or given passing attention as one supporting player among many in a larger cast whose lead roles belonged to others.[62] The luminosity of Szigeti's name, and of Koussevitzky's, quite naturally overshadows Victor Bator's own for later writers. Yet—to read his own account—Bator seems to have played a central role in orchestrating the aid.

> **As a result of a conference I had with Joseph Szigeti... I began a campaign** to collect funds to be donated to Columbia University out of which his Research Fellowship would be renewed. **I drew up a memorandum...** to explain the scientific purpose of the donations... **Using mostly Szigeti's name I sent out the memo in about 50 copies** to persons, institutions known to be patrons of music.
>
> **Meanwhile I negotiated with Columbia University** to create a cover up for the charity. On April 5th, 1943, **I had a conference with the Provost of the University,** Frank D. Fackenthal...
>
> Meanwhile some money was needed for the immediate living expenses of Mrs. Bartók and Peter Bartók... **So it was agreed between the President, Secretary-Treasurer of the Institute and me that I shall execute as Attorney in Fact the Note**, representing the debt that I shall deposit the check in Bartók's bank account without his seeing the "Artists' and Writers' Fund" printed on the check, and he would believe our story that this was a prize awarded for his excellence and merits...

---

62 The lone exception to this rule is Benjamin Suchoff, who in his writings about Bartók's American years often places Bator closer to the center of the picture than do other writers. See, inter alia, Suchoff, "Bartók in America," *The Musical Times* (February 1976), 123–24.

To describe the campaign and the efforts which were thought to be necessary to reach the goal, i.e., enough to assure a one-year extension of the Columbia appointment, would be voluminous. **I purchased many copies of the Sun carrying Kolodin's feature article. I wrote letters on my own behalf on behalf of Szigeti. I sent my original Memo as an enclosure in my letter. . . The costs of secretaries doing this work were heavy.**

The response to the request was devastating. . . The total donated altogether was $1067.04, <u>not enough for even one term of a half year</u>. **I added out of my own funds $500.00** (five hundred dollars). **Thus I deposited at Columbia $1567.00,** and Bartók's pride and minimum subsistence equaling the salary of $250.00 a month were made possible.

Highlighting his actions, as I've done here, allows us to see the distinctive nature of his role amid the many other names more familiar to us in this story. Long habit of authority left Victor Bator quick to assume command in groups of people. From that position he could actively steer and direct, using his experience, wealth, and staff support to cut through problems with relative ease. Once committed, he pursued projects with tenacity—a character trait that manifested itself just as readily in large, open ended projects (e.g., creation of Bartók Archives; litigation against communist government for his pension; post-war renegotiation of contracts with Boosey & Hawkes) as it did for more specifically targeted tasks (emigration of Peter Bartók from Hungary; negotiations over premiere of Third Piano Concerto). We see this temperament at work over and over again in the pages of correspondence published elsewhere in this book.

For the 1943 funds campaign he served as self-appointed banker, mail center, and attorney-in-fact.[63] He knew he could rely on his own staff to help: secretaries were on hand at Natvar and at his home office. (How easy can it have been, we might ask, to send out 50+ letters to solicit funds? Each typed separately, assembled, addressed, stamped? With his staff he could take on burdensome chores others would shy away from, or not even contemplate.) He knew his place, too, among professional musicians, and openly fell in line behind Szigeti, whose name recognition in musical circles guaranteed greater receptivity to the fundraising appeal. Later such deference would become more selective in its application.

---

63   To serve as attorney-in-fact requires a power of attorney. We can surmise that Bartók at the signing of his Will in March 1943 also signed a Power of Attorney document giving Bator the right to act on his behalf. That document appears to be lost. Upon Bartók's death it would have been superseded by the Will.

Chapter 2

Bator's witness account includes details only he could provide. With Bartók's two strongest advocates in the Music Department, Douglas Moore and Paul Henry Lang, he met on April 5th with the Provost to find a solution. They established a "Bartók Research Fund" to collect donations. Bator would be the banker for the fund. He then set to work soliciting donations, even making one of the largest ones ($500) himself—an amount that puts him alongside Koussevitzky at the very top of the list of those individuals who made the largest material difference in the Bartóks' circumstances that year. All of Bator's characteristic skill sets were on display in this one project: his ability to assemble people and draw on each individual's talents to achieve a goal; his openness to finding creative solutions to problems; his tendency to act quickly and decisively; his natural vitality when in control. A formidable intellect and ready pen gave these qualities external form. Lang and Moore themselves could move small mountains when needed; they had already done so to secure Bartók his honorary degree and first appointment at Columbia. Fackenthal, widely viewed on campus as a factotum for the President, possessed formidable administrative talent. Together, these four were quite a team. It's hard to imagine a more effective committee taking the reins—unless the Countess Széchenyi herself were to have taken a sudden interest again in Bartók's fate as she had done in 1928.

Even though he'd already been alerted to Bartók's decline in health, Douglas Moore's attention must have been riveted by the Kolodin article in the *New York Sun* that made public Bartók's plight (Fig. 2.4). Certainly the article reflected poorly on Columbia, though it refrained from naming that institution or Harvard. Seen in its original context here, the article's title stands out starkly from the routine classical music news around it, highlighting the distance between Bartók's personal crisis and the bravely persevering musical life of wartime New York—an extraordinary cry from the depths nestled against routine publicity photos of singers and Philharmonic news. Kolodin pointedly warns New York readers that they should not sit on the sidelines. He concludes:

> It would seem an obligation for the musical community of New York to assure him of the esteem in which he is held, to provide him with the material means and the mental stimulus to carry on his work. It would be an unpardonable slight to a man whose abilities are a matter of worldwide recognition if such homage were left to the lip service of eulogies, when they are too late to be of practical benefit to him.

Moore had already been at work, though. Even before he met with Bator and Lang in the provost's office he showed his mettle by arranging for the Ditson fund once more to come to Bartók's aid. On March 24 he wrote to Bartók with

Fig. 2.4. Irving Kolodin, "The Strange Case of Bela Bartok," *The New York Sun*, Saturday, April 17, 1943, shown here in its original setting among other general news from the classical music world.

news that the Ditson Committee had recommended "an additional appropriation of $1,000 as a subsidy to the Columbia University Press for your book on Jugoslav folk music . . . I believe now that things will go ahead fast and the book will be well on its way." He closed his letter with polite reference to Bartók's current poor health. "I am sorry to hear that your illness has continued and send you my warmest sympathy and best wishes for a rapid recovery."[64] These funds would not be released to Bartók directly, but they quickened the press's interest in moving forward more quickly towards publication. One more obstacle to Bartók's recovery was thus removed. Szigeti, on April 8, explained in a letter to Koussevitzky that Bartók's friends were trying to "feed him" with good news like this to boost his spirits.[65]

---

64 Douglas Moore, letter to Béla Bartók, on Columbia University letterhead stationery, March 24, 1943. Reproduced in facsimile in Lenoir, *Folklore et transcendence*, 116.
65 Joseph Szigeti, letter to Serge Koussevitzky, April 8, 1943 (Koussevitzky Collection, Library of Congress).

Chapter 2

Bator in his Memorandum twice uses the term "campaign" to describe the way Bartók's friends rallied around him in early 1943. The term is apt. When we view those months from Bator's perspective, rather than as many individual actions, we see coordinated layers of involvement, over time, on many fronts, by many people, with a specific goal in mind. He alludes to the "voluminous" amount of work he and others put in. Ultimately, the campaign failed to achieve its goals. "The response to the request was devastating," he remembers, in words still shaded with the full weight of his disappointment. Some donations, he recalled, were "so little that it was humiliating to accept it." With no love for Goddard Lieberson remaining in him after 1946, he singles out the Columbia Records executive's donation for special contempt: Lieberson, he writes, was one of only five members of the American Composers Alliance who, together, gave $13. (By implication Lieberson's donation was a few dollars.)[66] To marshall sufficient funds to offer Bartók another semester of work at Columbia Bator had to add in a large donation of his own, an outcome he was willing to accept. He transmitted the total of $1567.04 to Columbia that summer, allowing the university to proceed with offering another contract to Bartók.[67]

Bator Becomes Guardian of Bartók's Manuscripts. A New Will is Written.

Within two days of entering the hospital in early March, Bartók charged Bator with an important task. Bator was to collect all of his autograph manuscripts from their current storage site, at Boosey & Hawkes's downtown offices, and move them to his home on East 72nd Street for safety. On March 8 Bartók wrote from the hospital to Heinsheimer: "I should like to settle my manuscript business as soon as possible. As I can't attend to this matter for the time being because of my illness, I asked my friend Mr. Victor Bátor to do it on my behalf and gave him an authorization. He'll get in touch with you in a few days or next week in order to fix an appointment. You may, of course, keep the full

---

66 Details of the other donors can been found in a letter sent by Harrison Kerr, Secretary of the American Composers Society, to Joseph Szigeti, May 21, 1943. Bator's recollection in the Memorandum unintentionally slights the organization; the original letter apparently also included several personal checks from members (not specified)—not only the $13 from five members. How the subterfuge worked is shown in the letter's address. It was sent to Mr. Joseph Szigeti / Bela Bartok Research Fund / 14 East 60th Street / New York City. Copy preserved in BSCB Tampa.

67 Columbia's contract letter was sent to Bartók on October 11, 1943. It backdates the start of the appointment to July 1, 1943, and places its expiration at January 31, 1944, at the end of the fall term (Philip Hayden, Secretary, Columbia University, letter to Bartók, October 11, 1943). BSCB Tampa. The timing of this appointment has led to considerable confusion in the Bartók literature.

score of my violin concerto for the time being as it has been agreed between us a few weeks ago."[68]

The following day he and Bator crafted a more official-looking letter to Boosey & Hawkes, typed up by one of Bator's secretaries, this time conveying explicit instructions:

3242 Cambridge Avenue
Riverdale, New York
March 9, 1943

Boosey & Hawkes
43 West 23rd Street
New York, N.Y.

Dear Sirs:

I beg to refer to my letter sent to you direct concerning my manuscripts, held by you since 1940.

The holder of this letter is Dr. Victor Bator, whom I authorized to take over from you the above mentioned manuscripts. I gave him a list of the manuscripts enumerating 55 items. Concerning the Violin Concerto mentioned as Item 52, Dr. Bator will make arrangements with you enabling you to use those in the future as you have done in the past.

Dr. Victor Bator is hereby authorized to give you release on my behalf concerning all manuscripts which will be taken over by him.

Very truly yours,
Béla Bartók

In a handwritten postscript at the bottom of this letter Bator acknowledged receipt of the manuscripts: "I confirm herewith having received all manuscripts with the exception of N 49b (Mikrokosmos) 54 (Divertimento a) brouillon b) manuscript) 55b (VI. String quartet) and the full score of the Violon concerto (52b) as mentioned."[69] Probably this transfer took place sometime between March 10 and 31, 1943. Bator was never one to let the moss grow. Those few

---

68 Bartók, letter to Heinsheimer, March 8, 1943 (BBC-PSS Basel).
69 Bartók, letter to Heinsheimer, March 9, 1943 (BBC-PSS Basel).

manuscripts Bator couldn't collect from Boosey & Hawkes in March would come trickling in by early summer once the publisher no longer needed them. "I stored them in a metal cabinet in my home," he remembers in his Memorandum, "a not very satisfactory arrangement . . . by and large until his death they were in my house." From 1943-45 Bartók would periodically add manuscripts to the collection, making sure it stayed current.

On May 1, 1943, Bator wrote a news-filled letter to Heinsheimer. Every sentence in this letter speaks with easy authority on the composer's behalf, suggesting that an invisible line had been crossed in recent months, leaving Bator more in charge of Bartók's affairs than he had been in March. Heinsheimer could not have failed to notice the change in tone:

Dear Mr. Heinsheimer:

Many thanks for your letter of April 14. I am grateful that you sent me the list of the Bartok and Kodoly [sic] works which you published recently. I am going down early next week to see you and take over the three manuscripts and I will check up a few of those publications at that time.

I will use the same opportunity to discuss with you another problem connected with Bartok, where your advice may be very helpful for him and for me in connection with making arrangements for him.

May I remind you that you have not yet answered Bartok's last letter and he seems to be very worried on account of it. I told Mrs. Bartok to telephone you about this but since I am writing this letter, I mention it to you also.

Hoping to see you soon,
Very sincerely yours,
Victor Bator[70]

Hospitalization led Bartók to make another decision directly connected with the manuscript transfer. How long he had been thinking of re-writing his Last Will and Testament we can no longer reconstruct. (People often ponder this notion for months, or years, before they take action.) In Bartók's case the initial hospitalizations in May 1942 may well have triggered those first conversations. Now he could wait no longer. Under advisement from Bator, he autho-

---

70 Victor Bator, letter to Heinsheimer, typed, 1 p., on Bator's home stationery, May 1, 1943 (BBC-PSS Basel).

rized the preparation of a new Last Will and Testament in case he should die while abroad—a will that would be framed in American legal terms, for US court systems, in the event of his death. Bator turned to a young New York attorney who had been recommended to him. With Bator serving as intermediary, Harold Manheim drafted a will that met Bartók's wishes. The finished copy was presented to Bartók at the hospital for signature on March 28.

* * *

Just over two years had elapsed since Bator began to involve himself with Bartók's visa paperwork. Now the composer had placed his entire manuscript collection with him for safekeeping, and given him full responsibility to manage his estate after his death for the benefit of his family. Referring to the alchemical processes which led Bartók to place such faith in him, so quickly, Bator in his Memorandum concludes with candor and honesty, "It is difficult or hardly possible to give tangible reasons for Bartók's confidence in me as evidenced in the manuscript incident, the appointment as Trustee, and his reliance on my judgment in all his private and professional affairs." Bator's unwillingness to use the relationship "for prestige" counted a great deal, he suspects. "We never let him become conscious that he was 'Bartók'."

For the remainder of the war Bator continued to help the Bartóks in various ways. Respite breaks in Nonquitt were extended annually to both Bartók and his wife, together or individually. There the Bartóks joined other Hungarians guests to enjoy the hospitality of the Bator family at their home on the Massachusetts shoreline. Bator even arranged to have a piano available for the Bartóks' use while in Nonquitt.[71] Bartók always worked during these vacations: he never stopped working. To judge from surviving photographs, his hosts successfully rousted him outside for the occasional picnic or group excursion to the shore. He went on birding walks by himself for respite. Many years later Victor Bator set aside most of the photographs showing Bartók and gave them to the Archive to be catalogued and preserved in their holdings.[72] An Archive photo from the

---

71 Nicholas Milroy, letter to Elliott Antokoletz, October 21, 1986 (Collection of Elliott Antokoletz). Milroy, the son of Etelka Freund, recollected that Bator purchased his piano from him in 1943 "for Bartók's use in Nonquitt." The composer served as intermediary in this transaction. Milroy entered the U.S. Army in 1943 and had left his piano with Béla Bartók in New York City. That instrument, on indefinite loan to the composer after Baldwin withdrew their piano from his apartment, was subsequently taken up to Nonquitt and kept there for use by both Béla and Ditta Bartók during their visits.

72 These are currently preserved in binders in Florida. Several of the better ones were included as illustrations in the 1963 Bartók Archives catalogue. The images shown in Fig. 2.6, and many of the others, too, had originally been taken as slides, which he converted into photographs for inclusion in the Archives.

Chapter 2

Fig. 2.5. Two photographs of Béla Bartók at Nonquitt. Top) Picnic at Nonquitt, Summer of 1942. From left: Francis Bator, Gyula Báron, Victor Bator, Franci Bator, Paul Bator, Béla Bartók. Photographer: unidentified, possibly Peter Bator. Bottom) Heading out on a walk to the shore, Summer of 1944. Photographer: Victor Bator.
Source: both images CPB Homosassa.

summer of 1942 shows Bartók picnicking on the lawn with Gyula Báron and members of the Bator family. Two years later, at another of Bartók's visits to Nonquitt, the casually dressed, sunglasses-wearing folk music scholar was captured on film as he joined the party for a walk to the shore. (Fig. 2.5). In addition to the photographic record, most of which remains unpublished, approximately twenty letters from their correspondence survive, all dating from 1941-46.[73] In tone and content they deal matter-of-factly with visa documentation at first, then after 1943 grow more news-filled and personal. Bator brokered Ditta and Béla's living accommodations in New York in 1944 and 1945, helping them locate separate apartments. He knew of their ongoing marital strain. A flurry of letters back and forth to Ditta in July and August 1945 reveal him to be a thoughtful confidant, calming her worries, offering solutions as he always did. Routine back-and-forth exchange of family news fills these letters.

Earlier, on August 22, 1943, Bartók wrote a lengthy, 4-page letter to Bator from Saranac Lake with news of his health and pending business matters, including immigration. He mentions the editing process underway with Columbia University Press. He reflects back on Nonquitt and how pleasant those three weeks had been. Having been through so many visa and immigration conversations with Bator since 1941, he allowed himself to give full voice to his current pessimism:

> <u>Immigration.</u> This is now impossible: I have neither money nor the health. In the situation in which I find myself there is no possibility for me traveling and to take care of any kind of business activity. In addition to this I have no money because after all I have no income. And what is the purpose anyway. Also the counsel and other immigration authorities have certain prescriptions: they are not permitted to permit the immigration of a person which is ill and unable to make his living. Should I go out to Canada in this state I might not be able to come back. Peter cannot do anything either, because he has no money and on account of his military situation it is better not to undertake this activity.—The only problem is should I advise somebody, and whom, of the impossibility. And Peter too? Or is it enough if I am alone?[74]

With Bartók Victor Bator always acted the role of facilitator: Bartók turned to him when he needed help or advice outside the world of music. Over time,

---

73 Most of the surviving correspondence is preserved in BBC-PSS Basel. Because the two men met in person in New York and Nonquitt on so many occasions, even vacationing together, the volume of correspondence between them is disproportionately modest.

74 Bartók, letter to Bator, Aug. 22, 1943. English translation, ca. 1960s, Béla Bartók Archives. Translator not indicated. BSCB Tampa.

helper became friend. The term "friend" is difficult to square with Bartók's lifelong reserve, later writers are quick to note. But at the time others recognized the relationship for what it was. Douglas Moore, in 1943, referred to Bator as "Bartók's lawyer friend." Peter Bartók, reflecting generally on his father's relationships, explained that "when he was with people he could converse with; who were interested in what they could learn from him and from who he could also learn, i.e., who spoke his language, he could be relaxed, open, enjoy himself and give everyone a good time."[75] Bartók himself described Bator as "my friend" in a letter to Heinsheimer. In his Last Will and Testament he identifies "my friends Viktor Bator and Julius Baron" as executors and trustees. Bator in private communications such as his Memorandum and letters felt comfortable using the description; publicly he steered around it to avoid giving the impression he was clinging to Bartók's reputation. In a lecture he gave in New York City in the early 1950s he referred instead to the ways they interacted with each other in the United States. "My family and I," he said, "spent more private time with Béla Bartók than anyone between 1941 and 1945." (See Appendix A.)

While visa renewal issues may never gain much traction as a topic of serious musicological research, for Bartók they represented a source of ongoing concern during his years in the United States, reminding him with irritating regularity of his unsettled status as an immigrant in a country at war. More important to him personally was the successful escape of his son Peter from Hungary. The foundations for his friendship with Bator were laid during these specific actions.

In New York Bator became an island of stability for the three Bartóks: always present, always generous, always living in the same pleasant home with its Hungarian furnishings, always quick to come to their aid. It helped that one of his closest lifelong friends was Imre Waldbauer, and that he and his wife Franci had many other friends in common with the Bartóks, including the Hollós and the Bárons. For Peter he soon became, affectionately, "Viktor bácsi," or Uncle Victor. An important and (to date) underappreciated dimension of his relationship with Béla was their work together on the Movement for Independent Hungary. From this project they came to know and trust each other politically, too. Bator's work for the Bartók Estate after 1945 bore the continued imprint of his years helping the composer and the many conversations they had about family and business matters. From these clear memories he drew the certainty of purpose he would need in order to withstand the corrosive effects of the family disfunction and communist-led antagonism that would soon be coming his way.

* * *

---

75   Peter Bartók, *My Father*, 201.

After Bartók's death in September 1945 Bator stepped in immediately to continue care of Ditta and Peter. "I had one aim only," he recalled in the Memorandum, "to provide for the urgent needs of the Bartók family."[76] Ditta's mental health was poor. Peter was still in shock, grieving, too, having only been discharged from the Navy in August, six weeks before his father died. The story of what happened in those early days of the estate is best told by Bator himself. He writes:

> Béla Bartók's funeral was attended by hardly more than a score of friends. His bank account was practically exhausted. The credit balance amounted to somewhere between $200-300. Prior to his death he had an income of about $4,000.- a year. Yet, out of this amount the royalty income that could be expected to continue was less than $1,000.- a year. There was on the other side a family to be taken care of, Mrs. Bartók couldn't speak English, had never succeed to obtain or achieve any kind of income out of her musicianship except occasional fees among which the largest item was the fee paid to her by me for teaching occasionally my 2 younger sons piano. Soon after the death of her husband she fell into a serious state of depression. That made necessary the cure of [a] psychiatrist. With the help of a friend who was on the board of the Pratt-Whitney Institute, [the] mental institute of the New York Hospital, we succeeded to get her in there and put under good care both medical and otherwise. After she was released and her sorry state of mind was more or less cured, I succeeded to get her under further psychiatric treatment by Dr. Paul Hoch, now the Head of the Department in charge of mental hospitals of New York State. She was given by Dr. Hoch a post-hospital treatment with the help of which she recovered her balance of mind and soul, after which it seemed advisable to arrange her return to her native country, where living together with her mother, brother and many other friends and having the possibility of using her native tongue of Hungarian, the only language she speaks, her loneliness of living in a strange and foreign country could be eliminated.
>
> After the funeral I entrusted the personal care of Mrs. Bartók to friends, Mr. and Mrs. Paul Kecskeméti, who lived in the same house, to whom she and Mr. Peter Bartók had complete confidence because the sudden death of Bartók brought me back to New York without having done the unavoidable chores preceding the return to New York from my coun-

---

76 Bator, Memorandum on the History of the Bartók Estate, 44.

try home. ~~I was back in New York about the end of October~~. I discovered upon my return or soon after, that neither the fact that Béla Bartók by his Last Will had established a Trust out of his Estate, nor the significance of the existence of a Trusteeship, was known or appreciated by Mrs. Bartók, by Peter Bartók, or their entourage. Mrs. Bartók, Mr. Peter Bartók, with well-intentioned friends (some of them with an ax to grind) set out to handle the inherited estate as far as it lent itself to any activity.[77]

When I visited with him in 2010 Francis Bator told me a remarkable story. "My parents really were in many ways surrogate parents for Peter in those early years," he explained. "Peter initially behaved with great affection towards my parents." Apparently Victor and Franci Bator felt so worried for Peter Bartók that they considered taking the extraordinary step of adopting him into their own family. In light of the hatred Peter would direct towards his father later on, Francis remembered this family tale with no small amazement. He could no longer remember exactly when the idea took root, only that it was around the end of the war. (Peter turned 21 on July 31, 1945.) He and his brothers protested. "My mother and father presented the idea to us. My brothers and I warned them, though. We felt something was *off* about him. So in the end they decided not to proceed—which is good, because Peter would soon turn on my father."

---

[77] Victor Bator, Memorandum on the History of the Bartók Estate, Chapter C, 18-19. In the original typescript the sentence reading "I was back in New York about the end of October" was struck through by Bator during editing.

Battles in Philadelphia, I.
The Third Piano Concerto, 1945–46

In this passage from his unpublished Memorandum on the History of the Bartók Estate, Victor Bator recalls the behind-the-scenes dramas that threatened to derail the first performances of the Third Piano Concerto in early 1946.[1] In his first months as Trustee he learned that the Concerto had been given to Sandor to perform. Investigating further, he ascertained that this world premiere with the Philadelphia Orchestra would yield the heirs $17.50 in fees. This paltry amount would do nothing, he felt, to alleviate Mrs. Bartók's desperate financial need. Amazed at a system where an important work by a major composer could yield such low income, he immediately threatened to cancel the performances by withholding permission to perform, even though the concerts were already scheduled. No one knew, or even suspected, that he had that type of authority. Aggressive, hard-nosed negotiating earned him concessions from all parties. When the dust settled two months later he had secured $2,000 for the Bartók family. His unorthodox course of action, however, set off storms of displeasure within the walls of Orchestra Hall in Philadelphia, Columbia Broadcasting System in New York, and Boosey & Hawkes, as he relates here.

This was his introduction to managing the Bartók estate. The shock he felt when the economics of the composer's world were laid bare before his eyes still ring forth from his prose in this account, written a dozen years after the events it describes. As an outsider he quickly perceived the moral flaw in a system that allowed its producers to benefit so little, while performing organizations, soloists, and conductors earned substantial sums from ticket sales and broadcasting fees. His account makes plain his concern for Bartók's widow, who suffered an additional loss when "her" concerto was taken away from her through a decision made by her son and well-meaning supporters like Serly and Sándor.[2]

Word of Bator's successful negotiations soon spread in East Coast professional music circles, earning him brief notoriety. In 1946 Boosey & Hawkes felt his presence again

---

1   Victor Bator, Memorandum on the History of the Bartók Estate (1959–60), Chapter C, p. 19-29. BSCB Tampa.
2   Further perspective on the sequence of events can be found in George Sándor's oral history reminiscences (1983), preserved at Columbia University's Center for Oral History, available online at https://oralhistoryportal.library.columbia.edu/document.php?id=ldpd_4073512; and Robert T. Jones, "From Béla to Ditta," *The New York Times*, May 11, 1969.

when he took up the charge of renegotiating the contract for Bartók's music, now increasingly convinced that Bartók had not received appropriate compensation for his music. His success at negotiating increased fees met with unqualified admiration in the narrow confines of New York composers' circles: figuring out how to earn a decent living had become a pressing concern for them in the years around World War II. In December 1950 a conference on *The Composer's Place in Society and Industry* was held at Columbia University's McMillan Academic Auditorium, sponsored by the Guggenheim Memorial Foundation and the Columbia University Department of Music. Victor Bator was invited to speak. Howard Hanson, John Tasker Howard, and Alfred Wallenstein also appeared. At that event he repeated his story about the fees for the Third Piano Concerto to illustrate what can happen to modern composers who lack strong surrounding institutions for support. He had researched the latest income figures for the publishing and broadcasting industries in the United States. The latter, he stated, "live on music," but when it comes to paying the people who make it, "the composer is last in line." He argued in favor of setting a certain minimum price for a work, and "several milestones" that recognize stages of success, as seen, for example, in book contracts.[3]

Here is Bator telling the story of the Third Piano Concerto in 1959. By then he had reason to believe that the roots of the present litigation lay in aspects of Peter's behavior that were already on display in 1945. He makes little effort to conceal his present frustrations with the composer's son. We also see him grappling with his status as a musical outsider, and gaining certainty in his role as Trustee. As in other sections of the Memorandum published in this book, I have retained his references to supporting correspondence that would have originally been attached to the document, e.g., "Encl. C1."

Everybody in the family and among friends knew about a major work (now known in the world of music as "The 3rd Piano Concerto") that was composed, created by Bartók just before his death. But for a few missing bars it was complete, finished. Bartók wrote on the last page the word "finis." Yet, a few bars before the end were not written up. Nobody knows for sure whether Tibor Serly commissioned himself to do the almost routine job of completing with the missing little fragment or Mr. Peter Bartók made the agreement with him to do this. Nobody knows for sure who decided that with complete disregard of Béla Bartók's desire and plan to reserve the performance of the 3rd Piano Concerto for Mrs. Bartók, it should be given and permitted to anyone else. Tibor Serly, Mrs. Bartók, Mr. Peter Bartók all knew as I did that he planned the com-

---

3   A detailed report of this event was published as "What Price Creative Music?" in *The Musical Courier* (Jan. 1, 1951): 6-9.

position of that Piano Concerto with the idea that Mrs. Bartók would have exclusivity for performing not only at the first performance, world- and American premiere, but afterwards for a number of years. Bartók assumed correctly that symphony orchestras, with some supposed eagerness to perform a major Bartók work, will put it on their program and engage therefore Mrs. Bartók, without whom this would not be feasible, and that such appearances with major orchestras would set Mrs. Bartók in the higher echelon of concertizing pianists. With Bartók in the cemetery, the exceptional importance of the Concerto increased several times. No more major Bartók work could ever come up! The performance of such a "last" work must have grown in the estimation of the world of music manifold. Yet, Mr. Peter Bartók gave it away for performance to the Philadelphia Orchestra, Ormandy its conductor, George Sándor a pianist of Hungarian origin, obviously, because nobody put up a resistance, because Serly, Sándor, Ormandy, etc. thought it was a good move or just because he did not know what he was doing. Bartók told me the purpose of that work. That this is not imagination from me is firmly proven by a letter of Bartók to his son dated February 21, 1945 (Enclosure C1) in which he stated this. It is true that Mrs. Bartók in October 1945 was already in a depressed mental state, but I certainly would not have permitted had I been actually in charge or consulted, that she be dispossessed and despoiled even with the connivance of her son.

When I discovered what had happened without my consent, behind my back, and contrary to the interest of the Estate, I might have put down my foot and cancelled the whole project. I did not do it for several reasons. First, I disliked to put sharply and pointedly Mr. Peter Bartók to his place. Second, Mrs. Bartók was in fact in no condition to perform the work as pianist within a foreseeable time. Thirdly, the entire plan of first performance, broadcasting, had publicity already and its reversal would have been a bitter pill for the Philadelphia Orchestra, Ormandy, and George Sándor. Finally, had I been a recognized authority in music, I could have trusted that my veto would evoke approval from the Bartók family, musicians, daily press. But with no standing, name, and reputation, how to stand the storm that would follow from all quarters left me in a predicament.

Yet, in one respect, I had no hesitation. When I asked Mr. Peter Bartók, Serly who completed the work, how much would Mrs. Bartók, or the Estate be paid, the faces were blank. Nobody knew anything. "Ask the publisher."

Until this point my story was based on my memory. From here on letters, papers, are available which not only tell the facts, subsequent to all this, but support my memory as to the antecedentia related heretofore. I hastily studied the legal and business problems of my task and in December 1945 I went into action.

Battles in Philadelphia, I

I called the head of the New York office of Bartók's publishers, Mr. Heinsheimer, and asked him how much income will the Bartók Estate receive from the First Performance of that 3rd Piano Concerto by Ormandy, Sándor, and Philadelphia. The answer was 100% evasive. Or at least it seemed to me at that time 100% evasive. Mr. Heinsheimer said that it was very difficult to say what the performance would mean in terms of dollars and cents. He emphasized that the acceptance of Bartók's music may be later on very important, and such a concert by Philadelphia, with great publicity, is an important step in making Bartók's music accepted by the big orchestras, artists, and thereby, perhaps, by the public also. The answer did not satisfy me. I insisted to be told how much income in dollars and cents could be the result of the concert. Then, Mr. Heinsheimer told me that Boosey & Hawkes would get $75.- from the Philadelphia Orchestra, as rental for the orchestra material. "How much would the Bartók Estate get out of that money?" The answer was: "Seventeen dollars and fifty cents." Nothing else? was my next question. Yet, Mr. Heinsheimer said, the Philadelphia Orchestra pays $3,000.- yearly for the entire program of ASCAP for the use of any work in the ASCAP repertoire, or in the repertoire of all foreign performing rights societies of which any of the composers was a member (Bartók was a member of the British Performing Rights Society). By now [in 1959], I know that even that answer was incorrect, because the $3,000.- overall fee covers published works only, and the Piano Concerto was not a published work at that time. But, unfortunately, at that time I knew less about international copyright law than now. "In a year we shall know how much will the Bartók Estate receive out of those $3,000.-," but, he added, "in his opinion it wouldn't be of any significance or substantial sum." My answer was prompt and positive. I pointed out to him that as Executor of the Last Will of Bartók, I was the only person to decide the question whether the 3rd Piano Concerto should be published or performed, and that under the conditions communicated to me I would not permit the performance by Philadelphia. Heinsheimer became very excited indeed. Arrangements had been made, publicity was arranged, the concert was on the program, announcement had been made by Ormandy and Philadelphia, George Sándor, the pianist, had already begun to study the work, such a step by me would be unprecedented and would damage the reputation of his firm and would damage the interest of the music of Bartók. I was adamant and insisted that he should wire Philadelphia cancelling the license, granted by him. A storm followed. I got telephone calls from dozens of friends of the Bartók family, of George Sándor, from other musicians, all warning me that what I meant and wanted to do was an unprecedented step and shouldn't be done. Most of them questioned my authority to step in and upset and overturn the apple cart. But my indignation about the

$17.50 "remuneration" to the Bartók Estate out of the performance of the last important work of Bartók and in connection with such feverish activity by everybody, who obviously had a stake and an ax to grind—the pianist, the publisher, the orchestra, the conductor, did not share my knowledge that I was right—I felt sufficient moral stand to remain adamant and maintain the prohibition. Also I insisted that I was not consulted and therefore what I did was not going back on my word, but to prevent that an important value of the Bartók estate be used and exploited without proper remuneration and payment to the Bartók Estate. It was my impression that Tibor Serly, who completed the 3rd Piano Concerto by adding the few missing bars, might have been or probably was responsible for [the] consent of Mr. Peter Bartók and the arrangements with Philadelphia. I wrote him two letters, on December 11 and December 21st, 1945, making him responsible for the agreement without my knowledge (Encl. C1a). His irritated answer of December 23rd, 1945, denied his responsibility (Enc. C1b). I did not acquiesce, pressed my point against him in my letter of December 24th, 1945. I set forth that Boosey & Hawkes denies having made the arrangement. I told Serly that George Sándor, who was very eager to have that springboard of being the first performer of the 3rd Piano Concerto, could not possibly have the right to make such arrangement (Encl. C1c). In his answer, dated January 10th, 1946 (C1d), Serly insisted that he had no part in the negotiations with the Philadelphia Orchestra. Obviously, Mr. Peter Bartók could be the only person who did it.

Simultaneously, I telephoned to the musical director of the Boston Symphony, Mr. Koussevitzky, whether he was willing to pay a special fee for the first performance. His answer was that he might have done it, but he would not do now something that would appear as an anti-Philadelphia, anti-Ormandy move. "No, that I could not do."

Also, I did not want to be entirely negative. I respected and believed the information that such a festive concert connected with the general interest in Bartók's person and music occasioned by his sudden death, would help the acceptance of Bartók's work by artists, orchestras, and music loving public. Therefore, I wrote a letter to the Director of the Philadelphia Orchestra, Mr. Eugene Ormandy. In that letter [Encl. C2] I explained to him that according to information received from the publishers, the World Premiere of the 3rd Piano Concerto would *not* result in any payment to the Bartók Estate for the maintenance of the Bartók family, and that the amounts stated by the publishers were ridiculously small and negligeable, and asked him to arrange a substantial payment to the Bartók Estate in consideration of the right and privilege put upon the 3rd Piano Concerto. The answer came instead of Mr. Ormandy from the Manager of the Philadelphia Orchestra, Mr. Harl McDonald. It was entirely negative. He wrote, "contracts covering rentals of music are made with Boosey & Hawkes and I am afraid no exception can be made in the case of the Bartók First Performance. Unfortunately our blanket royalty payments covering the rights to perform contemporary works used by the Orchestra are subject to public audit, and this being a non-profit organization it will be impossible for me to make any special payment unless I did it from my own pocket. I am sure you will understand the situation and the reasons for my inability to do anything. The Bartók participation in ASCAP earnings is a matter determined by the Classification Committee action, and the Bartók Estate should have a just and equitable settlement from ASCAP."

I did not acquiesce. I maintained my prohibition of the performance and I insisted that payment be made to the Bartók Estate (Encl. C2c). Answering this, on December 27th another letter came from McDonald, promising that he would present the matter to the Board of the Philadelphia Orchestra and that decision will be made at the next Board Meeting on Jan. 9, 1946 (Encl. C3). Meanwhile I began to educate, train, and teach myself the facts and elements of music business. I spent several days in libraries doing research work, whether special fees for First Performance were usual or not. I could not consult easily counsels, because there was no money available for fees of such consultation. Though Bartók was not member of the American Association of Authors, Composers, and Publishers, I went to their office and succeeded to establish contact with the Head of the International Department and received from him the first instruction about the intricacies of the music business. I learned from him that since Bartók was not [a] member of ASCAP, he would not participate in the general distribution of the funds collected as performing fees by ASCAP, but that on the other hand some payment will be made by ASCAP to the British Performing Rights Society of which Bartók was [a] member, on account of which Bartók will receive some payment on account of the performance in Philadelphia. He told me that the Philadelphia Orchestra paid $3,000.- to ASCAP for all their performances, for the year-round use of any copyrighted music, out of which a very <u>un</u>substantial sum could be portioned out to one performance. He helped me in finding the source material for any special payments. On account of the storm that the prohibition of the Philadelphia performance created, I was under moral pressure from every possible direction, and in order to defend my action, I could not spare any effort to justify the prohibition, unless I was willing to throw in the sponge. That I did not intend to do. By December 31, 1945, however, I knew enough to take a definite stand. My letter to the Manager of the Philadelphia Orchestra (Encl. C4) is of such importance that I want to quote here what I wrote:

"When I began my activities in connection with the Bartók Estate and decided that the first performance of the piano concerto could not possibly be given over without a special fee, as a novice in this business I did not know that this was a quite customary an arrangement. Meanwhile I learned that the Philadelphia Orchestra paid Schoenberg a special fee, of which you are certainly aware, and which amounted to either one or two thousand dollars, although it was not a world premiere. I also learned that the agency handling the performance rights of the Russian composers charges a special fee regularly for the right of the first performance. I also learned, according to the newspaper reports, that for the first performance of the Shostakovich Stalingrad symphony, a fee of $10,000 was paid.

"Returning to the Bartók composition which, according to everybody's opinion, as I wrote you before, seems to be a very important work, I am convinced that you will want to pay an appropriate fee, particularly because Béla Bartók died leaving in his bank account an amount which is not sufficient for the most modest living expenses of a single person for a single month.

"I assure you that I do not want to take a purely mercenary attitude, but under the circumstances I cannot refrain from taking an intransigent stand."

At the same time on the same day I wrote to the publishers prohibiting the First Performance on the radio of the Philadelphia performance without a special fee (Encl. C5). On the very same day, that is, December 31st, I wrote to Peter Bartók sending him the copies of my letters, informing him about the fact that I was attempting to get in touch with his brother, and I sent him a $300.- check of my own (Encl. C6).

On January 8th, 1946, after my return to New York, I wrote another letter to the Manager of the Philadelphia Orchestra informing him about other fees paid to composers for first performances and asked him to confirm that (Encl. C7). In a letter answering mine, Mr. McDonald, the Manager, admitted that his first information that never special fees had been paid for the Premiere of important compositions was incorrect, but insisted that it had never been more than $500.-, and that mostly it had not been more than $250.- (Encl. C8). On January 11th Mr. McDonald informed me that the Board of the Philadelphia Orchestra voted a contribution of $500.- to Mrs. Bartók. He wrote: "This is unprecedented, but they felt that the circumstances warranted this action."

Meanwhile, I asked George Sándor, the pianist, to come and see me. I informed him at the time when he came that I would not agree to the performance in Philadelphia and his appearance as the first performer, unless he himself would contribute to the immediate needs of the Bartók family. In view of the fact that his fee amounted to $750.-, I asked $500.-. He agreed. Thus, I reached the $1000.- figure. That was much less than I expected, but on account of the publicity and the great pressure on me and of the immediate needs of the Bartók family, I agreed to the performance and released the music, by instructing the publishers to put the parts at the disposal of the Philadelphia Orchestra (Encl. C9 and C10).

Meanwhile, my prohibition of the broadcast was maintained, unless a special fee was paid. I had a telephone conversation with Mr. Julius Mattfeld, in charge of this broadcasting at the Columbia Broadcasting System. I asked him how much he was willing to pay. His answer was evasive, and he asked me how much I would demand. While I was hesitant, mainly because I had neither experience nor any knowledge about the possibilities, he bruskly interrupted my silence and told me the maximum he would consider would be $75.-. My answer was that he should forget about the broadcasting and the press reception to be given before the broadcast and all other festive arrangement of self-congratulation about broadcasting a modern important art work. What happened in the background I do not know, but I do know that within one hour Yehudi Menuhin appeared unannounced in my home and expressed sympathy with my stand, yet explained to me how much it meant for modern music that the broadcast should take place, and informed me that Columbia Broadcasting System would pay $250.- and another payment of $750.- would be forthcoming if I consented to the broadcast. The Columbia Broadcasting System duly paid $250.- to Peter Bartók, and the payment of $750.- was transmitted to Mrs. Bartók or Peter Bartók, both of them, on February 16, 1946.

This struggle for the first revenue resulted in obtaining, instead of $17.50, $2,000.- for the Bartók family. It taught me a lesson in another direction. I experienced and learned that the assumption of Bartók that he could not trust his son's spine and willpower, that he would not be strong enough to stand up for his artistic standards, was not untrue. Bartók's inheritance needed a Trustee indeed.

A fee of two thousand dollars does not sound like a great feat. Without the "give-away" it would have been more, too. But even so, it was in 1945 a sizeable sum. Before the post-war inflation that began in 1947 its purchasing power was more than 50% higher than now. In the all but complete impecuniosity of Mrs. Bartók, however, it meant the difference between destitution and a though modest but comfortable living standard for four to five months.

The "giving-away" of the 3rd Piano Concerto was not the only instance of mismanagement that happened.

The first years of my administration and office as Trustee of the Bartók Estate were filled with the problems and personal affairs of Mrs. Bartók and Mr. Peter Bartók, and with getting acquainted with the problems of a cultural treasure consisting mainly of musical compositions. I knew also, of course, all the time that Bartók was a great scholar on folk music. More especially I knew about his publications in the field of folk music. I had read his English-language book on Hungarian folk music that was out of print and not available on the market. I had some knowledge of his work on Rumanian folk music, all the more because I spent many hours, many days, with assisting him in the translating of the introduction and other textual material into English. I had quite much to do with prompting, urging, exacting pressure on Columbia University Press to bring about at last the actual publication of the Serbo-Croatian folk music work of Bartók on which he spent most of his life in the U.S. from 1941 until 1944. Yet, for about 3 years I did not become conscious of the fact that the manuscripts of the folk music works of Bartók, more especially of the one on Rumanian folk music, were supposed to be in my possession and they weren't there.

[In the Memorandum there follows seven typed pages retelling the story of how he tracked down the folk music manuscripts to George Herzog in Indiana and eventually forced their belated return in 1951.][4]

---

4   Bator included an abbreviated version of this story in his preface to the Béla Bartók Archives catalogue. He also retells it, in expanded form, in the preface to Vol. 1 of the Rumanian Folk Music. Here in the Memorandum he pairs it with the story of the Third Piano Concerto to illustrate the work he was forced into as Trustee by the family's hastily conceived arrangements with other musicians in the months after his father's death. He emphasizes that Peter's turning over of the Rumanian materials to George Herzog "was not done by Peter in bad faith," because Peter "either did not know or did not realize what a Trusteeship meant, and therefore had no idea that he was not supposed to do any such thing." Thus, he explains, "in 1949, it was up to me to get back into the Estate that valuable part of the Estate," which he tried to do "without hurting the sentiments of Peter Bartók" (Memorandum, p. 31).

Battles in Philadelphia, II.
The Philadelphia Orchestra and Bluebeard's Castle, 1951–52.

*I*n 1951 Eugene Ormandy signaled his plan to perform and record Bluebeard's Castle during the Philadelphia Orchestra's 1952–53 season. By contractual obligation, all recordings of the Philadelphia Orchestra were to be produced and distributed by Columbia Records. Victor Bator, in an effort to help Peter Bartók, reserved the right of producing the first American recording of the opera for the composer's son. He told Ormandy that the orchestra was welcome to perform Bluebeard but not record it. The letters presented here reveal why Bator was so insistent on helping Peter Bartók, even to the point of angering a prominent conductor. Bator donated $1,000 to the Philadelphia Orchestra to mollify the organization. Anger over his intransigence caused Ormandy and Columbia records to lose interest. The planned performances did not take place.

This exchange shows Bator's personality as Trustee in the early years. His commitment to the Bartók heirs was absolute. He is fearless when provoked into disputes with prominent individuals in the world of classical music, including two of the recording industry's most powerful figures in the 1950s, Goddard Lieberson of Columbia Records and Eugene Ormandy. He fiercely defends the rights of the Bartók family to receive more income from royalties and to record certain works first. Here, as elsewhere, he demonstrates the negotiating skills of a seasoned businessman used to working in the upper echelons of commerce. He could be forceful and direct. He certainly wasn't shy.

VICTOR BATOR, LETTER TO BETTY BEAN, BOOSEY AND HAWKES. TYPED, 2 P. ONIONSKIN COPY, UNSIGNED. IN ENGLISH. DECEMBER 6, 1951.

December 6, 1951

Dear Betty,

I discussed the recording of "Blue Beard's Castle" with Peter over the telephone on Monday. As a result, I sent you my wire reserving the right of recording as broadly as is legally possible for Peter Bartok.

Battles in Philadelphia, II

I know that you had your heart set in the performance by Philadelphia, and in so far as their performance is subject to the recording rights of Columbia, I regret that I am disappointing you.

As to the $1,000 pledge, we haven't made up our minds yet whether it would be given by me personally, as I would like to do it, or by the estate. This depends which donor carries more weight.

I won't drop this subject without reverting to a remark of yours about a possible boycott of Bartok's works. I hope that you didn't mean that, because though I appreciate forcefulness for argument, I think it is out of proportion and based on some kind of misinformation.

Let us review the "complications" to which you refer. Was it that I was unjustified in refusing to give my consent to the first performance of the piano concert without a special fee and that with an income of $17.50 accrued to the Bartok estate when the family was in distress? Or was it perhaps a contribution to the name of Bartok that this disgrace could not happen? Or did I damage so remarkably the reputation of Bartok by reserving the recording of the viola concerto for Peter in a much better performance, finer artistic quality, and better recording than the one planned by Victor, which certainly would not have been better than their other recording not to well reviewed by the music-loving public? Or was I perhaps the one who didn't do everything to bring about the production of the "Mandarin," not only with opening the purse but by the work I did with Kirstein? And here again, why can't Chicago perform the "Blue Beard's Castle" without recording or a $1,000 donation? And why should Philadelphia not be willing to do the same?

If there is a "vexatious" situation I am its only source by being neither composer, nor an artist, nor at the business of music. But I was put in this position by someone who certain did contribute to the artistic and material value meant by the name Bartok, and that was Bela Bartok himself. Perhaps his intention and his spirit that I represent without material or moral benefits should be respected and not boycotted.

I am sure that you agree with me. I am only writing this down as a source material argument for you; should someone from Philadelphia, Columbia, or any other place dare to speak of a boycott, I would be willing to challenge them to discuss this situation publicly. I would have a few things to say as you know.

Sincerely,

Miss Betty Randolph Bean
Boosey and Hawkes, Inc.
30 West 57th St.
New York City

Please pass this around to the rest of the family[1]

VICTOR BATOR, LETTER TO EUGENE ORMANDY. TYPED, 1 P. UNSIGNED. ONIONSKIN COPY. IN ENGLISH. DECEMBER 11, 1951.[2]

December 11, 1951

Dear Mr. Ormandy:

I heard with interest about your plan to perform "Blue Beard's Castle" in the Season 1952–53. It would be a memorable occasion to hear this work interpreted by you and your orchestra.

Unfortunately, for reasons which I am willing to explain to you if you are interested which I feel confident you may appreciate, I had to reserve the recording of the "Blue Beard's Castle" for Peter Bartok.

On the other hand, I realized that the recording would have been some kind of an additional incentive. Therefore, I conceived the idea to offer to you for the Orchestra Association $1,000 as a donation, should you with your orchestra perform in the season 1952–53 the "Blue Beard's Castle."

---

1   The annotation at the end of this letter appears to have been typed separately. The meaning of the word "family" is unclear, but it may refer to the Boosey and Hawkes staff.
2   Punctuation and spellings in this letter and in other letters reproduced in this volume are carefully retained from the originals. In his typed business correspondence Bator sometimes left off the accents in "Bartók," "Béla," or other Hungarian proper names even when writing to other native Hungarian speakers such as Ormandy.

Should this $1,000 not suffice you as a substitute for the recording please let me know and I will try to obtain some additional subsidy for that purpose.

I cannot close this letter without congratulating you on the occasion of the quite unprecedented recognition your work has been getting in connection with your last concerts recently.

As an admiring member of the audience at the Verdi Requiem I want to add my modest congratulations.

Sincerely,

Mr. Eugene Ormandy
Music Director,
Philadelphia Orchestra Association
1910 Girard Trust Company Building
Philadelphia, Pennsylvania

Victor Bator, letter to Goddard Lieberson, President, Columbia Records. Typed, 2 p. Onionskin copy. Unsigned. In English.

December 11, 1951

Dear Mr. Lieberson,

It is surprising to receive a letter from the head of a large organization with so many errors and misstatements. This is the only reason that I feel prompted to answer your letter of December 4th.

In the first paragraph of your letter you refer to the difficulties you encountered "in the attempt to record Bartok's Third Piano Concerto". Your files will show that you not only attempted but did, in fact, record Bartok's Third Piano Concerto after the first performance by Philadelphia and George Sandor. I don't know the date of the recording, because neither Boosey and Hawkes nor you informed Peter Bartok or myself of the recording. However, the world premier was in 1946, and the royalty statements of Boosey and Hawkes show that you sold in less than six months up to June 30, 1947, 69,112 sides of records. (Sixty nine thousand

and one hundred and twelve.) Thus it was not an "attempt", but a very successful business venture with considerable profit.

In the second paragraph of your letter you say, "the only Bartok we have every recorded in this company <u>was</u> not done for monetary gain." You are mistaken again; Columbia recorded not one Bartok, but twelve of his works so far. And as the above figures show, at least one of them was a hit. It is not my fault that in spite of this initial success of the Third Piano Concerto, you kept this work off the market. The unwarranted unavailability of the work during 1948–49 damaged considerably the public acceptance and response of the record and sales.

Your statement that you don't record Bartok for monetary gains seems to be in conflict with the opinion of Mr. Gilbert of your organization also. He, at his recent visit in my office, definitely stated that unless you included in your recording twentieth century music as that of Bartok and contemporary music also, you could just as well go out of business. Monetary gain is not only the one you collect in twenty-four hours, and I hope that you do not think that Columbia could stay in business with only Kostelanetz and Tchaikovsky. As a matter of fact, the sale figures of the Piano Concerto within on[e]-half a year amounting to 70,000, show that immediate monetary gain is possible though you do not use advertisements and other promotional means for modern music as you do otherwise[.]

I am sorry that you do not appraise the accomplishment of Bartok as a composer high enough to equal his greatness of man. Many people will disagree with this. This however, explains to me the negligence that Bartok found at the Columbia Recording Company. Let us see your record on Bartok music.

In 1941 Bartok was sixty years old. Most of his great compositions were then twenty to thirty years old. Yet Columbia Broadcasting was not interested in him until that time, and then mostly minor works. Prior to that date Bartok received tremendous recognition as the great composer of our generation in the whole world, and Columbia needed no prophetic inspiration in 1941 to record 4 of his minor works. But your organization saw it fit to keep the recording of the 2. part of the Mikrokosmos off the market for 10 years, during which time you succeed to lose irreplaceably one out of the six recorded parts of the second volume. The 1. part of the Mikrokosmos, which sold 3,000 in 1941-44 was unavailable after that date for 5 years.

You misrepresent the facts when you suggest that Peter Bartok and myself are "preventing six public performances in four large American cities" and "keep off the market the recording of one of his father's important work". Peter Bartok will record the "Blue Beard's Castle" before 1953, the date of your planned recording, and will thus advance the time when the public will be able to buy the record. Neither do I think that we are preventing the Philadelphia Orchestra from performing the work. After all, if the Chicago Orchestra can perform the work on January 31st and February 1st of 1952 without recording, I don't see why Philadelphia could not achieve the same. However, in order to further the performance by Philadelphia, 3 days ago I wired to Boosey and Hawkes that I was willing to donate $1,000 to the Philadelphia Orchestra Association if "Blue Beard's Castle" would be performed by them in the 1952–53 season. I hope that Columbia Broadcasting or you personally, as great admirers and friends of Bela Bartok, will match my contribution by an equal amount.

Your reverence toward Bartok and the fact that I have learned from your letter that he was your friend, makes me to hope that the deplorable omissions of your organization to do something for him while he was alive will be belatedly compensated by enthusiasm for his works in the future.

Sincerely Yours,

Mr. Goddard Lieberson
Columbia Records Inc.
799 Seventh Avenue
New York 19, N.Y.

VICTOR BATOR, LETTER TO EUGENE ORMANDY. TYPED, 2 P. IN ENGLISH. ONIONSKIN COPY. DECEMBER 17, 1951.

December 17, 1951

Dear Mr. Ormandy,

I have received Miss Colt's answer dated December 13th to my letter written to you.

It is difficult for me to believe that this is your final answer, though if it is there is nothing that I can do about it. The recording of BLUEBEARD'S CASTLE, it being a dramatical musical works, can be reserved for Peter Bartok not only as to the first recording but during the entire period of the copyright. This gives a tremendous advantage to Peter Bartok, and I feel that Bela Bartok would certainly want his son, as long as he is in the recording business, to have that privilege. I would fail the memory of Bela Bartok, who made me his testamentary Executor and Trustee of his estate if I sacrificed this privilege of his son just to avoid such conflict in which I found myself on account of yours and the Philadelphia Orchestra's desire to connect the performance of the work with its recording.

After all, you do perform many works without recording and without assistance such as I offered to you. It is true that you pioneered in presenting Bartok's works to the public, when audiences in the United States were apathetic to his compositions. But this was not true at the same time in other countries where he was already recognized as one of the great composers of the 20th century. Was not the performance of Bela Bartok's works by you one of the many milestones in your way to the summit of the musical career that you have reached? Has the Bartok Estate not given to you the first performance of the posthumous Piano Concerto and its recording, for which one year later, large amounts of cash would have been paid by other orchestras? Do you not by dropping the BLUEBEARD'S CASTLE, miss perhaps another monument in the long series of your achievements? You are the only person to answer this question to your yourself and it would be immodest from me to try to influence you. You are the best person to decide these questions which come to my mind.

I am sure that Mr. Lieberson has sent the Philadelphia Orchestra copies of his letters to me, though on his letter dated December 4th he omitted to mention those to whom copies were sent. Needless to say, I am not even going to answer his second letter, which was even more uncivil than his first one. Therefore, I want to give you the facts about the relationship of Columbia Recording Company to Bartok.

Columbia Recording Company first recorded Bartok when he was sixty years old, which was in 1940–41. They recorded the Roumanian Dance, the Contrast, the First and Second Rhapsodies and 12 sides of Mikrokosmos. The Roumanian Folk Dances, the Contrast, and the Rhapsodies did not receive any trade promotion by Columbia, and had a poor market. They published only the first six pieces of the Mikrokosmos. It sold between 1941–43 about 3,000 sides. Then they took it off the market for six years. The second part of the Mikrokosmos wasn't released at all for ten years. Two years ago Peter Bartok requested them to let him publish it. Mr. Lieberson refused this. The Third Piano Concerto was recorded after Bartók's death, immediately following the first performance by you in 1946. Then, it was taken off the market for two full years and reissued in 1950 on L.P.

The above record eliminates any thoughts about having moral obligations towards Columbia. However, this is not the reason that I don't let Columbia record BLUEBEARD'S CASTLE. I do this solely because of the relationship of Peter Bartok Recording Studio to the great composer, who in my opinion owes no gratitude to a recording company for having given niggardly recognition to his compositions. No amount of uncivil aggressiveness can now change *that* record.

I request you again to reconsider your decision. I and my friends are ready to help by contribution the Philadelphia performance. Yet, if you insist on the recording by Columbia, I cannot but express my regret.

Very truly yours,

Mr. Eugene Ormandy
Music Director
Philadelphia Orchestra Association
Philadelphia, Pennsylvania

Victor Bator, letter to Harl McDonald, Manager, Philadelphia Orchestra Association. Typed, 2p. In English. Onionskin copy. January 14, 1952.

January 14, 1952

Dear Mr. McDonald,

I am sorry that my last letter to you prompted an answer which necessitates a response from me.

I know the deep interest that the Philadelphia Orchestra Association has always shown in the music of Bartok, and nobody can appreciate this more than I do. However, it is an error on your part that "the Philadelphia Orchestra Association made a contribution of $500.00 to Mr. Bartok on February 28, 1946, when the financial hardships that the composer had endured was learned". Bela Bartok died in September 1945. Thus, you couldn't have possibly helped him at that time in his financial hardships. The $500 payment was made to the Bela Bartok Estate as a fee for the first performance of the Third Piano Concerto after the death of the composer.

If you look up my letters to you dated December 24th and December 31, 1945, January 6th and 14th, 1946, and your answer of December 21st, 1945, and January 2nd and 11th, 1946, you will see that we had a nice haggling about the size of the fee. I suggested $2,000. You went up from no fee to $200, and finally you agreed on $500. I would not have agreed to the figure of $500 had not Mr. George Sandor offered to pay another $500, and the Columbia Broadcasting Company $750 for the first broadcast performance. Thus, I collected almost $2,000, which was very nearly the figure originally asked for. Even so, it was generous of Mrs. Bartok to permit the first performance for $500.

This doesn't change in any way my opinion that the Philadelphia Orchestra Association and Mr. Ormandy were great friends and supporters of Bela Bartok personally and his music, which has been and will be appreciated by me and every other friend of Bartok.

Very truly yours,

Mr. Harl McDonald
Philadelphia Orchestra Association
1910 Girard Trust Building
Philadelphia, Pennsylvania

Chapter 3

One Will or Three? The Wills of 1940, 1943, and 1945

In August and September of 1945, in what would turn out to be his last months of life, Béla Bartók worked with singular purpose on the Third Piano Concerto and Viola Concerto. The war in Europe had recently ended. In Japan the two atomic bombs had been dropped. News of Japan's subsequent surrender was still sending shockwaves around the globe when, in August, Bartók's health took a sudden downturn. He and Ditta, growing uneasy, decided to return early from Saranac Lake. With his chronically poor health in mind, and no doubt for additional considerations we'll never be able reconstruct, he began to ponder making further changes to his Last Will and Testament. An unexpected hospitalization in New York City on September 21 made the matter urgent. There Bartók discussed the Will at his bedside with Victor Bator, who had been called in by the family to help. Bator promptly got in touch with Harold Manheim, the New York attorney who had prepared the 1943 Will.[1] Manheim crafted new language for the document. His staff prepared a revised Will for Bartók's signature. No one involved in this rush to produce an updated Will could have possibly known that the date arranged for Bartók to sign the new document—"September 26, 1945" is pre-typed on the signature page—would be the same day he died. Rapidly, too rapidly, the downward spiral of Bartók's late-stage leukemia accelerated towards its grim conclusion, overtaking them all.

Ordinarily a deathbed Last Will and Testament of a major artistic figure would have drawn the considered attention of biographers and scholars by now. This one hasn't. Only a handful of people around Bartók ever knew about this second American Will in late 1945—just those who were physically present in his last days or involved in the Will's drafting. In the wake of Bartók's death it

---

[1] Manheim was a name partner at Wachtell Manheim & Grouf, a small, well regarded New York firm that maintained a general practice and specialized in international business law, with additional practice areas in tax law and estate law. Its partners handled, among other matters, the legal work for the Republic of Austria's commercial interests in the United States. Harold Manheim (1900–92) was born in New York and educated at Columbia University ('20) and New York Law School (LL.B. '25). His firm represented Bator in several later actions, including the 1948 lawsuit against Boosey & Hawkes and Columbia Records over the recording of the 3rd Piano Concerto.

Chapter 3

faded quickly from view, long before biographers could notice it and incorporate it into their narratives of Bartók's last months of life. The reason is straightforward: it never got signed. There, in the hospital, his body failing rapidly, Bartók on September 26 no longer had the strength or presence of mind to sign the Will. Unsigned, it had no legal validity. It never became his Last Will and Testament. But yet it existed, and has existed all these years, on typed pages, minus a signature; it's an eloquent document on its own terms, mute proof of a life unfinished, of projects left incomplete, of an artistic life suddenly ended.

Bator was well aware that no amount of wishful thinking could make an unsigned will a valid legal instrument. As named executor in the 1943 Will, with the help of Manheim's office, he put forward for probate the earlier, signed Will. Under its terms he subsequently carried out his duties as executor and trustee.

Many years later the deathbed Will would come back to haunt the deteriorating relationships between Bartók's heirs and the Bartók Estate. None of the heirs had an actual copy in their possession. Some general awareness of its existence had been retained, however, and when tensions came to a boil in the Estate in the late 1950s, Peter Bartók asked Bator to locate a copy of the unsigned Will so he could see it again. Suddenly it developed new life. Resurrected, it became it another tool to justify and sustain litigation. As Béla Bartók's last thoughts on the disposition of his material affairs, dictated from his deathbed, the Will's dispositions carried great authority within a family shaped by habitual deference to his wishes when he was alive—and no small amount of destructive potential for their current relationships after his death.

On June 2, 1959, Victor Bator decided to take the matter up on behalf of the heirs. Faithful to his higher, moral charge as trustee on behalf of the family, he was curious himself whether the unused Will's terms might help them all sort through their growing tensions. He had retained the original document in his Estate files. He wrote two letters that day, one to Peter, one to Harold Manheim. He adopted a guarded tone with Peter, professing to know little about the document:

Dear Peter:

Mr. Rosen has told me that your attorney dropped remarks about some kind of a Will that was meant to change the Testament as it existed before the death of your Father. As I understand, you had told your attorney that your Father wanted to change his Will and sign a new one.

Even though legally that is of no importance because courts, trustees, and other official persons are not permitted or supposed to read the mind of the testator unless it is expressed in a legal form, privately they are allowed to be influenced within the limits of legal possibilities by such expression of desires and intentions.

It makes no difference to me whether you send your answer directly or through your attorney, but I would like to learn the facts about the intended new will of your Father. If there are no such facts according to your knowledge and the information is erroneous, please let me know also.

I look forward to your early reply.

Yours,
Victor Bator[2]

His letter to Manheim, by contrast, was more straightforward, written from one lawyer to another, requesting information.

Dear Harold:

In the files of the Bartók Estate I have found an unsigned Last Will of Béla Bartók dated September 26, 1945, that happens to be the day on which the composer died. Thus Bartók could not sign it, although the copy in my possession is all ready for his signature, complete with ribbon and seal, as prepared by your efficient office.

I do not remember the circumstances that prompted the preparation of this unsigned Will. Have you in your files any correspondence or memorandum instructing you to prepare it the way you did? If so, from whom did the instruction emanate? If papers relating to this new Will are available in your files, I would like to get their photostatic copy.

I know that this search may cause some loss of time which, naturally, should be charged to me.

The reason for this inquiry is that even though the signed Last Will and Testament of Béla Bartók is not involved in any dispute, the intentions of Bartók are being questioned; the family and I would like to read his mind retroactively and, should any new arrangement be worked out

---

2   Victor Bator, letter to Peter Bartók, June 2, 1959 (BSCB Tampa).

Chapter 3

among the members of the family, learn the facts about the background of this unsigned will.³

Manheim, overseas at the time, was unavailable to respond. One of his partners advised Bator that he had recalled the firm's "old Bartók file" from the warehouse to be available once Manheim returned.⁴ On June 18 Manheim replied. No, he had not visited Bartók in person in September 1945, he recalled. Instead he had prepared the Will based on instructions from Bator, which in turn came from Bartók himself while he was in the hospital. (This information allows us to date the Will's preparation precisely to September 21–26, 1945.) Changes in the Will, according to Manheim, "were dictated by the fact that Mrs. Bartók at that time was in an emotionally disturbed condition and it was felt that the interests of the family would be served better if any bequest to her was made in trust and was limited to the minimum required by the New York statute." He remembers running into Ditta later on, at a memorial concert held at New York Public Library; based on that encounter, he concluded, "it was unfortunate that the new Will could not have been executed."⁵

Half a century later, when he committed his memories to print in *My Father*, Peter retold the scene at his father's bedside in the hospital. As he remembers it, his father wanted to make some changes to his Will, and asked for Victor Bator while in the hospital.

> Victor Bátor was then staying in his summer house in Nonquitt, Massachusetts. When I reached him by phone he was in no great hurry to come to New York. He did not believe my father was in serious condition and, as neither did I, I could not convince him. He promised to inquire with my father's doctors about the situation. I learned much later that there were some changes my father wanted to make in his will, something Victor Bátor already knew about. He would come, eventually. [. . .] A day or so later Victor Bátor, whom my father was expecting in vain to see for awhile, finally arrived. On that day my father was already unconscious. Victor Bátor brought with him the matter needing to be attended to, a few typed pages; the draft of the new will. Seeing my father's condi-

---

3   Victor Bator, letter to Harold Manheim, June 2, 1959 (BSCB Tampa). Copy. A note on orthography: in this letter we see Bator using both lower-case and upper-case versions of the word "will." The accepted style among lawyers is to capitalize references to an individual legal document as Will, i.e., Last Will and Testament, but to refer to wills in the abstract, or generally, using the lower-case form. Some looseness and inconsistency is always tolerated, even among attorneys.
4   Hans Harnik, letter to Victor Bator, June 11, 1959 (BSCB Tampa).
5   Harold Manheim, letter to Victor Bator, June 18, 1959 (BSCB Tampa).

tion, he attempted pushing a fountain pen into his limp hand, trying to obtain a signature, but my father never regained consciousness. With my mother, Victor Bátor, myself, and a nurse standing by his bed, he died on that 26 of September, 1945."[6]

When I read this passage aloud to Francis Bator, curious about his response, he instantly protested. "This is gross!" he cried. "My father would have *never* done that!" The force and immediacy of his response impressed me at the time. Although his father never practiced law in the United States, he had a lawyer's trained mind, sharpened by decades of high-profile international legal practice. Lawyers know, in ways that lay people do not, that the circumstances of obtaining signatures must be handled with care. Ethical lawyers are automatically wary of situations like the one at Bartók's bedside; even the slightest whiff of misconduct can be grounds for a later malpractice lawsuit. The absence of Bartók's signature, in this light, should probably be interpreted as evidence that Bator exercised sound judgment that day in the hospital. (Manheim, moreover, had planned to be there to deliver the Will and supervise its signing; he was called off, apparently because it was already too late.)[7] The "pen in limp hand" image, in contrast, is the exactly the type of fiction a hostile heir might invent. So, too, is the accusatory tone in the expression that his father waited for Bator "in vain," and the insinuation that Bator knowingly dragged his feet on the new Will. These imaginative flights are wholly consistent with Peter Bartók's later habitual antagonism for Bator, and should be enough to cast doubt on the reliability of his witness to the event.

Ditta Bartók's only published memories of her husband's final days appeared twenty years later, in an Austrian music journal. She does not mention the scramble to revise his Will, though she sketches the scene at his deathbed with care. Nor does she indulge in casting blame. She seems studiously neutral—more factual, more emotionally contained. Of Bator she writes, "I do remember seeing Dr. Bátor there once [at the hospital], but Béla did not speak with him."[8] Looming larger in her memories are the roles played, instead, by the Kecskemétis and Dr. Holló, and, of course, her son, who helped her keep vigil during those final days at the hospital. Even when writing from Hungary in the mid-1960s, when battles over the Estate had entered their second decade, she does not impute malice to Bator, suggesting a core thread of commitment to their earlier supportive relationship.

---

6   Peter Bartók, *My Father*, 132–33; 137.
7   Harold Manheim, letter to Victor Bator, June 18, 1959 (BSCB Tampa).
8   Ditta Bartók, "26. September 1945: Zum 20. Todestag von Béla Bartók," *Oesterreichische Musikzeitschrift* 20 (1965): 446–49. As translated in Malcolm Gillies, ed., *Bartók Remembered* (New York: W.W. Norton, 1990), 198.

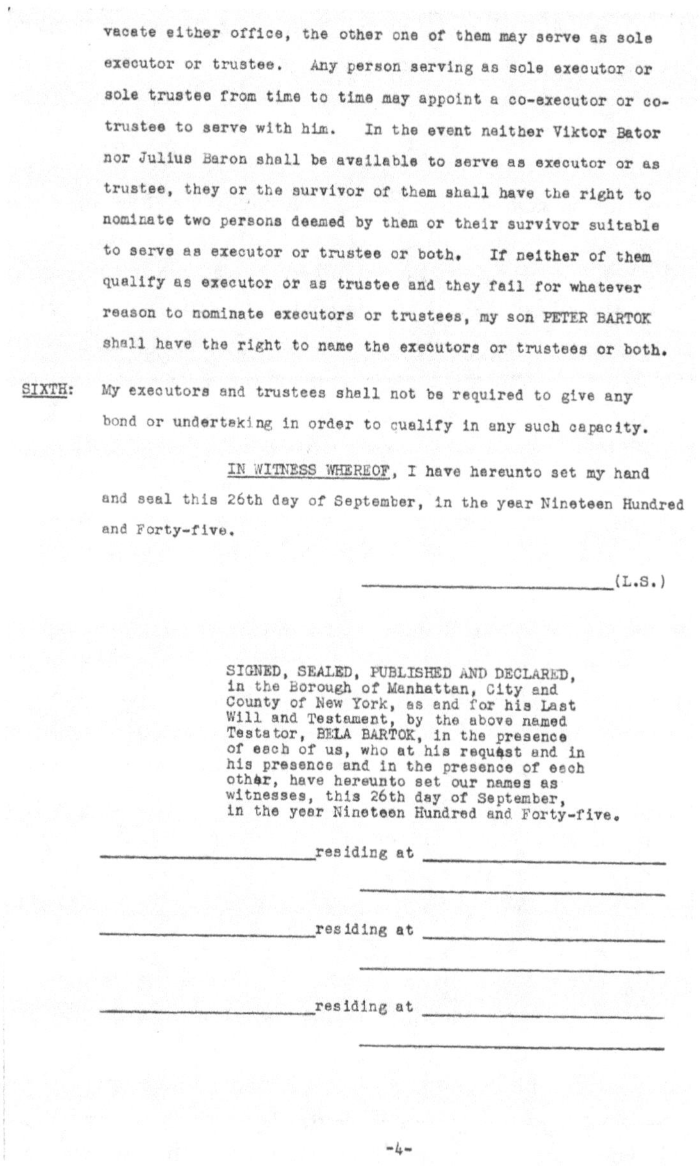

Chapter 3

> vacate either office, the other one of them may serve as sole executor or trustee. Any person serving as sole executor or sole trustee from time to time may appoint a co-executor or co-trustee to serve with him. In the event neither Viktor Bator nor Julius Baron shall be available to serve as executor or as trustee, they or the survivor of them shall have the right to nominate two persons deemed by them or their survivor suitable to serve as executor or trustee or both. If neither of them qualify as executor or as trustee and they fail for whatever reason to nominate executors or trustees, my son PETER BARTOK shall have the right to name the executors or trustees or both.
>
> SIXTH: My executors and trustees shall not be required to give any bond or undertaking in order to qualify in any such capacity.
>
> IN WITNESS WHEREOF, I have hereunto set my hand and seal this 26th day of September, in the year Nineteen Hundred and Forty-five.
>
> _____(L.S.)
>
> SIGNED, SEALED, PUBLISHED AND DECLARED, in the Borough of Manhattan, City and County of New York, as and for his Last Will and Testament, by the above named Testator, BELA BARTOK, in the presence of each of us, who at his request and in his presence and in the presence of each other, have hereunto set our names as witnesses, this 26th day of September, in the year Nineteen Hundred and Forty-five.
>
> _____residing at _____
>
> _____residing at _____
>
> _____residing at _____

Fig. 3.1. New York Bartók Archive photocopy of Béla Bartók's deathbed Will, showing the blank signature line and pre-typed date of September 26, 1945. Source: BSCB Tampa.

These few recollections by family members aside, we are left with little factual information to help us explain the mystery of the missing signature on Bartók's deathbed Will. Letters from Manheim help us understand the sequence of events. Even Bator himself, a central participant, by 1959 recognized that he could no longer recall the reasons why Bartók decided to revise a Will he had signed just two years earlier. The 1945 American Will itself is silent about its reasons for existing. It keeps its secrets. Its blank signature line under the pre-typed date—*this* date of all dates!—is eloquent proof of how suddenly Bartók was taken from this world (Fig. 3.1). My sense is that Bator, who remembers arriving at the hospital only 48 hours before Bartók's death, must have caught Bartók still lucid and able to talk with him about the changes he wished to make. Bator then rushed those changes to Manheim, who drafted the Will on Sept. 25, knowing that it would have to be signed as soon as possible. It would have to be the next day, in fact, so he pre-typed the date. When Bator went to the hospital on Sept. 26 he saw at a glance that all of this effort was too late. Ditta's recollection that Béla "didn't speak with him" is consistent with this scenario.

So the Will remained unsigned.

Once its language was revisited, in 1959, Bator to his credit considered a number of potential outcomes. Rather than take the narrow but legally correct view that there was nothing to learn from it, he acknowledged that in the present state of disharmony among the heirs there may be ways to use its directives to gain perspective on how Bartók himself might have wanted current tensions resolved. Since Peter brought it up, in other words, they might as well all look at its terms.

The 1943 American Will

Our review of Béla Bartók's three Wills starts by considering the legal language laid out in the first American Will. As his only legally valid Will at the time of death, it would go on to become the main governing document establishing the Bartók Estate and Trust. After it was probated, Bartók's 1943 American Last Will and Testament became a matter of public record.[9] The Will is reproduced in full below, apparently for the first time (Fig. 3.2).[10]

---

9 By longstanding practice, laws in the United States mandate that documents like this are public record once probated. (Prior to death—an important legal distinction—a person's last will and testament is considered private.) Unlike trust agreements, which by definition are private or secret, carrying no burden of public notification or reporting, wills are understood to have a necessarily public component. For the wealthy, or famous, tensions can arise between the dual goals of public access and individual privacy rights. For an overview of US and English law in this sometimes sensitive area, see Joseph Jaconelli, "Wills As Public Documents — Privacy and Property Rights," *The Cambridge Law Journal* 71/1 (March 2012): 147–171.

10 Bartók's will was recorded in New York Surrogate's Court on January 24, 1946, in Liber 1803, page 544. Copies of the document, if they existed, would have been few in number. At most three total would have been prepared for signing: Bartók's own, a copy for Bator, and the reference copy for deposit at Manheim's office.

Chapter 3

Provisions in this first American Will created a testamentary trust that would form upon Béla Bartók's death, with Victor Bator and Gyula Báron named as executors and trustees. Assets belonging to Béla Bartók would pour over into the trust unless otherwise specified. The trust's sole beneficiary was identified as Ditta Bartók. His two sons were given separate consideration. To Béla Jr. he bequeathed all his "property of whatsoever nature, real, personal or mixed property" in the Kingdom of Hungary and Germany. Peter, then still 19, received no specific bequests; as a minor, he was understood to be taken care of by his mother, Ditta. Paragraph 3 gave him status as a remainderman.

In harmony with the practice of estate law in the United States, broad powers were assigned to the two trustees. These powers were specified in detail to eliminate points of conflict that might emerge in years ahead. Copyrights, at that time the trust's main asset, were specifically addressed. Paragraph 4(a) gives trustees the right to sell any of the trust's property. Paragraph 4(e) gives them full power to take "any and all steps which may from time to time be required in order to protect" the copyrights of Bartók's works. Those copyrights are further identified as "any and all copyrights which may belong to me at the time of my death, whether at common law or by statute or by treaty." Paragraph 4(e) further charges trustees to be vigilant and comprehensive in their management of those copyrights. Finally, in a closing flourish, Bartók authorizes the trustees to "do any and all acts with respect to musical or literary properties which I may own at the time of my death which I could do if I were living." Many of Victor Bator's actions in later years can be read as his efforts to live up to the charge placed on him by this sentence.

Certain language in the Will reads like the boilerplate Manheim and his partners likely found useful for all their clients in New York City: it covers "securities purchased above par," for example, and the "foreclosure" of collateral securities. The trust provisions, however, are carefully tailored to Bartók's wishes. The language was prescriptive, in that it told trustees what they are being charged to do. The language was also preventative, in that it gave legal cover for trustees should the heirs feel wrongly treated. Equally, and even more important, it told heirs quite plainly where their rights lay, giving guidance to them, too, about what to expect in years ahead as they adjusted to the presence of two trustees in their lives.

Bartók already had some experience with trusts, we should remember, and had begun to appreciate their uses under US law. His 1940 autograph manuscript trust (see Chapter 2) named two trustees, Herzog and Hawkes, to carry out specific charges on his behalf. The new testamentary trust had a different purpose, but the concept was similar. Estate lawyers in the US often consider trusts as an option in situations just like Bartók's, where the beneficiary or ben-

IN THE NAME OF GOD, AMEN!

I, <u>BELA BARTOK</u>, of the City, County and State of New York, being of sound and disposing mind and memory, and mindful of the uncertainties of life, do hereby publish and declare this to be my Last Will and Testament, hereby revoking all prior wills by me made.

FIRST: I hereby direct my executors hereinafter named, to pay all my just debts and funeral expenses as soon after my death as may be practiceable.

SECOND: I hereby give, devise and bequeath all of my property of whatsoever nature, real, personal or mixed, which may be situate in the Kingdom of Hungary or Germany or in any country which at the time of my death may be subject to the control of the German Government, to my eldest son Bela.

THIRD: I hereby give, devise and bequeath all of the rest, residue and remainder of my property, real, personal or mixed, wheresoever situated, to my executors hereinafter named, in trust, however, to invest and reinvest the same, and to collect the rents, issues, income and profits thereof, to my wife EDITH PASZTORY BARTOK, and upon her death to pay the principal of such trust fund to my son PETER. There shall be deemed included in this residuary bequest all of my copyrights, all rights of renewal copyrights which I may now have or may hereafter acquire, and all rights in unpublished manuscripts. So long as the trust shall be in force my executors and trustees are specifically empowered to exercise any rights of renewal copyright which may arise with respect to any of my composition under the laws of the United States of America.

FOURTH: So long as the trust provided for in Paragraph "THIRD" hereof remains in existence, the following provisions shall apply: [p. 2]

(a) My trustees shall have full power of sale with respect to any real property which may at any time form a part of the trust estate.

(b) The trustees shall have the right to invest in any form of investment regardless of whether the investment is of a type sanctioned by the laws of the State of New York for the investments of trustees and specifically are authorized to invest in common stocks and bonds of all kinds, secured and unsecured, second mortgages and interest in real property of whatever nature.

(c) My trustees shall have the right to take any action with respect to investments which might be taken by the owner thereof.

Without intending to limit the generality of the foregoing, my trustees are specifically authorized to take part in corporate proceeds of all kinds; to institute and defend class actions; to cause themselves to be elected to the board of directors and to any other office of any corporation, the stock of which may form a part of the trust fund; to foreclose collateral security; to be purchasers at any such foreclosure; to administer the property thus acquired, whether real or personal; to execute leases of any property which may form part of the trust fund, now or hereafter, for any period of time regarded by my trustees as expedient and regardless of limitations imposed by law.

(d) The trustees shall not be required to amortize copyrights or the premiums on securities purchased above par.

(e) The trustees are expressly authorized to retain as part of the trust fund any and all copyrights which may belong to me at the time of my death, whether at common law or by statute or by treaty. My trustees shall be authorized to take any and all steps which may from time to time be required in order to protect such rights, including but not limited to prosecution or [p. 3] defense of actions arising out of alleged infringements of copyright, taking appropriate proceedings for the renewal thereof, instituting actions for the accounting of royalties, entering into license agreements to license or otherwise dispose of any such composition or copyright or rights therein upon such terms as the trustees deem appropriate at the time and in general, to do any and all acts with respect to musical or literary properties which I may own at the time of my death which I could do if I were living.

FIFTH: I hereby nominate and appoint as executors of this my Last Will and Testament, and as trustees of the trust hereinbefore provided, my friends VIKTOR BATOR and JULIUS BARON. In the event either of

> the said persons should not be available, or should be disqualified from serving as executor or trustee, or should vacate either office, the other one of them may serve as sole executor or trustee. Any person serving as sole executor or sole trustee from time to time may appoint a co-executor or co-trustee to serve with him. In the event neither Viktor Bator nor Julius Baron shall be available to serve as executor or as trustee, they or the survivor of them shall have the right to nominate two persons deemed by them or their survivor suitable to serve as executor or trustee or both. If neither of them qualify as executor or as trustee, and they fail for whatever reason to nominate executors or trustees, my wife DITTA PASZTORY BARTOK shall have the right to name the executors or trustees or both.
>
> SIXTH: I nominate my wife as the guardian of my son PETER, if he should be a minor at the time of my death.
>
> SEVENTH: My executors and trustees and guardian aforesaid shall not be required to give any bond or undertaking in order to qualify in any such capacity.
>
> IN WITNESS WHEREOF, I have hereunto set my hand and seal this 28th day of March, 1943.
>
> Béla Bartók

Fig. 3.2. Béla Bartók's American Will. The original typed document, 4 p., is dated March 28, 1943. It bears Bartók's signature at the bottom of page 3. Witness signatures from Dr. Julius Hollo, Dr. Elsa Hollo, and Eleanor Loebrich, RN, are found on the fourth page. In English.

eficiaries are either 1) under the age of majority, or 2) physically or mentally unable to manage property, or unlikely to manage it well. The idea is to appoint trustees who safeguard the integrity of the assets on behalf of the beneficiaries. Co-trustees, if specified, can serve as checks and balances on each other. In New York City the 1943 Last Will and Testament of Lorenz Hart, of Rodgers and Hart fame, also named two trustees for the trust that would form upon his death. One was his accountant. The other was his younger brother Teddy.[11]

---

11 Gary Marmorstein, *A Ship Without a Sail: The Life of Lorenz Hart* (New York: Simon & Schuster, 2012). The first chapter in Marmorstein's book tells how the terms of Hart's will introduced immediate tensions in the heirs.

Chapter 3

Artist Mark Rothko named three executors/trustees in his Will: a gallery director in New York, a fellow artist and friend, and a friend not directly involved in the art world. Igor Stravinsky assigned his wife Vera as co-executor of his estate; she shared that responsibility with New York attorney L. Arnold Weissberger. As sole trustee of the resulting trust Mr. Weissberger was given full authority to manage its affairs for Vera's exclusive benefit while she lived.[12] Many other instances of trustee selection are highlighted in the anecdotes told by New York City attorney Herbert Nass in his book *Wills of the Rich and Famous*.[13]

Typically, then and now, testators will appoint as trustee individuals who are known to them and trusted within the family; a trustee can also have significant business, accounting, or legal experience, or access to such skills. (The ability to maneuver comfortably in the financial and legal worlds is often one of the main job qualifications needed to be a trustee.) A trust department of a bank can serve this role. In the United States the responsibilities of trustees are carefully delineated in the Uniform Trust Code and by further state and local codes enacted over the years; in them particular emphasis is paid to the "duty of loyalty" concept that lies at the heart of the trustee relationship.[14]

In years ahead numerous attorneys would scrutinize these provisions in Bartók's Will, seeking guidance in the language, or probing for weaknesses or ambiguities that might help them advance a position desired by a plaintiff. A series of distilled versions found their way into court records as a result. Milton Goldman, writing for New York Surrogates Court in 1971, masterfully boiled the entire document down to a handful of sentences:

> In view of conditions existing in Europe at the time, [Béla Bartók's] will established two categories of property. The first included all property situated in Hungary or Germany and in any other country which at the time of his death might be subject to the control of the German government. The second included all his remaining property. The former he bequeathed to his elder son Bela, outright and not subject to trust. The remainder he bequeathed in trust, the income from which he directed be paid to his wife Edith during her lifetime, and the corpus of which he bequeathed to his son Peter as remainderman upon the death of his

---

12 New York State Supreme Court, decision in Re: The Estate of Igor Stravinsky, December 30, 2003. Available online at https://caselaw.findlaw.com/ny-supreme-court-appellate-division/1072944.html.
13 Herbert E. Nass, *Wills of the Rich & Famous: A Fascinating Look at the Rich, Often Surprising Legacies of Yesterday's Celebrities* (New York: Warner Books, 1991).
14 Karen E. Boxx, in "Of Punctilios and Paybacks: The Duty of Loyalty Under the Uniform Trust Code," *Missouri Law Review* 67/2 (Spring 2002), describes at length how the ancient duty of loyalty clause became codified in practice in English and American common law.

mother. The will specifically provided that the trust property included all of the decedent's copyrights, rights of renewal copyrights and rights in unpublished manuscripts of which he might die possessed.[15]

Peter's status as "remainderman" in the 1943 Will—the proper legal term, even though it was not used in the Will itself—placed him in a subsidiary position. Legally he was dependent on his mother to benefit from the trust. Later on, his standing to bring litigation, or any sort of complaint, was openly called into question by Bator, Suchoff, and other defendants—with justification. He possessed *in*direct standing by being named in the Will, and by his mother's later actions in 1946 giving him the power to act on her behalf. But after 1962, when she revoked that power of attorney, he would always sit in the outer circles of authority, a hard legal fact that had to have cut deeply as time went on and it became increasingly clear that his mother would remain isolated behind the Iron Curtain.

The 1945 American Will

When this Will was revised in September 1945, Manheim left intact the basic framework of the document, focusing his attention, as drafting attorney, on the dispositive provisions governing the trust. (Roughly 2/3 of the Will's language remained unchanged from 1943 to 1945.) He made substantive changes on Bartók's behalf that, had they become legally valid, would have fundamentally altered the history of the Bartók Estate in the 20th century. Peter was now 21, no longer a minor. In the past two years he had entered the US military, served in the war, and gained his US citizenship. Bartók now wanted to give him standing as a direct beneficiary.[16] Ditta's portion of the trust was correspondingly reduced. Changes were made in the following main areas.

> 1. In the paragraph covering disposition of his European property to Béla Jr., Bartók amends the language to leave "all my property of whatsoever nature, real, personal, or mixed, which may be situate in Hungary, Finland, Russia, Romania, Bulgaria and Poland, to my eldest son Bela."
>
> 2. The trust is now divided into two portions. After deducting funeral expenses and estate taxes, 1/3 of the value of the entire remaining estate

---

15 Milton D. Goldman, referee, "Report of Referee Dated May 14, 1971." Surrogate's Court, State of New York, County of New York, Index #P2751/1945.
16 A photocopy of the 1945 American Will survives in BSCB Tampa. The location of the original document, which Bator still had in his possession as late as 1959, is unknown.

Chapter 3

is to be held in trust "for the benefit of my wife Edith Pasztory Bartok." The remaining 2/3 "shall be held in trust for my son Peter Bartok."

3. Instead of Ditta Bartok being authorized to name executors or trustees in the event the two named trustees step down, Peter Bartok "shall have the right to name the executors or trustees or both."

Broadly speaking, these changes enhanced Peter's position and diminished Ditta's. Further language clarified contingencies for their two portions of the trust. Her 1/3 portion is directed to go to Peter Bartók after her death. His 2/3 portion shall be managed by trustees until he is 30 years of age, after which "my trustees shall pay the principal of the said second portion to him."

What he proposed for Béla Jr. shows Bartók trying to be more generous to his older son, too. The list of countries in Paragraph 2—where he allocates Béla Jr. his share of the inheritance—reads like a short list of the later Eastern Bloc. Bartók removed Germany from Béla Jr.'s bequest, a step made possible by the recent defeat of Hitler's government. In its place he itemizes a longer list of countries from a much larger swath of Europe, most of it soon to fall into communist hands. He adds in Russia, too. Royalty income from six countries would go to Béla Jr., including still, of course, Hungary. Undoubtedly shaped through discussion with Bator, whose well-informed opinions on foreign affairs Bartók trusted, this revised list of countries tacitly admits that already—in the fall of 1945—Bartók and Bator expected Hungary to fall to the Soviets. The new Will prepared for this eventuality.

By 1959, when this unused Will was revived, Peter Bartók had passed 30 years of age. (He was 35.) Instead of battling Bator through attorneys, 2/3 of the Estate's principal and revenue streams would have been his, if only the deathbed Will had been signed on that fateful day in September 1945. He could have replaced Bator as trustee, naming anyone else, even himself, to administer his mother's portion. In short, he could have taken full control: he could be managing all the income and deciding the fate of the manuscript collection. He could have been on the front line of all copyright permission decisions. Alas! Poor Peter! In a way I sympathize with him. To hold a copy of this document in his hands in 1959, and to see how his father had wanted to give him greater control of the trust—to see "what might have been" if only his father had lived a day or two longer to sign the new will. No wonder he began to dig in his heels further with Bator going forward.

Meanwhile, in dramatic counterpoint, the communist government in Hungary had taken the position that *another* will of Bartók's had legal priority.

The 1940 Hungarian Will

Anyone curious enough to investigate the rapidly growing body of writing about Bartók in the middle years of 20th century could learn that Béla Bartók had written a will in Budapest in 1940. Halsey Stevens included a passage from the Hungarian Will in his pioneering account of Bartók's final years (1953). He quotes verbatim the Hungarian Will's political protest clause as a telling statement of Bartók's state of mind in the weeks before he left Budapest. In Bartók's words:

> My burial is to be the simplest possible. If after my death they want to name a street after me, or to erect a memorial tablet to me in a public place, then my desire is this: as long as what were formerly Oktogon-tér and Körönd in Budapest are named after those men for whom they are named at present [i.e., Hitler and Mussolini], and further, as long as there is in Hungary any square or street, or is to be, named for these two men, then neither square nor street nor public building in Hungary is to be named for me, and no memorial tablet is to be erected in a public place.[17]

This iconic statement of the composer's political beliefs has proven irresistible to Bartók enthusiasts ever since. It's memorable. Vivid. Inspiring. It made its debut in print in one of the early Demény letters volumes (1951) published in Hungary.[18]

When Péter Ruffy published an overview of the international legal battle over Bartók's Estate in 1965, he summarized the circumstances behind the first two Wills. (He would not have known of the deathbed Will.) Titled "The Dispute Over Bartók's Will," Ruffy's article first appeared in *Magyar Nemzet* on December 25, 1965. The following year it was reprinted in English translation in Hungary's export magazine, *The New Hungarian Quarterly*. Later, Todd Crow selected it for inclusion in his volume of North American *Bartók Studies* (1976).[19] In the article could be found—complete—Bartók's 1940 Budapest Will, together with Ruffy's gloss on the history of the legal standoff. Ruffy's

---

17 As quoted in Halsey Stevens, *The Life and Music of Béla Bartók* (New York: Oxford University Press, 1953), 90–91. This passage from the will was not reproduced in later editions of Demény's letters volumes in Hungary (1955, 1976), nor did it carry over into the condensed, English language edition of 1971.

18 János Demény, *Bartók Béla Levelei* (Budapest: Művelt Nép Könyvkiadó, 1951), 153. Only this passage was included, not the whole will. Demény tucked it in between two letters from Bartók to Annie Müller-Widmann; he titled it "Detail from the Budapest will / Ending of Paragraph 8."

19 Péter Ruffy, "The Dispute Over Bartók's Will," *The New Hungarian Quarterly* 7/22 (1966): 206–9. Reprint. Todd Crow, ed., *Bartók Studies* (Detroit: Information Coordinators, 1976), 141–46.

article gained considerable exposure outside Hungary through Crow's volume of essays; the Vassar College pianist's book was one of only a handful of important Bartók publications in the English language in the 1970s. It found its way onto the shelves of many collegiate libraries across the United States. In its pages Ruffy's essay nestles side by side with essays by prominent Hungarian musicologists, including Szabolcsi, Lendvai, Bónis, and Kárpáti, their contributions, like Ruffy's, harvested for reprinting from earlier issues of *The New Hungarian Quarterly*.

Ruffy's article occupies a distant corner of the Bartók studies world today. It's quite old. It belongs to another era. This outwardly modest contribution to the world of Bartók studies, though, gave readers at the time a window into a rarely viewed world where the widening strategy by government agencies to lay claim to the Bartók Estate was openly on display. It voiced the substance of legal matters that had been all but invisible outside the inner circle of family, lawyers, and magistrates. Its author, moreover, functioned as an ideally impersonal agent of objectivity, a man with no history as a Bartók authority, either before or after. How the Hungarian communist regime could be backing this Will, when Bartók himself had expressly revoked it, is the tale we turn to for the remainder of this chapter.

A glance at the 1940 Hungarian Will shows many obvious points of difference with Bartók's later Will. Aside from its patriotic, anti-fascist, anti-Nazi clause that so beautifully captures Bartók's state of mind as he prepared to leave Europe, its provisions specify an even distribution of property among the heirs. It awards 1/3 portions of copyrights and income equally to three beneficiaries: Béla Jr., Peter, and Ditta. He also gives the three of them the necessary authority to manage all copyrights and income streams. The language, too, is more personal than what we find in either American Will; on its pages Bartók addresses his family members directly. Paragraph 1a covers, for example, the temporary conditions that prevail if Bartók were to die while Peter was still a student and a minor: 1/3 is to go to Béla Jr., ½ to Peter, and 1/6 to Ditta, the extra funding intended to help Peter finish his studies. "I expect from my son Peter Bartók to pursue his studies conscientiously, and to do everything possible to find employment as soon as possible."[20] He also addresses what should happen if Ditta were to later remarry.

---

20 Bartók, Last Will and Testament (Budapest, 1940). English translator unknown. New York Bartók Archives, ca. 1960? (BSCB Tampa). Two different English translations are preserved in the Suchoff collection, each originating during the New York Béla Bartók Archive era. They are typed and undated. Comparison with the version found in Ruffy's article, which is more polished overall, and more worthy of publication, suggests that these were in-house translations prepared by archives staff at Bator's direction.

In preparing this document the Hungarian lawyer, Ernő András, singled out for protection the US-based trust Bartók had created earlier in 1940 for his manuscripts.[21] Par. 2 specifically makes separate provision for the manuscripts in this trust, giving clear instructions about their treatment with regard to copyright and income:

> In the matter of the disposition of my musical manuscripts, and of the use and exploitation of the resulting income I made a so-called trust-agreement with the firm of Boosey & Hawkes, Inc., of New York, and with Dr. George Herzog, resident of New York, in accordance with the laws of the United States of America. I expressly maintain all the provisions which I made in this matter with reference to the disposition of the manuscripts and the use of the income; those provisions of the agreement which refer to the use and distribution of the appearing surplus I interpret in such a way, or rather, I modify them as regarding the mutual relationship of my successors so that as far as the income are concerned their shares should be determined according to Chapter I of this will.[22]

By accommodating the existence of a US trust like this, the 1940 Hungarian Will shows itself to be a fairly sophisticated legal instrument. András was a good lawyer. Bartók wanted the American trust to be recognized by his heirs and Hungarian courts. It was to continue on its own terms, keeping the two trustees already named; any surplus income from its operations could be distributed to the heirs according to the disposition in his new Will. Concerning "the two pianos belonging to me," he asks that Peter Bartók take his first choice; "that shall be his, the other my son Béla Bartók Jr.'s" Copyrights? "In case of an eventual exploitation or assignment of these copyrights, all my heirs should proceed in conformity," i.e., in conformity with the general divisions specified ear-

---

21 Two versions of the Hungarian Will survive in CPB Homosassa. They capture the Will in different stages of drafting. The first, a carbon copy typed in distinctive purple-blue ink, shows numerous pencil annotations and corrections in Béla Bartók's hand. The second, typed on heavily yellowed paper, is an original reference copy of the Oct. 4 Will, marked "Másolat" at the top, likely prepared for Bartók's personal use by András's office staff. Both documents show signs of folding and use as well as New York Bartók Archive processing stamps; they clearly came over the ocean with him in 1940, where they stayed. Ruffy would have liked to know about these two drafts. In 1970, still interested in the topic, he published a follow-up article describing recent interviews he had done with Ernő András, in which the aged Hungarian attorney told him about the drafting process. See Ruffy, "How I Found Béla Bartók's Will," *Magyar Hírek*, 23/19 (Sept. 19, 1970). An English translation of this interesting article was prepared for internal use in the New York Bartók Archive (BSCB Tampa). It shows little of the propaganda that mars his earlier article.
22 Bartók, Last Will and Testament (Budapest, 1940). New York Bartók Archives translation (BSCB Tampa).

Chapter 3

lier in the document (1/3 to each named heir). The goal is, however, to "prevent dispersion of the copyrights." The Will's most memorable passage is found in Paragraph 8, where he gives direction about his funeral, then stipulates how his name should *not* be used in Hungary, in the now justly famous political protest passage that caught Demény's eye and blossomed in importance through reproduction in later accounts. Some of Bartók's autograph corrections to an early draft of the 1940 Will, and his insertion of the soon to be independently famous Paragraph VIII, can be seen in Fig. 3.3.

The Will is dated October 4, 1940, and signed by Bartók and two witnesses, Mrs. Béla Csomós, and Dr. Ernő András. Table 3.1 summarizes the differences among the wills of 1940, 1943, and 1945.

Table 3.1. Comparison of Béla Bartók's Three Wills, 1940–45.

Informal name	*Country of Origin*	*Language*	*Signed?*	*Date*	*Status*	*Preparing Attorney*	*Dispositive Provisions*
1940 Hungarian Will	Hungary	Hungarian	Yes	Oct. 4, 1940	Revoked by 1943 will. Later published in Budapest, validating its terms under Hungarian civil law on Jan. 7, 1947	Ernő András	All copyrights and income divided equally among Ditta (1/3), Peter (1/3), and Béla Jr. (1/3).
1943 American Will	United States	English	Yes	Mar. 28, 1943	Valid Probated in New York Surrogates Court on Jan. 24, 1946	Harold Manheim	Two categories of property are created. Hungarian and German property bequeathed to Béla Jr. Rest of property placed in trust for Ditta Bartók, with Bator and Báron appointed as trustees.
1945 deathbed will	United States	English	No	Sept. 26, 1945	Never signed, therefore invalid	Harold Manheim	Two categories of property are created. Béla Jr. is bequeathed all property in six countries (Hungary, Finland, Russia, Romania, Bulgaria and Poland). Rest of property is placed in trust, with the trust beneficiaries identified as Ditta (1/3) and Peter (2/3).

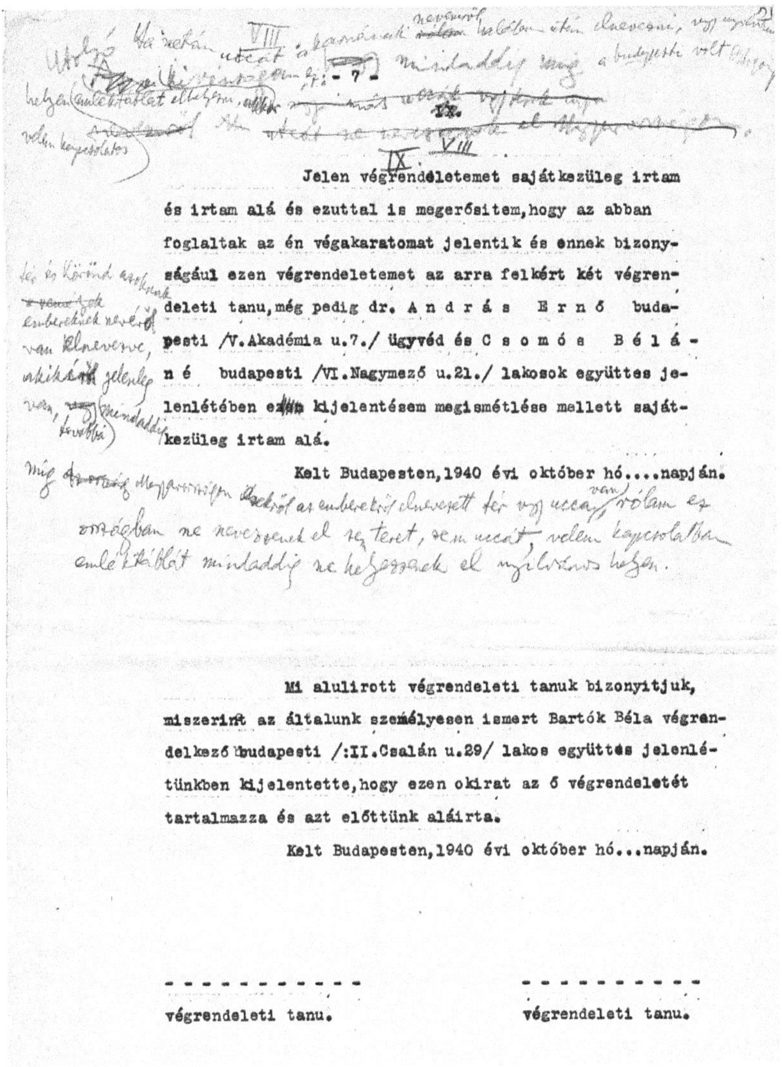

> Jelen végrendeletemet sajátkezüleg irtam
> és irtam alá és ezuttal is megerősitem, hogy az abban
> foglaltak az én végakaratomat jelentik és ennek bizony-
> ságául ezen végrendeletemet az arra felkért két végren-
> deleti tanu, még pedig dr. A n d r á s   E r n ő   buda-
> pesti /V.Akadémia u.7./ ügyvéd és C s o m ó s   B é l á -
> n é   budapesti /VI.Nagymező u.21./ lakosok együttes je-
> lenlétében ezen kijelentésem megismétlése mellett saját-
> kezüleg irtam alá.
>
> Kelt Budapesten, 1940 évi október hó...napján.
>
> Mi alulirott végrendeleti tanuk bizonyitjuk,
> miszerint az általunk személyesen ismert Bartók Béla végren-
> delkező budapesti /:II.Csalán u.29/ lakos együttes jelenlé-
> tünkben kijelentette, hogy ezen okirat az ő végrendeletét
> tartalmazza és azt előttünk aláirta.
>
> Kelt Budapesten, 1940 évi október hó...napján.
>
> - - - - - - - - - -   - - - - - - - - - -
> végrendeleti tanu.   végrendeleti tanu.

Fig. 3.3. Béla Bartók, early draft of the Hungarian Will (ca. September 1940) showing autograph corrections in pencil on the last page and his insertion of a new Par. VIII forbidding the use of his name on public spaces in Budapest unless certain terms were met. Source: CPB Homosassa.

Propagated in widely circulated books in the early decades of the Bartók studies field, the 1940 Hungarian Will won the publicity war by a large margin. This distinction is important to recognize. Bartók's *actual* Last Will and Testament stayed hidden in family circles and court systems. Its users were family, trustees, lawyers, and judges. The Hungarian Will had an entire secondary audience of

Chapter 3

students, musicians, readers interested in Hungarian culture, and academics around the globe. Historiographical imbalances like this can arise for any number of reasons, but in this case the differential rates of public exposure shaped a narrative about the Bartók Estate that allowed a communist-era strategy to gain far more traction than it deserved. We've never corrected the record. The communist regime's stubborn refusal to acknowledge the validity of the 1943 American Will fueled two decades of legal skirmishes with Bator. Dueling wills were unquestionably a factor, moreover, in the shifting alliances felt by the heirs as they were swept along by forces beyond their control. But all this still lay ahead.

Three Short but Critically Important Legal Documents from 1946

Ditta Bartók's decision to return to Hungary in December 1946 placed her in an awkward position with regard to the trust's management. As its principal beneficiary she was entitled to all income after expenses, but that income was now collected and managed in New York City, an ocean away from her home country. International banking systems could be managed easily enough by someone of Bator's experience. Far bigger worries were the chronic instability of Hungary's government, and, on a personal level, the unfortunate reality that Ditta was in no shape to make competent financial decisions on her own. Bator was unable to predict what would lay in store for Ditta once she was back home. He did what he could to manage the risks inherent in her departure. At the recommendation of counsel (probably Manheim again) he had some supplemental legal documents prepared: three short but far-reaching documents that offered protection for Ditta. Once signed, they gave Bator the authority to make discretionary distributions to Peter and centralize all decision making in the United States. They removed Ditta from any direct involvement in the Estate. No stressful decisions would be required of her. She could focus instead on recovering her health. Also, once she was back in Hungary no egregious theft or manipulation could happen; she was shielded from the effects of poor decisions. She placed her full faith in Victor Bator to continue taking care of her. <u>In practical terms her signatures also guaranteed the Estate protection against the gathering threat of Soviet dominion over Hungary.</u>

On December 18, 1946, just before her departure, Ditta signed an Assignation of Rights statement in which she assigned all her rights as beneficiary of the Will to her son Peter (Fig 3.4).[23]

---

23 A copy of this one-page, signed document is preserved in CPB Homosassa. It bears the date December 18, 1946.

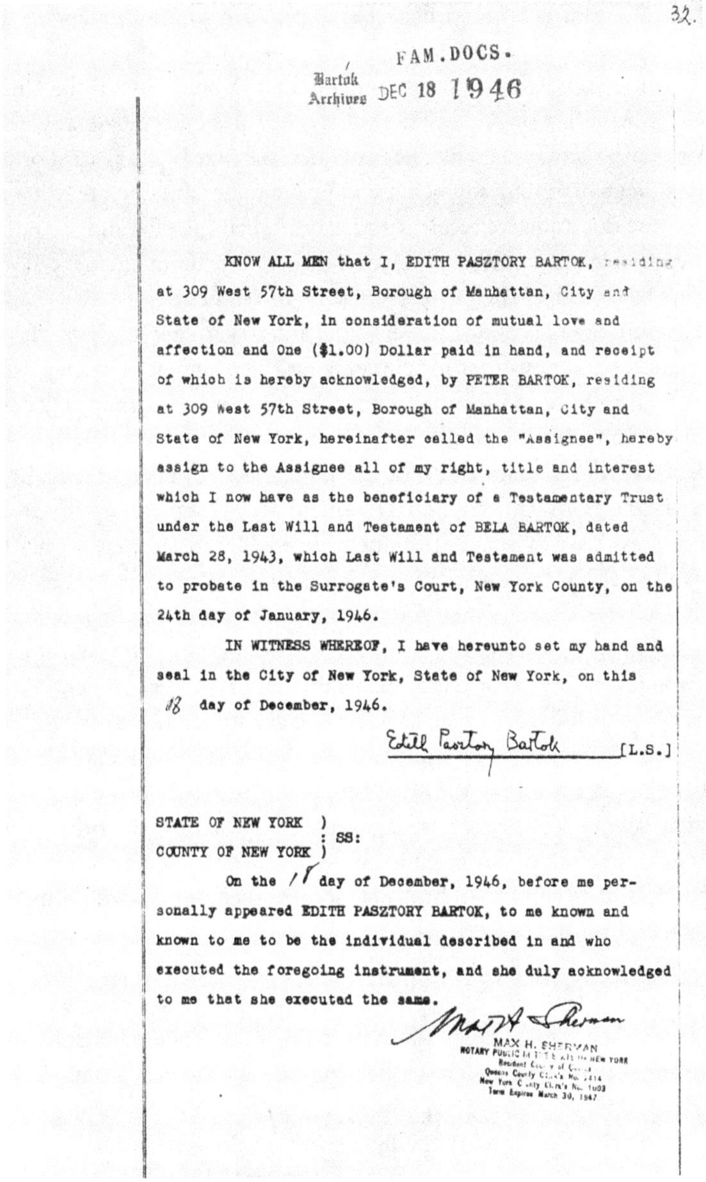

32.

FAM. DOCS.

Bartók Archives DEC 18 1946

KNOW ALL MEN that I, EDITH PASZTORY BARTOK, residing at 309 West 57th Street, Borough of Manhattan, City and State of New York, in consideration of mutual love and affection and One ($1.00) Dollar paid in hand, and receipt of which is hereby acknowledged, by PETER BARTOK, residing at 309 West 57th Street, Borough of Manhattan, City and State of New York, hereinafter called the "Assignee", hereby assign to the Assignee all of my right, title and interest which I now have as the beneficiary of a Testamentary Trust under the Last Will and Testament of BELA BARTOK, dated March 28, 1943, which Last Will and Testament was admitted to probate in the Surrogate's Court, New York County, on the 24th day of January, 1946.

IN WITNESS WHEREOF, I have hereunto set my hand and seal in the City of New York, State of New York, on this 18 day of December, 1946.

Edith Pasztory Bartok [L.S.]

STATE OF NEW YORK)
: SS:
COUNTY OF NEW YORK)

On the 18 day of December, 1946, before me personally appeared EDITH PASZTORY BARTOK, to me known and known to me to be the individual described in and who executed the foregoing instrument, and she duly acknowledged to me that she executed the same.

Max H. Sherman

MAX H. SHERMAN
NOTARY PUBLIC ... NEW YORK
Resident ...
Queens County Clerk's No. ...414
New York County Clerk's No. 1003
Term Expires March 30, 1947

Fig. 3.4. Ditta Bartók, Assignation of Rights, Dec. 18, 1946. Source: CPB Homosassa.

She also signed two Powers of Attorney: one granting Bator the power to act on her behalf, the other granting her son Peter legal authority to make any decisions in her name. The Power of Attorney for Peter gave him the following powers, which are worth noting in detail.

Chapter 3

(a) To make contracts in her behalf of any nature whatsoever and to execute the same.
(b) To bring and defend actions on her behalf in any court in the United States of America or any other country and to compromise any claim which may be brought against her or which she may bring against others.
(c) To collect any monies which are now due to her or which may hereafter become due and give receipts and acquittance therefor and to endorse any negotiable instruments which may be given to her in payment of such claims and to collect the proceeds of such instruments.
(d) To open bank accounts, in her name and to sign and endorse checks, drafts, notes and any other instruments for the payment of money which may be payable out of said account or which her said attorney may desire to deposit in the said account.
(e) To take all necessary steps for the protection of her rights as a beneficiary under the Last Will and Testament and Testamentary Trust created by such Last Will and Testament dated March 28, 1943, of her late husband, Bela Bartok, which Last Will and Testament was probated in the Surrogates Court, New York County, on January 24, 1946; and to specifically take all necessary steps for the protection of her statutory or common law rights of copyright in any literary or musical property which she may own individually or as a beneficiary under the Last Will and Testament or a trust set up under a Last Will and Testament of her late husband, Bela Bartok; and to institute any action which the said attorney may deem necessary for damages, for an injunction, or both, because of an infringement of any right which the undersigned may have in such property, and to appear in and defend any such action which may be brought against her.[24]

There follow provisions (f) through (k) further specifying situations where he may represent her. Collectively, these provisions cover the mechanics of managing her portion of the Estate (collecting checks, signing them, setting up bank accounts). They also (e) specifically grant Peter the power to protect her rights as beneficiary, naming that trust and its origination in the 1943 Will.[25]

---

24 Edith Pasztory Bartók, Power of Attorney, December 18, 1946. Copy of typed original notarized document. Max Sherman, notary public (BSCB Tampa).
25 In the litigation of 1959-61 Peter later claimed that he had no knowledge of this 1946 power of attorney; he also claimed to have never been shown a copy of the will. These positions were strongly discredited by Surrogate Court judge Samuel DiFalco, who wrote that it was "incredible" and "inconceivable" that Peter would not have known the documents. A summary of this court document can be found in Henry Ess's letter to Victor Bator, June 8, 1961. Collection of Francis Bator.

Most actions of the sort specified here would be carried out by Victor Bator in the coming years, acting on her and Peter's behalf. But we can easily see how Peter might have felt empowered to make decisions about folk song manuscripts, or to represent the family on plans for the Viola Concerto and other future projects. Bator did not encourage Peter to act independently like this. Nor did he discourage him. Final authority for Bartók family business matters still rested with the trustee. The new legal documents brought Peter into the fold as agent for his mother; they unquestionably nudged the balance of power in Peter's direction, giving him responsibilities for family matters that he didn't have the day before. Now, suddenly, a young man in New York City learned he could "take all necessary steps for the protection" of his mother's rights as beneficiary, and collect her money and income. He could even, if necessary, go to court on her behalf. It would be years before these seeds, now planted, began to sprout.

Ditta Bartók left the United States just days after signing this document. She arrived in Budapest around Christmas 1946.

Her timing was unfortunate.

* * *

In the months after the war ended, Hungarians began the slow, painful process of rebuilding their country. Approximately one million people had died during the war, including the majority of the Second Army sent to Central Russia and Ukraine in 1942–43. Another 500,000 had fled to the West. In Budapest the physical destruction was catastrophic. To Miksa Fenyő, one of the founders of the literary journal *Nyugat*, who had survived the war by hiding for over a year in the cellar of a home in Pest, the entire country by early 1945 was "a corpse. The crime of the Nazi abomination, crying to the heavens. A slaughtered country."[26] While international commissions ground forward, debating the terms of peace and the magnitude of reparations between states, in Hungary the new People's Courts asserted their own forms of justice, taking aim at war criminals and former politicians. The Soviet army ominously continued its occupation of the country. Not until the early months of 1947 did Hungarians learn that their country's borders would be returned to their post-Trianon state; the land grants given by Hitler would be stripped away. Internally, in this uncertain state of affairs, domestic politics boiled, and exhaustion from the war affected everyone, materially and emotionally. Free elections held on November 4, 1945, promised a new era, and briefly re-established the Independent Smallholders Party, a centrist alternative to the

---

26 Miksa Fenyő, *A Nation Adrift: The 1944–45 Wartime Diaries of Miksa Fenyő*, transl. Mario D. Fenyő (Reno, NV: Helena History Press, 2018): 579.

Chapter 3

Communist Party. The Smallholders, encouraged by this victory, formed a majority coalition in Budapest that committed the country to a path of judicious, democratic reform. Under their leadership Hungary declared itself a republic several months later, in February 1946. In response the communists, convinced that they could not ascend to power through democratic means, took control in other ways now familiar from their global playbook: asserting control over the police, the media, and the army, and attacking the church and other competing structures of a civil society. Soviet-trained secret police forces had been at work in the country since January 1945.[27] Soon the Smallholders coalition crumbled, having been successfully targeted as "reactionaries" and "fascists" by left-wing groups. Hyperinflation devastated the economy. Other developments in the global political sphere between Russia and the Allies gave Stalin little reason to hold back on the pace of his expansion plans in Eastern Europe. Despite opposition from a majority of Hungarians, by 1948 the country had been pushed forcefully into a nationalized, single party Soviet-style system. A new Hungarian Peoples' Republic was formally created on August 20, 1949.

Radical property rights reform had been enacted even before the war ended. In March 1945 the Provisional National Government in Debrecen passed legislation putting in motion the long overdue land reform many Hungarians had yearned for. Estates over 1,500 acres were confiscated, as were landholdings belonging to the Catholic and Protestant churches. Lands held by war criminals were similarly claimed. According to historian Deborah Cornelius, this revolutionary legislation resulted in forty percent of Hungary's land becoming state or collective property, and had the further distinction of being "the first direct Soviet intervention in Hungarian domestic affairs."[28] The nationalization of assets and property proceeded incrementally at first, then after 1948, precipitously. The Bator/Sicherman family lost ownership of their family vineyard in Mád (Fig. 3.5) during this period. All these changes pushed the middle class to continue its flight to the West, propelled by worries about the future. Remnants of the Hungarian aristocracy read the writing on the wall, especially if their family homes were in the more rural areas where land reform hit first. Many of them simply left the country, joining family and friends already resettled in London, Switzerland, Portugal, Canada, or the United States.

---

27 Anne Applebaum, *Iron Curtain: The Crushing of Eastern Europe, 1944-1956* (New York: Doubleday, 2012), 74–76. A comprehensive account of the rise of communism after World War II in Hungary, Poland, and East Germany, Applebaum's book meticulously documents the violent cruelty that accompanied the takeover.
28 Deborah H. Cornelius, *Hungary in World War II: Caught in the Cauldron* (New York: Fordham University Press, 2011), 385. Cornelius's revisionist historical account of wartime Hungary benefits greatly from post-communist-era perspectives. My account in these paragraphs draws freely from her narrative.

Fig. 3.5. Victor Bator (left) inspecting the crop at the Sicherman family's vineyard in Mád, Hungary, ca. 1935. Source: personal collection of Francis Bator.

Even had she wanted to write about her experiences in 1946, or been able to, Ditta Bartók left a scant trail for later researchers to follow. Unpublished documents from Victor Bator's desk offer insight into her return to Hungary, while also reminding us how much he tried to ease her troubles. Her travel, we learn, was arranged by Victor Bator and entirely funded by him. "The decision that she should return to Hungary was mine," he writes in his Memorandum. "I solved all the technical problems of traveling to Hungary; that task was not so easy after the war. She flew to Vienna. I arranged for the Hungarian Consul General in Vienna, who was a friend of mine, to meet her at the airport; he took care of her while she was in Vienna before she started on the last leg of the journey to Budapest."[29] Bator ensured Ditta's economic security back in Hungary: he contacted his former employer, the Pesti Magyar Kereskedelmi Bank, with instructions to pay Ditta from his own unclaimed pension funds. Archival records in Budapest show that Victor Bator asked the bank's president to personally intervene, and that Ditta received a monthly living stipend this way. Up to November 1947, at least, when the banks in Hungary were nationalized, Ditta was able to rely on funds designated for her use from Bator's pension. As Bartók's widow she also was entitled to receive payouts from the pension funds he was owed. (His 1940 Will directs that "under existing law" his wife "is entitled to a widow's pension on the strength of my appointment as a State official.")

---

29 Victor Bator, "The Hungarian Problem," in Memorandum on the History of the Bartók Estate.

Chapter 3

By now her poor health was chronic. Her American years left Ditta Bartók permanently changed. She was not a strong widow figure in the mold of Gertrude Schoenberg or Vera Stravinsky—quite the opposite. Remembered by Francis Bator many years later as "a somewhat fey, ethereal figure," and a woman who was "extraordinarily silent," Ditta Bartók had a complicated relationship with her fame as the wife of a great musician.[30] After her return to Hungary she lived humbly. She published very little by way of memoirs, and was known to be extremely private about the letters from her husband still in her possession. During her husband's final illness she began to show signs of a nervous breakdown. After his death her condition worsened, leading to a diagnosis of schizophrenia in 1946. American doctors hospitalized her for long stretches of time, improving her health through medically supervised rehabilitation. Peter Bartók visited her regularly in these facilities. Victor Bator helped her throughout this period, too, coordinating her medical care with Gyula Holló, and making sure that money was no obstacle. He quietly paid her bills. After she returned home he still worried about her. He viewed his concern as a natural extension of his role as trustee. In 1957, for example, he wrote to his old friend Andor Chatel in Budapest, trying to enlist his help in getting Ditta the best care possible in the Hungarian psychiatric community.

> It was around ten years ago that Ditta, Béla Bartók's widow, returned to Hungary. I sent her back because she became schizophrenic, and since she barely spoke English even before her condition, with her schizophrenia she would have been completely cut off from the world. I thought it would be a good idea to send her to a place where her melancholic, withdrawn soul could at least have some friendly, familiar and Hungarian speaking contact with her mother and relatives.

The intervening years had not been kind to her. In 1956 Peter Bartók was able to visit her on two occasions; for the second, after the Revolution, they arranged to meet in Rimaszombat, Slovakia, her home town, with her mother and brother.[31] Her health was still poor. Peter reported back to Bator that "beyond a couple of words a day it is impossible to keep a conversation going with her, except for food related conversations and the like." Worried, he brought his concerns to Bator after returning to New York. He had heard from Pasztory family members that her doctor, Tibor Hajnal, was not doing enough for her. "Ditta's

---

30 Francis Bator, interview with the author, Oct. 25, 2010. On the difficulties of writing biographically or musically about Ditta Bartók see Virág Büky, "Bartók's Heiress," *Studia Musicologica* 53/1–3 (March 2012): 187–98.
31 Peter Bartók, letter to Victor Bator, August 31, 1957 (BSCB Tampa).

schizophrenia is critical," Bator wrote to Chatel, summarizing the situation, "and it continually is getting even worse. At this point we have to make a choice of either letting her roll further down this slope and possibly ending up in a mental institution like a raving lunatic or in an apathetic half-dead state, or we can try to find a way to fight her condition." Bator urged Chatel's intervention. Ditta, he felt, deserved better than what she was getting.[32]

The question of whether Ditta developed actual schizophrenia, or instead suffered from a related mental health disorder, lies well outside the scope of this book. Medical records in Hungary may be able to give insight, if records of this sort even survive. How her condition was treated during her lifetime is germane, too, but I cannot determine anything about this from the records I have on hand. All we can safely conclude from the Bator family documents is that Ditta Bartók by 1946 manifested signs of mental illness sufficient to give her a working diagnosis of "schizophrenia" by physicians in New York, presumably a medically responsible diagnosis made by well-regarded psychiatric specialists.

Dueling wills. The international contest over jurisdiction begins.

What happened next set in motion one of the more protracted legal battles to engulf the estate of any major 20th-century composer. Someday additional documents may surface that allow a fuller narrative to emerge from the account sketched below and elsewhere in this book. The more I investigate, the more loose ends I find. The source document situation remains stubbornly unstable after all these years: no single scholar in the field of Bartók studies knows the full extent of the family archival holdings that remain in private possession. Homosassa is a large part of this mystery. What follows here is necessarily incomplete: inductive reasoning has its limits. Even with gaps in our knowledge, unavoidable for now, it's a strange and incredible story.

During the war little communication took place between Béla Bartók and his oldest son. Béla Jr. did not even know his father had written a new Last Will and Testament to replace the Hungarian one.[33] He learned of the American Will in early 1946 through correspondence with his brother Peter; he received a copy that April courtesy of Manheim's office, together with signed statements from Peter in both Hungarian and English.[34] Whether or not receipt of a legal document from America meant that Béla Jr. absorbed its significance—or chose

---

32 Victor Bator, letter to Andor Chatel, April 16, 1957. Reproduced in full elsewhere in this book.
33 Victor Bator, "The Hungarian Problem," in Memorandum on the History of the Bartók Estate.
34 Peter Bartók, letter to Victor Bator, March 29, 1946 (CPB Homosassa).

to—is a more nuanced question. Confusion was inevitable. Trusts, and trustees, were never encountered in Hungarian civil law. The whole concept was deeply unfamiliar to Béla Jr. "An institution like a Trusteeship does not exist and is foreign to Hungarian law," Bator later explained. "Béla Jr. assumed that outside of some life interest of Mrs. Béla Bartók, he would share the inheritance half and half with his younger brother."

In Hungarian law the property of the deceased transfers at point of death. During probate the heirs develop an inventory of assets and certify their relationship to each other and to the deceased; debts or other financial obligations of the estate are enumerated and taken into account. A highly trained civil-law notary takes inheritors through this process. Unlike US law, where a probate judge approves the Will in court, in Hungary the notary at the close of investigation "publishes" the will, an action that certifies the will's terms, making it legally valid.[35] Among other tasks the notary must verify proper jurisdiction in consultation with local authorities, i.e., that the will is being probated in the correct administrative region for the decedent's residence. Inheritors named in the will are summoned to appear before the notary, together with any other parties holding direct interest in the outcome. Prior to 1959 the laws governing inheritance were established through generations of case law which yielded a common understanding for the principles and practices to be used in each individual situation. In 1959 this area of law was comprehensively codified for the first time in Act IV of the Civil Code of the People's Republic of Hungary.[36]

In Hungarian civil law, then, Bartók's death automatically set in motion the terms of his Hungarian Will. Béla Jr., Peter, and Ditta were vested in his estate at the moment of death on September 26, 1945. Uncertainty over the future may explain why Béla Jr. was unwilling to put a stop to the probate process in Hungary after April 1946, by which time he certainly knew of his father's American Will. Since laws govern these situations, though, not heirs' individual desires or

---

35 Many summaries of this process can be found online. See, for example, the excellent explanation found on one modern notary's site, http://akozjegyzo.hu/en/services/the-succession-procedure. Useful scholarly introductions in English to Hungarian inheritance law can be found in Hella Molnár, "The Position of the Surviving Spouse in the Hungarian Law of Succession," *ELTE Law Journal* (Budapest), 2014(2): 89–105; and Zoltán Csehi, "The Law of Succession in Hungary," in Miriam Anderson and Esther Arroyo i Amayuelas, ed., *The Law of Succession: Testamentary Freedom. European Perspectives* (Groningen: Europa Law Publishing, 2011), 177–84. This area of civil law, Molnár indicates, has proven to be one of the "most durable parts" of Hungarian law, more impervious to change than contract and business law.

36 Hella Molnár, Email communication with the author, Dec. 18, 2019. See also Molnár, "The Position of the Surviving Spouse in the Hungarian Law of Succession." Act IV of Hungary's 1959 Civil Code is available online in English translation at https://www.refworld.org/docid/4c3456fc2.html.

impulses, a more likely scenario is that he received counsel from his notary that the Hungarian Will took precedent due to his father's status as a citizen of Hungary at the time of death. What we know for certain is that on January 7, 1947, Béla Bartók's Hungarian-language Will was published by the notary in Budapest, i.e., certified and made valid in terms of Hungarian law. Ditta had arrived home just one week earlier, a sequence of events that cannot be coincidence. Her return to Budapest must have triggered publication of the Will, probably by making it possible for her and Béla Jr. to appear together at the notary's office in early January to answer questions.

Thus rumbled to life the Hungarian Will. Improbably, two Wills were now in force in two different countries.[37] How could this happen? It's a situation lawyers do everything in their power to avoid. Innumerable difficulties would arise for the Bartók Estate and heirs in the years ahead as a result of this new development.

Few facts present themselves to explain why the Hungarian notary decided to overlook the existence of a superseding American will. Hungary was emerging from a brutal war experience, and still reeling from the economic disaster brought on by the world's highest ever recorded rate of inflation. Partisan political fighting threatened the rule of law. Diplomatic relations between Hungary and Allied nations, moreover, still were under repair, or unsteady at best, slowing restoration of the economic and foreign policy frameworks necessary to foster a stable legal environment. It's possible that the notary felt disinclined to consider as valid an American legal document presented to him under these conditions. It's possible, too, that Béla Jr. and Ditta knowingly withheld information about the American will's existence, although this explanation seems unlikely. Ditta, in particular, had freshly arrived from the United States. She had been apprised of the terms of the American Will and had just executed further legal instruments to ensure its smooth functioning internationally. Did she neglect to mention those documents? We'll never know. Bator himself, far closer to these events and individuals than we'll ever be, rued the general lack of "information, factual and numerical, about what happened in Hungary, except a few occasional scraps of facts."[38] We can only echo his lament.

---

37 Multiple wills in different jurisdictions are not unknown in the world of estate law. They may be recommended, in fact, as a strategy for estate taxation purposes, or for certain advantages to heirs. In such cases the wills should ideally be coordinated, with attorneys in each jurisdiction working closely with each other and inserting complementary language. On the challenges of multiple wills in different jurisdictions, see the American Bar Association's recommendations for "Estate Planning with Foreign Property," available at https://www.americanbar.org/groups/gpsolo/publications/gp_solo/2011/april_may/estate_planning_withforeignproperty/.

38 Victor Bator, "The Hungarian Problem," in Memorandum on the History of the Bartók Estate.

Chapter 3

Expediency probably played a role, too. A Hungarian will governed by Hungarian civil law, and granted a ruling in Hungarian, promised to raise far fewer questions for Béla Jr. and Ditta in months ahead. For these and other reasons the Hungarian notary, who identifies himself on the published Will as "Dr. Keszthely," decided to move forward with probate of the earlier Will. The facts as he knew them argued in favor of this decision. Bartók's status as a Hungarian citizen could not be brushed under the carpet.

With this Hungarian ruling in hand Béla Jr. now gained honest possession of chattel that survived the war—if, indeed, in those difficult post-war years such claim was even needed or possible.[39] Ditta could reclaim some of her furnishings from their home on Csalán út. Also, the heirs now had proof of their right to receive royalties generated in Hungary through sales and performances of Bartók's music. Funds could be released directly to them in correct allocations. For Ditta the document eased conversations about her husband's pension—its widow benefits—and about her status on future income vis-à-vis Béla Jr.

That the notary in Budapest validated Bartók's Hungarian Will under such circumstances is our first indication that *jurisdiction* would be a sticking point going forward. What happens to personal property when citizens of one country die in another country? Many variables come into play. Whether or not, for example, a person dies intestate is of primary importance in determining outcomes. If a will does exist, where was it written? Where are the beneficiaries domiciled? Where is the property physically located? Such questions form the daily bread of attorneys around the globe who are charged with ensuring proper legal succession when someone dies. Because Béla Bartók was living in United States at the time of death, and had written a new Will there, the handling of his personal property at time of death became subject to the laws of that country, a fairly common practice then and now. Once the Hungarian communist government decided on a path to assert control over Bartók's legacy, it became convenient to assert the primacy of the earlier Hungarian Will on grounds that a) Bartók was a Hungarian citizen at the time of his death, and b) the trustee concept did not exist in Hungarian civil law historically, and, regardless, carried no weight in a country they were trying to rebuild into a fully functioning communist state with a wholly separate conception of property rights. Hungary held the right of jurisdiction, in this view, not the US. As late as 1984, lawyers

---

39 Thanks to a document executed by his father in the fall of 1940, Béla Jr. already had been granted significant rights in his father's absence, including the right to receive monies due to Béla Bartók from Hungarian publishers and music organizations; to receive his pension and housing allowance; to collect any earnings and resolve debts; and to pay rent and otherwise manage the Budapest home. A draft copy of this document showing Béla Bartók's autograph corrections survives in CPB Homosassa.

for the Hungarian government were still claiming jurisdiction, after Ditta's death, demonstrating the longevity of this point of conflict for the heirs and the Estate, including Béla Jr.[40]

Had democratic norms won out in years ahead, Bator would likely have used litigation to force a resolution in favor of the American Will. He had the wishes of the deceased in his favor. And he had sat at the top of the legal profession in Budapest just a few years earlier, an acknowledged expert in aspects of Hungarian civil law. He knew how to proceed. By 1948, though, the communists were in power. And everything changed. Once the takeover of Hungary by the Communist Party began, communications with Béla Jr. and Ditta became unreliable, even dangerous. "The situation was aggravated," Bator wrote,

> by the fact that Government and the Communist Party group surrounding it has always been equally feared and disrespected by everyone in Hungary. People hide and conceal every facet of their life because as soon as anybody not belonging to the inner circle of the Communist Party shows independent (including income not paid by the Government) suspicions, restrictive methods and arbitrary expropriations may, and mostly do, happen. Letters going and coming from abroad are censored and therefore are not used for disclosure of facts and figures which may be used for such interferences, arbitrary taxation, confiscation, or any other purpose.[41]

With these changes, too, came an unwanted—but in communist ideology, necessary—overhaul of the laws governing society. Inheritance law changed radically. No longer could a dispute over legal jurisdiction be resolved by common allegiance to rational rule of law as practiced in civil societies around the globe. In classic Marxist thought, property inheritance perpetuated the dominance of the ruling class, and therefore needed to be dismantled to establish rule by the proletariat.

The imposition of rigid ideology on inheritance law sharply circumscribed the types and amount of personal property that could pass to heirs. Even the sternest communist ideologues, however, could not abolish the right to inherit. Only its terms were changed. And there the changes were predictably far-reaching. A large literature explores the rule of law in communist countries in

---

40 Petition for a Voluntary Accounting, Surrogates Court, County of New York, Feb. 1, 1984. Index No. P2751/1945. In this document Béla Jr.'s standing in the proceeding is explained by reference to the longstanding dispute over the two wills. It further explains (p. 5) that "The Budapest Office of State Notaries Public exercised jurisdiction over the estate on the basis of the decedent's nationality" (BSCB Tampa).
41 Victor Bator, "The Hungarian Problem," in Memorandum on the History of the Bartók Estate.

the 20th century. In Russia the Bolshevik curtailment of inheritance had been swift. Practical guidelines for the new legal system took many more years to develop, though, much longer than anyone could have predicted.[42] The body of law imposed on the Eastern Bloc after World War II by Moscow-backed ideologues was, it soon became apparent, still a work in progress. During the Rákosi era what settled over Hungary was an approach to civil and criminal law—known derisively in the West as "Soviet legality" or "socialist legality"—that Soviet courts had established as precedent.

Communism required estates of even modest size to be recaptured by the state after the death of the testator. It didn't matter if the deceased's personal property was located at home or abroad. Courts in Russia had established that when Russian citizens died abroad, their estate was treated as if the death had taken place in Russia. From 1922 to 1961 the policy of Soviet jurists was to apply Soviet civil law to all inheritance, *regardless of the place of death*, even when foreign nationals died inside Russian borders; the right to make or revoke a will was also governed by the laws of the country of citizenship. Kazimierz Grzybowski, in his authoritative review of Soviet inheritance law, explains that after 1961 mild liberalization led to the adoption of the Principles of Civil Legislation, which reversed the situation by stating that "matters of succession are governed by the law of the country in which the deceased had his last permanent residence."[43] Citizenship was replaced by "permanent residency" as the litmus test for jurisdiction. Testamentary dispositions in turn were to be interpreted according to the laws established in the place of permanent residence.[44] In fundamental ways Soviet inheritance law changed after 1961. Winds of change were felt in other socialist countries in the Eastern Bloc, too, where Soviet legality, because of its forceful ideological nature, had always rested uncomfortably upon the distinctive civil law cultures each nation already possessed.

An expansive approach to jurisdiction, then, was a cornerstone of communist-era inheritance law. It gave the state a forceful tool to pursue reclamation of property from the estates of citizens who had fled abroad. Even the right to

---

42 The chapter on "Inheritance and Socialism" in John H. Hazard, William E. Butler, and Peter B. Maggs, *The Soviet Legal System*, Parker School Studies in Foreign and Comparative Law (Dobbs Ferry, NY: Oceana, 1977) is the best introduction in English to the topic. Excellent for its investigation into the underlying spirit and philosophy of Soviet law is Harold Berman, *Justice in the U.S.S.R.: An Interpretation of Soviet Law*, rev. ed. (Cambridge, MA: Harvard University Press, 1963). An outstanding period account of the rise of Communism in Hungary is Ervin Laszlo's *The Communist Ideology in Hungary: Handbook for Basic Research* (Dordrecht, Holland: D. Reidel, 1966).

43 Kazimierz Grzybowski, *Soviet Private International Law*, in the series Law in Eastern Europe, ed. Z. Szirmai, vol. 10 (Leyden: A.W. Sijthoff, 1965), 135. Grzybowski provides a thorough review of the recent statutory changes in inheritance law as practiced in Soviet Russia. See pp. 134–40.

44 Grzybowski, *Soviet Private International Law*, 136.

revoke one's will was constrained by jurisdiction. (This explains later Hungarian attorneys' refusal to acknowledge Bartók's revocation of the 1940 Will while living abroad.) Sympathetic foreign attorneys could always be hired to pursue the state's claims in international courts. For Róbert Palágyi and the Hungarian attorneys who helped him in the 1950s, or who later succeeded him, including Ernő Vajda, jurisdiction was at its core an ideological issue, and therefore not subject to compromise, particularly when pitted against an opponent cursed with the misfortune of living in a decadent capitalist society. They had no choice. They *had* to press claims against Victor Bator and the Bartók Estate with the goal of bringing its assets under state control. Whether their zeal was genuine, or the fruit of reluctant compromise with the hard reality of practicing law in a communist system, cannot be determined from their actions.

Since 1852 a distinctive feature of Hungarian inheritance law has been the principle of "compulsory share," which requires testators to allocate a portion of their estate to all lineal dependents. Similar concepts are found in Norway, Spain, and many other European countries. As its name suggests, compulsory share offers certain guarantees. It protects members of a testator's immediate family from being cut out of the Will or treated unfairly; it assures any sons or daughters a share of the estate. Remarkably, the principle survived communism, albeit much altered by the experience. Molnár describes it as a "cultural tradition" that became "an integral part of the Hungarian private law culture."[45]

This principle of compulsory share explains several features of Bartók's 1940 Will that might otherwise pass unnoticed. Each heir is allocated an *equal proportion* of the estate. Peter Bartók, though only 16 years old, is given a full third, his portion not being allowed to be determined by his mother. Béla Jr. is given the same. (Arbitrary distinctions between children were not permitted.) Laws governing compulsory share also explain—if explanation is needed—the absence of Márta Bartók from the document. Even had Bartók been interested at all in granting his first wife some form of recognition from his estate, the compulsory share principle does not apply to former spouses; it more narrowly restricts the guarantee of inclusion to lineal dependents, each of whom can expect to inherit something, even though they may not end up succeeding the deceased. Without even seeing the Will Márta Bartók knew, in other words, that she would have no claim to her former husband's estate unless he decided to specifically list property under her name as a bequest—which he didn't. She would never be a presence in any of the legal proceedings.

---

45 Molnár, "The Position of the Surviving Spouse in the Hungarian Law of Succession," 102. Csehi, in "The Law of Succession in Hungary," neatly summarizes many aspects of the compulsory share principle.

Chapter 3

Whether Béla Bartók's heirs paid attention to the terms in this soon-to-be-revoked Will scarcely mattered. As Hungarians they would have absorbed the underlying cultural expectations for succession simply by living shared lives with other Hungarians who occasionally went through this process when family members died. They knew they were guaranteed a portion of the estate's property—a claim, in their case, buttressed by the actual terms of the Will. Béla Jr. had every reason to believe he would get his fair portion, and he could further assume it would be equal to his brother's. We can only imagine his surprise at learning (eventually) that he was granted only a geographically circumscribed portion of the overall estate, and that everything else would go to his step-mother, all by terms of another legal instrument prepared overseas in a country he had never visited.

* * *

By the time Demény included a portion of the 1940 Will in his 1951 letters volume, what Bator called "the subjection of the Bartók Estate to the complete control of the Government" had developed new urgency for the Communist regime. The government was not after just "a few dozen musical works," nor even "the substantial foreign exchange income," but, instead, the new regime sought "the possibility to exploit the name, reputation, and fame of Bartók—the Bartók legend—for the political, propaganda, soul- and mind-control scheme of the Government."[46] Around this time Bartók's suitability as a role model for the new People's Democracy was subjected to intense scrutiny and public debate. As Danielle Fosler-Lussier explains in her monograph on the history of Bartók's music in Cold War Hungary, the 1948 Soviet Communist Party decree denouncing Muradeli's opera *The Great Friendship* quickly rippled outward to the emerging East Bloc countries, launching a wave of internal struggle as countries tried to clarify their own artistic principles in response. Hungarian composers such as Ferenc Szabó and András Mihály, both committed communists at the time, believed initially that the examples of Bartók and Kodály pointed to a promising ideological "third path" that allowed Hungarian music to position itself aesthetically between the decadent capitalist West and the Soviet East.[47]

Through lectures and debates the new government worked out its political position on Bartók's legacy, using Soviet models as a guide. Internal bans on

---

46 Victor Bator, Affidavit in the litigation proceedings of 1958–61 (see Appendix).
47 In these paragraphs I draw freely from the account of Hungarian cultural policy found in Fosler-Lussier's *Music Divided: Bartók's Legacy in Cold War Culture* (Berkeley, CA: University of California Press, 2007), 4–27.

certain Bartók works arose from shifts in socialist ideology. Ideologues, Fosler-Lussier explains, had to "dismantle his prestige as an art music composer" in order to turn him into a suitable socialist hero. This involved some rewriting of history.[48]

Victor Bator viewed the year 1951 as a turning point in the Hungarian government's approach to the Estate. "Until about 1950 or 51," he wrote, "not even what is called 'socialist legality' existed." As a result, his trustee relationship with the Bartók family "until 1951 cannot be given a well confined and definite description. Everything was informal about it." From his prominent perch in the US Hungarian community he watched on, appalled, as the communist government imposed changes that brought such disorder. In the period 1947–51, he observed,

> Government was exercised completely arbitrarily, the new Communist bureaucracy, untrained in administrative procedures, ran every part of the political, economic, social machinery by arbitrary decisions. No individual rights were respected, and nobody had the courage to assert even the slightest measure of independence. Between Hungarians who lived in Budapest and their relatives, friends, who were abroad the relationship was based on principles of charity. Every Hungarian abroad spent half of his life and time in attempts to send to his Hungarian relatives and friends some kind of material support, mostly by charity packages. The former currency of Hungary disappeared. The inflation erased and eliminated its value 100%, and until the new currency could assert itself and acquired the minimum confidence of the populace, remittances in money were not important and had very little purchasing power.[49]

By Victor Bator's calculations, Béla Jr. collected "about $5,000 worth of Hungarian currency" in a four-year period from August 1946 to the end of 1950.[50] The material needs of Bartók's oldest son were being met. But his ability to continue collecting royalties was threatened by political changes. In this tumult Bator came to his aid in early 1951 with the so-called "Interpretive Declaration," a document that would later cause such trouble for them all. (See Chapter 6.)

Once Béla Bartók's name emerged from the ideological debates of 1948–50, the New York Bartók Estate and the new government in Hungary began to

---

48 Fosler-Lussier, *Music Divided*, 63.
49 Victor Bator, "The Hungarian Problem," in Memorandum on the History of the Bartók Estate.
50 Victor Bator, "The Hungarian Problem," in Memorandum on the History of the Bartók Estate.

Chapter 3

square off more firmly. For Bator these new developments were all part of a messy post-war continuum. "The entire relationship until 1951 cannot be given a well confined and definite description," he later explained. Conditions in Hungary undermined all their efforts to establish an orderly method of managing the Estate.

> People were struggling with establishing and rebuilding a modest frame of existence in which normal life could be lived again, and therefore problems like should be the relationship in regard to copyrights, authors rights, how to share a more or less nominal income, how to get hold of income from abroad that wasn't coming anyway, played a very secondary role in the thinking of Hungarians… Government was exercised completely arbitrarily, the new Communist bureaucracy, untrained in administrative procedures, ran every part of the political, economic, social machinery by arbitrary decisions. No individual rights were respected, and nobody had the courage to assert even the slightest measure of independence.[51]

Once Bartók's reputation as an acceptable if compromised national hero had been worked out, his socialist credentials validated and affirmed, he became newly interesting to the Communist Government as an internationally famous Hungarian, known for his moral integrity, whose name could be exploited for propaganda purposes. Demény's 1951 letters volume opens with a substantial preface extolling Bartók as a Hungarian who, ahead of his time, bravely anticipated the current era. (No political endorsement had been needed for his 1948 volume.) Written by András Mihály—or in his name—the essay positions Bartók as a worthy socialist hero. "As the dawn of the Hungarian People's Democracy grows brighter, day by day, Bartók's musical legacy, his folk culture program, his human greatness, were one of the creation forces for our people's rich and important heritage."[52] Nine-and-a-half pages of similar socialist effusion follow.

And here is where the 1940 Hungarian Will makes its first public appearance. Situated among other Bartók letters that denounced German wartime aggression—all familiar to us from later reprintings and translations—the Will's anti-totalitarian provision helped position Bartók politically as a committed leftist, feeding nicely into the Communist Party's moral claims for governance. Demény's editions of Bartók letters, published in Hungarian, circu-

---

51 Victor Bator, "The Hungarian Problem," in Memorandum on the History of the Bartók Estate.
52 Mihály, "Elöszó," in Demény, *Bartók Béla Levelei*, 3.

lated widely among musicians, and also abroad in the international Hungarian diaspora. (My copy of the 1948 first volume, for example, was inscribed in English by "John Demény" to Yehudi Menuhin; I have two copies of the 1951 edition, one from the library of Fritz Reiner, the other bearing a bookseller's stamp from Pannonia Books in Toronto. My 1955 volume is signed "Waldbauer" on the title page.) These books got around. In the Cold War they served another master, too, as propaganda for the international communist movement. They issued from the depths of the most repressive period in Hungary's experience with communism.

Demény's ability to locate caches of Bartók correspondence proved so successful, ironically, that he soon caught the attention of the only man alive who could equal him in this skill. By 1954 Demény's ever-expanding production of new Bartók source material goaded Bator into action. Many letters to and from Bartók were being published without consideration for copyright. State publishers in Hungary cared nothing for the conventions of international copyright law. In October 1954 Bator sent a firmly worded cease and desist letter to Demény, having failed so far to extract meaningful concessions from the publishers of these volumes. Thus Demény earned the distinction of being the first Hungarian Bartók scholar to find himself on the wrong side of the American Estate for copyright reasons.[53]

In years ahead the communist government would continue to assert the validity of the 1940 Hungarian Will. As sticking points go, this was a big one. The litigation of 1959–61 laid bare numerous points of disagreement whose foundations lay in the principled assertion of conflicting views over which of Bartók's Wills controlled the Estate's disposition. Because of their relevance to the escalating battle for control of the Estate, these episodes in the afterlife of the three Wills are discussed below, in Chapters 5 and 6, where they can be placed in proper context.

All of this helps us see why Ruffy's 1965 article and its two English-language reprints were so useful to the communist government's political agenda. In its pages estate law and propaganda merge. Ruffy, a respected journalist and writer in Hungary, known for his interwar reporting on Transylvanian politics and economic matters, was well aware that he could not give his journalistic

---

53 Bator expresses his principled objection to Demény's activities in a letter he wrote to Paul Sacher on Nov. 1, 1954. "The memory of Béla Bartók has not been served or enriched by the publication of letters, lumped together fortuitously as they may turn up, without preconceived plan or system." He wonders if Sacher "unwittingly abetted the infringement committed by Dr. Demény" by agreeing to have a letter published, and suggests that further cooperation with the trustee may lead to better long-term results that honor Bartók's memory more appropriately. For reference he includes a copy of his recent (Oct. 10, 1954) cease and desist letter to Demény (Paul Sacher private correspondence files, PSS Basel).

Chapter 3

imagination free rein. It's to his credit, actually, that the first two-thirds of his article are factually accurate as he reviews the 1940 and 1943 Wills' contents and the events up to 1945. Then he turns on the spigot. The propaganda starts to flow. He blackens Bator's eye by launching into a critique of the current legal standoff, parroting positions the regime and Bartók's two sons had been articulating for the past six years. Quoting "experts in international law," he explains that "for eleven years Bátor presented no accounts" for the Estate. "When finally he produced them it became apparent that the legatees, Ditta Pásztory, Béla and Péter Bartók, had received 'barely a quarter' of the very considerable sums amounting from royalties. Three-quarters of the royalties were charged by Bátor to expenses." He continues in this vein for another nine paragraphs, discrediting Bator and openly suggesting that his actions were criminal. "It is somewhat depressing that so many difficulties have had to be surmounted before the heirs of this great Hungarian could enter into their rightful inheritance." He then reveals his main target, the New York Bartók Archives, which Bator "treats as if they were his own, and in fact declared them to be his property"—a trope originating in the legal standoff of 1959–61 that Peter Bartók would go on to assert relentlessly, and unjustly, for the next six decades. "Bátor's duplicity over the manuscripts came to light," and his actions "raised new and unjustified claims to certain autograph manuscripts." Hungary's claims to the Estate take precedent, he asserts, because "under Hungarian law probate of Bartók's Will undoubtedly is subject to Hungarian law." He ends by expressing hope that "the final disposition of the Estate" will "speedily be settled…. Settled, as Bartók intended in his last will."[54] Should any reader still have any doubts about the right path forward, he appends a complete copy of the Hungarian Will—an extraordinarily public salvo in this battle between dueling Wills.

When do the wills of famous artistic figures get reproduced in full in multiple international scholarly publications? This one did.

Bartók's Hungarian-language Will thus made its musicological debut comfortably nestled on a bed of propaganda that advanced the goals of the Hungarian communist regime. No one used to reading communist-era publications will find this statement a revelation. What stands out here, making the article worth our reconsideration these many years later, is how closely Ruffy's claims match plaintiff's complaints that were developed in the course of litigation in the late 1950s and early 1960s. By being aired in *The New Hungarian Quarterly* in 1966 these positions gained false currency, long after being discredited by Samuel

---

54 Ruffy, "The Dispute Over Bartók's Will," 142–43. I suspect Ruffy simply didn't know the other side of the coin. He had no way of checking whether the "facts" he was being told were suspect.

DiFalco in his 1961 Surrogate's Court judgment.[55] Crow's reprint edition gave them further life in the 1970s and 80s. "Ruffy had no idea what he was talking about," commented Ben Suchoff when I spoke with him, sighing at the memory. "How could he?" That old political saw about mudslinging certainly applies here. Bator disdained engaging with the communist government at this level. His record of involvement shows quite clearly his preference for fighting in courts of law and through private communication. His decision to create the Béla Bartók Archives can be seen as a vigorous assertion of his rights as Trustee—a transformation in his tactics of resistance. With a cultural institution he could fight back more publicly. Béla Bartók conferred trusteeship on him back in 1943, he knew, to protect the Estate against encroachment from *any* totalitarian government—not just from the right, but also from the left.

---

55 How much the field of musicology has unconsciously absorbed the allegations transmitted in Ruffy's article is shown in Donald Maurice's book on the Viola Concerto. (See his chapter titled "The Future and Legal Issues.")

Correspondence: Estate Management, 1957–59

*V*ictor Bator's trustee duties placed him at the center of the Bartók publishing and recording world after World War II. The letters below show him engaged in daily matters of estate administration: correspondence with publishers, with Hungarian musicians, with prospective authors, and with staff of the Archives. They offer a rare window into the inner workings of the estate. Of particular interest is the letter of inquiry he wrote to John Rockefeller in 1959, in which he initiates discussions about a possible institution home for the Bartók Archives at Lincoln Center. A letter to Dr. Andor Chatel urges the Hungarian doctor to intervene in the matter of Ditta Bartók's mental health care: she was slipping "deeper and deeper into a half-dead state."

Several letters reveal how carefully Bator controlled licenses to record Bartók's works in the 1950s. His letter to George Mendelssohn, of Vox Records, is breathtakingly direct, a masterpiece of the rejection letter genre. In 1958 came the rupture with Peter Bartók, ignited when Peter's recording of the First Piano Concerto with Leonid Hambro failed to meet high expectations for its quality. Letters to Tibor Serly and Michael Kiely document the ruffled feathers that happened when Bator decided to forbid its release. Here we see another side of Bator: his fidelity to Béla Bartók's high standards, and his willingness to forcefully defend those standards even when faced with incredulous reactions from the musician community. His support for Peter's recordings activity had been generous, but far from absolute. These letters show him ever alert for ways he might give Peter strategic advantage in the recording industry, whether facilitating licensing arrangements in France (letter to Serge Moreux), or suppressing competition by reserving for Peter the exclusive right to record certain works (letter to Serly). A letter to Oxford University Press shows Bator in yet another mode: courting publishers for Bartók's folksong research in an effort to move these long simmering projects forward.

Correspondence: Estate Management, 1957–59

VICTOR BATOR, LETTER TO DR. ANDOR CHATEL. TYPED, 4 P., UNSIGNED. ONIONSKIN COPY. IN HUNGARIAN. TRANSLATED BY DAVID NAGY AND ETELKA NYILASI

April 6th, 1957

Dear Andi,

On this occasion instead of a private letter, you are receiving a request from me.

It was around ten years ago that Ditta, Béla Bartók's widow, returned to Hungary. I sent her back because she became schizophrenic, and since she barely spoke English even before her condition, with her schizophrenia she would have been completely cut off from the world. I thought it would be a good idea to send her to a place where her melancholic, withdrawn soul could have at least some friendly, familiar and Hungarian speaking contact with her mother and relatives.

Oh, as you must know, she was a pretty talented pianist before, as she often played two-piano recitals with her husband. She never had a very extensive repertoire, not big enough to play anything beyond these two-piano or other appearances performing Bartók's music, but she taught the instrument pretty well to my sons Péter and Pali among others, and she also sometimes performed smaller, less demanding programs. Ever since she became sick she stopped playing the piano completely. She writes to us or to me twice a year, a three to five line long letter, short and sweet, but she does not go beyond that. Her son Péter visited her recently in Rimaszombat, Slovakia,[1] where he planned to stay for October, November, December, and perhaps even January, and he too reported that beyond a couple of words a day it is impossible to keep a conversation going with her, except for food-related conversations and the like.

Her doctor is Tibor Hajnal, who was also her son's doctor, however he does not seem to pay much attention to her. I suppose if she had a more serious condition, and I do not mean the serious disorder she already suffers from, but some type of internal medical problem, he would take better care of

---

[1] Rimaszombat, Slovakia, where Ditta had grown up, and still had extended family.

her. I hope so at least. The family, Ditta's I mean, is upset with him because while he has regularly been charging them a fair honorarium, when Ditta had the need to see another doctor he sent her straight to the free clinic where she had to stand and wait in line which in her age and condition is unacceptable, therefore he did not take the best care of her. But I have something a lot more serious against him. Ditta's schizophrenic condition is critical and it continually is getting even worse. At this point we have to make a choice of either letting her roll further down this slope and possibly end up in a mental institution like a raving lunatic or in an apathetic half-dead state, or we can try to find a way to fight her condition. I believe if her health was in the hands of a fair, caring, and competent physician, she would have been taken to a psychiatrist a long time ago, especially in the past 3 to 4 years, who would have been able to help her.

I do not have to tell you how much medicine has advanced in this field during the past three to five years. I did extensive research on the subject and many psychiatrists tell me that the electrical and mainly the chemical treatments, especially the combination of the two, yield amazing results: patients' conditions not only improve, but in many instances patients with seriously advanced conditions who had been permanently hospitalized were able to leave the mental facilities cured or partly cured in large numbers.

Here we are facing two different cases again. First, it might be that Ditta's condition is already, as they say here, "beyond the point of no return." In this situation in America: they try operations.[2] Dr. Walter Freeman, a specialist in psycho-surgery from Washington, D.C. has worked with hundreds of seemingly incurable cases with success. Only a third of the operations are successful but in cases where the choice is between surgery and a half-dead state or even worse, this is not a low percentage rate.

Even more important, and actually what I wanted to bring your attention to, because I think or I hope that Ditta's condition is not too serious yet, is the application of rauwolfia (commercially what they call serpasil, or tranquillizer in the common language).[3] This is what I had on my mind.

---

2   The last three words in this sentence are typed in English, as if reproducing a saying Bator heard frequently in North America.
3   Rauwolfia is a chemical compound derived from leaves from members of the dogbane plant family. In powdered form its use in clinical treatment of patients with hypertension, cancer, autism, schizophrenia, and other diseases was widespread in Western medicine in the 1940s and 1950s.

I don't even want to go into further explanations since I am writing to you. All I want to say is that serpasil therapy combined with some other medications has yielded unbelievable results in this country.

I have no doubt that Hungarian psychiatrists know exactly as much about this as Americans do. Here we have Béla Bartók's widow, who has the means to afford the treatment, therefore I cannot see any reason why Tibor Hajnal has not arranged or initiated some kind of treatment for her. The intention of my letter to you is to ask you in Péter Bartók's and my name to take Ditta in your care as her physician. As soon as you see fit, also get a first-rate psychiatrist involved who could, along with you, evaluate the possibility and necessity of either of those treatments. Most important, someone who would at least be willing to give the serpasil therapy a try on Ditta.

I shall send a copy of this letter to Péter today. Péter will either write to his uncle and grandmother about this on his own or he will attach his personal note to my letter. Whatever happens, the initiation must come from the other side, except if Péter decides to write to you himself and with his letter in hand you could get in touch with Ditta; or you could send his letter ahead to her, in which he asks you to take her in your care. Please don't do anything until you receive a follow-up letter from Péter, which might be in this envelope. However, once Péter's letter reaches you, him being Ditta's only son (as Béla Bartók Jr. is not her son) I believe in cases involving psychosis, he has the right to authorize these provisions, as the closest relative. Meanwhile, if my letter reaches you before his, please think about whether you are willing and/or able to help her.

I am certain this letter reads rather naively, especially because it was not my intention to fix it up too much after transcribing it from the dictaphone. If I were not writing to a doctor, I would probably tweak it some more to make it sound more sophisticated. My only aim with this letter is to express my concern and thus to support my wish to somehow initiate serious action to save Ditta even if a successful cure is not guaranteed, and even if the most caring and most conservative people think that the cure might carry slight risks that occur occasionally. To sink deeper and deeper and end up in a half-dead state is not in any way a desirable result. I thus have no doubt that it is my and Péter Bartók's duty to try and prevent that from happening.

I don't want to mix personal news into this letter, but I will mention that we spent two weeks in Jamaica with Franci and granddaughter Nina. We have been fighting late winter colds and other minor things ever since we got back. Soon it will time for Nonquitt, so we can have a break from the tiring problems of urban living.

Hugs to you, dear Andi, and to the family of course, to Toni and the children. By the way, as for myself, I will support your decision and determination regarding this major problem, even if it's a personal sacrifice on the part of your friends here.

Hugs,

Mr. Andor Chatel
Mátyáskirály utca 32
Budapest, Hungary

VICTOR BATOR, LETTER TO GEORGE BANHÁLMI.[4] TYPED, 2 P., UNSIGNED. ONIONSKIN COPY. IN HUNGARIAN. TRANSLATED BY ETELKA NYILASI.

April 19, 1957

My dear friend,

I am responding to your letter to Peter Bartók, dated March 18th. The reason why I am responding instead of Peter is because in your letter there were actually two points that concern me more than they would concern Peter.

First of all, I'm interested in your comment about playing from manuscript works in Budapest, such as, for instance, the 5th movement of the Opus 14 Suite. I am the trustee of the Bartok estate, and other than

---

4   A gifted pianist and composer, born in Budapest, Banhálmi (1926-1985) was brought to the US by Fritz Reiner in 1956 to serve as pianist for the Chicago Symphony Orchestra. He served in that capacity from 1957–58. He remained in the Chicago area for the rest of his life, serving for many years on the faculty of the Music Institute of Chicago.

handling his legacy, 10 years ago I began to collect all kinds of Bartok memorabilia, such as manuscripts, letters, photographs, programs, reviews. Therefore, from this perspective, I would be most interested to learn more about this unpublished 5th movement. To be honest, I had no idea that this 5th movement even existed. I would therefore like to ask you about everything you know about it, including, of course, if you happen to have a score or a recording of it; please send it to me and I am not only willing to reimburse you for the related expenditures, but I am also willing to pay an honorarium for your help in getting a copy made of this work, or just of this particular movement. So, apart from everything else, I would like to ask of you a timely response regarding this matter.

After reading your letter, I gave my friend Ottó Herz a call, and he provided me with some more information about you. He, thank goodness, confirmed everything that was in your letter. So now it would be a matter of when you could come to New York. I don't know if you were here on March 28th, but if you were or weren't, I would like to know when you will be here next time; in that case I would suggest that you find me, and I'll call and invite Peter Bartók so that he can also be here, as well as perhaps a few other musicians who'd be interested; you could perhaps play a little, and of course we could discuss future plans that you could potentially get involved with.

As far as the making of an album is concerned, Peter of course has his own preferred pianists, in part because he is accustomed to them, and in part because they are all excellent musicians. Naturally, this does not mean, of course, that if we were to "discover" you for the American and record-buying public, that would primarily be in your interest, and of course in the interest of the Peter Bartók Recording Studio as well.

Do you have a Budapest record that could be listened to in the meantime? Of course, after assuming that you did not travel from Hungary abundantly loaded down, perhaps you should obtain material (discs, scores, etc.) by correspondence with Budapest, the acquisition and showing of which would greatly promote co-operation.

Please telephone the Chicago university teacher, Steven Rothman, and mention my name when you do so. István Rothman is an old friend of mine, a great music lover and enthusiast who just loves to play piano duets. Today, he is America's leading, comprehensive authority in the field of dermatology. He has a very nice family as well. You will certainly become good friends with him, his wife and his family. The other "Amerikásh"-Hungarian contact who I would recommend, if you have a way to visit him on a weekend or some other time if you are free, is a wonderful amateur pianist, Dr. Gyula Báron. His address is 317 Fairview Avenue, Iowa City, Iowa; telephone: Iowa City 8-3720. He also is a great pianist, much better than Rothman, as Rothman will probably tell you. Imre Waldbauer's widow also lives in Iowa City; she is in his inner circle of friends, just like we are. Just prior to moving to Iowa City, Gyula Báron was my co-trustee at the Bartók Estate and knew Béla Bartók well. It would also be nice to hear about you from them, as their opinions about you would be greatly beneficial for the purposes of future possible contributions.

I will send a copy of this letter to István Rothman and Gyula Báron, therefore you can refer to these letters if you telephone them. István Rothman's address: 5801 South Dorchester Road, Chicago 37, Ill. Unfortunately his telephone number is not in my address book. But it will be simple for you to find it in the telephone directory.

Frigyes Reiner of course is a great Bartók friend; he was one of those who stepped forward sooner than the American conductors in the cultivation of Bartók's music. He was also a personal friend of Bartók. I, too, know him. Please extend my greetings to him. I hope you are satisfied with your position there, although a pianist is never really a member of an orchestra. I'm sure you remember Ivan Waldbauer, who is now at Ithaca University. He is now trying to settle in New York.

I look forward to hearing news first and foremost about the unknown 5th movement, but also, of course, in due time, about the other matters.

Many greetings,

George Bánhalmi
Commonwealth Hotel
2757 North Pinegrove
Chicago 14, Ill.

Correspondence: Estate Management, 1957–59

VICTOR BATOR, LETTER TO SERGE MOREUX. TYPED, 1 P., UNSIGNED. ONIONSKIN COPY. IN ENGLISH.

May 15, 1957

Mr. Serge Moreux
24, Rue La Rochefoucauld
Paris 9, France

Dear Mr. Moreux:

I have just received your letter of May 7th. I thank you for your information regarding the Spanish and French editions of Bartok's writings.

I am passing on to Peter Bartok your comments on Verseau and the future of the French market. I will ask him to answer your question about recording on stereo.

As to the Hungarian tapes you have heard and found so impressive, I want to call your attention to the fact that these Hungarian tapes have been made without license from the Bartok Estate. Should anyone attempt to use these tapes for publication of records or for performances, the Bartok Estate would immediately institute legal proceedings and would attach the infringing and piratical reproductions. I do not think that Ducretet-Thomson will want to get involved in such a venture.

The various Hungarian government agencies are publishing music, making tapes, issuing phonograph records without license and on account of the lawless situation on the other side of the Iron Curtain, as long as the regime does not change, there is nothing I can do to prevent this. On this side of the Iron Curtain, however, whoever would use those infringing reproductions would become a party to the infringements. I am preparing a legal action against two English firms who ventured into such activity. The same will be done against a German and an Italian firm. Legal proceedings are already in course of preparation.

Please let me know whether your firm is interested in taking over the sale of the Bartok records. I am pretty sure that Peter Bartok is recording on stereo. In fact, he was perhaps the first to do this in the United States and he is doing it in cooperation with the Massachusetts Institute of Technology which is the highest ranking teaching and research instituted in the United States.

With best regards,

VB: EH

Victor Bator, letter to Béla Börösmény-Nagy.[5] Typed, 2 p., unsigned. Onionskin copy. In English.

May 29, 1957

Dear Bela:

I apologize for the delay in answering your letter of April 25th (and for answering it in English because I have no Hungarian secretary).

The reason for this delay is that I wanted to study thoroughly your idea of writing a book on Bela Bartok and it was quite hard for me to clarify my own thoughts on the subject.

My appraisal of the problem and your relationship to it is that if you try to write a book in six months, as you indicate in your letter, I have serious doubts whether you would excel over and above the standard set by Halsey Stevens.

The first writer who rushed into print with a work on Bartok which has been published in several languages, was Serge Moreux who wrote a weak, watery "soufflé" but succeeded to cash in on the first waves of interest for Bartok. Halsey Stevens wrote a much better book. He is already preparing another edition which, I assume, will be probably published in 1958. There is no point in writing a third book unless one is willing

---

5   Eminent Hungarian pianist (1912–90), appointed to the piano faculty at Indiana University in 1953 as Resident Pianist. He taught there until 1962. He left Hungary in 1948, moving first to Canada, where he taught at the Toronto Conservatory. He later taught at Boston University and Catholic University.

to spend two or three years on that task doing some preparatory work so that the book should not be written until some time in 1960.

If I were you, having—as you mention—important material already on hand, I would rather write about one or the other facet of Bartok's personality. It is not the length and the volume of a book that counts, especially when already two large-sized books and hundreds of articles have been written on Bartok. Only the general intrinsic value of writing would attract public attention to such a publication.

Answering your questions one by one:

1) I do not think that any Foundation would sponsor a publication. The maximum I can visualize is a Guggenheim fellowship.

2) As Moreux's book proves, once a work is worthy of publication, there is no problem to have it published in all the important languages.

3) I do not think that anybody in the Bartok Archives would accept to be your <u>assistant</u> in this work. They all want to write their own book.

4) Lang would never lend his name to such an undertaking. I do not quite understand your idea about an editorial committee. What can an editorial committee have to do with your book or mine? I doubt that Lang would even write a preface to such a book.

I hate to give you so many negative answers to your questions, but this is what I think about all this and I should not keep it from you before you bite into this new task.

Meanwhile Zathureczky[6] has come up with a conclusion which is not different from what psychologists would have anticipated anyway. This did not keep me from giving him my candid opinion on the matter, even though I had very little doubt that his decision would go the other way. His hesitations are not much different from yours or mine when we face

---

6   Ede Zathureczky (1903–59), eminent Hungarian violinist and student of Hubay, taught at the Liszt Academy until 1957, where one of his frequent recital collaborators was Béla Nagy. From 1943 to 1957 he was general director of the Liszt Academy. He left Hungary in 1957 to join Nagy at Indiana University, where he died suddenly two years later.

a situation where the pros and cons do not all point in the same direction. I am sure he will be in Bloomington next year.

We enjoyed having you at our house and we hope that there will be a repeat performance soon.

Yours very sincerely,

Mr. Bela Borosmeny-Nagy
Indiana University, School of Music
Bloomington, Indiana

Victor Bator, letter to George Mendelssohn. Typed, 2 p., unsigned. Onionskin copy. In English.

December 12, 1957

Dear Mr. Mendelssohn:

As Trustee of the Bela Bartok Estate, I feel I should not leave without comment the conversation which took place between you and me last night.

It seems to me that you are so accustomed to the compulsory license system of the U.S. Copyright Law that my thinking and handling of the recording problems of the Bartok works appears to you as a mysterious and insulting procedure.

This is not so. I am not insulting anybody by not inviting someone to my house or to ride in my automobile, still less by not permitting to drive my automobile or refusing to give up my privacy. In the same way I have complete liberty to have my photograph taken only by people to whom I go for such purpose, or to have my writings printed. Nobody thinks that he is entitled to any such activities unless specifically requested to do so.

Without going into the technicalities of the compulsory license system, the laws of the United States and four other countries permit record manufacturers to record such musical composition[s] which have been licensed for recording by other record manufacturers. Whatever I think about it, this is the law of these five countries. Fortunately, many other countries have not adopted such a system. While I am compelled to tolerate the practice of compulsory licenses by record manufacturers and dealers who want to exploit these special privileges in their favor, I am certainly not under obligation to help them in such activities, and by refusing to do so I behave exactly in the same way as when I do not offer a trip in my automobile to outsiders just because granted such favor to someone else.

This being so, I was somewhat taken aback when I was taken to task by you for not allowing the publishers to give to your company a license for recording the "Cantata Profana," although I did grant a license to Peter Bartok. I do not see how it can be interpreted as a slight against you or your company. I know that you are a bona fide record manufacturer doing everything that enables you to make a profit and is permitted by law. Still that does not give you the moral right to drive my automobile or for recording a musical composition or, as it happens to be the case, a dramatic musical work and most certainly, when you threaten that you will be able to get around my refusal to grant a permit, I have every reason to say that should you do that, I will use all legal remedies available to me to prevent you from doing so.

I do not quite understand why you insist on including in your business activities such recordings where your activity is not welcome. Certainly the literature of music is big enough to give you sufficient scope for your business practice without having to do something that is not welcome, though most certainly I did not intend to slight you in the least by not licensing to you a recording which I do not intend to license to anybody else either.

Yours sincerely,

Mr. George H. Mendelssohn, President
Vox Productions, Inc.
236 West 55th Street
New York, N.Y.

Victor Bator, letter to Benjamin Suchoff. Typed, 1 p., unsigned. Onionskin copy. In English.

January 7, 1958

Dear Ben:

I don't want any misunderstanding and hence I want to put on paper what is the present state of our relationship in regard to your work in the Archive.

I want you to continue to do everything that is and will be necessary to complete the publication of the Roumanian Folk Music material that is supposed to be included in the four volumes now under preparation. Three people will be responsible for the proper result of the work of editing. First of all, Constantine Braioloiu; you, and finally, myself. I want you to assist me, advise me regarding every point where you feel that by doing so the result will be improved. Whatever work will be done by you in this regard will be appreciated, given credit, and naturally the usual fee will be paid also.

On account of the special nature of the Archive being in very large degree contingent to knowledge of the Hungarian language and the Hungarian world of music, I have made up my mind, as you know, that the leading role there should be played by Ivan Waldbauer. I want him to get acquainted with the material fully, and for that reason I prefer him to do his work now without assistance from you to enable him to feel himself completely at home, and to show me how far by doing only a part time job now he can acquire complete control over the material. He will have the assistance of Elma and Marie, but he should be the intellectual head of the Archive. I hope that whenever he may get lost, he and I will have the privilege to turn to you and ask you to help us with your recollection, because on account of the tragic disappearance of Nike from the Archive family, we unfortunately cannot turn to her memory and knowledge.

As soon as Ivan Waldbauer will be able to start, and I will see that he has acquired that complete control I refer to above, I shall be able to make an intelligent decision as to which way and regarding what part of the work we can make use of your talent and past experience in connection with the Archive.

Yours sincerely,

Mr. Benjamin Suchoff
225 Smith Street
Woodmere, L.I.

VICTOR BATOR, LETTER TO TIBOR SERLY. TYPED, 2 P., UNSIGNED. ONIONSKIN COPY. IN ENGLISH.

January 6, 1958

Mr. Tibor Serly
10 West 58th Street
New York 19, N.Y.

Dear Tibor:

Many thanks for writing me your letter of December 30th and having taken the trouble to clarify the history of the unfortunate and unsuccessful recording of the First Piano Concerto. As you can easily imagine, I have received a full-scale report about all this from Peter himself and from a number of other sources. Also in addition to the subjective description of the happenings and description of the details how the tape came into being, I have an impartial appraisal from a musician of high rank whose judgment I trust, according to which the tape did not record a top quality performance no matter what the reasons happened to have been.

As you know, I don't want, and I don't let myself be involved in the management and the control of Peter's recording business. If and when he comes to me for advice, I don't close my ears. I listen to him and I might express opinions but decisions should be and are made by him without interference from me. There is even one point where just in this particular connection I have gone a little bit beyond the above limit. In the last five to six years, quite a number of great and important Philharmonic societies approached me for license to record the First Piano Concerto. I refused to give permission for the reason that it should be Peter who does the first recording. In fact, I have urged Peter for quite a while already to tackle the task but each and every time I emphasized that the challenge being great, it must not be a good record but a superior quality production. This being so and having learned from you and from every other source that this recording does not satisfy the standard set by me and would not be proper justification for my refusals to other orchestras, I have told Peter that as Trustee of the estate, I am not willing to license the publication of this tape. How he will solve this impasse must be his business. Fortunately, that is not my responsibility and it would be anyway beyond me.

I am sorry that you are personally involved in this but I assure you that not only nobody wants to insult or question your great abilities and musicians but I have not heard from anyone any implication in this direction.

Yours sincerely,

VICTOR BATOR, LETTER TO MICHAEL KIELY, JR. TYPED, 1 P., UNSIGNED. ONIONSKIN COPY.

February 12, 1958

Mr. Michael J. Kiely, Jr.
Myles, Wormser & Koch
60 East 42nd Street
New York 17, N.Y.

Dear Mr. Kiely:

I read your letter with amazement. I think that a little more modesty and less haughtiness would be in place in a matter where a job was done, costing many thousands of dollars, the result of which is unusable and means complete or almost complete loss. Doctors do not ask the full fee from the patient who died on the operating table. Lawyers usually reduce their fees when a case they advised was good is defeated in court. Regardless of whose fault it was, the other soloist in the debacle immediately volunteered that no fee be paid to him.

I do not let Peter Bartok suffer from this experience more than he does anyway and, therefore, I prefer to send the check myself. Thus the world of music will be spared from witnessing the Hogarthian spectacle of a court trial in "Serly versus Bartók."

Yours sincerely,

VICTOR BATOR, LETTER TO OXFORD UNIVERSITY PRESS. TYPED, 2 P., UNSIGNED. ONIONSKIN COPY.

February 13, 1958

Oxford University Press
Music Department
44 Conduit Street
London W. 1., England

Gentlemen:

I have before me letters exchanged in 1951 about the re-publication of Bela Bartok Hungarian Folk Music.

At that time I asked you to quote for the reprinting of the book on my behalf. You made a bid in your letter of January 10, 1952.

Later in 1956, I wrote to you about the publication of Bartok Roumanian Folk Music and you declined to quote for the work.

At this time I am considering the publication within a period of two or three years:

A. Bela Bartok's Roumanian Folk Music. (First Volume "Colinde," Second Volume "Roumanian Folk Music of Maramures", Third and Fourth

Volumes "Roumanian Folk Music", Fifth Volume "English Translation of the Roumanian Poetic Material").

B. Re-publication of the "Hungarian Folk Music".

C. "Slovakian Folk Music" (probably three volumes, but its editing is not yet in a sufficiently advanced stage to determine exactly its size).

D. "Turkish Folk Music".

Three of the above works will be ready for publication in 1958, the Roumanian, Hungarian, and Turkish works. The manuscript on Turkish Music is complete and it is probably somewhat less voluminous than the Hungarian book.

I am now asking bids regarding the fourth or fifth volumes of the Roumanian group. (It has not been decided yet whether the English translation of the Roumanian poems will be published as Volume 5 or not.)

I am enclosing herewith the specifications. Though it specifies the paper and many other details, among them those in regard to binding, if you can suggest better alternatives more suitable or customary in England, please do not hesitate to do so. These specifications were written by my assistant who knows the American specifications only.

Remembering your refusal to bid for the similar job in 1956, should you not be willing to undertake this now, please advise me whom else you would suggest in England and/or the Continent, i.e., Copenhagen, Vienna, or elsewhere.

My inquiry is alternative. Would you undertake to publish the entire collective work that embraces the entire non-musical, scholarly, posthumous material of Bartok? If so, please state your terms. Or, should you not be willing to undertake the publication as such, would you print it for the Estate of Bela Bartok?

Yours sincerely,

VICTOR BATOR, LETTER TO IVAN WALDBAUER. TYPED, 2 P., UNSIGNED. ONIONSKIN COPY. IN HUNGARIAN. TRANSLATED BY ETELKA NYILASI.

April 3, 1958

Dear Ivu,

I have the following comments on your text for 5 Songs, which we intended for the "Critical Edition," and my queries are indicated as follows, with question marks in red pencil:

1) Bartók wanted to play the 3rd song not only in Berlin, but also in Vienna, according to his letter.

2) As Bartók wrote that the songs are from 1916, I find this to be very accurate and, consequently, it would be inaccurate to say that there is no "exact date," as the month and the day are written on it and we already know the year.

3) In a publication from 1958, the words "general disorder" cannot be used when referring to the events of 1918–19. A better text would be: "revolutions, civil war and social disintegration following end of World War I."

4) I do not know if composers generally deposit their manuscripts with publishers, especially since Universal Edition had no definite and long-term contractual relationship with Bartók until 1923. It would therefore be better to say that Bartók sent the songs to U.E. for the purpose of publication.

5) The fact that Bartók sent 5 songs to U.E. for publication (see the April 11, 1918 letter) shows that he wanted to publish five. Nevertheless, the letter from April 28, 1918 suggests the publishing of 4 songs.

6) Never has any Bartók letter spoken of "Securing of Copyright," only of "Unannehmlichkeit" [inconvenience] because the author of the poems is "unbekannt" [unknown].

7) The date of the April 4 letter seems to have been changed by Marianne correctly to the 11th.

8) I do not share your view that we cannot refer to some unnamed person familiar with Béla Balázs's poems.[7] However, I would like to note that the following text is barely legible at the beginning of the fourth song: "Béla Balázs: The Woman and the Garden." If Bartók had written this, it would be a good indication that perhaps Bartók was in possession of this unknown Balázs poem. In any case, it would be interesting to mention this, despite the fact that we do not know about such published Béla Balázs poems.

9) I therefore find it unnecessary to discuss recovering the manuscript, as I see no reason whatsoever to mention in the text how and why the manuscripts appeared, (which—according to the Bartók–U.E. contract—belonged to Bartók) as well as when they were returned.

My general answer otherwise, is that I made this an urgent matter because you didn't spend March in New York. So I wanted all the text, music, and copies to be in perfect and final shape before you left. If I had known you were coming back at the beginning of April, and you were not prepared anyway before the end of your week here in March, I wouldn't have felt this urgency.

My expectation is that when I give someone a task, I get a completed job where I don't have to deal with any describing, numbering, checking, rendering, dotting the i's and crossing the t's, or any other insignificant details.

Hugs,

---

[7] These poems were later discovered to be written by two teenage girls that Bartók had befriended in 1915 while researching Slovak folksong, Klára Gombossy and Wanda Gleiman. On the early confusion with Béla Balázs in the songs' reception history, see Dille, "L'Opus 15 de Bartók," in Denijs Dille, ed., Yves Lenoir, *Regard sur le passé* (Louvain-la-Neuve: Presses Universitaires de Namur, 1990): 257–77.

Correspondence: Estate Management, 1957-59

VICTOR BATOR, LETTER TO JOHN ROCKEFELLER. TYPED, 2 P., UNSIGNED. ONIONSKIN COPY.

April 10, 1958

Mr. John D. Rockefeller 3rd
President
Lincoln Center for the
Performing Arts, Inc.
10 Columbus Circle
New York City

Dear Mr. Rockefeller:

From the April 9 issue of the New York Times I learned that the Lincoln Center Project has been enlarged to include two more buildings, one of which is planned to be a Museum and Library of the Performing Arts.

The writer of this is Trustee of the Estate of the late Béla Bartók, who died in 1945 as a resident of this city. Besides taking care of the administration of his works and their copyright, in 1948 I began to collect manuscripts, letters, photographs, pictures and all other kids of documents and mementos connected with the great composer's life and work. At the time of his death I had already in my possession almost all of his manuscripts and many hundreds of letters and papers which he has had entrusted to me during his lifetime and which are now in my custody as Excutor and Trustee of his inheritance. The material is now being indexed, catalogued and classified in the Archives and all the necessary work is under way to prepare it for public use. This work will be completed in one or two years.

At that time I shall face the problem where to deposit the material as part of a museum or library serving similar kind of scholarly use. The news item published in the New York Times suggests that perhaps the new addition to the Lincoln Center Project may be the suitable accommodation for the Béla Bartók Archives as part of the Museum of Performing Arts.

Should this idea appear to be worth of consideration, I shall be only too pleased to explore together with your Committee the possibility of its realization.

Yours very sincerely,

Victor Bator
Trustee
Béla Bartók Estate

Victor Bator, letter to President Grayson Kirk, Columbia University. Typed, 2 p., unsigned. Onionskin copy.

Oct. 16, 1959

Dear President Kirk:

I am writing this letter because our discussion the other day broadened in a way that may make appear the immediate problem before you and me as if it had been by-passed. That was not my intention.

I believe that the Manuscripts now on deposit belong to the Estate of which I am a Trustee. This is so because Béla Bartók, who died in 1945, had never expressed the idea and never stated verbally or in writing that he had intended to make the deposit a "permanent" one. As far as I know, the intentions to give a gift can never be construed, assumed or presumed. Papers in the files testify to the fact that the Officers of the University themselves have serious doubts about the nature of the deposit. I am sure that if you ask whether Béla Bartók ever signed a letter or statement to the effect that the deposit was permanent and not revocable, my above summary of the facts will be confirmed.

I do not find the argument that the University is a depository of the intentions of the depositor prevents you from recognizing that the Manuscripts belong to the Estate. Our disagreement concerns the intention itself. Would the intention of the deposit be clearly established, I would not have made my demand to have the Manuscripts delivered into the Estate.

The above does not change my desire to find a settlement not because I have doubts about the legal situation, but because I concede that the University would be a worthy depository. However, being a fiduciary, I can not give up the title without consideration. With that in mind I took the liberty to suggest to you that the University find a way to contribute to the expenses of the publication that was so dear to the heart of Béla Bartók. Hence, this publication is one of the important aims of my administration. A contribution would justify the recognition of the title of Columbia.

Yours very sincerely,

President Grayson Kirk
Columbia University
116 Street and Broadway
New York City

Chapter 4

Old Ties Bind

In New York Béla Bartók found himself in one of the largest communities of expatriate Hungarians in the world. An estimated 50,000 Hungarians lived in the greater New York City area in 1940. The steady flow of arrivals from Europe formed a new layer in the émigré community. Already in place were older layers of first and second generation immigrants, too, men and women whose American roots extended back to the 1920s, or even well into the 19th century, including the earliest waves of immigration from the Austro-Hungarian empire to the U.S. Many of the older generations were working class men and women. Immigration reforms of the 1920s meant that most of the newer arrivals came from Hungary's broad middle class: lawyers, doctors, bankers, professors, musicians, writers, businessmen, and journalists, together with their children and families. Bartók, within minutes of landing in the U.S. in April 1940 found his way into this Hungarian community: Tibor Serly and his wife Judith met him at dockside. For the next five years the Hungarian community in New York supplied both Bartóks with their main network of support. Fellow Hungarians helped them settle, find housing, line up concerts, navigate visa processes, process the news coming from Europe, and manage daily life in a new city. Ditta, especially, since hers was largely a domestic role, supporting her famous husband, situated herself almost exclusively within this community. She "never had any other friends but Hungarians or Hungarian born Americans," Victor Bator later recollected.

Writing specifically about Hungarian Jewish immigration in the early 20th century, Tibor Frank observes that "most émigrés were confined in their own social circles," and usually "they were left to themselves" in the new country, a feeling that could deepen their sense of alienation, on the one hand, or spur them to assimilate more quickly by learning English.[1] A large literature documents the sociological effects of emigration from Europe to the US by the pro-

---

[1] Tibor Frank, *Double Exile: The Migration of Jewish-Hungarian Professionals Through Germany to the United States, 1919–1945*, Exile Studies 7 (Oxford and Bern: Peter Lang, 2008), 207.

fessional classes at this time.² Ethnomusicologist Bruno Nettl, whose parents left Prague to settle in the US in 1938, recalls that after arriving his mother and father surrounded themselves primarily with other Europeans, chiefly Austrians and Swiss, but also German-speaking Czechs and Hungarians. "These," he explains, "were the people who, one might say, 'understood.'" Few Americans could enter this circle, unless they had spent substantial periods of time in Europe and spoke some European languages.³

For these Hungarians in North America, bonding and networking became "more intense" in the war years, not just in New York, but in other cities like Cleveland, Toronto, and Los Angeles with strong Hungarian minority communities.⁴ "Over here there was a tightness of community among the Hungarian émigrés," Francis Bator explained. "Once these people came to the U.S. their sense of Hungarian-ness was strong."⁵ As a group, and in some cases individually, they suffered from the shadow of wartime suspicion: their country had aligned itself against U.S. interests in the war. Bartók, before he could be hired by Harvard, was quietly investigated by the Music Department's chairman. Tillman Merritt didn't expect that their prominent guest would bring "pro-Axis" views to campus, but out of an abundance of caution he still needed to check. For many Hungarian émigrés, American foreign policy stimulated the natural propensity to turn inward.⁶ It was easier to congregate with and among their own people, avoiding political conversations with outsiders who couldn't be trusted to find the country on a map. Here in the United States Hungarians who were not necessarily friends or acquaintances back home, or who might not routinely cross paths, could in their new environment strike up warm relationships based on language and shared experience. This is how Victor Bator came into Bartók's orbit again in 1940, and how our tale now circles around, finally, to Gyula Báron.

***

2 The essays found in Brinkmann and Wolff, eds., *Driven into Paradise: The Musical Migration from Nazi Germany to the United States* (Berkeley and Los Angeles: University of California Press, 1999) focus on musicians at this time. More general studies include Bodek and Lewis, eds., *The Fruits of Exile: Central European Intellectual Immigration to American in the Age of Fascism* (Columbia, SC: The University of South Carolina Press, 2010); Endre Szentkiralyi, *Being Hungarian in Cleveland* (Reno, NV: Helena History Press, 2019); and Donald Fleming and Bernard Bailyn, eds., *The Intellectual Migration: Europe and America, 1930–1960* (Cambridge, MA: Harvard University Press, 1969).
3 Bruno Nettl, "Displaced Musics and Immigrant Musicologists: Ethnomusicological and Biographical Perspectives," in Brinkmann and Wolff, eds., *Driven into Paradise*, 60.
4 Frank, "Budapest-Berlin-New York: Stepmigration from Hungary to the United States, 1919–1945," in Bodek and Lewis, eds., *The Fruits of Exile*, 207.
5 Francis Bator, interview with the author, September 24, 2010.
6 Frank, "Budapest-Berlin-New York," 198.

Today we know Gyula Báron's name from Bartók's Last Will and Testament, but a deep dive into the Bartók literature reveals almost nothing else about him. New York Bartók Archive holdings contained only one letter from him to Bartók, written from Chicago in September 1945 to recommend French pianist Emile Baume.[7] Other than that lone document, which has never been published, no record of close interaction, or even passing interaction, survives. He is utterly absent from biographies. His name cannot even be found in Victor Bator's 1963 Archives catalogue.[8] Yet Bartók gave him rarefied status as a Co-Trustee of his Estate. Why? Who *was* he? The timing of my interest in studying Bartók's American years meant that I was able to interview a number of individuals who still remembered Bartók personally. Some were well known in the Bartók world. Others, less so. Their personal impressions of Bartók remained vivid despite the passage of time. David Diamond, for example, recalled several occasions when he found himself in Bartók's presence in New York City in the early 1940s, backstage or at gatherings put on by the League of Composers. "What struck me most, you'll find this interesting, is the way Bartók *smelled*," he told me. "He always wore eau de cologne. He had a very distinctive smell about him. I had never met anyone who wore cologne like that. It seemed so European to me." As for young American composers of that time, he assured me, "rhythmically we were *all* influenced by Bartók." Storm Bull wrote me with detailed memories of studying the Second Piano Concerto with Bartók in Budapest. Arthur Berger remembered meeting Bartók at Mills College around 1940 at a reception at someone's home. "He sat by himself in a corner, looking quite lost," so "I went over to him and tried to have a conversation with him. It was not the language that bothered him. He was just quite reticent or shy. He was fascinated by the native Indians."[9]

Francis Bator and Iván Waldbauer, in my interviews with them, both zeroed in quickly on Gyula Báron as part of the history of the Bartók Estate. They had known him personally. Waldbauer spoke of him with the warmth accorded a favorite uncle. To understand how Báron became involved in Bartók's Estate, they emphasized, it was first necessary to recognize how the Waldbauer and Bator families were connected. The origins of that story lay in the early years of the 20th century in Budapest, when a handful of boys became friends in school, their families encouraged those friendships, and they continued to socialize as they set out on careers.

---

7 Gyula Báron, letter to Béla Bartók, September 4, 1945 (BBC-PSS Basel).
8 I suspect Bator omitted Báron's name on the advice of attorneys, to shield him from the litigation surrounding the Bartók Estate.
9 David Diamond, interview with the author, 2003; Storm Bull, letter to the author, August 26, 2002; Arthur Berger, letter to the author, August 25, 2002.

Chapter 4

By the time I caught up with them, Francis Bator and Iván Waldbauer were both in their 80s, fully retired from their careers. Waldbauer, then living in Oberlin, Ohio, freely shared with me his childhood impressions of Béla Bartók, delivered with zest, humor, and the practiced delivery of a natural raconteur. Asked about Bator and Báron he became pensive. Multiple points of contact linked Bator to Bartók's world, he explained. Victor Bator was one of a group of 8–9 men, all born in the period 1890–92, who grew up together and became lifelong friends, extending those friendships in many cases to the United States. They informally called themselves "The Club" (which Iván always pronounced "cloob.") Imre Waldbauer, Iván's father, was a member of this Club (in Hungarian, originally, "Klub"). Another was Gyula Báron. Other members of the Klub were Pál Sebestyén, later a distinguished member of the foreign legation, Alfons Weiss de Csepel, scion of Hungary's leading industrialist family, and "the three Raj boys," as Waldbauer referred to them. Their friendships, born in shared family experiences in Hungary, remained in place their entire lives.[10]

Fig. 4.1. "The Klub." Membership as reconstructed from interviews with Francis Bator and Iván Waldbauer, 2010-13.

Imre Waldbauer	Pál Sebestyén
Gyula Báron	Alfons Weiss de Csepel
László Raj	Viktor Bátor
Ferenc Raj	_____ Raj

With only one professional musician among them, this group of Hungarian men (Fig. 4.1) developed its core identity not by schooling, or profession, but by a shared personal and family outlook. Ivan Waldbauer explained that this connection was very important to all of them.

What bound these people together was kind of a shared outlook, which for lack of any better words I would call 'liberal free thinking.' That was

---

10　Two of the Raj brothers died in World War I. László Raj was a talented painter. His brother Feri, who survived, "was probably Victor Bator's closest friend." Feri Raj stayed in Hungary his entire life and was godfather to Victor Bator's oldest son Francis (Waldbauer, interview with the author, 5 January 2011). László Raj painted a very fine oil portrait of Imre Waldbauer in 1911 that the violinist brought to the U.S. when he emigrated. Other close friends of the Bators, but not members of the Klub, were Ferenc Eckhardt, a Hungarian historian, and Andor Chatel. "The whole Chatel family were our friends," Francis stated. "A distinguished medical family. His wife Marie was a close friend of my mother's. My godmother." (Francis Bator, interview with the author, January 11, 2013).

their family heritage. And that was throughout their lives. That's what I am now, and what Francis [Bator] is, I am sure. These people were friends in that sense that is rare in this country. Perhaps if you think of *Beau Geste*… a kind of absolute, unquestioning loyalty to each other.

Some of them had gone to school together. Some had Jewish heritage. Some were Lutheran. Some were Catholic. "But these differences didn't matter," Waldbauer emphasized. "The most important connection was that they were all liberal free thinkers."[11] Most had intellectual parents. By the mid-1920s all had situated themselves firmly in the prosperous professional class. Based in Budapest, their collective home, they also enjoyed meeting each other abroad while travelling. They vacationed with each other and their families. After 1918, the Waldbauer-Kerpély Quartet travelled widely, giving concerts. They would sometimes find themselves in the same European cities as Victor Bator, then just establishing his international legal career.

Iván repeatedly used the word "family" when he described the Klub members' relationships. For their wives were friends, too, he stressed to me, and their children, too, forming a multi-generational array of personal relationships that carried on through the years. They raised their children together. They socialized in ways many of us recognize as hallmarks of middle class and upper middle class lives: dinners at friends' houses where they bring the children along, sailing outings on Lake Balaton, walks through the Buda hills, attendance at school choir concerts, skiing trips to Austria at Christmas time, and (in season) frequent games of tennis for those who liked to play the game. They were godparents to each other's children. "It was a very good, civilized life," Francis remembered. Geographic closeness in Budapest deepened their friendships. The Waldbauers lived next door to the Bators on Gellért Hill.[12] The Weiss family and the Sebéstyens lived a short distance away. So, too, the Bárons. Both the Bators and the Weisses had private tennis courts. Their children played the game, occasionally adding in one of the adults for sport. Francis remembered playing tennis with Imre Waldbauer —a boy in his early teens playing against an adult. "He was temperamentally a very difficult man. Highly strung. As a boy I'd play tennis against him, and if he didn't win, he didn't like it." He also played tennis with Tibor Eckhardt on the family court in Budapest, and later in Nonquitt.

Gyula Báron (1891–1973) came from a prominent Hungarian medical family. His father, Dr. Jónás Báron, was a major figure in Hungarian academic

---

11 Iván Waldbauer, interview with the author, January 5, 2011.
12 The Waldbauers lived at 13 Somlói út; the Bators at 19 Somlói út, directly adjacent. The homes were on the same property. Iván Waldbauer referred to his boyhood home as "the garden house." Claudia MacDonald, Email communication with the author, December 3, 2020.

Chapter 4

medicine and head of the Jewish hospital in Budapest. Gyula and his brother Alexander followed in their father's footsteps to become doctors. Both left Hungary in the late 1930s during the exodus of Jewish professional families. Gyula, a respected radiologist in Budapest, at the height of his career, came to the U.S. in October 1939.[13] Like his brother he settled in Chicago, at the University of Chicago's Billings Hospital, where many Hungarian physicians, especially Jewish physicians, would relocate during the war years due to liberal relicensing regulations. The hospital sponsored his visa paperwork. Almost immediately he anglicized his name to Julius Baron, retaining his Hungarian first name as a middle name: Julius G(yula) Baron. Citizenship being a requirement for medical licensure in Illinois, he promptly put in motion his naturalization paperwork. As Dr. Julius Baron he practiced medicine in the University of Chicago system for sixteen years. (Billings was a research and teaching hospital affiliated with the university's medical school.) In 1956 he moved to Iowa City, capping off his career with a stint at the Veterans Administration hospital and teaching medicine for the University of Iowa until his retirement in 1966.[14] At the VA hospital he was chief of radiology. In retirement he and his wife Maria moved back east to Rye, New York, just outside of New York City, where he died in 1973 at the age of 84. At the time of his death he was a 20-year member of the Mathematical Association of America.

Báron's professional work in radiology nurtured his natural inclination for physics, mathematics, and medical research. He was blessed with a curious, analytical mind, as seen in articles he authored or co-authored for academic journals such as *Radiology* and *Archives of Internal Medicine*. Among his American publications in the 1950s was a substantial overview of radiation hazards for physicians.[15] His expertise in the science behind X-ray protection drew him to medical conferences as a presenter, including the 1958 American Roentgen Ray Society national meeting in Washington, D.C., where he contributed to an exhibit on the elements of radiation protection, a collaborative venture with the University of Iowa's radiation research lab.[16]

Friends knew him as a gifted pianist. "He was as good an amateur pianist as you could be," remembered Francis Bator. "He aspired to play piano at a very

---

13 U.S. immigration records show that Báron arrived in the U.S. by plane from Cuba on Oct. 24, 1939, through the Miami airport. Like Bartók a year later, his immigration was preceded by an exploratory visit to America ahead of time, in his case, a visit to New York in May 1939. His older brother travelled the same route to the US through Cuba and on to Chicago.
14 An obituary for Báron appeared in the August 4, 1973, issue of the *Iowa City Press-Citizen*. He died in Rye, New York, on July 22 of that year.
15 Julius G. Baron et al., "Reviews of Internal Medicine: A Primer on Radiation Hazards for Physicians," *Archives of Internal Medicine* 103/2 (Feb. 1959): 308-28.
16 "Medical Radiation," *Public Health Reports* 74/1 (Jan. 1959): 36–38.

high level." Admiration for his talent didn't keep friends from teasing him now and then, especially because he took his piano playing so seriously. Henry Lax, another friend and Hungarian émigré physician, would explain to him, "Gyula, look you can practice all you want and you still won't play like Schnabel."[17] Victor Bator esteemed his friend as "a great pianist" who played much better than another Hungarian émigré doctor of their acquaintance in Chicago, Dr. Steven Rothman.[18] Iván Waldbauer, a fine pianist himself, remembered Báron as an exceptionally talented piano-playing doctor. "He and I had many, many good four-hands sessions both before and after the war. I consider himself as good as most of my professional friends. My father did, too."[19] In an interview Francis told me the following story.

> One time, I think in the summer of 1936, there was a polio epidemic in Budapest. We had just come home from Italy in August. One of the neighbors' children had polio. My parents decided that living at home I would be too exposed, so I was sent to spend a couple of months during this contagious period to live with Gyula and Maria Báron, who lived about a half mile away. I have wonderful memories of going to sleep in their apartment at night with him playing Chopin études at the piano. It was just a pleasure.[20]

For Iván Waldbauer the relationship may have been even closer:

> By the mid-1930s Gyula had sort of adopted me as a surrogate father figure. I was a pianist and he was interested in me quite apart from the fact that I was my father's son. I inherited his piano when he left Hungary—that piano came to me. And also his record collection, including Backhaus playing Chopin études among other things—this, to my mind, was the acme of piano playing at the time.[21]

Báron's interest in the piano extended well beyond the performer's art. Already by the mid-1930s he had co-authored a substantial article (Fig. 4.2) in a German scientific journal arguing for the presence of a distinguishing human touch when playing a single tone on the instrument, something musicians had always felt was possible, but which had come under fire from physicists skeptical of the

---

17 Francis Bator, interview with the author, Sept. 24, 2010.
18 Victor Bator, letter to George Banhálmi, April 19, 1957. Published above in this book.
19 Iván Waldbauer, interview with the author, Nov. 29, 2010.
20 Francis Bator, interview with the author, Sept. 24, 2010.
21 Iván Waldbauer, interview with the author, Nov. 29, 1010.

Chapter 4

notion.²² The science of piano sound intrigued him. In a review of the topic published 22 years later in the US, he explains that while the velocity of the hammer determines the sound originating from the strings, piano tone also contains elements caused by the mechanism and the impact of the finger on the key, and, further, the key bed. He continues:

> All these elements are noises. They are present only at the beginning of the piano tone and, to a much lesser extent, at the very end. They were not recorded by Hart, Fuller, and Lusby. Their curves are strictly periodic, showing no decrease of the amplitude of subsequent cycles. Therefore, these curves represent late, that is, noiseless parts of the piano tone. On the other hand, if the average spectrum of the whole piano tone is recorded, as it was done by Meyer and Buchmann, then, in addition to the lines of partials, an impressive continuous spectrum becomes evident.

Close review of the relevant acoustical science, he feels, makes obvious the possibility that noise elements may influence the tone of a struck piano key in a perceivable manner. "Therefore," he concludes, "there is no reason to deny the physical possibility of the role of touch in piano playing. Many people (among them the present writer) firmly believe that they are able to perceive the effects of differences in touch. They have been told many times that their contention is based on imagination. This is not necessarily so. Piano touch may have sound physical foundation. This possibility should not be disregarded because it may pave the way to rational teaching of the art of piano touch."²³

The appeal of this research to someone like Béla Bartók is obvious, with its emphasis on rigor and scientific method. Reminders of their shared interest lay very near the surface in New York, too, as they had in Budapest: Báron's co-author in the study (Fig. 4.2) was none other than Gyula Holló, Bartók's own personal physician. Holló, Báron, and Bartók were all interested professionally in the art of playing piano, it seems: Báron and Bartók as practioners at the artist level, and Holló and Báron as medical doctors exploring the physics of piano tone. (Holló was also a violinist, described to me by Iván Waldbauer as "so-so, but very knowledgeable.") Báron already had met Bartók several times in the 1920s and 30s. In the US they simply continued their existing relationships, with Bartók triangulated in strongly through Holló, who had been his personal physician in Budapest, too. That Holló also was Victor and Franciska Bator's

---

22 J. Báron and J. Holló, "Kann die Klangfarbe des Klaviers durch die Art des Anschlages beeinflusst werden," *Zeitschrift für Sinnesphysiologie* 66/1–2 (1935): 23–32.
23 Julius G. Báron, "Physical Basis of Piano Touch," *Journal of the Acoustical Society of America* 30/2 (1958): 151–2.

> **Kann die Klangfarbe des Klaviers durch die Art des Anschlages beeinflußt werden?**
>
> Von
>
> J. Báron und J. Holló (Budapest)
>
> Es ist oft behauptet worden, daß die Farbe des Klavierklanges mit der Klangstärke eindeutig bestimmt ist. Am klarsten wurde das von Tetzel[1], auf Grund von Gutachten namhafter Physiker, ausgesprochen. Demgegenüber meint die Mehrzahl der Musiker und Konzertbesucher, daß der Klavierklang auch unabhängig von seiner Intensität, verschiedene (weiche, harte, singende usw.) Färbung haben kann. Im folgenden wollen wir versuchen, dieser Behauptung eine physikalische Unterlage zu geben.
>
> Die Klaviertaste ist in der Hauptsache ein doppelarmiger Hebel, dessen innerer Arm beim Anschlagen hochsteigt, den auf ihm ruhenden Hammer mit sich nimmt und gegen die darüberliegende Saite wirft, wodurch diese in Schwingung kommt. Mit Ausnahme der obersten Töne sitzt auf jeder Saite ein Dämpfer

Fig. 4.2. Title and opening sentences of a study on the sensation of piano tone, co-authored by Budapest physicians Gyula Holló and Gyula Báron. Published in 1935 by the Leipzig-based neurological journal *Zeitschrift für Sinnesphysiologie*.

personal physician in New York, and someone Ditta Bartók considered her closest friend by 1943, would have struck them all as perfectly natural.[24] The Hollós had been family friends with the Waldbauers in Budapest, too.

A respected pulmonologist, in New York Dr. Gyula Holló had a mix of American-born patients and many people he had known from Budapest. His gentle, soft-spoken, somewhat resigned personal demeanor appealed to patients. Francis Bator knew him well; the Hollós were frequent guests in his parents' home in New York in the 1940s and 50s. He remembered the legendary stories that circulated in the Hungarian community about Holló's perfectly pitched bedside manner. "How are you feeling today?" he would ask a patient. "I feel terrible," they'd reply. Holló would pause for several seconds, look at the patient with a long face, then reply, in a quiet voice, "So do I."[25] Holló and his wife Elsa got along particularly well with the Bators because they shared a disdain for the habitual complaining of many other recent émigrés. "Holló was the kind of person to whom everybody listened on those rare occasions he spoke," Ivan recalled

---

24 In her application for visa renewal in 1943, Ditta Bartók was asked to list the names of three "close friends in the United States." Gyula Holló was the first name she listed, then Tibor Serly and Ernő Balogh. U.S. Department of Justice, Immigration and Naturalization Services, Form I-55. CPB Homosassa.

25 Francis Bator, interview with the author, Sept. 24, 2010.

Chapter 4

separately. "When I arrived in the U.S. in 1947 he struck me as the voice of reason and sanity." His role in bringing Báron more firmly into Bartók's orbit after 1940 should not be underestimated. These two Jewish physicians lived up to the promise of their name: like the Gyula of ancient Hungarian history, they were wise men both.[26]

As his career unfolded in the Midwest, Gyula Báron regularly found reasons to visit New York, in part to talk over trustee business with Victor Bator. He usually stayed at the Bator's house in New York. He spent time most summers in Nonquitt, vacationing with Victor and Franci and whoever else came to visit. He and his wife Maria (1896–1984) had no children, which allowed them to travel more freely. As trustee he let Victor Bator handle all management matters. His role was more informal out of necessity. We may assume that he offered regular counsel, too, helping shape the growth of the Archive and Estate through countless conversations with Victor over the years. Sometime around 1955, in New York, he took the time to make a beautiful manuscript copy of Bartók's Op. 15 songs in an early step towards getting those songs published.[27] When Peter Bartók drew up his own Last Will and Testament in 1954, he borrowed the model used by his father and also appointed, as Co-Executors, Victor Bator and Gyula Báron.

Acknowledging the general sentiment that Báron was, in his words, "a superb radiologist," Francis Bator also remembered him more personally as "a very driven, obsessive man, very strict… a complicated figure." Waldbauer remembered Báron as "a man of *very* strong character." Sometime in the mid-1950s Báron fell ill and had to undergo surgery. His life took a sharp turn. Ivan remembered what happened:

> The doctors gave him Demerol to help him recover, and somehow he became addicted to the drug. Gyula recognized what was going on, though. He knew what he had to do. He came east for detox. Victor Bator helped pay for the treatment. After that he resigned from Billings hospital, he returned his license to the governing board—I don't know what that is, but he *returned* it. He got a limited license to practice at Veteran's Hospital in Iowa City.

---

26 Iván Waldbauer, interview with the author, Nov. 29, 2010.
27 Iván Waldbauer (interview with the author, January 5, 2011) gave credit to Báron for preparing this publication-ready manuscript of the Op. 15 songs, at that time still unpublished. "That was Gyula's handiwork. I don't remember the circumstances. I don't know why Gyula copied this manuscript. It was published for copyright purposes and I myself put a copy in the Harvard Library."

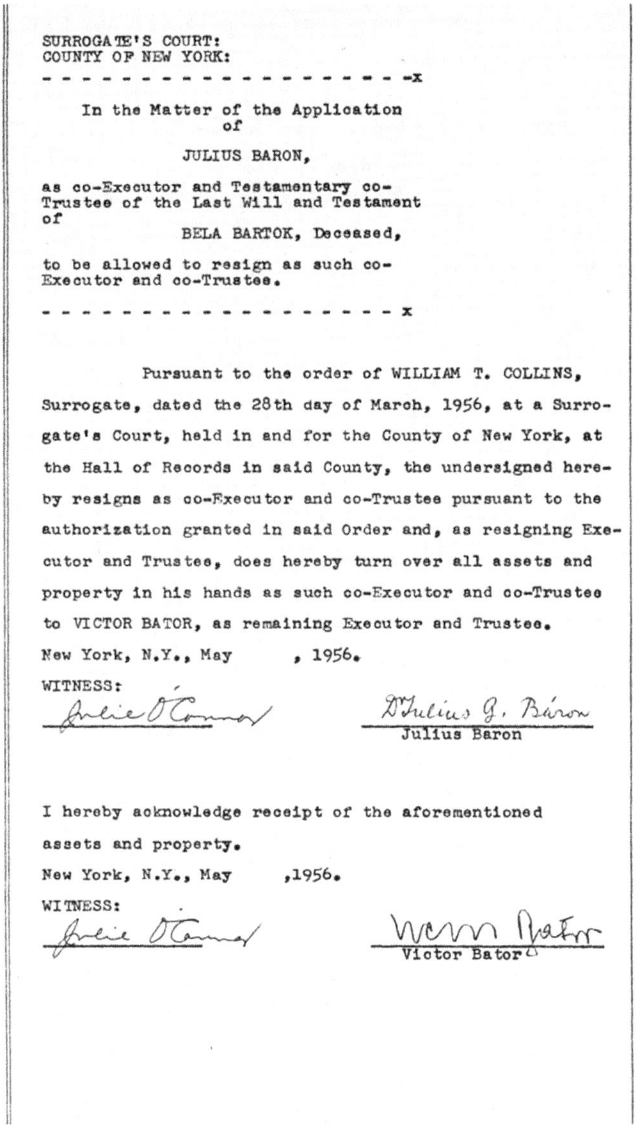

```
SURROGATE'S COURT:
COUNTY OF NEW YORK:
- - - - - - - - - - - - - - - - - -x
         In the Matter of the Application
                        of
              JULIUS BARON,
         as co-Executor and Testamentary co-
         Trustee of the Last Will and Testament
         of
              BELA BARTOK, Deceased,
         to be allowed to resign as such co-
         Executor and co-Trustee.
- - - - - - - - - - - - - - - - - x
```

Pursuant to the order of WILLIAM T. COLLINS, Surrogate, dated the 28th day of March, 1956, at a Surrogate's Court, held in and for the County of New York, at the Hall of Records in said County, the undersigned hereby resigns as co-Executor and co-Trustee pursuant to the authorization granted in said Order and, as resigning Executor and Trustee, does hereby turn over all assets and property in his hands as such co-Executor and co-Trustee to VICTOR BATOR, as remaining Executor and Trustee.

New York, N.Y., May   , 1956.

WITNESS:

_____   _____
                                              Julius Baron

I hereby acknowledge receipt of the aforementioned assets and property.

New York, N.Y., May   ,1956.

WITNESS:

_____   _____
                                              Victor Bator

Fig. 4.3. Signed document dated May __1956 setting forth Dr. Julius Báron's resignation as Co-Trustee of the Bartók Estate.
Source: BSCB Tampa.

Ivan revealed this story to me to make a point. Báron, he felt, had the strength of character to directly confront his post-operative addiction and seek outside help. His willingness to relinquish his Illinois state medical license testified to a personal integrity his friends all recognized as inviolable.

Chapter 4

The decision to leave Chicago in 1956 prompted him to reassess his desire and willingness to continue as co-trustee for the Bartók Estate. Iowa City was one step further removed from New York geographically, requiring additional travel anytime he returned east. Whether for this reason, or from a growing sense of weariness over his recent health challenges, on February 14, 1956, Báron formally resigned as co-trustee. The action was not forced on him. It was his own decision. Some pro forma paperwork that spring made it official. A court order on March 28, 1956, formally revoked the Letters of Trusteeship granted to Báron in the Will, and directed him, as a matter of routine, to surrender all Bartok-related assets to the remaining trustee. Two months later the process was complete. A legal document (Fig. 4.3) certified that he had turned over any Estate property he might have had in his possession. He had never kept in Chicago any property of the Estate, as far as I know. From May 1956 onward the Bartók Trust's management was entirely in the hands of Victor Bator. No one who knew the two Co-Trustees was surprised at this turn of events. Bator had effectively been managing the Estate single handedly since September 1945.

When Klub members and their families spent time together someone always seemed to have a camera on hand, ready to snap spontaneous photos. Francis Bator shared with me his parents' photograph albums from the 1920s and 30s. With his permission I reproduce a sampling here. Dozens of other photographs like this survive, all documenting a family's life in Budapest's prosperous upper middle class.[28] Gyula and Maria Báron figure prominently in these photo albums.

Within this group of friends some relationships were closer. László Raj was his father's best friend, Ivan told me, before he was killed in World War I. His brother Feri, in turn, had been probably Victor Bator's closest friend. (Mrs. Raj, their mother, "was a surrogate mother to me," Ivan reminisced.) Some had known each other since early childhood. Imre Waldbauer and Paul Sebestyén became friends as young boys in school together, as did Bator and Báron. The slight difference in their age meant that, at one point, Victor Bator had been a tutor for both Báron brothers while growing up.[29] Alphons Weiss's great wealth eventually complicated his friendships from earlier days. Neither Francis nor Iván dwelled at any length on the Weiss children their age, even though in Budapest they had often spent time together. Klub members' families could grow apart with time, too.

---

28 After Francis Bator's death in 2018, these photo albums were dispersed among his extended family.
29 Francis Bator, interview with the author, September 24, 2010.

Fig. 4.4. Photographs from Bator family photo albums.

1. Dr. Gyula Báron, on vacation in Nonquitt, Mass., ca. 1954. Photographer: Victor Bator.

2. The Báron family and Bator family vacationing in Europe, ca. 1936–37. Standing, from left, Maria Báron, Gyula Báron, Franciska Bator, Victor Bator, with the two Bator twins, Peter and Paul. Location unknown, possibly Northern Italy or Sweden. Photographer: unidentified.

Chapter 4

3. On vacation in Switzerland. From left, Gyula Báron, Franciska Bator, unknown, Francis Bator, Victor Bator. Photographer: unidentified.

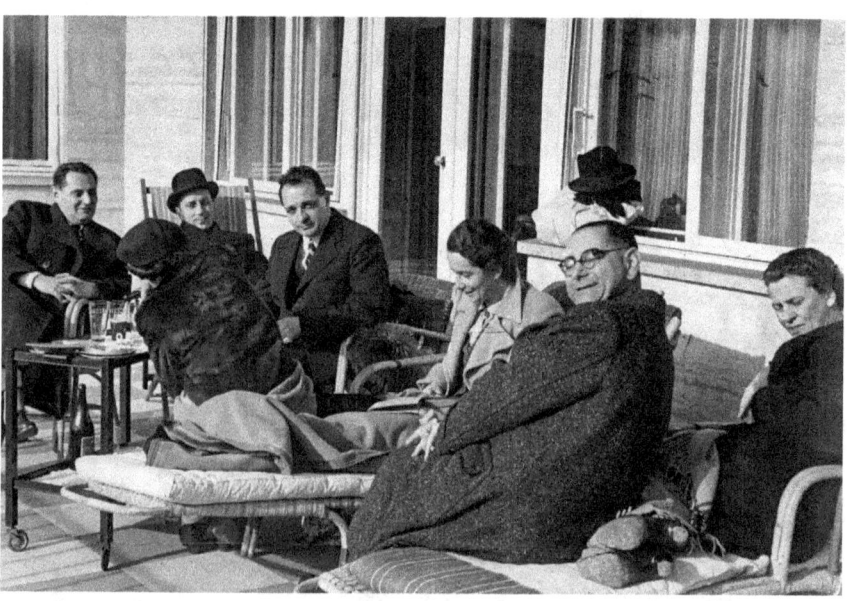

4. Gathering of friends, ca. 1937, on the terrace of the Bators' new home on Gellert Hill, Budapest. Imre Waldbauer at far left. From right, Maria Báron, Gyula Báron, and (in tan coat) Franciska Bator. Woman with back to camera, Isabella Waldbauer. Others not identified. Photographer: Victor Bator.

5. Francis Bator, at left, sailing as a boy on Lake Balaton with the Chatel family, ca. 1937. Photographer: unidentified.

A particular school in Budapest explained a great deal about how these families became more closely knit through their children. The school was tied to the Chatel family, and run by Luigia Chatel, known affectionately to the kids as "Babszi." Francis remembers:

> My godmother's school, called the Chatel Iskola, was in walking distance of the Commercial Bank, where my father had his office. My father would drive to the Margit Island, play tennis in the morning, with famous tennis pro Franzi Schmidt, and I would play with someone else. After that he would drive me to his office, and drop me off at school along the way. Babszi Chatel was the older sister of Andor Chatel.
>
> The Chatel Iskola was a private elementary school, non-denominational, grades 1-4. The circle of friends' children all went there. The Chatels founded the school, and all the Weiss kids—all the Manfréd Weiss descendents' kids—, my brothers and I went there, Ivan and Márta Waldbauer went there, Ferenc Chorin's children went there (Daisy and Erzsébet, his two daughters, and his son Ferenc), and Tamás Vietorisz.[30]

---

30 Francis Bator, interview with the author, January 11, 2013.

Chapter 4

"Most of the people I knew growing up," Francis told me, "came from the prosperous upper middle class." Hungarians will recognize some famous names in their country's history on this list. Chorin (1879–1964), scion of a prominent Hungarian business family, was a member of the upper house of parliament and Vice President of the Commercial Bank, where he worked alongside Victor Bator. His marriage to Daisy Weiss, daughter of Manfréd Weiss, created an empire of manufacturing entities that made their extended family by many magnitudes the wealthiest in Hungary. (The Weiss-Chorin family was "Like the Rockefellers, Guggenheims, and Astors all wrapped up in one," Waldbauer drolly explained.) Chorin's forced capitulation to German occupiers in 1944 drew international attention to Hungary's abasement before the Nazis. Though Jewish, the family had stayed in Hungary to hold their business empire intact, a matter of national economic security. By 1944 the family could no longer ignore the threats to their safety. In what amounted to a forced barter, in exchange for protected passage for 40 members of the family to Portugal and Switzerland Ferenc Chorin ceded to the Nazis the entire business empire. The family escaped. Chorin himself relocated eventually to New York City. (Francis Bator: "He later had an apartment on Park Avenue a few blocks up from where we first lived.")

* * *

In North America, Klub members and their adult children dispersed over a wide geographical area. Imre Waldbauer came to the U.S. after the war, in 1946, and relocated to Iowa City, where he taught violin on the faculty of the University of Iowa until his death from cancer in 1952. Báron and his wife, as we've seen, lived in Chicago. Distance intensified and also attenuated these friendships. Still, they remained deeply connected to one another. "Maybe one instance will show you what membership in the Klub entailed," I was told by Iván. "Somewhere in later years one of the members played away money entrusted to him. Victor was by then rather well to do. Without a word he put his hand in his pockets and paid it off, and the whole matter was covered up. It was as a matter of course."[31]

Béla Bartók, it should be clear by now, was not a member of The Klub. He was ten years older, attended different schools growing up, and did not form social relationships easily in the way that these men did. His contact with certain members of the group came through Imre Waldbauer, one of his oldest musical advocates in Budapest and a longtime colleague at the Liszt Academy.

---

31 Iván Waldbauer, interview with the author, Nov. 29, 2010. He did not divulge the name.

To Imre's son Ivan, reminiscing many years later, these old family histories explain how Victor Bator and Gyula Báron eventually became drawn into Bartók's personal affairs. He put it like this: "Gyula was a periodic visitor to New York, and he usually stayed at Victor's house. He was probably on hand at the time. Bartók trusted him, too—again, as his *friend's* friends. His friend, of course, being my father." Báron was "a natural"—Ivan's words—for the role of Trustee. Dr. Holló's endorsement of the new arrangement is easy to imagine: at the time of the Will's signing Holló was seeing Bartók almost daily as his supervising physician in the hospital. Holló knew them all.

Old ties bind.

Had I not asked, and had Iván Waldbauer and Francis Bator not still been alive, most of this information would have died with them. I've quoted them extensively in this chapter because their perspectives restore some sense of the thickly overlapping relationships that surrounded Bartók and his wife in the Hungarian émigré community immediately upon their arrival in New York City. Knowing that Victor Bator and Imre Waldbauer had been *neighbors* in Budapest, for example, as well as longtime friends, opens a window of fresh understanding into this world, allowing us to see more clearly why Béla Bartók felt so comfortable with Bator in the United States. (Francis: "I remember the Waldbauer Quartet rehearsing in my living room.") Knowing that Bator tutored Gyula Báron when they were both young boys in school together, and that their friendship blossomed over coming decades, through marriage and the addition of other married couples to their close group of friends, likewise explains how they fell in together as co-trustees for Bartók's Estate. They had always done things together. They enjoyed each other's company. Báron's fascination with science and music, and his near-professional skills as a pianist, illuminates an inner logic behind Bartók's decision to add his name as co-trustee—especially when we remember, too, that Ditta Bartók considered Báron as one of her closest friends in America. No matter that he lived in Chicago. He came east often enough to vacation with the Bators.

"Carl, these types of friendships don't exist here in America," Ivan took care to explain to me, sensing my struggles to piece together the jigsaw puzzle of names and relationships he had just laid out. "They're an Old World thing. In countries like Hungary you make your friends when you are in your teens. You make friends for a lifetime. In America you can't afford to do this—the country is too big. You move around a lot and have to keep making new friends."

Musicologists who have spent time in this small corner of the Bartók studies world will remember that Iván Waldbauer worked for Bator for a number of years at the New York Bartók Archives office; he served as an on-staff musicologist for the nascent archive from 1957–66, working there mainly during the

Chapter 4

summers. He helped prepare the first edition of Bartók's Op. 15 songs that Gyula Báron had copied out by hand. He also spent several years assembling what would have been the first thematic catalog of Bartók's music. (A project that never got off the ground due to later litigation.) Neither he nor Bator would have viewed the work arrangement as unusual.

Bator always looked out like this for his friends and the children of those friends. Many of them were able to emigrate to the United States in the 1940s and 50s because of his determination to rescue them from their collapsing country. Charles Szladits (1911–86), son of his former law professor, came to the US in 1949, his journey funded and arranged by Victor Bator, who also coordinated a landing spot for him on the library staff of Columbia University's law school, a position for which the young lawyer amply qualified. Szladits remained in New York to become a leading figure in law librarianship. He spent his career at what is now the Parker School of Foreign and Comparative Law, where he also held a faculty appointment. Deeply loyal to Bator, he agreed to serve on the board of directors for the new Bartók Archives when it launched in 1963, and even, for a while, served behind the scenes as his appointed successor-trustee for the Bartók Estate.[32] Another young man rescued by Bator from post-war economic turmoil was Tamás Vietorisz, who fled from Hungary in 1947 with Bator's financial support. Vietorisz (1926–), still living at the time of this writing, established himself in the US as an eminent economist and engineer after receiving his Ph.D. from M.I.T. As a boy he had been a schoolmate of Francis's at the Chatel Iskola in Budapest; he and Francis would remain lifelong friends who both, as Bruno Nettl might say, "understood."

No story exemplifies the tightness of Klub members' bonds more than the tale of the Waldbauer family's emigration from Hungary. In late summer of 1946 the University of Iowa learned of the famous Hungarian violinist's availability. Paul Rolland at the University of Illinois had contacted Phillip Clapp, head of the Music Department at the University of Iowa, to suggest he look into hiring Waldbauer, his former teacher, who was urgently seeking a way out of Hungary. Clapp pitched the idea to Dean Allin W. Dakin. They decided to make it work. In early September the university sent a cable to Waldbauer offering him an appointment for three years at $4,000/year, starting September 15. Visa and travel arrangements tumbled forward quickly from there. But Waldbauer could not meet such an ambitious schedule; he needed more time to prepare for departure. So he brought in Victor Bator to mediate discussions among the embassies and the university. "Negotiate by telephone professorship

---

32 Szladits served as Successor Trustee for the Bartók Estate from 1963-68; a notarized copy of the legal document appointing him to that role on Feb. 28, 1963, survives in BSCB Tampa.

with my representative Victor Bator," Waldbauer, still in Budapest, cabled the university on October 11. From that point forward Bator acted as Waldbauer's agent, generating correspondence that has been preserved at the University of Iowa's Philip Greeley Clapp collection.[33] Bator offered to travel to Washington to meet with embassy staff if necessary. At one point he called the university president to negotiate salary and a revised start date. He advised the university about the precise form their offer should take in order to meet eligibility requirements for a non-quota visa. Months later, after Waldbauer had arrived in New York, Bator wrote to Dean Dakin on December 17 with final arrangements. "His coming over here was made possible by the fact that I paid his travelling expenses from Budapest by remitting him $500.00. It would be a hardship for him to repay this sum now," Bator explained to his friend's future employer, "when he must go to considerable expense in setting up a new home for himself and his wife and children, who are expected to arrive here in January."[34]

These same months in late 1946 found Bator wading into a variety of tasks for the Bartók Estate, all new to him. He continued negotiations with Boosey & Hawkes to revise the contract for Bartók's music, and decided, with her consent, to send Ditta Bartók back to Hungary, a large undertaking that required, as we have seen, the crafting of critically important legal documents and extensive travel arrangements. Imre Waldbauer finally arrived in Iowa City a few days before the New Year—to the day almost exactly when Ditta Bartók arrived safely home in Budapest.

More than six decades later, Iván Waldbauer remembered with gratitude what Victor Bator had done for his parents. And for him. "The reason I got out," he told me frankly, "is because Victor Bator helped." His mother, Isabella Waldbauer, could not make her way to Iowa City until early April 1947; she had to leave Ivan and his sister in Budapest. Iván spent the immediate post-war years as a pianist on the faculty of the Liszt Academy and, briefly, a piano class instructor at the conservatory in Székesfehérvár. In 1946 he had been appointed soloist for the Hungarian state broadcasting system. Like his parents he needed to navigate US immigration laws if he were to emigrate successfully. Over the summer his parents heard that Tufts College in Boston might be willing to sponsor Iván. On August 11, 1947, in a heartfelt letter, Isabella Waldbauer pleaded with Tufts music chairman Thompson Stone to hire her son. Internal

---

33 I am grateful to Sarah Lucas for directing my attention to this correspondence file and for sharing her copies with me. The Philip Greeley Clapp Papers are preserved in The University of Iowa Archives, Special Collections, The University of Iowa Libraries.
34 Victor Bator, letter to Allin W. Dakin, Administrative Dean, University of Iowa, Dec. 17, 1946. Philip Greeley Clapp Papers.

Chapter 4

correspondence preserved by Tufts shows that the President, Leonard Carmichael, hesitated to hire Ivan because no funds were available.

Enter Victor Bator. The Waldbauers appealed to their friend to advocate for their son. In an extraordinary deal of the sort inconceivable in today's academy, Bator offered to cover a full year of Ivan's salary, $1,500, as long as Tufts would pay for one year at the same rate. On September 18 he laid out his proposal to the President. "I suggest that you extend the appointment of Iván Waldbauer for two years. In order to enable the college to do this, I deposit herewith my own check for the other $1500, covering the salary of Professor Waldbauer for the second year of his appointment. I do this mainly because of my old friendship to the Waldbauers." Knowing the intricacies of the visa process, and assuming that his offer would be met favorably, Bator included with his letter drafts of the cables and embassy letters that should be sent from Tufts over with the President's signature.[35]

The following day, President Carmichael cabled to Budapest with an offer for Iván Waldbauer to teach for 2 years at Tufts College (now University)—a telegram presumably the same one Bator had drafted. Ivan immediately accepted. Thus Iván received a 2-year offer at Tufts, his lifeline out of Hungary. His American career in academia was launched. The position had been crafted for humanitarian reasons; it paid approximately half a regular professor's salary, and in exchange required a roughly half-time commitment of him, with the expectation that he live nearby and actually perform services for the college. A note in the personnel file indicates that in making this offer Tufts was trying to "get this man out of Budapest before the Russians get him." Ivan had been active in the underground, they were told. He was in very real danger for his life.

As it turned out, Ivan stayed at Tufts only for one year. When he discovered that the position was really only half time, and a term appointment at that, he began to look for other work. In 1948 he moved to the New England Conservatory to take a position as Instructor in the piano and music theory departments. But at least he had gotten out.

A rather interesting letter from Báron to Bator, written in 1958, finds the two old friends quietly conspiring to provide financial help to Imre Waldbauer's widow in Iowa City.[36] She was then working at the university hospital as a

---

35 Some 20 letters and documents for the hiring of Iván Waldbauer at Tufts College have been preserved in the university's vertical files (Digital and Special Collections, Tisch Library). I am grateful to librarian Adrienne Pruitt for her help accessing these documents during the coronavirus era.
36 Gyula Báron, letter to Victor Bator, April 10, 1958, sent from Iowa City. Personal collection of Francis Bator. Francis knew her as "Böce" since childhood, and always referred to her that way in our conversations.

nurse's aide. She covered the night shifts from midnight to 8 a.m. Lonely and bored on her off days, which she spent doing housework by herself, she had lately been expressing her unhappiness to friends and family members. Word somehow got back to Bator in New York. He asked Báron for his honest assessment of the situation. Báron in his letter reviews her income and expenses in detail, and speculates about the best path forward for her in retirement. She had been constantly sending financial assistance to her older sister back in Pest. Böce, as she was known to her close friends, should probably stay in Iowa City instead of moving back east. He and his wife were her only Hungarian speaking friends, but all she needed to do was spend three more years in her current job, which was secure, to reach the age of 62; then she could collect Social Security. Leaving for a different job in a new city would be "catastrophic" for her, Báron explained. If Bator wanted to help, send her money to fix her car. Otherwise, he and Maria would continue to look out for her.

They had all been friends for a very long time.

Correspondence: Estate Correspondence with the Bartók Heirs, 1957–63

Of Victor Bator's correspondence with the three Bartók heirs after 1946 only a few dozen letters were found among the papers preserved by Francis Bator, most from the period 1957–63. While limited in number, these letters offer rare insight into the inner workings of the estate at a time when it was experiencing considerable tension. The first letter is reproduced in facsimile to show the form in which most of this correspondence has survived: typed carbon copies on "onionskin" paper, as this type of paper was known at the time. Typically these copies lack the closing signature which would have been on the original letter that went out in the mail.

Estate Correspondence with the Bartók Heirs

Victor Bator, letter to Peter Bartók, May 23, 1957. Typed, 2 p. Onionskin copy. In English. Reproduced in facsimile here.

VB Bator

May 23, 1957

Mr. Peter Bartok
113 West 57th Street
New York, N.Y.

Dear Peter:

Further to my letter of May 21st I would like to point out to you that your father seems to have had a very definite idea about the ultimate destination of his manuscripts. The trust agreement between him on one side and Boosey & Hawkes and George Herzog on the other makes it fairly clear that he did not want his heirs to have the right of free disposition (sale or dispersal). I do not know what his instructions to Boosey & Hawkes and to Herzog were, but it would not have made any sense to go into a complicated trust agreement, had his purpose simply been to follow for the manuscripts the same course as for his copyrights and other worldly belongings.

Whatever his intentions were with the trust-agreement, that arrangement was terminated and dissolved some time before March 1943. On the other hand, in March 1943 he suggested to me personally to take over the manuscripts. At that time he expressed the wish that the manuscripts be kept together as the physical embodiment of his creative work and be preserved as such. He instructed Boosey & Hawkes to deliver them to me and they were in fact handed over to me in my personal physical possession.

At that time, as far as I can remember, I had no information or knowledge about his will and his other possessions, and my office and appointment as holder of the manuscripts had no connection with the will which was then in existence or with the will which ultimately became his last testament.

In fact, my desire and intention to incorporate the manuscripts in a foundation having for its purpose their preservation are motivated by my wish to reconcile my duties as his "alter ego" with regard to the manuscripts with those of Executor of his will and Trustee of the estate. I wish I were not the Trustee. In such case I could negotiate an agreement for the solution of this task entrusted to me by your father, that I do not want to forsake. This way, having several not quite parallel responsibilities, I am in an embarrassing position. I certainly do not want the manuscripts to be exposed to the dangers and losses which occurred in the past to many of his writings and pieces of correspondence which were

> P. Bartok   - 2 -   May 23, 1957
>
> not handled with the minute attention and care which I hope I have succeeded to bring to bear upon them from the beginning of my activities until now.
>
> Yours sincerely,
>
> Victor Bator

Victor Bator, letter to Peter Bartók, June 1, 1957. Typed, 2 p. Onionskin copy. In Hungarian. Translated by Etelka Nyilasi.

June 1st, 1957

My dear Peter,

I am writing to you about the very serious issue of your mother's health and treatment. I am aghast since I heard from you that your Hungarian family is generally of the view that your mother is not ill or not very ill and thus does not require any medical treatment. I cannot recover from the consternation this news has given me and I am not willing to assume the responsibility of not doing anything upon hearing this news.

The treatment and general perception of mental diseases has changed dramatically over the last 10 years, with a lot of progress taking place over the last one, two, three, four, five years. The psychiatrist used by your uncle is either incompetent or your uncle has mis-interpreted what the psychiatrist has said. However, we do not know when the consultation took place, what he said a year or five years ago, and what he would say today.

Dr. Andor Chatel is the most respected internist in Budapest. The correct procedure is for your mother to go and see Dr. Andor Chatel, and he should refer her to a psychiatrist, or any other specialists, and he should be in charge of the final decision regarding her health and treatment. I do not have any trust in Dr. Hajnal since I've heard the treatment he gave your mother during a previous illness. I do not trust a treatment that has probably been devised based on financial aspects: savings and cost avoidance.

I would like to ask that you entrust your mother's treatment to Dr. Andor Chatel. Since she is not fully competent and you are her only child, you have the right to decide what is best for her without any interference from other relatives. You also have the right to instruct your aunt and uncle to take your mother immediately to see Dr. Andor Chatel. In the letter to your uncle and aunt you should also specify that costs are not an issue, that Dr. Andor Chatel will be in charge of billing the costs directly to the Estate and I will make sure that the bill is paid. These costs include Dr. Chatel's fee, the fee of the psychiatrist, medication, and the cost of the institution in which your mother might be temporarily admitted. Your letter should also explain that your mother's disease has dormant periods, in which there are some improvements, but a crisis could happen anytime and getting out of the crisis is much more difficult than preventative long term treatment.

You should also emphasize in your letter that once under the supervision of Dr. Andor Chatel the group of doctors that has examined your mother has reached a final decision, they also need to give a final written report on their diagnosis and treatment plan. I want to consult some US psychiatrists on the diagnosis and treatment. It is hard to know whether Hungarian doctors know about all the progress that has been made in the US, and I want to get the opinion of an American doctor as well.

You can write your letter to Dr. Andor Chatel in English since he speaks fluent English. I would like to ask you to send me a copy of your letter to Dr. Andor Chatel. Please do not postpone taking definite steps towards addressing this important issue.

Many hugs,

To: Mr. Peter Bartok
2727 Palisade Avenue
Bronx, NY

Victor Bator, letter to Peter Bartók, November 9, 1957.
Typed, 2 p. Onionskin copy. In English.

November 9, 1957

Mr. Peter Bartok
113 West 57 Street
New York 19, N.Y.

Dear Peter:

As I told you last night, the accountant and the lawyer are preparing the 10-year report on the finances of the Bartok Estate, income, expenses, etc. Thus, the books and the checks are not available at this moment and it will take about a week before they come back into my office and enable me to account for the expenses of the Estate spent on manuscripts and other maintenance activities.

On account of the above, I am unable to give you now final figures. However, sometime about a year ago, I went through the expenses from that viewpoint and as far as I can remember, almost all payments made by the Bartók Estate in connection with what we usually call "The Bartok Archive" were spent until about a year ago <u>on the manuscripts and other papers which are the property of the Estate.</u>

As you know, the manuscripts and other papers of your father were, at the time of his death, in a fairly neglected physical state. They were mostly in envelopes, all of them in different suitcases, some of them in my possession, others in his own apartment and later carried away from New York by Herzog. At a given time, I realized that it would be contrary to my duties and certainly against the interests of the Estate if I did not do everything to preserve in good condition the manuscripts and other papers of your father. This did not mean their maintenance in the condition in which I took them over in 1943 and later after his death. It has been my duty to put them in a condition where they would resist deterioration and depravation which go with longevity. Most of the paper on which they were written was not of the finest quality but a cheap kind which, without proper care, would deteriorate. Their handling by publishers and interested musicians may also have damaging effect.

In the last six years, we have more or less completed the following tasks: We put every page in a plastic cover and stamped each of them separately to make it impossible for anybody to embezzle them. We put them in bindings. All of them are described, catalogued, indexed in many ways and are being kept in big fire-resistant safes. Quite a lot of work was done in order to identify some of the manuscripts and especially to organize the non-musical manuscripts in a way they have never ever been before your father died. Since all these papers are the property of the Estate, the expenses incurred for that work were paid by the Estate. Further, to eliminate the physical handling of the manuscripts and other papers by interested people, we had them all photographed (negatives, positive copies, microfilm, etc.), then had these photostats bound. That was a costly operation, also. Naturally, the Estate had to pay these expenses, too.

There was a time when the Estate did not have sufficient funds to pay these expenses. At that time, I advanced the money to the Estate for the above expenses. All these advances have been repaid to me, naturally free of interest. On the other hand, many of the expenses were paid by me while the Archive had no separate office and it was located in a room of my office. Such expenses were telephone, light, secretarial, rent, and were paid by me directly.

On account of the above situation, when I started to work on collecting other Bartok mementoes which did not become property of the Estate but my own, the expenses were not always strictly separated. Some of them were paid by the checks of the Estate. I have the feeling that these two amounts will more or less balance each other—that is, the payments made by the Estate which were not strictly spent on Estate property, and my payments spent on Estate property. However, an analysis of the expenses will be made to discover the details.

Now that the Estate has sufficient funds and the work on the manuscripts is about to be completed, the time has come to examine all these facts and figures and to separate the two groups. Should any balance exist in favor of the Estate, I shall pay it into the Estate's account. On the other hand, should a balance result in my favor, I shall ask you, Peter, to repay to me that balance. I do not think that the amount could be substantial either way.

This accounting a posteriori will be done for the period ending December 31, 1957. It is my suggestion that from January 1, 1958, on, payments should be made with checks of the Estate and that they be marked with a capital A or capital B. Capital A will designate those which should be borne by the Estate, and capital B by those which will be necessitated by the existence of the Archive. At the end of every half-year or every year, I would then repay to the Estate the amount spent on the Archive. On the other hand, from January 1, 1958, the Estate will have to pay me all my expenses in connection with administration and a fee we shall have to agree upon.

Please let me know your reaction to the above.

Yours sincerely,

VB/sm

VICTOR BATOR, LETTER TO BÉLA BARTÓK, JR., DEC. 21, 1957.
TYPED, 2 P. ONIONSKIN COPY. ORIGINAL IN HUNGARIAN.
TRANSLATED BY ETELKA NYILASI.

December 21st, 1957

My dear friend,

Please find attached a copy of the letter I sent to Mr. Róbert Palágyi today. The purpose of sending a copy directly to you is merely to allow for easier and faster communication between the two of you in order to consider and discuss it.

There is however an issue in this letter that I would like to bring to your attention. This problem is discussed under point "A" on the third page. I am sure you will notice the level of significance I attribute to the handling of the estate as one single unit in point "A," even though I essentially endorsed you to handle it in 6 countries—while keeping the unity—as if the unity was nonexistent. The reason for this is as follows:

One of the things your father considered when he gave the rights to handling the estate to the trustee named in the will was that he was not sure and could not have been sure whether members of the family would always be in a position to properly handle the copyrights—which make up most of the estate—for the 50 years after the death of the composer. When I write that your father did not know whether members of the family would be in a position to handle the artistic value of the estate in the "best" possible way, I refer to the legal, financial and artistic significance altogether. We are all mortals, subjected not only to the risk of premature death, but also to the physical and spiritual trials of our lives. By having a trustee handle the estate, the quality of the work is assured by the idea that a trustee during his time of service can name a successor who would be intellectually and spiritually compliant with your father's standards and principles. If for some reason a successor would not be named, the court would appoint a new trustee who surely would be from qualified circles. Therefore, on one hand we have the security that a well-chosen trustee means, and on the other the uncertainty of fate that members of the family face.

Therefore when I continue handling the estate as a single unit, I want to assure you that your father's intention is that if for some reason you would not be able to handle the values of the inheritance in those six countries, the handling rights and liability would return to the trustee, who by then would surely not be me but my successor, whom I will name first as co-trustee in the near future. After all, you are much younger than me, and your ability to work will surely outlive mine.

I am happy to hand over the managing rights of the estate in those six countries to you, because in the end who could be a better man for the job than the son of the testator, my late great friend. However, it is very important for me to know that it will not be decided by chance who takes over the managing rights of the estate in those 6 countries if any of the aforementioned unforeseeable events occurred in the next 40 years. It shall not be exposed to the unsupervised dealings of publishers or some bureaucrat's whimsy, but instead, someone should handle it who was appointed according to the final will of your father.

By the way, I hope that by the time I see you at the festivities in Basel we will have all these issues worked out.

Greetings,

Béla Bartók Jr.
45 Daroczi St.
Budapest, Hungary

Victor Bator, letter to Peter Bartók, January 29, 1958.
Typed, 2 p. Unsigned. Onionskin copy. In English.

January 29, 1958

Dear Peter:

After having acted as Executor and later as Trustee of the inheritance of your father and having spent a considerable part of my working time during those twelve years on the problems of the inheritance, your own personal problems and those of your recording company, I realize now that the way of handling all these problems as to procedure has required so much of my time and attention that it became necessary to subject it to some scrutiny, to analyze it, and to try to put it in proportion to the amount of time I can possibly spend on it, and the compensation for the expenses I am incurring in order to do it well. As you will remember, I took over the Estate when the income amounted to a few thousand dollars, no agreement existed between the Estate and Universal Edition, Universal Edition was in a state of paralysis and dissolution, the Hungarian publishers were completely out of touch with the world outside of Hungary, and Boosey and Hawkes had a contract which was not only very unsatisfactory, but also wasn't even abided by them. Today, outside of the controversy regarding the first 21 compositions published originally by Hungarian firms and the controversy and the conflict with the Hungarian Government Agencies, there is a more or less well-regulated situation. This would imply or entail less work for me, but for the fact that, on account of the tremendous increase in the acceptance of Bartok music, of income, and supervisory work necessitated thereby, I find myself busier than ever with Bartok matters.

Under such conditions, I cannot possibly continue as Trustee unless an agreement is concluded with you, on your own behalf and that of your mother, from whom you have broad power of attorney, that will not give adequate financial compensation for the work I am doing, but at least will carry the burden of the office, travel, and other expenses.

I am perfectly willing to resign. Naturally, in that case you will have to retain a good attorney because most of the activities require knowledge of law, understanding of legal problems and accounting, most of which activities have been taken care of by me with the help of my legal and business training. It is my suggestion that we conclude an agreement in regard to the administration of the Estate from January 1, 1958, as per the enclosed draft.

Yours sincerely,

Mr. Peter Bartok
2727 Palisade Avenue
Bronx, New York

[attached is a two-page draft agreement proposing specific conditions and financial arrangements necessary to retain Bator in the position]

Victor Bator, letter to Peter Bartók, March 7, 1962. Typed, 2 p. Onionskin copy. In English.

Dear Peter,

I confirm receipt of your letter of March 1st.

My suggestion that you come and see me has nothing to do with the accounting. Whatever information you will want to get about accounts you will have to obtain it from Helphand; he has the data, he is preparing it. The purpose of my proposed conference was the same as of previous invitations, that is, to bring you up to date in Estate matters, to have the benefit of your views as well as those of your Mother's on problems which come up for decision. However, this time I had also another subject matter in mind and there is no obstacle in setting it forth by writing.

The work connected with the administration and management of the Estate is not decreasing. This is contrary to my expectations. There are daily problems to be attended to and be settled, requests for licences come in, demands for assistance which are beneficial to the Estate increase in number. All these are connected with expenses about which decisions need to be made on the spot. Last but not least, I have to check on the publishers, watch the records of sales and performances, and many other facets of the work of the publishers if they do not come up to expectation or if some of the works stay behind; good management requires that I inquire, investigate and put pressure on those whose duty it is to bring about more sales, more performances, more recordings, etc.

This being so, what I hoped for and expected, decrease of my work, has not happened. On the other hand, I do not want to continue to spend the major part of my working time on the daily management of the Estate—what I have been doing until now and am still doing—even if I were well paid for it.

Would you be willing to undertake this management job? There is a certain field in which the law obliges me to make decisions myself, but outside of that reserved field I have the intention to hire a person who could do that job. This would be a very interesting, intellectual, inspiring field of activity, no second grade person could possible do it and therefore, I could not find a suitable person to that without substantial fee.

My suggestion is that you take over this job from me and whatever salary your Mother will find appropriate, it will be paid. This arrangement would have another advantage. Since expenses will be first checked upon and passed by you as manager, you would have opportunity to express approval or disapproval before the payment is made and hence, the periodic accountings would not create problems or retroactive approval or disapproval where hindsight plays a strong role. Accounting problems would be restricted to such payments which would be made contrary to your advice.

All the above is a general idea and requires further careful thinking before it can be put into execution. My mind is open to consider any other kind of solution. That is the reason why I wanted to discuss this project personally, but perhaps it is just as well your read it now in a more tangible form and let me know what your response is. Needless to say, I would like to begin with a new system very soon, thus if you refuse to take over that work I will have to look for another suitable manager.

Incidentally, I have a very good special secretary who assists me in the Bartók Estate matters, who knows it thoroughly and therefore, the temporary problem of take-over could be solved without too much great difficulties.

Yours sincerely,

Mr. Peter Bartók
Bartók Records
111 W. 57th Street
New York, N.Y.

Victor Bator, letter to Peter Bartók, January 30, 1963.
Typed letter, 2 p. Carbon copy.

Dear Peter,

I have your letter of January 28, as well as your letters of January 10 and January 17. All of your letters overlook certain fundamental facts which have been brought to your attention before, but which I am bringing to your attention again in the hope that you at length understand the considerations under which the trust under your father's will must operate.

In the first place, I have received notification that your mother had revoked the power of attorney which she had heretofore given you, and, therefore, I must deal with you not on the basis of your being your mother's attorney-in-fact but on the basis that you are the remainderman of the trust under your father's will. Legally, you have no interest in the income from the trust and I can only look to your mother for requests and instructions with regard to income. It follows, therefore, that I am not under any obligation to, nor could I properly, pay you any income from the trust under your father's will.

In the second place, so far as payments to your mother are concerned, you should recall that Surrogate DiFalco specifically referred to this matter in his opinion in the litigation which you commenced, to set aside the accounting decree. In his opinion, Surrogate DiFalco reiterated what has long been the law of New York that payments of income to beneficiaries living behind the Iron Curtain may be made by a trustee only to the extent that the trustee is satisfied that the beneficiary will receive the benefit of such income payments. This principle has been my guide in making remittances to your mother, and, in my judgment, further remittances to her in excess of the amounts now being sent would not be justified in the light of all the circumstances.

The considerations which underlie the rule of the New York courts regarding payments to beneficiaries living behind the Iron Curtain also apply in equal force to instructions issued by income beneficiaries living behind the Iron Curtain with regard to any payments to be made out of income even if such payments are directed to be made to persons in the United States. On the basis of the material now available to me, I do not feel justified in making any payments to you on the basis of your mother's instructions, coming as they do from Hungary.

You speak in the first paragraph of your letter of expensive litigation. I should bring to your attention that it was not I who commenced the expensive litigation which concluded unsuccessfully for you and which imposed very heavy expenses upon the estate. As a lawyer in Hungary for many years, I came to know the perils and expenses of litigation and I have never engaged in any unnecessary litigation.

I am pushing forward as rapidly as possible with the completion of the accounting to which you refer. It will be necessary in this accounting, in contrast to the prior informal accountings, to go into a number of questions some of which you yourself raised in the proceeding which you brought to set aside the former accounting. Included among these questions is the one which Surrogate DiFalco himself raised in his opinion as to whether all of the payments received by the trust from performances of your father's works should be treated as income or whether part of such payments should be treated as principal. These and other problems that have to be dealt with are not simple. I have no desire at all to postpone the day on which the accounting is filed; rather I am bending every effort to see that the accounting is filed promptly.

Yours sincerely,

Mr. Peter Bartók
Bartók Records
200 West 57th Street
New York 19, N.Y.

Estate Correspondence with the Bartók Heirs

Victor Bator, letter to Peter Bartók, January 30, 1963. Typed, 1 p. Carbon copy. Unsigned. Accompanied by a pretyped reply letter for Peter Bartok to sign and return, signaling his acceptance of the offer to serve the new Archive's board of trustees.

January 30, 1963

Dear Peter,

The Bartók Archives will be transformed now into an independent organization administering everything that is now being held by the Archives. The new institution will be called "Bartók Archives" and will have 5 or 6 trustees. I shall be one, one of my sons will be one, Dr. Charles Szladits will be the third, probably a member of the law firm of Davis, Polk, Wardwell, Sunderland and Kendel will be the fourth, and I hope that Paul Lang will accept to be the fifth. I also hope that you will join and that will make up the members of the Board of Trustees.

With best regards,

Yours sincerely,

Mr. Peter Bartók
Bartók Records
200 West 57th Street
New York 19, N.Y.

[On an adjacent page, just the following sentence and a blank signature line are found. These pages, signed by each trustee, were designed to be forwarded as a group to New York State Regents for registration with the Secretary of State's office as a non-profit organization. Peter Bartók did not sign his copy.]

I hereby agree to be appointed and serve as Member of the Board of Trustees of the Bartók Archive.

_____

Peter Bartók
January 31, 1963

Chapter 5

The Early Years of the American Bartók Estate, 1945–53

> The communists succeeded in destroying the Archives.
> The Hungarians didn't want anything to be in New York.
>
> —Francis Bator, 2012

> I have never been, am not now, and never expect to be interested in the legal shenanigans connected with the turbid story of Bartók, the Bartók family, and Estate. I leave these for History to eventually record.
>
> —Tibor Serly, 1975

In 1981 *The New York Times* published a Page 1 story about the history of the Bartók Estate. Its timing was inspired by the forthcoming decision in Surrogate's Court over whether to award Peter Bartók $1.3 million in legal fees and expenses for his pursuit of claims against the Estate. The reporter, Edith Evans Asbury, reviewed the Estate's history and the Trust's origination in Béla Bartók's Will. She mentioned in a general manner several of Peter's complaints, including the fight over whether the Stefi Geyer concerto manuscript belongs to the Estate or the Archives, and his allegation that the Bator sons were at fault for dragging out lawsuit. She included background information that few readers could have known, using Peter as her main source, supplemented by historical facts and perspectives she was able to ferret out from litigation documents preserved in Surrogate's Court.[1]

Despite the reporter's honest effort to summarize the litigation and its turbulent history, no one close to the Estate was happy. Even the title of the article seemed to take sides: "22-Year Battle By Son of Bartok Over Estate Is Nearing Decision." Within days both Peter Bartók and Francis Bator leapt into action, one from his home in Florida, the other from his home in Massachusetts. Separately they wrote long letters to the editor, pointing out the injury that had been done to the truth. Throughout the Estate's history, Peter asserted, claims had been presented against him. He had to defend himself. In a follow-up letter written one month later he repeated his points. To emphasize his continued objection to the news article he included for the Editor's use a prepared

---

[1] Edith Evans Asbury, "22-Year Battle by Son of Bartok Over Estate Is Nearing Decision," *The New York Times*, March 23, 1981.

statement marked "For Release" that lists further clarifications.² He vigorously disputed the statement that Suchoff had been chosen as successor trustee with his consent, and took exception to the declaration that it was he who had continued to press the suit after Bator's death. Quite the contrary, he explained. At fault were the attorneys representing his mother, who refused to settle. Sentence by sentence he picked apart the article.

When I met with him for the first time at his home outside Boston, Francis Bator showed me his own letter of rebuttal to the *Times* editor, a faded photocopy of which he had saved in his files for almost three decades. "In the end my brothers and I decided not to send it," he told me. "We saw no point in provoking Peter further." In that letter he objected to the reporter not doing her homework by reaching out to them. "The first that my brothers and I knew of the Times story was when we read our papers on Monday morning… (A senior partner of Davis Polk Wardwell, and two professors at Harvard University, we are not especially hard to find.)" Had she made inquiries, he wrote,

> she would have discovered that this is a pathetic story of an unhappy young man, who engaged in a pointless 24-year vendetta, the net outcome of which was to generate a lot of lawyers' fees, and to malign a man who had devoted extraordinary energy to the enhancement of the estate in an attempt to establish a national institution in Bela Bartok's name, whose purpose would have been to honor Peter Bartok's father's work, and to enrich musical scholarship.

In support of this statement he quoted from court opinions that fully exonerated his father. "The courts have rejected all of the substantial claims," he averred. He and his brothers had considered sending a Letter to the Editor of the *Times* for publication, just to straighten out the story. "However, experience in these matters suggests that the truth will never catch up. Moreover, it is very likely that a response on our part would merely stimulate Peter Bartok into a further bout of publicity-seeking activity at my dead father's expense." Instead, he indicated, he would write privately. What the newspaper had just published about the Estate's history, he told the Editor plainly, "was a thoroughly irresponsible piece of journalism and wholly out of character for *The New York Times*."³

---

2   Copies of these letters found their way into the Tibor Serly papers at Columbia University, suggesting that Peter circulated them to those he considered friendly to his cause at the time.
3   Francis Bator, letter to *The New York Times*, March 1981. Copy furnished to the author by Francis Bator. Because neither his nor Peter Bartók's rebuttal letters made it into print—one by design, the other noted but ignored by *Times* editorial staff—the original article went uncorrected.

Its flaws notwithstanding, the *Times* article stands to this day as one of only a handful of public-facing news reports to have been written about the Bartók Estate's litigation. Shortly after it ran the Surrogate denied Peter Bartók's claim, another in a long string of defeats for Bartók's youngest son. Surrogate Marie Lambert ruled that Peter was not entitled to legal fees because he was not a lawyer; even if he was a lawyer, she explained, he was not entitled to fees from the Bartók Estate.[4]

By the 1970s as many as 15 law firms had become involved in litigation over the Bartók Estate, on both the plaintiff side and the defense side. Those firms represented parties in Budapest, Boston, New York, Basel, London, Vienna, and Homosassa. In any litigation stretching over such a spectacularly long period, from 1958 to 1985, inflection points can be seen: important judicial decisions, sudden changes in an heir's status or position, involvement of new parties, or external events. Below I identify some of these inflection points and critical moments in the Estate's early history. (Its later history, post 1967, will have to await separate treatment.) To understand why so much bitterness consumed the Bartók Estate we must turn back to the years 1948, 1951, 1958, and 1961. Long before the first lawsuit was filed, the seeds for conflict had already been sown.

* * *

Critically important to the premise of this and the next chapter are the hundreds of pages of original Estate correspondence that Francis Bator saved in his home in Massachusetts as a memorial of his father's involvement in the Bartók Estate. Highlights from those letters are published throughout this book. I conducted extensive oral history interviews with Francis Bator and Benjamin Suchoff while they were still alive. Specifically and generally, those interviews inform the following pages. Thousands of pages of legal documents survive in New York State Surrogate's Court from decades of hearings, depositions, petitions, motions, preliminary rulings, and legally-binding intermediate decisions by justices. "The entire history of the Bartók Estate is in the Surrogate's Court records," Suchoff told me. Fortunately, earlier court decisions already took this mass of information into account. These court decisions sifted through the accusations and hyperbole to establish relevant facts, yielding a series of legal decisions that confirm an account of the Estate's management that bears little resemblance to the darkly criminal version Peter Bartók has propagated through the years. Finally, we have as evidence Victor Bator's own extensive analysis of

---

4   "Bartók's Son Loses Plea on Court Fees," *The New York Times*, March 27, 1981.

Chapter 5

the Estate's history up to 1960, which he documented in a massive, 310-page typed Memorandum intended to serve as a factual guide for the legal teams involved in the first litigation of 1959–61. Excerpts from Bator's Memorandum are published in this book for the first time.

As a group these documents force us to reconsider what we thought we knew about the Bartók Estate and its troubled history. My own fascination with this topic, I might as well admit up front, began when I first realized that almost everything I had heard about Victor Bator's management of the Bartók Estate was wrong, and that he had been the victim of decades of disparagement and slander by a bitter, frustrated Peter Bartók, abetted by communist agencies and their lawyers who had their own reasons for challenging Bator. Peter Bartók had sixty years to tell his side of the story. He told it often.[5] Musicologists and musicians, eager for any scraps of information, curious about the causes of the Estate's well-known troubles, drank it in. It played into our own grievances about lack of access to Bartók's manuscripts and unpublished letters, and fed our natural human fascination with family disfunction. Surely someone must be at fault for this mess? Collective imagination supplied the name of a long-dead trustee. A rich oral tradition of stories did the rest. *Victor Bator didn't trust Hungarians* ran a common theme. Or *He sent his three sons to college on proceeds from the Estate*, a comment I overheard spoken with conspiratorial seriousness at a Bartók conference in Budapest in 1995. (Amazed, I believed it at the time.) Still other allegations of criminal misconduct got laid at Bator's door: *Bator tried to steal the manuscript of the Stefi Geyer concerto. He robbed the heirs of 3/4 of the Estate's income. He didn't present an accounting of the Estate for the first ten years. He refused to pay for the viola concerto manuscript when it came up for sale through a dealer in Switzerland. He let Peter Bartók and Ditta Bartók starve by not paying them income from the Estate.* Or these: *Bator claimed that Bartók's manuscripts actually belonged to him. He set up the Archive so he could donate the manuscripts and*

---

5   Among the print sources that express Peter Bartók's views on the Estate's history are: Stephen Wigler, "Composer Bela Bartok's Legacy of Litigation," *Orlando Sentinel*, Nov. 27, 1983; James Roos, "Bartók's Son Recalls Life With a Master Composer," *The Miami Herald*, June 30, 2002; Carolyn Russo, "Dad's Music Was a Lullaby For Me," *The Tampa Bay Times*, October 13, 2005; Paul Hume, "Decision Expected Soon in Suit By Bartók Son Over Estate, *The Washington Post*, March 24, 1981; and *The New York Times* article from 1981 discussed above. Earlier sources include Fritz Kuttner, "Der Katalog des Bartók-Archives in New York City," *Die Musikforschung* 21/1 (Jan-March 1968): 61–63; and Ruffy, "The Dispute Over Bartók's Will." Kuttner, to his credit, reported an update the following year that shows his awareness of recent legal decisions (*Die Musikforschung* 22/1 [Jan.-March 1969]: 75–76). Direct expressions of Peter Bartók's views can be found in his own writings. Among these must be included the Estate history published on the Bartók Records website (https://bartokrecords.com/articles/bela-bartoks-manuscripts); various passing comments in his book *My Father*; and the reviews of the Estate's history he has placed on deposit at the Sacher Stiftung in Basel.

take a tax deduction for himself. And on and on. As musicologists we weren't warned away, in so many words, but as a group we certainly intuited that any investigation into the Estate's history would be thwarted immediately by Peter himself, still very much alive, and still making decisions (after 1985) about whether or not to authorize or license propagation of any previously unpublished materials. No point in provoking him.

Somfai, Tallián, and an earlier generation of Hungarian scholars experienced different sorts of impediments, even more frustrating to their research goals, in the 1960s and 70s, when Suchoff was Trustee. György Kroó spent two months at the Archive in January and February 1968, a rare degree of access for a Hungarian scholar in those days.[6] One day while he was working, the FBI knocked on the door, asking questions about him. "You should have seen him," Suchoff remembered. "He was as white as a sheet." The agent soon left, apparently satisfied that Kroó posed no threat to national security. "György was relieved." Shortly after Kroó's visit the boom dropped: Suchoff, under advisement of his attorney, who was worried about litigation exposure, put a stop to most outside visitors.[7] After Victor Bator's death Peter Bartók actively policed Suchoff's actions, intent on keeping all outsiders away from his father's manuscripts and letters. Access grew more limited. The practical requirements of his job as a high-school music teacher for the Hewlett-Woodmere Public School system deterred Suchoff from hosting long-term visitors at the Archive. He was typically available only in late afternoons, on weekends, or during holidays, including summers. From 1965–78 he supervised the school district's music programs as Director, a full-time administrative position out on Long Island. In the face of outside commitments like these, Suchoff remained admirably devoted to building the Archives' musicological profile through further publications of Bartók's folk music studies and other writings. One can read Elliott Antokoletz's overview of the New York Bartók Archive's history, published in 2012, and see the distinguished Bartók scholar carefully avoiding the quicksand; his account remains resolutely positive. He emphasizes the achievements of Suchoff during his tenure as Successor-Trustee, including the folk song publications and the *Béla Bartók Essays* volume (1976).

---

6   Suchoff, letter to Francis Bator, March 23, 1968 (BSCB Tampa). Suchoff wrote to Francis asking him to allocate extra funding to Ida Kohler for the supervision and hours she spent helping Kroó on site at the Archives. Kroó's visit itself was the product of years of on-again, off-again diplomatic negotiations between Bator, Dille, and the embassy staffs of both countries.

7   László Somfai was in the middle of a multi-month research visit on site in 1968 when Suchoff felt compelled for legal reasons to discontinue his access to the Archives. Suchoff's attorney worried about the ramifications of Somfai's research and the likelihood of it contributing to further claims against the Bator sons by Peter Bartók (Suchoff, interview with the author, June 19, 2002). Extensive documentation for Somfai's interrupted research residency has been preserved in BSCB Tampa.

Chapter 5

It's easy to lose sight of those achievements amid the deepening muck of litigation and conflict that swamped the Estate by the mid-1960s. Peter Bartók, still in New York, became consumed by the litigation. His career sputtered, then stalled. Because he and Bator were physically located in New York, and Suchoff was, too, most of the legal dramas played out in New York Surrogate's Court. Peter voiced his opinions among friends and sympathizers. People were inclined to believe him. He was, after all, Bartók's son. Greater skepticism greeted him from the lawyers and judges who encountered him in court proceedings, however. What intrigued them about Peter Bartók was his dogged determination to represent himself in all matters. How many people, after all, would even consider wading into a lawsuit with no legal representation? Especially when the opposing attorneys were from Sullivan and Cromwell? Other attorneys across the United States snap to attention when dealing with Sullivan and Cromwell. Peter didn't. He stubbornly refused to hire his own counsel. He always appeared *pro se*. (The exception was in the first litigation of 1959–61, where he was represented by Barbara Zinsser.) He couldn't afford attorneys, he claimed. He had to work full-time on his own defense. By purchasing law textbooks and studying relevant statutes and case law, he taught himself what he needed to know. He subscribed to the *New York Law Journal*. He purchased the standard reference volumes on copyright law. He learned how to file complaints in court. "They all said he could have been a good law clerk," Suchoff told me. Year after year, in hearings and in court, Peter sat by himself with no legal representation, while attorneys from one of America's most venerable firms sat on the other side of the table representing the Bartók Estate and Archives, and still other New York firms represented the Hungarian government. It was a spectacle the court didn't see very often. As one bemused judge remarked in 1971:

> At these hearings the parties and their counsel were afforded the fullest possible latitude in the presentation of their proofs, a latitude which this referee deemed particularly necessary in light of Peter Bartók's representation of himself. I am constrained to observe that Peter Bartok's efforts on his own behalf were conducted with unusual skill hardly to be expected from a layman. Although the latitude afforded to Peter Bartok in particular may well have tended to enlarge the record at these hearings, at least it can be said without doubt that he has received his day in court without discernable disadvantage because of the absence of counsel.[8]

---

8   Milton D. Goldman, Referee's Report, May 14, 1971. New York Surrogate's Court.

With no lawyer by his side to guide him to reasonable solutions, or to speak plainly to him of his options, Peter Bartók plunged ahead throughout the 1960s and 70s, intransigent, always guided by his own North Star. Whether or not to continue battling on wasn't a difficult decision. No one was billing him. Why quit? He footed his own costs, hence his eagerness to recoup them later in the litigation's life cycle. Setbacks and judicial decisions against him only stiffened his resolve. He would occasionally consult with lawyers in New York, but he didn't retain them.[9] They told him things he didn't want to hear. His many letters from this period express profound distrust for the legal profession. Lawyers dithered. Lawyers ran up fees. Lawyers misled him. Judges were in on it, too: their inertia allowed the litigation to plod along. A defining feature of his crusade was its slow descent into paranoia, which in the end left him, as it must, further alone.

The writings of Victor Bator reveal a lucid, bracing intelligence that instantly reassures. There is no question whose is the more reliable guide to events. Bator's letters, lectures, and other writings offer an additional advantage: he was uniquely positioned at the very center of the Estate's activities. His business correspondence shows us the history of the Estate as it's taking place, in engaging and lively prose, bristling with facts and, when necessary, lengthy explanations. Readers of this book can judge for themselves. "My father was a wonderful letter writer," Francis told me. He was right. Some allowances should be made for the polarizing political atmosphere of the Cold War, which gave a sharp edge to Bator's prose during those years. A marked contrast can be observed in Peter Bartók's letters and other writings, which even in the 1960s infrequently dwell on communism or politics of any sort.[10] From the beginning, for Peter, this battle was more personal—truly, a vendetta. He felt Bator had tried to rob him of his inheritance. For Bator, in comparison, it was always about fidelity to Bartók's wishes, and about keeping Béla Bartók's legacy free from the grasping hands of communism.

When I told Francis some of the things that I'd heard repeated about his father, he was incensed. "Do people in your field even know who my father

---

9   Paul Sacher grew concerned about Peter Bartók's refusal to hire attorneys. He once offered to pay for Peter to obtain first-rate legal counsel in New York in the later 1960s. It didn't work. The attorney, Irving Moskowitz, met with Peter Bartók several times, but Peter never returned, having not liked the advice he received, and uncomfortable accepting Sacher's largesse. Moskowitz was convinced that Peter's commitment to acting as his own lawyer had drawn out the litigation. Peter, he concluded, rather enjoyed being a martyr. Moskowitz, letter to Paul Sacher, Nov. 3, 1967 (Paul Sacher Correspondence, PSS Basel).

10 Peter Bartók prepared two confidential documents on the history of the Bartók Estate that he deposited in the Paul Sacher Stiftung to accompany the collection of his father's manuscripts and letters. Though their content is highly subjective, the documents have their uses for later scholars, chiefly as a way of verifying certain events. I am grateful to Peter Hennings for granting me permission to review them in 2018.

Chapter 5

was?" He sharply rebutted the notion that he and his brothers had gone to college on funds their father stole from the Bartók family. "Are you kidding?!!" he exclaimed. "My father didn't need that money! Why would he have done that?!" He was incredulous. His disgust with Peter Bartók rekindled—he assumed Peter was behind these allegations—, Francis encouraged me to settle back in my chair while he told me about his father, and about his father's troubled relationship with Béla Bartók's youngest son. He patiently started at the beginning. The earlier chapters of this book owe themselves to those many conversations. Now we turn to the less pleasant parts of the story.

Ben Suchoff lived through the entire lifespan of the litigation. He had known Peter Bartók since 1954, and he became directly involved in defending the Estate after 1968. He, too, felt that its story was worth preserving. He remembered pitching a book to the University of California Press in the 1990s. "I was planning to call it *The Rise and Fall of the Bartók Estate*. But when they learned what it would be about they said no. It's all law, they told me, and not musicology. 'We don't have a legal division.' That's what they said."[11] He drifted away from the idea. He decided instead to leave his extensive personal papers to the University of South Florida in the hope of inspiring a Center for Bartók Studies in North America.[12] Fortunately, I recorded two days of interviews with him at his office in Florida in 2002. While Successor Trustee of the American Bartók Estate and Trust, until it was completely unwound from litigation in 1985, Suchoff was properly professional in that role; he framed his actions within the boundaries set by attorneys, litigation, and New York state law. His personal lawyer Shirley Thau stood by his side for the entire period. He took in stride the slings and arrows hurled at him by a grievance-filled collective of musicologists, musicians, plaintiff's attorneys, and especially Peter Bartók. Such stings came with the job. Many wished him to be something he could not be. They wanted a helpful archivist. Instead they found a Trustee, whose actions were defined by law and the Uniform Trust Code, his primary duty not to aid scholars but to fructify the Estate and care for its beneficiary. The musicological stings hurt most, because he had always viewed himself as part of the scholarly community; he had, in fact, written the first American doctoral dissertation on Bartók's music. Musicology was his home. Like a longtime faculty member appointed as dean, he regretted that his new position forced him to say no to so many requests.[13] To serve as court-appointed Trustee for Bartók's

---

11 Suchoff, interview with the author, June 19, 2002.
12 A finding aid to the collection can be found at https://digital.lib.usf.edu/SFS0032063/00001. The collection is preserved in the library of the Tampa main campus of the University of South Florida.
13 Asked about this sensitive topic, Suchoff told me had had thoroughly enjoyed his days as Curator of the Bartók Archives, 1954–67, when he could help everyone who came through the doors

American Estate required a thick skin. It also ensured that in Hungary, where no cultural tradition of trusteeship existed, he could be viewed by some as an interloper. (He was aware of that perception.) Those suspicions eased with time, though they never entirely disappeared. "I had established a personal reputation by my books," he told me many years later. "People knew that I wasn't a greedy trustee. I was also a musicologist! And a teacher. That was very important as far as Hungary was concerned."

Suchoff regularly attended American Musicological Society meetings in the 1990s and early 2000s. He and Antokoletz would convene Bartók specialists and paper presenters at these conferences for spontaneous dinners at local restaurants. These were some of my earliest memories of the Bartók studies field. Many years later I realized that in all my conversations with Benjamin Suchoff he had never said a single bad word about Victor Bator. I should have paid attention more closely.

* * *

The year 1951, Victor Bator felt, changed everything for the Estate. Before that year "everything was informal" about his relationships with the three heirs; their individual activities were varied and mutually supportive. "There had been undisturbed harmony within the family," he wrote in his Memorandum, "also between the family and me." The rapidly shifting political environment in Hungary from 1947–51, however, permanently reset the foundation of their working relationships with each other. Suddenly two heirs, including the beneficiary of Béla Bartók's trust, found themselves locked up behind the Iron Curtain in a brutally repressive political state.

When the communist regime in Budapest began to take interest in Béla Bartók for its own reasons, whatever the heirs and Estate did or thought with regard to Bartók's music became politicized by default. The consequences were fatal to the harmony that had existed. Skirmishes throughout the 1950s put the heirs and the Trustee on a collision course that led, eventually, to warfare. Fought out of sight through courts and through lawyers, these troubles brought considerable tension to the heirs: by the mid-1960s a rupture developed between

---

to do research. "As Curator, it was another life. I had personal contact with people. Conductors, composers, pianists, musicologists, students who came to the archive. We talked . . . it was just wonderful for me. To share with them the things I was learning myself about Bartók. I had no responsibility [for legal matters]. Except to build that archive and make it better. And to write books. I relished it thoroughly." After his appointment as Trustee he recognized that he missed the cordial friendships his earlier, public facing role had given him. Suchoff, interview with the author, June 19, 2002.

Chapter 5

Peter and his mother that would never heal. Bator, committed to opposing the spread of communism, especially in his homeland, dug himself in. His Somme, his Flanders would be the battles with communist agencies over ownership to the copyrights of 21 works published by Hungarian publishers. Heat from those battles touched Béla Jr., as we will see in Chapter 6. Bator energetically fought to bring control of all Bartók copyrights under a single umbrella. He *knew* they belonged to the Estate. Bartók's Will said so. He had talked about these matters with the composer himself.

Peter Bartók Establishes Himself in the United States. Bartók Records is Born

After the war Peter Bartók took up residence in greater New York City. He was newly discharged from military service. Six weeks after returning home he watched his father die in the hospital, a stunning personal blow. Family friends, including the Bators, Kecskemétis, and the Hollós, offered him practical and emotional support in those difficult days in late 1945; they helped him with his mother, too, who had fallen into a state of profound depression that she could not shake off. For the U.S. Navy Peter Bartók had served as an Electrician's Mate in the Canal Zone. There he worked in the Navy's electric shop, repairing and maintaining equipment. He developed severe asthma while in Panama, requiring hospitalization and, eventually, a medical discharge. Correspondence with his father and mother during his nineteen months of service is filled with parental worries about his health and safety, in addition to expressions of lively curiosity about his experiences.[14] Béla Bartók had his own personal history with asthma back in Budapest. He sympathized and offered paternal advice. Peter traced the asthma's likely source to the blue smoke which filled the electronic shop from all the soldering taking place. Asthma would affect him his entire life. His later decision to relocate away from the Northeast Corridor to a relatively remote and quiet region of Florida was driven in part by his desire to get away from air pollution. "I couldn't breathe the air in New York," he told an *Orlando Sentinel* reporter in 1983. "It was so brown."[15]

During the war he earned his American citizenship. Military service in those days offered an automatic pathway to naturalization, subject to certain terms and conditions. While in Panama Peter took advantage of this arrangement. He served sufficiently long in the armed forces to meet the requirements. He became an American citizen on October 26, 1944, in a ceremony on base in

---
14 Many of these letters are reproduced in full in *My Father*, 274–327.
15 As quoted in Stephen Wigler, "Composer Bela Bartok's Legacy of Litigation."

Ancón, Panama. Neither of his parents had yet gone through this process; they still kept their Hungarian citizenship. This distinction along citizenship lines would have lasting effect on the Estate's subsequent history.

Just 21 years old in 1945, like multitudes of other servicemen Peter Bartók decided to take advantage of the U.S. government's generous post-war education subsidies. Through Roosevelt's new GI bill he enrolled in college courses free of charge. For three and a half years he took courses at the Pratt Institute, known for its science and engineering programs and its proud tradition of vocational training. Pratt, located in Brooklyn some three miles southeast of Manhattan, experienced a large wave of GI enrollment after the war. It also had a campus in Manhattan. There Peter explored his interests in radio engineering and electronics. He didn't amass enough credits to receive a degree, but these courses gave him advanced electronics training and other skills he could use in his future. Contact with collegiate life yielded a side benefit, too: acclimatization to American culture, and ongoing practice reading and writing in English as part of his studies. The GI Bill made available modest living stipends to veterans who enrolled in approved programs of study. During these first years after the war Victor Bator, acting in loco parentis, reached into his own pockets to make sure Peter stayed solvent financially, just as he was doing for Ditta. By 1947 he was able to start making small periodic distributions of Estate income to them both. Between government checks and the occasional check from the Estate, Peter carved out a humble living in New York after the war, enough to establish himself, at least. His circumstances would soon change dramatically.

New York Surrogate's Court issued letters of trusteeship certifying Bator and Báron in their new roles on January 23, 1946. Under United States law trusteeship carries a strong "burden of care" expectation, as discussed above in Chapter 3. Ditta's health collapse meant that Bator needed to step in immediately to support her. He had no time to work his way into the trustee position; before the Will was even filed for probate he had already been compelled to make decisions on her behalf. The dynamics of their trustee/beneficiary relationship got established immediately. Bator assumed his natural position as a strong, capable executive figure who wielded authority with ease.

As the Co-Trustees and beneficiaries lived into their new roles in those first months and years, the accumulating impressions they gained of each other prepared them for their shared future. They were bound to each other by law, and, through that connection, to the expressed wishes of Béla Bartók, whose legacy they all wished, in their ways, to honor and serve. Ditta Bartók, for the time being, was helpless and utterly dependent on the care of others. The relationship between Peter Bartók and the Trustee in New York was shaped by differences in age and socioeconomic status that gave Bator authority well beyond the legal powers vested in him by his deceased friend. Bator occupied a commanding position in the Hungarian émigré community. By almost every conventional measure of social standing—wealth, intelligence, education, friends, business connections, political connections, family accomplishments—he stood high among his peers. The weight of these qualities lived in him, giving him a confident manner. Suchoff remembered meeting Bator for the first time in 1953.

> He had a very prestigious address. I was quite impressed to even *enter* the building. Here I was, you know, living out on Long Island. I went up on the elevator and I walked in. The secretary took me into his office, right off the corridor. I introduced myself, and I told him what I was doing, how I'd read Halsey Stevens's book, and so on. And he looked at me. He was a very *stern* looking man… When I got through with my recitation, he looked at me something like this [crosses arms, looks serious], and says, "I'm not going to write your thesis for you." And I looked at him, "But you're not *qualified* to write my thesis for me!" [laughs] I was so angry. You know what happened?! He broke out in a beatific smile—the only way to describe it. He got up, said "follow me," and he took me over to the family apartment across the corridor. He opens the door to this closet. The only thing in the closet was an enormous olive green cabinet.[16]

Peter Bartók had much more reason to feel comfortable with Bator, but he, too, had to have been affected by Bator's strong personal presence. (In a later claim he alleged that Bator's "dominant position" was a contributing cause to fraud and mismanagement.)[17] He was also prone to crises of confidence in his personal and business affairs, as Bator would soon find out. Yet he had pride, and a famous name that earned him quick acceptance in musical circles and within the Hungarian émigré community.

Francis Bator remembered Peter as "obsequious" in their younger days, a term that carries polyphonic layers of meaning, some bound up with social class distinctions. What Peter thought of Francis he seems to have kept to himself. Like many adolescents of similar age whose parents are friends, these two Hungarian-born young men managed to associate pleasantly enough in the context of family gatherings, but over time, on their own, the chemistry of their relationship could not sustain itself. They had no common ground for friendship beyond those early times together, which might have been sufficient for lifelong

---

16   Benjamin Suchoff, interview with the author, June 19, 2002.
17   Estate of Bela Bartok. Opinion of Mr. Surrogate S. Samuel DiFalco, *New York Law Journal*, May 3, 1961.

The Early Years of the American Bartók Estate

Fig. 5.1. Franci Bator reading in the living room of her home in New York City, ca. 1955. At right is the grand piano where Ditta Bartók taught piano lessons in 1944-45 to the teenaged Peter and Paul Bator. Photographer: Victor Bator. Source: personal collection of Francis Bator.

cordiality had the Estate litigation not permanently curdled the relationship between them. I can easily imagine Peter Bartók feeling tentative or eager to please in Francis's presence in the 1940s. Every time he visited the Bators at their East 72nd Street home, or at Nonquitt, Peter found himself in elegant surroundings and a stable domestic environment that contrasted starkly with his own circumstances (Fig. 5.1). Left on his own following Ditta's return to Hungary, Peter could no longer count on his mother to mediate his relationship with the Bators.[18] He possessed his fair share of what George Eliot, in *Adam Bede*, expressed as "the wakeful suspicious pride of a poor man in the presence of a rich man." He had no reason not to feel comfortable with the Bators. But the difference in their social position always hovered in the background, a gap that widened over time.

In the spring of 1947 Peter Bartók made his first recording in the living room of his apartment, using equipment he had purchased on Canal Street for $30.[19] A friend of his, a singer, wanted to submit a recording for an audition. He

---

18 Francis Bator told me that his mother felt sorry for the way Peter had been left abandoned by his own mother. Francis Bator, interview with the author, October 25, 2010.
19 A number of profiles of Peter Bartók were published in the early 1950s in newspapers and magazines. My information in these paragraphs draws freely from John Watson, "Monument of Music," *New York Journal-American*, April 7, 1955, and the private memories of Victor Bator as writ-

Chapter 5

volunteered to help. Sound recording developed into a new hobby. He made audio recordings for third parties, including Vox Productions and Tibor Serly, or friends needing audition recordings to submit. New equipment purchases were funded by written requests to his father's Estate. Bator sent the money promptly. Since Peter Bartók was attorney-in-fact for his mother, all he had to do was ask for money and it would be sent to him by check. His dreams, he learned, could be achieved with little resistance. He bought more and finer equipment. Other equipment he built himself. On December 21, 1948, he wrote to Bator excitedly about a Steinway concert grand piano he had the opportunity to purchase for $1,450. His current piano could be purchased for $550 from its owner, he explained, and refurbished for another $150. Erzsi Kecskeméti, with whom he consulted, reminded him that the touch of a Steinway was better than the current piano he used in his recording studio. If it's not too much, he would like to buy the Steinway. Two days later Bator approved. "If the Steinway concert piano is the kind of piano you should have in the studio, I am for it. The money is available."[20]

During his first years as an audio engineer, from 1946–48, Peter Bartók recorded other people's projects on a fee basis, advertising his business through word of mouth—what was called "service work" in those days. He built his apartment recording studio with equipment funded by his father's Estate and income he earned on his own. He tinkered continuously with his microphones, cables, and recording equipment, applying his expanding engineering skills to create optimal studio recording environments for the musicians who came to him. Editing the taped masters sharpened his ear, allowing him to exercise the exacting habits for which he would later become known in the industry.

In September 1949 he moved his studio into Steinway Hall, on 6th Avenue, where he paid $186/month in rent for a prime location with generous space and what he felt were "excellent acoustics." To make this move possible friends at Boosey & Hawkes interceded on his behalf. From that point forward he felt like he had a professional setting for his work. He had just recorded, for the first time, one of his father's works, the Third String Quartet, played by the New Music String Quartet. (The Bartók-Serly Five Pieces from *Mikrokosmos* were also included.) This record was released in September 1949. By November 1st it had already sold 700 copies. It and some of his early recordings were made in his apartment living room, with artificial reverberation added by placing a loudspeaker in the bathtub, a creative touch that captivated early reporters who cov-

---

ten down in his Memorandum, often with very specific dates and information. See also a May 1953 press release, "Up to Now," 2 pages long, prepared by Peter Bartók with information for reporters to use in their stories (copy in BSCB Tampa).
20 Victor Bator, Memorandum on the History of the Bartók Estate, 221 (BSCB Tampa).

ered the emergence of this talented young recording engineer. Energized by this flush of success, Peter contemplated recording more of his father's works. He wrote enthusiastically to his brother Béla Jr. in Budapest on November 1, 1949, with news. The production of records has gone well, he writes. It's at least as good a business as a recording studio. He has "grandiose plans" to record his mother playing with the Budapest Philharmonic.[21] The members of the New Music Quartet suggested further ideas. They liked working with him. Bartók Records was born.

Reading Bator's Memorandum, surviving correspondence, and legal documents from those early days of the Bartók Estate, one gets the impression that all of the Bartók family friends in New York wanted Peter to find success and to establish himself independently in the United States. In running his own business, however, like many first-time small business owners he began to rack up problems he was not equipped to solve. Close friends noticed. So did his business associates. So did a few sharp-eyed reporters. By 1950 Peter Bartók had settled on a plan to record all his father's music. "Very few of his compositions had yet been recorded then," he explained.[22] The project had genuine commercial merit, even some astute timing: the post-war boom of interest in Bartók's music had just started. To suitably honor a project of such scope and ambition, he committed to using excellent musicians and top-quality production standards. He himself would produce the LP's. That meant not just recording the albums, but also distributing them and selling them through record stores and his own studio office.

At first he did well, making studio recordings of solo and chamber ensembles. He expanded to making orchestral recordings in London, and recording in concert halls around New York City, using portable equipment. He recorded the Berg Opus 3 string quartet at a church in Stonington, Connecticut. In *The New York Times* in 1951 his photograph accompanied a news report about one of his new records. Many Hungarian musicians came through his studio to record. His growing reputation for top quality recordings drew younger American musicians like Robert Mann and Leonid Hambro to his studio. Mann recorded the Solo Sonata for Peter Bartók in 1953, a recording regarded to this day as one of the finest interpretations this work has ever received. Peter recruited several friends

---

21 Victor Bator, Memorandum on the History of the Bartók Estate, 228 (BSCB Tampa).
22 The website for Bartók Records offers a 2-paragraph summary of the company's history and achievements written by Peter Bartók in 2010 (https://bartokrecords.com/about-us/). Remarkably long-lived for an independent record company, it ceased to exist only after Peter's death in December 2020. In Florida he kept these legacy recordings available for purchase by making new pressings from the original masters. Altogether 35 LP records were produced, most of them in the decade 1950–62. See also Peter Bartók's updated catalog, *Bartók Records & Publications*, printed privately on October 1, 2012.

Chapter 5

> **COMPOSITIONS OF BÉLA BARTÓK**
> **IN THE CATALOG OF BARTÓK RECORDS:**
>
> (1) ORCHESTRAL:
> Deux Images*
> Two Portraits*
> The Miraculous Mandarin, Suite*
> Rhapsody #1 for Violin & Orch.*
> Rhapsody #2 for Violin & Orch.*
> Divertimento for Strings*
> Concerto for Violin & Orch.*
>
> (2) PIANO SOLO:
> Allegro Barbaro
> Roumanian Dance #1, Op. 8a
> Suite, Op. 14
> Suite—Out of Doors
> Improvisations, Op. 20
>
> Three Rondos**
> Sonatina**
>
> (3) MISCELLANEOUS:
> String Quartet #3
> Contrasts for Violin, Clarinet & Piano**
> Sonata for Unaccompanied Violin**
> 44 Violin Duets*
> Eight Hungarian Folk Songs
>   (On disc "Folk Songs of Hungary"—
>   Vol. 1)
> Twenty Hungarian Folk Songs
>   (On disc "Folk Songs of Hungary"—
>   Vol. 2)**
>
> 30—15000 cps. range indicated by *
> 20—18000 cps. range indicated by **
>
> For further information consult your dealer or write for catalog to:
> **Bartók Records, 135 Central Park West, New York 23, N. Y.**

Fig. 5.2. An October 1953 advertisement showing recent offerings from Bartók Records. From the Béla Bartók issue of Sam Goody's *The Long Player* 2/10 (October 1953): 12.

to help him run the business side. At its peak in the early 1950s his company produced 4–6 new records a year. He moved his studio to a prestigious penthouse location on Central Park West, one block up from the Dakota building.[23] In the Béla Bartók Issue of *The Long Player* in October 1953—a source already known to us for its reminiscences of the composer's American years by Balogh, Moore, Dorati, and others—Peter Bartók placed a dignified, subdued advertisement (Fig. 5.2) showing works of his father recently added to his list.

The notion of a famous composer's son committed to recording all of his father's works held obvious emotional appeal for a wider audience. A feature profile in the *New York World-Telegram* in June 1953 highlighted the deeply personal nature of Peter Bartók's enterprise. "I did not feel so close to my father until I began to record my father's music," Peter told the reporter. "I had to grow older and hear a lot of him before I came to realize what he was saying. Now it's the most thrilling music I can imagine. But naturally I'm prejudiced."[24] His

---

23 This location placed him directly across Central Park from Victor Bator's home and office. Future scholars curious about the psychology of the Bator/Peter Bartók relationship might find this drive for geographical proximity in one of the world's most highly priced, prestige real estate markets (even in the 1950s) a useful matter to consider.
24 Ed Wallace, "Bartók's Son Dedicates Life to Recording Father's Music," *New York World-Telegram*, June 25, 1953. Additional reporting on Peter Bartók's early achievements as a recording engineer can be found in John Watson, "Monuments of Music," *New York Journal-American*, April 7, 1955; Peter Bartók, "In the Groove…," *The Nation*, Dec. 4, 1954; "Bartók's Music Lives

COMPOSER'S SON DEVOTES BARTOK RECORDS TO FURTHERING FATHER'S MUSIC

Fig 5.3. Front page of an industry trade publication, *The Presto Recorder*, Vol. 5, No. 8 (August 1953). Source: PBC Homosassa.

plans had evolved by then. He hoped to make one recording a month of his father's music, the article reports, while remaining small enough "to make a fetish of quality in recorded sound." That he had most definitely arrived as a record producer is shown by the generous news coverage he received in the years 1953–55. In 1953 he won Audio Engineering Magazine's First Annual Audio Engineering Award, in the vocal category, for his recent recording of *Folk Songs of Hungary* (Fig. 5.3). This prestigious award catapulted his name to the top ranks of the recording engineer profession. He was invited to write a technical

---

Again," *Audio Record* 10/1 (Jan/Feb. 1954). A British fluff piece on Peter Bartók from 1955 retells the story of his flight from Europe in 1942, aided by a "mysterious girl" in Italy who helped him get to the train station (Joseph Johnston, "From a Son's Perilous Flight to Freedom Comes Recognition At Last For a Great Composer," *Sunday Mirror Magazine*, March 6, 1955).

feature article for a "High-Fi Special" issue of *The Nation* magazine; his name received lead billing on that nationally circulated magazine's front cover. Now "one of the best recording engineers in the country," Peter Bartók was considered "Big League" by the old established firms, one reporter pronounced.[25]

As trustee Victor Bator threw his support to Peter's recording business, firm in his belief that Béla Bartók would have wanted Peter to find success in his chosen career. Sending checks to Peter from the Estate's proceeds fell clearly in the "duty of care" realm for a trustee. Access to ready funding from his father's Estate may have allowed Peter Bartók's ambitions to get out in front of his ability to build a flourishing enterprise. But Bator let that pass. His wouldn't be the first business to overextend itself in its early stages, exhausting its founder. The press Peter was getting, meanwhile, was gratifying to them both. Evidence suggests that Bator served more or less as an open checkbook for Peter in the later 1940s and early 1950s.[26] To be clear, it was not Bator's money, but the Trust's, collected and administered for the beneficiaries by the Trustees. Bator wrote to Béla Keresztes in 1954:

> If Peter Bartók wants me to pay him every cent of the income in excess of sums required for the purposes set forth above [i.e., money for Mrs. Bartók, and for care and preservation of Bartók's manuscripts], the entire balance will be paid to him. What amounts not sent to Mrs. Bartók were spent according to Peter Bartók's instructions. I have no power to do anything else.[27]

Bator's position allowed him to help Peter in other ways, too. During the 1950s when he was approached by conductors, pianists, orchestras, and soloists for permission to record certain works, he sometimes declined their requests. He wanted to reserve those rights for Peter Bartók. He turned down a number of requests to record the First Piano Concerto; for similar reasons he refused to let Ormandy and the Philadelphia Orchestra record *Bluebeard's Castle*. (See the

---

25   Wallace, "Bartók's Son Dedicates Life."
26   In the Memorandum, p. 217–58, Bator offers a sustained analysis of Peter Bartók's recording career. Peter's decreasing attention to sales, he observed, brought about a crisis in the company by the mid-1950s, by which time it already suffered on a deeper level from Peter's ambivalence about the company's mission: was it just to be Bartók Records, or was it also to provide audio recording services on a contract basis to musicians and record companies who approached him? Peter felt pulled between these two overlapping areas of activity; the overcommitment exhausted him. To write a fair-minded history of Bartók Records is a task that awaits the right scholar. It won't be attempted here. It needs better representation of Peter's viewpoints than I am able to offer at present.
27   Victor Bator, letter to Béla Keresztes, October 19, 1954. As translated and included in the Memorandum.

correspondence published elsewhere in this book.) Fewer overall Bartók recordings got made in the 1950s as a result. In exchange Bartók's son was given an important competitive advantage. It worked, at least in some instances: Peter's recording of the Viola Concerto, with William Primrose as soloist, became Bartók Records' highest selling LP by 1955.

One of his regular working relationships in those years was with Jac Holzman, who had just founded Elektra Records (1950). Holzman's business instincts had not yet propelled him into the fame he later enjoyed as one of America's leading record producers and technology executives. He was still feeling his way forward in the new LP business, recording folk acts he heard in Greenwich Village, just 19 years old, when someone at Caedmon Records told him about Peter Bartók. His very first record, *New Songs by John Gruen*, he recorded in Peter Bartók's studio in a single three-hour session in December 1950. His second record, *Jean Ritchie Singing the Traditional Folk Songs of Her Kentucky Mountain Family*, he asked Peter to master. Surely Peter would do a better job than RCA had done on the masters for Elektra 1, he felt. He was right. Soon he was bringing all his recordings to Peter to master. Most of them were folk music, a genre close to Peter's heart as well, a family legacy. "Every record I had for probably the first three or four years was mastered by Peter," he told me in a recent interview.[28] Peter had a facility in his apartment that was better than anything he'd ever seen in New York. "I used him for years. His apartment was filled with equipment that no one had ever seen before, even at major radio stations like CBS. The tubes that he used were *radio* tubes, and they were very big. He could put a lot of power on a disc which the major labels couldn't, because they weren't ingenious like him. Peter was ingenious."

Holzman found himself amazed by the creative solutions Peter would devise to produce top quality sound or special acoustic effects. One involved a fantastic array of interconnected equipment whose key design element was one of those classic 1950s children's toys, the Slinky, which somehow helped produce the faint echo effect they were seeking for that record. "His attitude towards record making and the technology involved really rubbed off on me," he told me. Up to 1960 Holzman used Peter's mastering services whenever he could. He valued Peter's incredible ear, his sensitivity, and his creative solutions to technology problems that would defeat other engineers.

Through Bartók Records he learned something else, too. Peter never spoke about his famous father, Holzman recalled. "But I bought some records of

---

28 Jac Holzman, interview with the author, May 21, 2021. Holzman eventually rose to become Chairman of Panavision and Chief Technologist at Time Warner; he signed and worked with some of the leading singers and bands in the United States, including the Doors and Judy Collins.

Bartók's music because they were Peter's dad. Some of them I liked a lot." This experience, he realized years later, had produced a deep impression. "I found that my ability to be comfortable and hear the value of his dad's music made it very easy for me to be comfortable and hear the value of the very odd records that I put out on Elektra. It stretched my ears and *my willingness to try something*, even if I wasn't sure about it." The lessons he had learned while watching Peter Bartók work stayed with him his entire career, he is quick to point out. Already independent minded by nature, he learned to harness his independence to pursue results. Peter modeled this habit of mind. "I learned from Peter to think something through, figure it out, and execute, rather than have somebody else tell me how to do it." In his published memoirs Holzman warmly remembers Peter Bartók as "one of the most instinctively ingenious sound engineers I have ever known."[29] Elsewhere he credits Peter Bartók with instilling in him a "thirst for 'quality without compromise'" that guided him his entire career."[30]

Victor Bator deliberately kept an arm's distance from Bartók Records, allowing Peter to make all his own decisions. In his Memorandum he emphatically disputes the later allegation that he steered Peter towards the idea and "invested" the family's money in producing records, thereby causing great loss of funds. All the losses were incurred by Peter, as were, by extension, any gains or profits. More important by far, Peter was making a living. Privately, he questioned the wisdom of Peter's move to Steinway Hall in 1949. He worried that Peter was letting his ambitions take flight without considering how he would pay for it all. Unlike string quartets, folk singers, or pianists, hiring an entire orchestra could get expensive. For his debut recording of *Bluebeard's Castle*, made in London in 1953, Peter incurred expenses of $15,000 for singers, conductor, travel, hotel, hall rental, and recording session fees for the orchestra musicians; before he was finished he realized that actual outlay would be closer to $17,000, an amount simply spectacular for the time, equivalent to $165,000 in 2020 dollars. No independent record producer could afford expenses like this and hope to stay in business. The Trust quietly paid for it all.

A number of documents got introduced in the upcoming litigation to demonstrate that Peter Bartók suffered bouts of profound emotional distress while running his record company. He had a nervous breakdown of sorts in the mid-1950s for which he sought counsel from Bator. Some deeply personal documents that presented him in a poor light became known within the inner circle

---

29 Jac Holzman and Gavan Daws, *Follow the Music: The Life and High Times of Elektra Records in the Great Years of American Pop Culture* (Santa Monica, CA: FirstMedia Books, 1998), 6. Some factual information in these paragraphs is drawn from early pages of this book where Holzman describes the start of Elektra Records.
30 Jac Holzman, email communication to Peter Bartók, May 9, 2018. Reproduced with permission.

of family and their lawyers. In the world outside, meanwhile, he kept solidifying his reputation as a technician of rarefied skill and exacting standards. "Peter was no businessman," Suchoff appraised. "But he was remarkably good as an engineer. His output was *excellent*." Holzman admired him without reservation, even after he had met and worked with many other sound engineers at leading American record labels. "He was amazing." Jack Pfeiffer, a senior record producer at RCA Victor Red Seal who oversaw many of the recordings of Van Cliburn and Horowitz, agreed. "At RCA, we always admired everything he did. It's a great loss to the whole industry that he didn't fulfill his destiny."[31]

* * *

Against this unfolding backdrop of Trust support for Peter Bartók's career, the events of 1948 left a lasting impression on the history of the Bartók Estate. Hungary's rapid slide into single-party dictatorship in 1946–47 had been achieved in part because of US passivity in the face of alarm bells sounding from State Department offices. American foreign policy shifted dramatically a year later when it became clear that hopes for a peaceful cooperation with Russia in the region were shattered. The deepening civil chaos in Hungary touched off two specific events with long-term ramifications for the Bartók Estate: 1) the new government stripped Victor Bator of his Hungarian citizenship; 2) over in New York City, Victor Bator decided to start collecting memorabilia that would eventually become the Béla Bartók Archives.

As we saw in Chapter 1, Bator's citizenship had been revoked once before, by the Nazified government in Budapest in 1941; it was restored to him after the war during the brief window of time a democratic coalition held sway in the government from 1946–47. Now the communists revoked it again in retaliation for his increasingly public anti-communist activities in the United States.[32] Separately, in the early summer of 1948 Bator filed a lawsuit against his former employer in Hungary to force the return of back pay and pension funds it technically still owed him from the war years. That lawsuit got swallowed up by the

---

31 As quoted in Wigler, "Composer Bela Bartok's Legacy of Litigation," 4. Wigler, an excellent reporter to judge from his work in this article, went to the trouble of interviewing a number of individuals about Peter Bartók; his article is one of the most reliable and balanced reports of the litigation to appear in an American newspaper.
32 I have not been able to determine the exact date of this action. Francis Bator could find no documentation in his family records, but his memory was clear: he remembered it as a retaliation for his father's increasingly visible stature in the United States as an opponent of communism. Likely it took place in later 1948, possibly even early 1949. On June 20, 1948, the newspaper *Szabad Nép* published an article claiming that Bator was the handler of Horthy's fortune that had been smuggled into the United States (Botos, "The Stages of Victor Bator's Career").

Chapter 5

communist overthrow of government and subsequent developments in Hungary's history, although it did progress far enough internally at the bank to generate a typed memorandum on June 21, 1948, summarizing the specific allegations and his history with the bank during the war.[33] At some point in 1947–49 the communists seized his wife's family vineyard in Tokaj. His home on the Gellért Hill would soon be claimed by the state, too. The Bator family's losses were enormous. He had been opposed to communism before. The year 1948 hardened him into an active foe.[34]

The immediate post-war period also found Bator wading vigorously into the business side of running the Estate. Here was an area where his natural talents could be put to use. To Boosey and Hawkes he signaled that he would be coming back to them to renegotiate the contract for Bartók's music. From 1946–48 he threw himself into learning everything he could about the music publishing business. He met monthly, sometimes more often, with staff at Boosey & Hawkes and at ASCAP. He exerted steady pressure on Boosey & Hawkes to support Ditta Bartók financially, and to increase their promotion of Bartók's music. "I was a harder man to handle than a real composer eager to hear his music," he later explained.[35]

Before he died Béla Bartók had extended his existing contract with his publisher through 1949. The occasion of its pending renewal drew from Bator a determined effort to improve its terms. Neither he nor Ralph Hawkes particularly cared for each other, they soon realized. (Victor Bator: "I have never seen a businessman from whom one can ask with more justification, seeing his yacht and his automobile, where are the yacht and automobile of his customers?" Lawyer to Bator: "Mr. Hawkes does not seem to hold you in very high esteem,

---

33 Memorandum, Tárgy: Bátor kontra Pesti Magyar Kereskedelmi Bank / 1948. június 21. Magyar Országos Levéltár. Personal collection of Francis Bator. In the chaos of 1948–50 Bator's lawsuit against the bank failed to obtain resolution; he obtained a ruling transferring it to New York State Supreme Court. There it limped along until at least 1953, hampered in its prosecution by the State Department's hard-line sanctions against communist countries. In the United States his lawyer for the lawsuit was none other than Harold Manheim, who had drafted Bartók's two American wills. Manheim filed Bator's lengthy amended petition in New York State Supreme Court in February 1950. It lists 26 causes for action, most of them failures to remunerate Bator properly. His director's share of bank profits, we learn, was 0.75 %, or "at least 75,000 pengos" for the years 1940, 1941, and 1942. The bank had agreed to cover his necessary living expenses in New York City, too, up to July 1941, "in the sum of $12,000," none of which was reimbursed to him at the time. By 1950 Bator estimated the total amount he was owed at "$95,381.80," plus interest.
34 Comments Ben Suchoff made to me suggest that a considerable part of the Bator family's animus for communism came from Franci Bator. Franci deeply resented the loss of her family's cherished vineyard property in Mád.
35 Bator, Memorandum on the History of the Bartók Estate, 49. Bator devotes 90 pages of his Memorandum, approximately 30% of its entire length, to a detailed account of his business relationships with Bartók's publishers and with ASCAP.

a fact which I do not believe will bother you very much.")[36] In his Memorandum he outlines the concessions he wrung from Hawkes through canny, tough-minded negotiation, including increases in all royalty rates and specific language requiring the firm to promote Bartók's music more vigorously. The lawsuit Bator filed against the publisher in March 1948 forced the parties to the negotiating table. He threatened to terminate the Bartók contract on its renewal date for non-performance (generally) and copyright infringement for the Third Piano Concerto (specifically). That lawsuit—the Estate's first—also named Columbia Records, alleging that like Boosey & Hawkes it had profited at the expense of the Bartók Estate with regard to the Sándor and Philadelphia Orchestra first recording of the Third Piano Concerto. Specifically, Columbia Records had undertaken to make, license, and sell the records "without the consent of the deceased or of the plaintiffs (Bator and Báron)."[37] At the ensuing trial in U.S. District Court Bator took the stand for two days, undergoing examination and cross-examination; Ralph Hawkes underwent the same experience for another two days, with Victor Bator assisting in the cross-examination.

Unfurling his formidable business talent like this, Bator pushed and drove Hawkes into agreeing to more favorable terms. Instead of "routine treatment" by the publisher, he sought for Bartók's music "individual attention, drive, and special effort"—superior effort, in other words, commensurate with Bartók's stature in their catalog. So unyielding were his demands that he even alienated his own attorney, Harold Manheim, who as the litigation proceeded accused his client of overtrading and argued in favor of settling, which led to substantial attorney-client disagreement. By mid-1949 they came to terms with Hawkes. In a new contract back-dated to January 1, 1949, a raft of changes were made to this most important of all contracts for Béla Bartók's music, foremost among them a new royalty rate of 16 1/2% for all sheet music sales (previously 15%), increases in all rental rates (a major source of Estate income going forward), and an agreement that Boosey & Hawkes should issue printed editions of *all* Bartók's works and keep them in print in sufficient numbers.

In a significant victory Bator also got the publisher to commit to purchase and acquire from Hungarian publishers the 21 works that had been published in Hungary prior to Bartók's transition to Universal Edition.[38] He made them

---

36 Bator, letter to Arthur Garmaize, August 7, 1947; and Garmaize, letter to Victor Bator, July 8, 1947. Copies in BSCB Tampa. Garmaize helped Manheim during the Boosey & Hawkes contract negotiations in 1946-49. His expertise was in entertainment industry law and music publishing contracts.
37 Bator et al. v. Boosey & Hawkes, Ltd. (Columbia Records, Inc., Third Party Plaintiff), U.S. District Court for Southern New York. July 13, 1948.
38 These and other terms of the new 1949 contract with Boosey & Hawkes are summarized in Bator's Memorandum, p. 58-60.

Chapter 5

go after the Hungarian publishers. For Boosey & Hawkes, exerting an occasional effort to acquire those Hungarian copyrights would not be sufficient. Their staff now had to actively pursue them or be in breach of contract. All manner of trouble would come from this one obligation in years ahead. It guaranteed friction. For the privilege of poking at rattlesnakes like this, Boosey & Hawkes agreed to pay the Estate a minimum of $8,000 once the Hungarian copyrights were acquired. Together these renegotiated terms kept Bartók's music in the Boosey & Hawkes catalog.

Bator consistently remembered 1948 as the year the idea first came to him for collecting papers and miscellaneous "mementos" associated with Béla Bartók's life and career. He never expressly linked the start of the Cold War with his idea of starting an archive. Not in so many words. When he started collecting Bartók mementos the lifespan of the political standoff between the US and Russia could not be foreseen. Nor, for that matter, did the growing holdings yet have a physical space or sufficient materiality to give them form; at present they were little more than the contents of that olive green cabinet.

The Bartók Estate now turned an important corner. Soon enough new troubles would arise, rippling out from these early events. They were inevitable. For as Indira Ghandi once said, in a wholly different context, you cannot shake hands with a clenched fist.

Correspondence: The Litigation of 1959–61

*N*umerous letters from the years of litigation survive. Because they lay bare the texture of the original legal drama between Bator and the Bartók heirs, these documents provide an important corrective to the misunderstandings and falsehoods that have become part of the lore surrounding the Bartók Estate. I reproduce a small handful here.

Communications from the Hungarian side are scarce. Neither Béla Jr. nor Ditta Bartók wrote many letters to anyone in the United States except Peter. During these years the Hungarian government spoke for them in the litigation, primarily through Róbert Palágyi and lawyers whose names have not been recorded, and to a lesser extent through Béla Keresztes and government notaries. Peter Bartók may have saved some of the Estate's voluminous correspondence files that he inherited. If so, we will learn the extent of those holdings in coming years. Litigation churns out legal communications of all sorts. What survives sixty years on, though, will always be spotty. Business correspondence has a way of disappearing. Records retention policies at law firms invariably require old paper files to be destroyed, usually through shredding, unless the matters remain open or have the potential to be reopened. Public court records in the United States, on the other hand, are typically archived and available to intrepid later researchers willing to wade through them. Documentation for the litigation of 1959–61, in other words, will always show unavoidably large gaps in coverage. Enough survives, however, to discern the inner machinery of the dispute.

The most important court document from the early years of the Bartók Estate is the *1961 Opinion of Surrogate S. Samuel DiFalco*. Its findings are summarized in Chapter 6.

Glimpses into the litigation's main themes can be found in the five letters and documents printed below. An important Hungarian document reaffirming the government's official position on the matter of Bartók's Hungarian Will shows how the government maneuvered to assert control over the American Estate. A letter Bator wrote to his son Paul in 1959 shows gallows humor that could not be revealed outside family circles.

Victor Bator, letter to Ernest Roth, January 14, 1958.
Typed, 1 p., unsigned. Onionskin copy. In English.

January 14, 1958

Dr. Ernest Roth
Boosey & Hawkes, Ltd.
295 Regent Street
London W.I, England

Gentlemen:

I confirm receipt of your letter of January 9th regarding the request of the Bureau Hongrois pour la Protection des Droits d'Auteur re directing the Composer's share of mechanical fees to Bela Bartok Jr. in Hungary.

I request you to maintain the refusal communicated to the Hungarian office. On the other hand, I want to inform you that recently the same Hungarian office finally gave up its Molotoff approach of "Nyet" to all proposals I formulated for a constructive solution of the disagreement by the Hungarian authorities appearing under half a dozen names including that of Bela Bartok Jr. and showed some willingness and possible sense of inclination to bring about peaceful co-existence. Thereupon I sent them a definite proposal in the middle of December, copy of which I am not transmitting to you because it was written in Hungarian. I have not received yet an answer, which seems to indicate to me that instead of repeating their old story, they are examining it. I am not overly optimistic because Communist bureaucrats don't usually dare, when it comes to the final step, agree to anything in a positive sense, but I am not entirely pessimistic because I have succeeded, as you know, to block their attempts to sell Bartok music and collect fees from abroad, not only in England, Australia, Switzerland, France, but in other places too, and that is the language they seem to understand.

The above is the reason that I am holding back the intention of suit against whoever would see Bartok music or perform it.

I shall keep you posted about further developments.

Yours sincerely,

Correspondence: The Litigation of 1959–61

VICTOR BATOR, LETTER TO HIS SON PAUL BATOR, DECEMBER 18, 1959. TYPED, 1 P., UNSIGNED. ONIONSKIN COPY, WITH HANDWRITTEN INSERTIONS AND CORRECTIONS. IN HUNGARIAN. TRANSLATED BY ETELKA NYILASI.

Dec. 18th, 1959

My dear son,

Since it's clear that the thought seemed to have formed in your mind that during my 14 years of Bartók administration—which is now under scrutiny—there may have been some small little things swept under the rug that could now be seized on by the Bartók family or an ill willed lawyer, I felt obliged to write to you and talk this out.

What I personally think of all this is irrelevant, because most people in my situation tend to be more anxious and more timid than an outsider would be. In other words, it is not the case here that I am the braver and more critical one. Just the opposite, actually. Even if someone's nature, like mine, is hardly given to excess cowardice.

I had already made available all the details to Helphand and Rosen when the settlement was prepared in 1958, and they were of the opinion that there was no point in the settlement that could be criticized. There is nothing in the correspondence I could not take pride in. Once the lawsuit appeared, I immediately set about assembling my own conscientious review of the Estate's history.[1] Rosen, who is now over 70 years of age and is a careful, rational and cautious lawyer, re-stated his previous opinion and underlined to Henry Ess and DeGenaro at the hearing at Sullivan and Cromwell that he, who is acquainted with every detail, believes this case is to be laughed at and that it is mostly based on ignorance.

Now that I have examined every piece of paperwork, my worries have vanished. While before I only believed that everything was accurate and proper, now I know it for certain. Please do not spend a minute worrying. I have no doubts about how this case will terminate. The only problem is

---

1   This appears to be a reference to his 310-page Memorandum. The "settlement" term in this letter refers to the First Intermediate Accounting, which was judicially settled in New York Surrogate's court on January 6, 1959. See Chapter 6.

that I cannot follow Christo's advice to shoot Peter Bartók instead of all the "rabbits."[2] Neither can I follow my own inclination that tells me all Bartóks should be drowned in the Danube, because the role of a trustee is not to constantly fight the beneficiaries. Therefore, I will carry on with this little war, philosophically speaking, in which they have no atomic bomb and I don't dare or even want to use mine.

Fondly,

Paul M. Bator

VICTOR BATOR, LETTER TO GUSTAVE ROSEN, JANUARY 22, 1960. TYPED, 2 P., UNSIGNED. ONIONSKIN COPY. IN ENGLISH.

January 22, 1960

Dear Gus:

I take the liberty of outlining my idea about the way the suit against Bela Bartok Jr. should be framed. I am of course influenced by the fact that the day after tomorrow I shall go into the hospital to be operated on the following morning, and for a few days afterwards I may not be available for consultation. Since the complaint has to be filed within 20 days from yesterday, the preparatory period, as far I am concerned, will be shorter than that number of days.

I suggest that the suit be directed at two different objectives:

1. To oblige Bela Jr. to pay to the Estate all sums collected by him (from the income of royalties, licenses, publications, sales, performances, mechanical reproductions, films, broadcasting and television, etc., regarding any and all works of Bela Bartok, and especially the 21 compositions orig-

---

[2] In the original letter the word "rabbit" is typed in English, with quotation marks, suggesting an inside reference among members of the Bator family. The "Christo" here refers to his grandson, Christopher Bator, who was five years old at the time. In a recent interview he had no recollection of making this particular remark, of course, but it prompted fond memories of the abundant rabbits that lived in the gardens and lawn at Nonquitt. Apparently as a young boy he had overheard his grandfather grumbling about Peter Bartók and the lawsuit. An innocent, playful remark he made one day lodged in the mind of his grandfather, who found in it some welcome humor.

inally published by the Hungarian publishers) originating from outside the territory where the income should ultimately be collected by him,— whatever that territory may be, depending on the court's construction of Paragraph 2 of the Will.

2. To restrain Bela Jr. from any act aimed at controlling, influencing, exploiting, and using any Bartok works, musical and non-musical like, <u>anywhere</u> including the territory from which (according to Paragraph 2 of the Will) the income and proceeds of Bartok works may be due and payable to him.

I suggest that the amount claimed on the basis of the above Paragraph (1) payable by Bela Jr. to the Estate be set at 1,500,000 Forints ($135,000) as appraised by his brother, Peter Bartok. This figure shall be based on the statement that it is not only improbable but wholly irrational to assume that Peter Bartok demands the repayment or inclusion in the accounting of such sums which, under the Will and its Paragraph 2, would be due and payable to Bela Jr. anyway. Nobody can have any doubt that under Paragraph 2 of the Will some part of the income must ultimately go to Bela Jr. Since Peter Bartok demands the inclusion in the accounting and maybe the repayment by me of $135,000, I have to assume that he knows that this is the amount by which Bela Jr.'s collections exceeded the amounts due to him under Paragraph 2.

As it is clear from the aforegoing, I would not specify which countries belong to the territory where the income is due to Bela Jr. Let the court construe Paragraph 2. Whatever the court's construction will be, it will be acceptable to the Trustee.

As to (2) the purpose of this is twofold. First, I want the court to decide the question whether, according to the court's construction of the Last Will and Testament in regard to the territory from where the income may belong to Bela Jr., he has or has not the control of and/or title to the Bartok works and their copyrights. This regards even those countries (Hungary, etc.) from where under the construction of the Will by us, by the court, or by anybody else, the income does belong and is payable to Bela Jr. Second, such framing of the prayer eliminates the possibility and the danger that instructions or consent of Peter Bartok on his own behalf and on behalf of his mother compel me to drop the claim. Peter and his mother may withdraw their complaint against me for letting Bela Jr.

collect any part of the Estate's income, in which case the rug would be pulled out from under my feet in maintaining the suit for repayment of past collections by Bela Jr. But by the prayer directed at restraining Bela Jr. from interfering and disturbing my rights as Trustee in regard to all Bartok works and their copyrights, such danger would be eliminated. No instruction given by Peter now would relieve me from seeking such a restraining order and indemnity for past violations, as my duties as Trustee to hold the right to copyrights and their exploitation cannot be delegated either inside or outside the territory from where the income may have to be paid to Bela Jr.

I hope that the above ideas may help you to frame the prayers of the complaint.

Yours sincerely,

Mr. Gustave J. Rosen
14 West 46th Stret
New York 36, N.Y.

cc: Mr. Henry N. Ess III

Government decree. Office of the Government's Public Notaries in Budapest, August 26, 1961.

This official translation was prepared in Hungary for consideration by American and European attorneys. It records a critical step in the litigation whereby the Hungarian Office of Public Notaries re-certified in 1958 the primacy of Béla Bartók's 1940 Hungarian Last Will and Testament, dressing up in legalese and official stamps the same position it had always held. The petition demands termination of Bator's office. Vienna-based attorney Erich Habernal received a copy of this document directly from Bator in late 1961, accompanied by Bator's dismissive interpretation of its content (see following letter). In the transcription found here the original document's spellings, punctuation, and syntax errors are carefully retained.

TRANSLATION FROM HUNGARIAN

OFFICE OF THE GOVERNMENT'S PUBLIC NOTARIES IN BUDAPEST No. Kjö: I-II, 4340/1958/43

Decree and Certificate of Inheritance.

The Office of Government's Public Notaries in Budapest takes due note of the fact that in the matter of the inheritance of

the late Béla Bartók

who had been an inhabitant of Budapest II, at 29 Csalán Street the Kjö: I-II 4340/1958/29 temporary letters testamentary has become absolute, the parties with adverse interest have not—in the 60 days beginning with the receipt of the decree 51.Pkf.23764/1961/40—commenced an action for vacating and voidance of the decree absolute; the parties have not filed evidence of any such action in conformity with 3rd alinea of Para. 60 of Government Decree 6/1958 I.M.

Consequently, the temporary letters testamentary have become of full validity and effect.

Hence,—on the basis of the testament dated March 28, 1943, Paragraph 2 and the notarized statement dated February 28, 1951, now listed among the testamentary documents,—all author's rights and copyrights of testator in Hungary, Austria, Czecho-Slovakia, Poland, Yougoslavia, Roumania and Germany have become owner by and the property of Béla Bartók Jr. (Budapest XI, 10 Köbölkuti Street).

Likewise the ownership of all other chattels in the territory of Hungary belongs to Mr. Béla Bartók Jr.

On the basis of Para. 3 of the testament all such author's rights, copyrights and other chattels not adjudicated to Béla Bartók Jr. have become the property of and owned by Peter Bartók, son of the testator by his second marriage, domiciled at 111 West 57th Street, New York 19, N.Y.

According to the last will all annuities, profits, income and gain realized out of the assets acquired by Peter Bartók are due to the second wife of the testator, Mrs. Béla Bartók, born Edit Pásztory, domiciled at Budapest I, 17 Krisztina Krt., during her lifetime and become her property,—this to include her dower.

In the course of the hearings of December 30th, 1958 and January 2nd, 1959, the heirs, Béla Bartók Jr., Peter Bartók and Mrs. Béla Bartók stated their views in regard to the revocation of the letters testamentary and of commission of administration of the Executor of the Testament, Dr. Victor Bator. They have requested the cancellation of his commission and for an order for accounting.

The Government's Public Notary officiating in this case takes due note of these statements and informs of this decision Dr. Victor Bator by delivering him this decree. Further he is hereby informed that his office and commission terminated otherwise also at the time when this procedure of inheritance ended. Therefore he is directed to deliver his accounting to the heirs within 15 days from the date of delivery to him of this decree.

The inheritance consisting of chattels only is not subject to inheritance tax.

The officiating Government's Public Notary requests the Internal Revenue Office of Budapest to determine the tax of procedure and to collect it.

The inheritance of the testator with a "Last Will and Testament" and with descendants in life had to be disposed of according to the last will and testament dated March 28, 1943, taking in consideration also the notarized declaration of Peter Bartók, a testamentary and legal heir and Victor Bator and Gyula Baron, testamentary executors dated February 28, 1951, interpreting Para. 2 of the Last Will and Testament,—with special regard to the fact that the parties of adverse interest did not avail themselves of the right to sue for the voiding and vacating of the decree absolute secured to them by alinea 3 of Para. 60 of the I.M. Government Decree No. 6/1958.

Decreeing the full effect of the letters testamentary was done ex officio.

In consideration of the fact that Germany as of now consists of two parts, both Germanys are within the term "Germany."

Within 15 days from the delivery of this decree appeal may be lodged at the Office of the Government's Public Notaries

Budapest, August 26, 1961

Dr. András Vuits, m.p.
Government's Public Notary

Certifying the copy:
Luskén m.p.
Head of Office

Seal: Government's Public Notary, Budapest

Victor Bator, letter to Dr. Erich Habernal, October 24, 1961. Typed letter, 3 p., unsigned. Onionskin copy. Original in English.

October 24, 1961

Dear Dr. Habernal,

Our last exchange of correspondence was in late 1960, almost a year ago. This short letter was preceded by a letter of yours to me dated October 17th, 1960, which set forth the terms which—should the proceedings be resumed and be subject matter of further motions by Béla Bartók Jr.—would be used by you as the line of defence. It is my guess that soon, or sometime in the next future, such a step will be taken by the Hungarian Government which controls this whole affair, using Béla Bartók Jr. as their dummy or agent for the purposes that they want to realize. The time since the end of 1958 until now, has been used by the Hungarians for putting through in Hungary a procedure which would produce and has brought about semi-judicial decisions in Hungary handing over the inheritance to Béla Bartók Jr. and to Peter Bartók and Mrs. Bartók in a way that suits the Government's desire to acquire the control over the entire property that seems to represent for them substantial financial and prestige value.

I send you herewith enclosed marked "A", the decision of the Government's Public Notary's Office rendered in August 1961, that was sent to me by registered letter from the Legation of the Hungarian People's Republic and reached me on Saturday, October 21st. You will find marked "B" its English translation. As you will readily see, the Hungarian Notary Public, who has a jurisdiction which corresponds roughly to the Surrogate Court in New York, issued letters testamentary in favor of Béla Bartók Jr., Peter, and in a restricted sense to Mrs. Béla Bartók, and at the same time declared my office as Executor and Administrator of the Estate as terminated, and obliged me to give an accounting within 15 days from the day when this decree was delivered to me. I have not signed any receipts. The receipt of the registered letter was signed by the doorman of the house in which I live, and though the decree was accompanied by a demand that I send to the Legation a receipt confirming the arrival of the papers, I am not going to sign or send anything.

I am sure nobody expects in Budapest that the New York Courts or I will abide by their decision. It is my guess that this whole procedure was instituted for one purpose only, that is to present the Court in Vienna with a legal-looking document according to which Béla Bartók Jr. has been recognized by a Court as the owner of all Bartók rights in the seven countries which have often been mentioned in the papers, which include Austria and Germany, though restricted to copyrights and author's rights. (Other chattels and movable properties were adjudicated by Béla Bartók Jr. only insofar as they are physically in Hungary today). As you know, the opinion of the New York counsels and of the Surrogate Court of New York is, that all copyrights, without exception, whether they cover Hungary or any other country, are part and parcel of the Estate, and I have the duty and the right to administer the copyrights and to appear in every relationship as their legal owner. This point has been sufficiently covered in our previous correspondence and I do not think that you need further clarification or explanation. The question to be decided in the Vienna Court will be whether a testament that was drawn up and signed in New York by the testator who immigrated in the U.S., was a resident of New York, whose testament was drafted by New York attorneys, has to be construed by and executed according to New York law, or is on account of the nationality of the testator a purely Hungarian matter under the jurisdiction of the Hungarian and other authorities.

For the full understanding of the Hungarian proceedings, I am sending you herewith enclosed in photostatic copy the minutes of all the proceedings that took place in Hungary in regard to the Bartók Estate. They

Correspondence: The Litigation of 1959-61

are, of course, in Hungarian and it would be a much too heavy task for me to have them translated into English as long as I do not need to use them in Court in this country. Also, should you want to use them, you would need a German translation anyway. Further, I do not think that there will be any real difficulty to find in Vienna legally-trained translators who know the Hungarian legal language and can translate them in proper and understandable legal German. Should you not know about such suitable interpreters, it may be useful for you to know that a former colleague of mine who worked in my law office in Hungary is now in Vienna, is an Austrian citizen, and is perfect both in Hungarian and in German language. His name is Dr. Thomas Mezel and his address is: Esteplatz 7, and his telephone number was, the last time I heard from him, U-17-2-40. I have not been in any connection with him for almost 10 years, but knowing his very high abilities and intelligence, should he be willing to undertake this job, he certainly will do a good one.

Perusal of the Minutes and other papers (marked "C") will show up that they are in sharp conflict with this last decree that was delivered to me a few days ago. For further clarification, I am enclosing letters of a Hungarian lawyer who is in confidential contact with me. I send these letters of my friend to you for your confidential information, and under no circumstances must these letters be even mentioned to any third party because without great difficulty the name and identity of the author would be discovered and that would endanger if not his life, at least his liberty.

The essence of all this is that there is a kind of conspiracy between the Hungarian Government and Béla Bartók Jr., not helped, but neither prevented or contradicted by the two other members of the Bartók family. In fact, Peter Bartók told me in July of this year, between two journeys to Hungary, that neither his Mother nor he is in control of what is happening in Hungary, that the Hungarian Government is actively directing every step, and because of the presence of his Mother, Mrs. Bartók, in Hungary,—he and his Mother—simply could not take the risk of contradiction or opposition.

In one respect, the position of Universal Edition has improved. I know that Dr. Kalmus and his colleagues were, up to a certain degree, disturbed by the fact that the delivery to me of Bartók's manuscripts might be objected to on the basis of the thesis that everything that is or was in Vienna belongs to Béla Bartók Jr. This claim has now been given up.

Outside of author's rights, this decree gives into the ownership of Béla Bartók Jr. only chattels and other movables which are in Hungary, distinguished this way, between copyrights and other properties. Thus, the manuscripts which were handed over to me are not subjected to any claim from the viewpoint of Universal Edition.

I repeat this time what I have said often in the past, that I am not party to this litigation and for the time being, I do not see any advantage for me to become involved in it. Therefore, this letter to you should serve only the purpose to help Universal Edition with facts which otherwise might have not been known to you.

Yours sincerely,

Dr. Erich Habernal
Mahlerstr. 13/7
Vienna, Austria

Chapter 6

A Thorn in the Rosebush

> There are always thorns in rosebushes. One such thorn, ever since the establishment of the Hungarian Communist regime, has been the existence of the Bartók Estate.
>
> –Victor Bator, 1960

To chronicle in great detail the meandering history of decades-long intercontinental litigation—the original complaints, the parties to the lawsuits, their positions, all the court rulings along the way—would bring little reward to any writer, and even less reward to the reader. Litigation is, and always has been, a joyless affair for many people involved. Voltaire and Mark Twain jabbed at its folly, as did French moralist Jean de La Bruyère, who delivered himself of this epigram in his *Caractères*: "Avoid lawsuits beyond all things: they pervert your conscience, impair your health, and dissipate your property." Rare are the humans unwillingly ensnared in the net of litigation, apart from many of their lawyers, who find in its pursuit even the remotest sliver of pleasure. Still, our appetite for seeking redress, real or perceived, through rule of law has immeasurably advanced the cause of justice around the globe. Correctly applied, lawsuits curb human aggression and greed. They push back against injustice. Abused, they visit destruction on individuals, families, and businesses at staggering cost to human society, particularly in democratic countries like the United States which liberally empower citizens to seek resolution of complaints through legal action.

An especially virulent strain of litigation thrives in the wills and estates arena, where families work out disputes in court after a death. For broken families burdened with historic grievances, this moment when assets transfer can turn brother against brother, sister against sister, children against their parents, and form camps actively devoted to the high art of antagonism. What sets off family feuds, estate attorneys recognize, can just as easily be the little things: sentimental objects, or personal effects like mom's favorite earrings, a favorite painting, or dad's watch.[1] Neither wealth nor fame protects a family from suc-

---

1 A light spirited but informative review of family behaviors during estate litigation can be found in Paul Sullivan, "When Heirs Fight Over Assets with Sentimental Value," *The New York Times*, April 4, 2015.

Chapter 6

cession tussles, of course. Quite the reverse. For prominent families, high-stakes estate litigation can drag on for years, steeping a bitter brew of allegations, recriminations, distrust, and anger. In music the estates of Igor Stravinsky and Arnold Schoenberg devolved into epic, cinematic battles among each composer's surviving heirs that resulted in, among other actions, the wholesale transfer of the Schoenberg Institute from Los Angeles to Vienna in 1998. The estates of George Gershwin, Billy Strayhorn, or, more recently, Prince are not particularly happy places. In a category of its own for the frequency of its public brawls is the estate of Martin Luther King, Jr., which perseveres in the news not for its concerns over money—King had little money when he died—, but for his three children's long trail of disputes over how to honor his substantial spiritual and cultural legacy.

Given Béla Bartók's prominence as a cultural figure in Hungary, and internationally in the world of music, it would have been a remarkable feat had his estate sidestepped all encounters with litigation. Disputes were bound to materialize somewhere. In this chapter I review the history of the American Bartók Estate's notorious legal dramas, not with an eye to completeness, but, instead, with the specific purpose of examining the Hungarian communist government's role in stirring up disputes after 1950. Communist state offices and their lawyers destabilized the Estate for most of its history, at times actively manipulating heirs into conflict with each other in pursuit of a larger goal, the reclaiming of the American Bartók Estate for Hungary. Animated by their commitment to the larger struggle between communism and Western democracy, the principal parties quickly grew entrenched against each other, hardening battle lines around legal issues that stayed completely out of public view in the 1950s. All three Bartók heirs became pawns on this geopolitical chessboard, each moved and controlled by larger forces in an invisible game to establish dominance. Shifting alliances brought them brief periods of power. But the larger game played out over their heads, with Victor Bator, a determined anti-communist on one side, and the Hungarian communist government, equally determined, on the other. Parties joined to the lawsuits, like Boosey & Hawkes, Paul Sacher, or Universal Edition, could do little more than watch on. And wait.

Ignorance of the actual sources of tension in the Estate was widespread. It could hardly be otherwise. In estate litigation the determining action plays out in law offices and in court systems. While court decisions (in the U.S.) are generally a matter of public record, in the pre-internet era those judicial decisions were anything but easy for the general public to locate. It took savvy to navigate those waters. Additionally, many of the litigation documents are not in the public record. This tendency towards a closed system, sealed from outside eyes, was also maintained by strong force of habit among lawyers, whose standards of professional conduct constrained them from talking publicly about their cases. For the Bartok Estate litigation the Bator family—father and sons—kept their counsel. Their lawyers *never* talked out of school. Nor did, apparently, any other lawyer associated with the case, including those suing on behalf of the Hungarian government. What spilled into public view usually passed through the mouths of the heirs, who were hardly impartial observers, or through an occasional journalist. The gears of justice, meanwhile, ground forward on their own terms and schedule.

After the communists seized power in Hungary, any scraps of information that managed to leak through the Iron Curtain got bent immediately by the prism of Cold War politics. Family and friends outside the country's borders tried desperately to find out what was happening. A dense fog of propaganda floated outwards, hard to penetrate. It soon became apparent that within its borders Hungary was a police state. With Béla Jr. and Ditta muted by the effects of totalitarianism, only Peter Bartók, living in New York City, could give full voice to his complaints without fear of retribution. Certain actions in the Estate's legal history progressively removed his actual authority. When an American court judgment in 1961 repudiated his allegations of trustee malfeasance, an emboldened Peter felt the tug of higher calling and settled into a new role—the aggrieved heir. Any inhibitions he may have once felt about speaking publicly of private matters soon fell away.

In the absence of facts Winged Rumor spreads her own mischief. By the mid-1960s the foundations of a new mythology began to accrete around Peter Bartók's opinions. That mythology, in its American version, omitted from its creation stories the role of communist agencies in the Estate's early history. Instead, it framed the Estate's problems as a conflict of personalities between a supposedly corrupt trustee, Victor Bator, and an embattled heir, Peter Bartók, whose crusade for control of the Estate claimed all virtue for itself in the manner of crusaders since antiquity.

Bator's death in 1967 removed his steadying hand from the tiller. By then he had formally established the Béla Bartók Archives, though, in one bold step adding another layer of legal protection for its holdings through New York state law. The new institution was placed under the care of a star-studded board of trustees that included Yehudi Menuhin, Jozsef Szigeti, Eugene Ormandy, and Antal Dorati. As a beacon of light shining brightly from American shores in the cultural Cold War, the new Archives carried symbolic weight in view of Hungary's decision in 1961 to establish its own institution for Bartók research, the Bartók Archívum. After his death his sons inherited his place in the litigation, as *his* heirs. They got drawn into the morasse, too. Active management of

Chapter 6

the Estate fell to Benjamin Suchoff. As the court-appointed Successor Trustee Suchoff now became an attractive target for attacks by Peter Bartók, whose sharp pen left an epistolary record of staggering proportion: hundreds upon hundreds of tartly worded letters that fill archival boxes around the globe wherever remnants of this litigation can be found.

* * *

To judge from Victor Bator's letters and later chronicles of the Bartók Estate's history, his work as Trustee in the 1950s fell into three broad categories:

1. Attention to the wellbeing of Bartók's three heirs, expressed in a variety of ways; Trust financial support for Ditta and Peter was a paramount objective.
2. Battles with Hungarian publishers and their lawyers over copyright matters, with specific emphasis on the 21 works whose copyrights were owned by Hungarian publishers before they were liquidated under communist rule.
3. Management of the copyrights for Bartók's music across the globe through licenses for publication and recording.

These fiduciary duties were expected of him as Trustee. They consumed most of his available time. For the growing Archives he also worked on:

4. Acquisition of new materials.
5. Conservation and organization of manuscripts and other materials coming in.
6. Planning for a future institutional home for its holdings.

Extensive documentation of Victor Bator's fiduciary activities is preserved in his Memorandum. There can be found a detailed chronicle of his contract renegotiations with Boosey & Hawkes and Universal Edition (1946–54), and an exhaustive listing of actions he took on behalf of the Estate. A chapter from that Memorandum titled "The Hungarian Problem" can be found in complete form in the appendices to this book. Of the extraordinary volume of correspondence he generated while Trustee no estimate can yet be attempted for how much has survived into the modern era. Most of it is probably lost or discarded—a common fate for business correspondence.[2] In this chapter I selec-

---

2 According to a Memorandum dated December 30, 1968, Suchoff received into his care that

tively review his writings to establish an inner architecture for the Estate's actions in the 1950s.

The Interpretive Declaration of 1951

Early in 1951 Victor Bator heard of changes taking place in how Hungarian government agencies were managing the flow of income from sales and performances of Bartók's music. Here it was. This was the battle he knew would be coming his way. By either version of his Will Béla Bartók had granted to his oldest son Béla Bartók Jr. some property and rights in the Estate, which at the time was comprised largely of copyrights. At issue was how much income he should receive, and from where, and how those decisions were made. Bator in New York wasn't in any position to supervise or manage royalties generated by performances of Bartók's music in Hungary. Even if he'd wanted to, the severity of the country's postwar economic and political turbulence ruled out oversight from abroad. As a result, from 1946 to 1951 Bela Jr. and Ditta were left to collect whatever they could from Hungarian publishers and performers, supported from afar—in a principled way—by their American counterparts.[3] "The idea behind every step taken by me or Peter B. [after the war] was to have the Hungarian income collected wherever it could be collected, and to use it for the benefit of the two members of the family living over there," Bator wrote in the Memorandum. Practicality ruled.

Until it didn't.

As we saw above, in Chapter 3, this matter of dueling Wills became the principal source of *legal* tension in the Estate once the communist regime had decided on its strategy of laying claim to Bartók's material legacy. The Hungarian side had one Will. The American side had another. In early 1951 the troubles—we can use the Irish term—began in earnest, on a number of fronts. As his father's namesake, and by virtue of his 1/3 claim to royalty income through the Hungarian Will, Béla Jr. had received a portion of royalty income generated in post-war Hungary. Late in 1950 he noticed that the new ministries in charge

---

    month all of the Estate correspondence and business papers from Victor Bator's former office on the 16th floor of E. 72nd Street. He collected these papers from their temporary storage in the Archives offices and moved them to his own office in Cedarhurst, New York (BSCB Tampa). Suchoff indicated to me that he gave "all of that stuff" to Peter Bartók in 1985 (Interview with the author, June 19, 2002).

3 In his Memorandum Bator mentions one instance. He and Peter instructed Béla Jr, in a letter sent November 10, 1949, to seek a fee of 30,000 forints (=$3,000 at the official exchange rate) for the first performance of the Viola Concerto in Hungary. That fee, Peter directed, should "be paid in the proportion 50:50 to you and my mother."

Chapter 6

of culture were leaving him out of discussions; he was being ignored in other ways, too. Worried about what this might mean for him personally in the new regime, he wrote to his brother, risking the censors. Most Hungarians in North America were deeply concerned about the communist takeover. An atmosphere of urgency and worry gathered around any communications from back home. After learning of Béla Jr.'s worries, Peter Bartók conferred with Bator, who in turn consulted with his lawyer. They jointly decided to send over a formal statement of support on behalf of the Estate. This "Interpretive Declaration" was dated February 28, 1951, and signed by Bator, Co-Trustee Gyula Báron, and Peter Bartók. As its title suggests, it was not a legal document in the narrow, binding sense; but it did transfer to Béla Jr. the right to act on behalf of the Estate and the beneficiaries with respect to the family's affairs in Hungary. It represented a concerted statement of intent by the two American trustees, backed by Mrs. Bartók's son, who had power of attorney to speak for his mother.

The basic idea of this document, Bator later explained, was to let Béla Jr. "get hold, collect, and take possession of everything that couldn't be taken out of Hungary anyway, and unless collected by him would be lost." (Bator's own rueful summary of the Interpretive Declaration's effects on the Estate, and on Béla Jr., form a large portion of his chapter on "The Hungarian Problem.") Its timing couldn't have been better. The same day Béla Jr. received it in the mail from New York, he also received word that the Ministry of Education and Culture had ruled on a new payment plan. According to decree 1732/51, from henceforth, i.e., early March 1951, all Hungarian payments to the family would be divided as follows: 1/4 to each of the two sons, 1/2 to Bartók's widow. On the surface these ratios showed a certain fairness.

But now three entirely different royalty allocation plans existed for Béla Bartók's music, each with its own supporting claims for legal authority. No single person or entity even knew them all.[4] The new, communist-dictated formula bore no relation to the ratios Bartók expressly laid out in his Hungarian Will—not to mention the entirely different, trust-based plan laid out in the valid American Will. Readers interested in how this tangled knot got resolved will find Bator's narration of subsequent events fascinating (see "The Hungarian Problem" and the Affidavit of 1960 at the back of this book). Enough grist now existed for a decade's worth of legal jousting.

Bator came to regret the Interpretive Declaration. It brought more trouble than it was worth. Its goal had been to position Béla Jr. favorably with the new

---

4   Victor Bator claimed to not know the specific details of the Hungarian Will until the mid-1950s. I see no reason to disbelieve him. Béla Bartók had preserved a draft of his 1940 Hungarian Will in his papers when he came to the United States. That Will's final version appears to have been left in Hungary, either with Béla Jr. or with Ernő András.

Hungarian regime, or, as Bator put it, "to make an attempt to build him up into the strongest possible position" (Memorandum). In that respect it succeeded. By 1953 and 1954, though, Béla Jr. started to turn against Bator and the American Estate—a significant and worrisome development. He increasingly appeared to act in concert with Hungarian government agencies, lending his name to their actions and fronting for them in communications abroad. Bator viewed this transformation as a tragic betrayal of the Bartók family legacy of principled resistance to totalitarianism: "Despite the lure and bribes, I believe that it could have been expected from the son of Béla Bartók not to join the Communist bureaucrats engaged in these intrigues, schemings, and practices." In the Memorandum he shrewdly analyzes the psychology of Béla Jr.'s accommodation, not without sympathy, for he knew, or felt he knew, what pressures Béla Jr. would have faced to lend his name to the new regime. Why should any of this be surprising? he asks rhetorically. "Why would it be surprising and not the most natural and human experience to see Béla Jr. disengaging himself from the Estate, the Trustees, his brother and Mrs. Béla Bartók? How could Béla Jr., living in Hungary, strewn by government favors, be expected to resist the temptation to ally himself with the Hungarian authorities?" In his analysis, Béla Jr.'s understandably human desire for security, recognition, and privilege left him open to manipulation by the regime. Bator, seeing the damage the Interpretive Declaration had done, formally revoked it in late 1954.[5]

Between the Interpretive Declaration and the new communist government's energetic assertion of rights to ever-increasing shares of revenue across Europe, the question of who controlled the rights for Bartók's individual works, i.e., who held copyright control, became hotly contested ground after 1951. The main conflicts were felt in two areas:

1. Early works brought out by Hungarian publishers that had been liquidated to become Zeneműkiadó Vállalat. Did the copyrights for these "21 works," as they soon became known in litigation circles, revert to the trust, as Bartók specified in his American Will, or did they now belong to the state? Legal maneuvering in this highly technical area of international copyright law created steady turmoil for the Estate and Bartók's publishers. Seeking to strike back against unjust infringement, Bator vigorously claimed them for the Estate, and brought bat-

---

[5] Bator sought counsel in New York from an attorney at Manheim's firm who was familiar with international copyright conventions. Charles Seton recommended specific and immediate action in a letter delivered to him on October 15, 1954. Based on that advice he "withdrew and repudiated" the Interpretive Declaration via a letter written to ASCAP on October 27, 1954, signed by both trustees and Peter Bartók (Memorandum).

tle to communist authorities over these 21 copyrights. They just as vigorously asserted their rights to promote and control those works not just within Hungary, but, eventually, abroad as well.

2. Any publication or recording in Hungary that infringed on copyrights controlled by the Estate in New York. Examples include the Demény letters volumes.

The Interpretive Declaration muddied the waters by giving Hungarian state publishers, through Béla Jr., new leeway to conduct activity beyond the country's borders, in Germany, Austria, Czechoslovakia, Poland, Yugoslavia, and Rumania—seven countries total, including Hungary. Though it had been revoked in late 1954, the Hungarian government kept using its expansive powers to lay claim to more and more. What had been a *private* right given to Béla Jr. became by 1955, apparently, a *state* right *fronted* by Béla Jr., in whose name it was claimed. Here, in a nutshell, stood the essential ideological conflict between Western capitalism and communism.

In 1952 Nemesis emerged in the form of Dr. Róbert Palágyi, an attorney who before the war had been one of Hungary's few specialists in copyright law. (Bator seems to have known him by reputation in their earlier days.) It would be three more years before Bator learned his name. Palágyi claimed to represent as counsel an extraordinary number of offices and organizations in Hungary. In the Memorandum Bator enumerates them, almost in awe, as "a) Béla Jr.; b) Office for the Protection of Authors Rights, c) Performing Rights Society, d) Office for the Publication of Music, e) Corvina, f) Association of Hungarian Musicians, g) other companies or agencies engaged in exploitation of copyrights, h) company for the production of films." How can one man speak for all these agencies, as well as for Béla Jr.? Bator was incredulous. In one typical action, Palágyi accompanied Béla Jr. to Vienna in the mid-1950s to retain Austrian attorneys to file suit against Universal Edition, claiming royalty collection violations on behalf of Hungarian state offices. In 1955 Palágyi claimed control of the copyrights for the 21 works not just in Hungary, but for the whole world. (The works in question included Bartók's early piano works published by Rozsnyai or Rózsavölgyi.) In 1959–61 Palágyi spearheaded the Hungarian government's litigation against the estate, using Béla Jr. and Ditta as fronts for claims of mismanagement and fraud. The Interpretive Declaration resurfaced at that time—as did another legal document that had been slumbering quietly for 14 years, and now was called by destiny to wreak its havoc.

Bator came to see Palágyi as not only "the mouthpiece of the Hungarian government," but also "the mover, promoter, and leading spirit of their anti-

Bartók scheme" (Affidavit). Elsewhere he is "commander of the Government task force against the Bartók Estate." Palágyi first identified himself in letters to the U.S. in 1955. He had been actively directing decisions for the propagation of Bartók's music since 1952, he indicated; until 1955 he concealed his name behind a facade of bureaucratic anonymity. Through his various offices the communist regime asserted legal claims to Bartók's legacy. They nibbled away year after year through licensing contracts made illegally for compositions the state purported to own, lawsuits filed in foreign courts against Boosey & Hawkes or Universal Edition, threats of those same lawsuits, and publications that openly infringed on copyright. (See the many instances detailed in "The Hungarian Problem" and the Affidavit of 1960 at the back of this book.) These actions all demanded careful monitoring and response by those publishers, each of whom had negotiated separately with Bator for licensing rights, all carefully laid out and defined with regard to territory.

Bator was not without allies in Hungary. His sister was a doctor in Budapest, and he had many friends and acquaintances among the people who had stayed, even such close family friends as the Chatels. His sister, because of her profession, enjoyed certain protections in the new regime, and was able to get news out to Bator.[6] In 1954 he discovered another sympathetic ear in the form of Dr. Béla Keresztes, a lawyer who represented Ditta Bartók. Keresztes had a daughter who had married János Bartók, a cousin of Béla Jr. and of Peter's. Bator came to see him as a "trusted friend and 'in-law' relative." Keresztes served as Ditta Bartók's personal counsel in the 1950s; after 1961 he would be replaced in that role by Ernő Vajda. Keresztes and Bator appear to have struck up a cordial understanding based on their joint efforts to make sure Ditta was cared for.[7] Keresztes wrote with candor and confidentiality to Bator, and from his comments Bator felt reassured that Ditta Bartók still expressed solidarity with his actions as trustee.

"The Hungarian Problem"

"The Hungarian Problem" opens with a lengthy, itemized list of what Bator knew about Ditta's positions and opinions through 1957. Through Keresztes he discerned her positions on essential Estate matters. She approved of his use of

---

6   Suchoff, interview with the author, June 19, 2002.
7   Bator in his Memorandum refers to his "voluminous" and "confidential" correspondence with Keresztes after 1954, at least through the end of 1957. These letters may yet exist. If found, they would provide invaluable insight into Ditta Bartók's physical condition and state of mind in the 1950s.

Chapter 6

trust funds for maintenance of the Archive (#3); she endorsed the position that "all income no matter which country, which publisher, whatever other source it may come from, should be collected by the Trustee (#2); she repudiated the stand of Hungarian government agencies "in regard to the control of copyrights, the distribution of income" (#5); she had not approved or endorsed the stand taken by Peter Bartók after 1958, that is, the present litigation in Surrogate's Court (#7). Collectively, these and other positions by Mrs. Bartók were tremendously important to him, because they validated—in his eyes—the actions he had taken as Trustee. To a skeptical eye, or a plaintiff's attorney, these itemized "facts" might be discounted as self-serving and biased. That possibility must be acknowledged. Bator's willingness to report her positions at face value contrasts noticeably with his close scrutiny of the two sons' actions.

The more important truth revealed in this chapter of the Memorandum is that Victor Bator himself felt that he stood on solid ground with Ditta up to the time of its writing (late 1959/early 1960). As internal fault lines in the Bartók Estate grew more defined, it became increasingly apparent that Béla Jr. stood on one side, allied with the communist regime's interests, while Victor Bator stood on the other side, with the American Estate, in solidarity (he felt) with Ditta. Where Peter stood on this chessboard seemed to be changing. Until 1958 he had been firmly on Bator's side. That year, after the incidents described below, his allegiance shifted.

Irked by his recitation of Palágyi's many official positions, Bator came up with a visual metaphor to describe his own corresponding role in the Bartók Estate's history. The metaphor is so striking that I made it the title of this book. It drew from him one of his most impassioned statements about Bartók's legacy during the Cold War.

> Yet, there are always thorns in rosebushes. One such thorn, ever since the establishment of the Hungarian Communist regime, has been the existence of the Bartók Estate. This sounds ridiculously disproportionate. It would be if Béla Bartók were but a composer of music, no matter how great or important as such. But a legend surrounding his name made out of Béla Bartók, the scholar and composer, the "greatest Hungarian" of the past generation, as just now, in our contemporary period, the name of the "greatest living Hungarian" would no doubt be voted by all Hungarians to be another musician, composer, and scholar, Zoltán Kodály. Thus, the subjection of the Estate of Béla Bartók to the complete control of the Government is not a problem of rule over a few dozen musical works, not even over the use of the substantial foreign exchange income, but the possibility to exploit the name, reputation, and fame of Bartók—

the Bartók legend—for the political, propaganda, soul- and mind-control-scheme of the Government.

If the Bartók Estate was a thorn to the communist government, Bator was the sharp tip of that thorn. He used his position as Trustee to relentlessly push back, to prick, to wound. He was good at it. He refused to let a communist regime take control of Bartók's spiritual legacy and pervert it into support for socialist ideals. Against such a broad ideological front he could only do so much, of course. But as Trustee he held exceptional legal power. Tales of his battles with Hungarian publishers fill the pages of his correspondence. (Letter to Ernest Roth in 1958: "I am not entirely pessimistic because I have succeeded, as you know, to block their attempts to sell Bartok music and collect fees from abroad, not only in England, Australia, Switzerland, France, but in other places too, and that is a language they seem to understand.")[8] Two lectures he gave in the United States (Appendix) show him as a principled advocate for keeping Bartók's name clear of Hungarian communist propaganda.

After 1951, friction from these many skirmishes pushed heat into the Estate, filling it with energy that had to dissipate somehow. With each passing year the Estate collected more money from royalties and licensing agreements. By the end of the 1950s the American Bartók Estate was generating significant annual income for the Trust and its beneficiaries. A table of annual income figures shows the rapid growth after 1946 (Fig. 6.1).

Fig. 6.1. Annual income for the Bartók Estate, 1946-61. All figures taken from the court-approved First Intermediate Accounting, supplemented by information found in the Second Intermediate Accounting (1958-61). Source: Referee's Report, Index #P2751/1945. Milton Goldman, Surrogate's Court of the State of New York (May 14, 1971).

1946	$2,891.04	1954	$40,717.14
1947	3,693.50	1955	34,652.54
1948	10,571.50	1956	42,856.83
1949	23,853.22	1957	59,111.19
1950	13,577.66	1958	62,914.19
1951	16,987.66	1959	82,611.17
1952	22,898.95	1960	62,297.57
1953	36,205.40	1961	112,149.03

---

8   Victor Bator, letter to Ernest Roth, January 14, 1958 (Collection of Francis Bator).

Chapter 6

These figures reflect income received from four principal sources: ASCAP, Boosey & Hawkes, Ltd., Boosey & Hawkes, Inc., and Universal Editions Ltd. of London. Additional, minor amounts of income came in during these years through Boosey & Hawkes Canada, Ltd., Edward B. Marks Music Corp., and Carl Fischer and several other sources. They omit, of course, any revenues that accrued to government agencies in Budapest.

Victor Bator's analysis of the Estate's "Hungarian Problem" confirms what anyone might have suspected about the ways communist governments went about their business. What I find fascinating are the details. Bator's narrative chronology amasses facts and statements from a variety of individuals who were directly involved in the propagation of Bartók's music after the war. He *shows* us how the communist government took control away from the Bartók heirs. He introduces us to individual communist bureaucrats. He does not disguise his impatience with their actions, but he's reasoned and detailed in his grievances. Ever the professional lawyer, he patiently builds his case. He quotes extensively from letters he received during this time, avoiding generalizations, his mind always fascinated with the details. His Memorandum, and the Affidavit, record events and impressions while they were still fresh, preserving in amber the attitudes and positions that introduced so much conflict into the Estate by 1960.

Benjamin Suchoff lived with the consequences of the Estate's disfunction. He felt that the root of its problems went back still further, to late 1945, when Peter Bartók made decisions about the Third Piano Concerto and Viola Concerto without consulting with Bator. "That's when the estrangement really began with Victor," he told me. The relationship between the two men had gotten off to a rocky start. It never fully recovered its equilibrium, despite many years of cordial relations. As time went on Bator tried to conceal behind his actions a growing impatience with Bartók's youngest son and what he called Peter's "inclination to desponding." Peter, on his part, while grateful for Bator's generous support of his Bartók Records business, and appreciative of the Trustee's handling of all contracts and licensing agreements, eventually grew weary of Bator's strong management style and archives ambitions. As expressed in the litigation of 1959–61, he felt Bator too often spoke "as if he had inherited the decedent's [Béla Bartók's] authority to advise, guide, and direct his family."[9]

Still, he and Bator had reason to keep common cause with each other. A letter from Bator to Serge Moreux in May 1957 shows him to be genuinely sup-

---

9   S. Samuel DiFalco, Opinion re Estate of Béla Bartók (1961). The purest expression of Peter Bartók's complaints against Bator that I have found is a 7-page typed "Memorandum in Reference to the Bartók Estate" that Peter prepared in 1961 for use by European attorneys, while the litigation was still pending and all the history was fresh in his mind. A copy of this document was sent to Paul Sacher, who saved it (BBC-PSS Basel).

portive of Peter's recording business (see Correspondence). Peter kept the affectionate "Viktor bácsi" salutation in his correspondence through the mid-1950s. Tensions over the whereabouts of the Viola Concerto manuscript peaked in those years. Bator still blamed Peter for letting the manuscript out of their hands in the first place, and the 1952 Bartók Records recording re-aggravated those grievances. ("No more Uncle Victor after that!" Suchoff commented wryly.) When the final break came, in late 1957 and early 1958, it arrived on two fronts: Peter's disastrous recording of the First Piano Concerto, and his response to seeing for the first time a full accounting of expenses and income for the Estate dating back to its inception.

The Events of 1958. Peter Bartók's Recording of the First Piano Concerto. The Premiere of the Stefi Geyer Violin Concerto in Basel.

In February 1958 Peter Bartók recorded the First Piano Concerto up in Boston with a string orchestra known as the Zimbler Sinfonietta, augmented by winds, brass, and percussion from the Boston Symphony Orchestra and other professional ringers. The Zimbler ensemble had already made over a dozen recordings for Decca, Unicorn, Boston Records, Deutsche Grammophon, and, recently, RCA Victor. It was a versatile and experienced group, used to the rigors of recording sessions. For the Bartók concerto Leonid Hambro was the pianist. Robert Mann conducted. The only problem with this recording is that it had already been attempted once before.

Several months earlier Peter had arranged to record the same works with Hambro, but in London, and with a different orchestra and different conductor. Those London sessions in December 1957 went poorly. Peter showed up late for his own recording session. He scrambled to assemble his equipment while the musicians waited. Hastily they ran through the pieces in the remaining time, but the results were declared unusable by all involved, whether from microphone placement, uneven sound levels, or rough spots in the ensemble that couldn't be patched in time. The recording was a failure. A very expensive failure. Suchoff, who was working at the Archives at the time, vividly remembered the First Piano Concerto incident and how angry it made Victor Bator.

> Peter had the opportunity to record the First Piano Concerto with a friend of his, Leonid Hambro, who was a very fine pianist. It would be recorded in London with an assemblage of musicians. I don't remember the ins and outs of the story. Maybe it was the London Philharmonic? Or another group of musicians. But it was arranged that they would record it in Lon-

Chapter 6

don and Peter would do the recording in London with this well-known pianist. And Tibor Serly would be the conductor. So I guess it was a pickup orchestra that Tibor probably arranged. Anyway, this is what happened. The parts were passed out, the musicians got started, and Serly took them through their paces a little bit. They got started. They might have gone through it, for all I know. But where was Peter? So Peter comes in, and they had to stop practicing. And Peter set up his microphones, and his cables, his recording apparatus. Time was running out. They were getting paid by the hour. A big orchestra! By the hour! Finally, they cut the record, as they say. And it was a disaster. The masters were packed in a storage case and Peter brought it home. But he could not publish it. And Victor paid out $10,000. *Ten. Thousand. Dollars.* This was when the real break with Victor began. Because he realized he had to account for this to Mrs. Bartók.[10]

Using his power as Trustee, Bator curtly refused to license the tape, blocking Peter from putting it into production. A letter he wrote to Tibor Serly on January 6, 1958, thanks him for taking the trouble to explain what went on in the recording session (see correspondence, above). "I have an impartial appraisal from a musician of high rank whose judgment I trust," Bator wrote, "according to which the tape did not record a top quality performance no matter what the reasons happen to have been." Having refused to allow a number of major philharmonic orchestras to record this piece earlier in the 1950s, Bator felt embarrassed at the outcome. Peter Bartók's recording needed to be "a superior quality production" in order to justify those earlier refusals. When he learned from other musicians, including Serly, about Peter's "unfortunate and unsuccessful recording," he decided he couldn't let it be released. "How he will solve this impasse must be his business," he declared. Peter himself, of course, would have been the first to refuse releasing a substandard performance; his exacting standards as a recording engineer were well known. How he found himself going into a recording session unprepared we'll never know. Apparently the sessions in Boston two months later, with a new orchestra and new conductor, were part of his solution. In that later form the First Piano Concerto recording was released the following year (Fig. 6.2).

---

10   Suchoff, interview with the author, June 19, 2002. By the time I spoke with him Suchoff could no longer remember all the details, but he expressed no uncertainty about the importance of this incident to the Bartók Estate's subsequent history. I believe the possibility exists that in this recollection he inadvertently conflates two episodes from Peter Bartók's recording career. Peter was in London frequently for recordings in the 1950s; I have found no supporting evidence that the first, failed recording of the First Piano Concerto took place there. A firmer account of this episode may be possible someday should any of Peter Bartók's personal files for his recording business emerge from storage in CPB Homosassa and become accessible to scholars.

Fig. 6.2. Front cover of the Bartók Records LP of the First Piano Concerto (BR 313, released 1959). Source: CPB Homosassa

Bator didn't absolve Serly of blame for the mishap, either. In a follow-up letter he bluntly suggested that Serly, as "captain of the ship and first in command" for the recording sessions might have shown more initiative to find out why he "received no call, or request for conferences" from Peter in the days before the session. Out of fairness to Peter, he wrote, "I don't think that the fault lies on one side of the gallery only."[11]

From Peter's various writings over the years we know he viewed this incident as the end of Bartók Records. From that point forward, he was fond of saying, his involvement in the litigation proved so time-consuming that he no longer had time for the record business.[12] (Suchoff's take was less charitable. Peter, he said, "ran his record business into the ground.") His reaction and later reminiscences suggest that some emotional cord must have finally been cut, too—a cord

---

11 Victor Bator, letter to Tibor Serly, January 15, 1958 (Collection of Francis Bator).
12 See, for example, the history of the Bartók Estate he placed on deposit in BBC-PSS Basel. Peter eventually released the Hambro recording, pairing it with the Rhapsody, Op. 1. As of 2020 copies of the LP can still be purchased through the Bartók Records website.

Chapter 6

that tied him to his faltering Bartók Records enterprise, and also to Bator. Thereafter, in quick succession, the following incidents and events took place, all of which together turned what was essentially a private dispute into the opportunity the Hungarian regime, through Robert Palágyi, had been waiting for.

One of the great Bartók discoveries after World War II was the long-lost early Violin Concerto, which came to light in 1956 when Stefi Geyer, its muse, arranged for it to be placed with Paul Sacher for longterm keeping in Basel after her death. She authorized the transfer to Sacher of the autograph score and violin solo part that Bartók had given to her. To highlight the new discovery he planned a Bartók Festival in Basel for three days at the end of May 1958. He made arrangements for a very fine Swiss violinist, Hansheinz Schneeberger, to give the premiere performances; Geyer had expressly wished that Schneeberger be the soloist. News of the previously unknown work and its upcoming premiere electrified the Bartók world. Peter Bartók wrote to Sacher excitedly, hoping to record the work.[13] When Bator learned of the proposed performance, however, he immediately opposed it, using as his argument the principles enshrined in Bartók's Will: that the right to manage and control copyright for all his works was vested in the Trustee. A battle royale erupted. These two men with strong personal ties to Bartók, both determined to do the right thing for their deceased friend, launched into a heated dispute that stretched into late 1957 and early 1958, right up to the weeks before the performance. (Victor Bator on Sacher: "He may be a good musician, but he is certainly not a good copyright lawyer. Neither is he a good psychologist, having tried to cut corners and ignore the simple fact that it wasn't he whom Bartók appointed as trustee. The matter is in the hands of lawyers.")[14]

A rich trail of documentation survives for this controversy, both in Basel and in the Collection of Francis Bator. As an important episode in the post-war reception of Bartók's music, it warrants extended consideration separately. I cannot do it full justice here. Bator wanted Menuhin or a violinist of comparable international stature to give the premiere, not a (to him) fairly obscure Swiss violinist who happened to be on friendly terms with Sacher. Both Sacher and Bator claimed certain ownership rights to the manuscript. Bator felt that legally it belonged to the Bartók Estate. He claimed the right to arrange publication of the new work—a concession he was granted. Sacher felt that Geyer's bequest, and his previous demonstrated commitment to Bartók's music, gave him a moral right to arrange the first performance and select the violinist. His ownership of the manuscript had been specifically intended by Geyer. Bator, yielding an inch,

---

13 Peter Bartók, letter to Paul Sacher, October 1, 1957 (BBC-PSS Basel).
14 Bator, letter to Sándor Veress, January 28, 1958. Collection of Francis Bator.

requested that a photostatic copy of the manuscript and its violin part be sent to America immediately. The matter ended with a compromise both men deeply resented. Bator refused to allow the performance unless the manuscript itself would be delivered to him afterwards for the Bartók Estate in New York. Sacher, as a concession, was allowed to keep the manuscript (score + solo part) for a period of three years. At the end of that period, in 1961, he was to deliver the autographs to Bator in New York. In the unsteady truce that followed, Sacher boiled with anger over how he had been treated. Neither he nor Bator had walked away victorious. But having won the right to use Schneeberger, he went on to program the piece and give the Bartók Festival. The concerto received its premiere under his direction in Basel, Switzerland, on May 30, 1958.

In attendance at the festival to witness events were Victor and Franci Bator, Peter Bartók, and Béla Jr. and his wife. Ditta, invited, was unable to attend.[15] All stayed at the Drei Könige, Basel's famed 5-star luxury hotel. Only at the last minute did Hungarian authorities allow Béla Jr. and his wife to attend by issuing them the required passports; he arrived 24 hours after the opening events. Bator as a courtesy supplied him with $1,000 of spending money, or he wouldn't have had any western currency to spend; the Hungarian government hadn't provided for that need. (See Bator's description of the Basel event in the Affidavit.) He used Trust money to support Peter's travel and expenses, too. The Bartók sons spent two weeks in Basel that year as honored guests of Paul Sacher and the City of Basel. Amid the dinners and public appearances they made time for private conversation about the new concerto, the Estate's management, and other matters of mutual interest.

They had much to talk about. Since mid-1957 Victor Bator had been pondering alternatives to the Estate's current management structure. He had lost Báron as Co-Trustee the previous year. A vacancy existed in that position should he wish to have it filled.[16] Correspondence with the Bartók heirs, included above in this book, shows quite plainly the types of changes Bator was mulling. The dismal outcome of the Hungarian revolution demoralized him. He was more aware than ever of the ever-expanding volume of work required to manage the Bartók estate. Reviewing the options before him, Victor Bator considered passing more of the Estate's active management to Bartók's two sons. He had zero faith in Peter's ability to administer the Estate; he foresaw a spreading disaster. But with

---

15 One possible reason: were she and Béla Jr. to leave the country at the time, both to meet with Bator and with Peter, the risk of defection existed. Another possibility is that travel was simply too difficult for her to manage in her current state of health.
16 Tibor Serly remembered (1975) that he had been asked at one point if he might be willing to take a more formal administrative role for the Estate. From the information I have at hand it seems possible that that offer came to him from Bator in the late 1950s.

Chapter 6

help from good lawyers and accountants that Bator could arrange for him, perhaps he could carry on. Bator also recognized that was not getting any younger. He was 66. People lay plans for their retirement at that age.

In a letter to Béla Jr. sent at Christmastime in 1957, he suggested one possible way to eliminate some of the tensions over in Hungary. "I am happy to hand over the managing rights of the estate in those six countries to you, because in the end who could be a better man for the job than the son of the testator, my late great friend." After all, he writes, "you are much younger than me, and your ability to work will surely outlive mine." But he would only countenance such a move if Béla Jr. assured him that he would not yield those rights to the Hungarian state. A legally binding agreement agreeing to these terms would be required. To help Béla Jr. envision what that might look like, he drafted a detailed proposal and sent two copies to Hungary, one to Béla Jr., the other to Palágyi.[17]

To Peter in January 1958 he wrote a candid assessment of the current state of affairs. Other than the still unresolved controversy over the 21 works in Hungary, he indicated, everything in the Estate's purview has been brought under control and is running smoothly. Because of the dramatic increase in interest in his father's music, though, "I find myself busier than ever with Bartók matters." He then makes an extraordinary confession: "I am perfectly willing to resign." But, he warns Peter, if that were to happen, "you will have to retain a good attorney, because most of the activities require knowledge of the law, understanding of legal problems and accounting." (See correspondence, above.)

The controversy over the Stefi Geyer violin concerto landed squarely in the middle of this internal ferment. Bator had just been signaling his willingness to step down as Trustee, or to make concessions under the right conditions. It's no wonder, then, that in Basel the two Bartók brothers determined to seize this moment. Each for his own reasons chafed under the present circumstances. In the summer of 1958 they commenced their push to remove Bator as Trustee, aided and abetted by Palágyi, who marshalled the forces available to him—including his ability to speak for Ditta—in support of this now seemingly achievable goal. Their open rebellion began. A reluctant, confused, but ultimately compliant Ditta got pulled into the conflict when her name was needed to front the lawsuit that issued from Hungary in 1959. Bator's solemn insistence on using the power of his office to assert control over the violin concerto had done him no favors with Bartók's two sons, it must be acknowledged. Both

---

17 Victor Bator, letter to Róbert Palágyi, December 21, 1957 (Collection of Francis Bator). Translated by Etelka Nyilasi. In this enormous letter spanning 8 single-space typed pages, Bator reviewed the legal disputes over the 21 works and proposed modifications to the current arrangements.

were quick to perceive his actions as a disservice to their father's memory, and an embarrassment to the family. Peter, from this point forward, turned against Bator more consistently, challenging his actions and decisions, disputing them, picking fights, knowing that he had the support of his brother.

Sensing that he had Sacher's ear, too, Peter Bartók began to send letters to Basel with news of the concerto manuscript, news of the Estate, and, eventually, appeals for advice on legal matters.[18] Sacher became his new confidant, a potential ally to be cultivated for the fight that lay ahead. Of primary concern to Peter by 1961 was whether Sacher intended to transmit the manuscript for the violin concerto to the Bartók *Estate*, or the Bartók *Archive*. The distinction hadn't mattered much before. But now, due to the litigation, it mattered very much. To Peter, at least.

The First Intermediate Accounting

In mid-1957 Victor Bator hired an accountant in New York to prepare a report on income and expenses for the first ten years of the Bartók Estate. He did so partly to quell Peter's questions, and partly to settle in his own mind a proper path forward now that both the Estate and the Archives had grown significantly in size. It seemed like a good time to take stock. As part of what he called "this 'putting-everything-in-order' business" he appointed his son Paul as Successor Trustee. His other son Peter he added as Trustee, too, by early 1959, making them his Successor Co-Trustees.[19] His renegotiated contracts with Boosey & Hawkes and Universal Edition were churning out more revenue than ever before. "Something like 16 1/2 percent royalty," Suchoff remembered appreciatively. "He squeezed that out of Boosey & Hawkes and Universal Edition, and they screamed bloody murder. That brought in an awful lot of money."[20] Interest in Bartók's music seemed to keep expanding with each passing year, as measured in recordings, live performances, and sheet music sales or rentals. Bator sat down with Peter Bartók in January 1958 to review the report. He showed Bartók's son the annual levels of income and explained where that income was coming from, and in what amounts. He also showed him the breakdown of annual expenses since 1946. What was later described in court docu-

---

18 A collection of 35 letters between Sacher and Peter Bartók, dating from 1957 to 1975, has been preserved in the Paul Sacher Stiftung.
19 Victor Bator, memorandum to his three sons, January 13, 1959. The co-trustee model made sense in their current circumstances, he explained, because Peter was a member of the New York Bar.
20 Suchoff, interview with the author, Jan. 19, 2002. The exact royalty percentages for licensing of sheet music, recordings, and live performance are exhaustively detailed in Bator's Memorandum.

Chapter 6

ments as the "First Intermediate Accounting" comprised a detailed summary of how the Trust's income had been spent over the first twelve years, from its inception in 1946 up to Dec. 31, 1957.

More ink got spilled in later court proceedings over this First Intermediate Accounting than even the most curious later historian would wish to wade through. What appears to have mattered for the Bartók Estate's history is that after January 1958 Peter Bartók, and through Peter, the Hungarian heirs and the Hungarian government lawyers, had access to specific figures for the Estate's income and expenses. Peter knew much of this information already: Bator had kept him informed, at semi-regular intervals since 1947, of how much income was coming in.[21] Now those figures stared up at the heirs from the page in black and white. The Hungarians saw how much money had been going to Peter for his record company and living expenses.[22] The report tallied the amounts Bator had spent on staff (Varga, Suchoff, other assistants, secretaries) and materials (binders, storage systems, safe, microfilm and photography, office supplies) needed for "maintenance and improvements of the manuscripts" still housed on the 16th floor of E. 72nd Street.

It also showed that Bator himself had never collected a penny for his work; his remuneration as Trustee from 1946–57 was exactly $0.00 for the entire span. By longstanding practice in American law, Trustees customarily receive a small percentage of Trust income as compensation for their time and effort, in the range of 1–2% as a minimum, sometimes higher. The generosity of Bator's decision to forego this practice drew only passing appreciation from Peter, and (we may safely infer) zero appreciation over in Hungary. What really mattered to the heirs was the eye-popping amount of money Bartók's music had started to generate in royalty income—in 1956 and 1957 combined, a total of $101,968, an amount equivalent to $945,000 in 2020 dollars. Money like that will turn peoples' heads. Peter responded as most of us might have done, very humanly. He decided that he might have allocated some of this money differently if he were in charge.

Of course, he wasn't in charge. Not even remotely. And therein lay his problem.

---

21 A letter from Peter to Bator dated March 15, 1947, acknowledges having received a "detailed accounting" of the income for the Estate; he indicates that he sent a copy of the report to Béla Jr. in Budapest (BSCB Tampa).

22 I have not yet located an actual copy of the First Intermediate Accounting report. My comments here are derived from later judicial accounts that refer specifically to its content. Exact figures for Peter's income in the later 1950s got reported elsewhere, too. A 2-page typed document titled "Payment to Peter Bartók, from 1956 January" shows every Trust distribution to Peter from 1956-59 (BSCB Tampa). The subtotals are: 1956, $12,642; 1957, $21,052.65; 1958, $30,3982; 1959 (Jan–July 31), $4,000.

The Second Intermediate Accounting

As litigation dragged on into the mid-1960s, it became important to bring the estate's financial figures current for all parties to examine. What became known as the Second Intermediate Accounting added four more years to the span under consideration, from Jan. 1, 1958, to Dec. 31, 1961.

The Litigation of 1959–61

Several months after they returned from Switzerland, Bator summoned Peter Bartók to his home again, this time to have him look at a revised version of the accountant's report. Peter had asked valid questions about the report when he first saw it. To allay his concerns Bator had requested the accountant to make adjustments to the ways certain expense categories were itemized. As before, Peter approved the report, signing in writing that he had reviewed the report and found it accurate. His release and consent had been recommended by Bator's legal counsel, Gustave Rosen, who also took the precaution of filing the accounting report in Surrogate's Court, together with Peter's signed approvals. The sons' discontent had reached the point where precautions were necessary. On January 6, 1959, the First Intermediate Accounting was judicially settled by decree of the Surrogate's Court.[23] This had the effect of certifying the financial accounts of the Estate's first 12 years, making them a matter of court record.

This year-long process of looking closely at the finances of the Estate turned up loose ends that needed to be addressed going forward. First, it showed quite plainly that managing the Estate required a considerable investment of time and expertise—one later judge called Bator's Trusteeship "essentially a full-time job." Bator had passed the point where he felt comfortable doing that work for free. Peter had been telling him for years that he deserved to take some form of compensation. Bator always resisted. Now it was time. Second, the status of the Archives needed clarification. Were its holdings Bator's personal property? Did they belong to the Estate? Had expenses for Estate and Archive been commingled in the past, or handled loosely? Should costs be segregated more carefully going forward? Finally, the accountant's probing into the movement of funds had revealed some tax irregularities. Peter had been paying state and fed-

---

23 Because trust law in the United States is state specific, any claims and litigation over the Bartók Estate usually needed to be resolved in state court, which in New York is called, for wills and estates matters, the Surrogate's Court. In New York, judges presiding over wills and estates matters are called "surrogates." Even when the Hungarian government became involved, after 1959, most of those disputes had to pass through Surrogate's Court.

Chapter 6

eral income tax every year on the money he received. Careful review of tax procedures, however, pointed instead to his mother as the individual in whose name some of the annual forms should have been filed.

Meanwhile, in Hungary Béla Jr. reported back to Palágyi about the conversations that had taken place in Basel. The offer Bator had made the preceding December was still on the table. Subject to certain conditions, Béla Jr. was still welcome to assume control of managing copyright matters for Hungary and other countries behind the Iron Curtain. One condition was non-negotiable, however: Béla Jr. would be assigned control as Bator's *agent*, and should he ever be unable to serve in that capacity, the rights to administer that portion of the Estate would revert to New York. Such an agreement, Bator thought, would empower Béla Jr. and give him some negotiating clout within Hungary by expanding and making semi-permanent the intentions of the Interpretive Declaration. He recalled the Basel conversations like this:

> I explained to him that that will help him and that he can use this construction to his own advantage because whenever he doesn't want to do something that the Government would want him to do, he could bottom his refusal upon the threatened or expected withdrawal of his authority and my resistance. During our negotiations in Basel, Switzerland, in May 1958 Peter Bartók strongly supported that argument and tried to impress upon Béla Jr. that this was in his own interest. It seems that in 1958 and ever since his Ego problem was already beyond rational thinking. He wanted unconditional surrender of the Trustee's rights in the countries behind the Iron Curtain and in Austria and Germany. It is difficult to decide how much and how far this is at the same time a "fronting" for the Hungarian Government. His acting is in unison and synchronized with the Hungarian government agencies. It serves not only what I called his Ego, but serves at the same time the aims and purposes of the Communist bureaucracy.[24]

Palágyi decided, instead, to take Bator's offer and go one step further, making a determined grab for control using the full force of his position. He was tired of dealing with Victor Bator. In a judicial proceeding in late 1958, the Office of Government Notaries formally upheld the validity of Béla Bartók's 1940 Hungarian Will; to that formality it attached further claims to control Bartók's music for the six countries identified in the Interpretive Declaration of 1951. Bator, when he learned about these legal actions, felt that these "semi-judicial

---

24 Bator, Affidavit in the litigation proceedings of 1959-61. See Appendix C.

decisions" in Budapest were aimed at "acquiring the entire property for Hungary," and establishing a legal-looking document with which to assert further claims in Vienna, London, and New York.[25] He was right.

By now Peter Bartók was actively colluding with Béla Jr. to unseat Bator. He had allowed himself to come under the sway of his half-brother as a way to gain some measure of control and standing for himself. The psychology behind his shift in allegiance fascinated Bator, who watched it happen. In a letter he wrote to Gustave Rosen in the fall of 1959 he mused freely about the recent changes he had observed in Bartók's youngest son:

> There is not the slightest doubt in my mind that Peter's frustrated psychological state is responsible for the aggression he is engaged in against me. It is a well-known reaction of dependent persons. They first turn against those who had sheltered and protected them, and make such persons responsible for all their failures and frustrations. Even if some of the factors could be attributed to the pressure of the Hungarians, that too, though indirectly, is a consequence of his frustrated state of mind.[26]

Letters sent back and forth across the Atlantic helped Peter and Béla Jr. cement their plans. Peter spent more and more time in Budapest. Hearings between all three heirs and government lawyers took place in late December 1958 and early January 1959. After those hearings Peter returned to New York to consult further with his attorney, Barbara Zinsser, who had taken the case on a contingency basis. (She represented Peter and his mother both.) In April 1959 he returned to Hungary again, this time with Zinsser's exact instructions on the next steps needed for all three heirs to join forces together most effectively in an American court. At those meetings Ditta Bartók was asked to sign some documents. She upheld the power of attorney (1946) granting Peter Bartók authority to act on her behalf. She simultaneously revoked Victor Bator's power of attorney (1946); he could no longer act on her behalf or represent her interests as Trustee. A third document directed the New York Surrogate's Court to appoint Peter Bartók as Successor Trustee. Ditta's brother Jenő Pásztory was present at these meetings to support her; he later sent a report of the three heirs' conclusions to Bator, who recognized the conspiracy afoot against him, controlled and directed by the Hungarian government. Mrs. Bartók's "limited consent" in this affair was apparent. (See Affidavit published as Appendix C in this book.)

---

25   Victor Bator, letter to Erich Habernal, October 24, 1961 (Collection of Francis Bator). Reproduced in full in the correspondence ahead of Chapter 6.
26   Bator, letter to Gustave Rosen, September 8, 1959 (Collection of Francis Bator).

Chapter 6

The Bartók heirs, backed by the communist state bureaucracy in Hungary, went to court in the summer of 1959. The petition was filed in New York Surrogate's Court by Zinsser. It claimed a number of injuries:

1. Bator had permitted Béla Jr. to collect royalties and income from Hungary, when, in fact, that income should have been collected for Ditta Bartók in New York. The total misdirected income was estimated at 1,500,000 Forints, or $130,000.
2. Bator had wasted more than $70,000 on Peter Bartók's Bartók Records business.
3. Bator had wasted large amounts of income for preserving the manuscripts belonging to the Estate.
4. Bator had wasted large amounts of income to establish a Bartók Archive, in which Bartók's letters, memorabilia, manuscripts and other papers connected with Bartók's life and works were included.
5. Bator had included in that same Archive a large number of manuscripts which belonged to the Estate.
6. Using his influence over Peter, Victor Bator had persuaded him to agree that the Estate should pay to offset his office expenses, including those allocated to the Archive, and also that the Estate should pay him 10% of the income as a fee for his special work.
7. Bator had neglected to file New York Estate Tax Returns, and that no Estate Tax was paid to New York State.[27]

In support of these allegations Peter Bartók filed a detailed Affidavit that became a matter of court record. To commence the litigation Zinsser pressed her attack on the Estate's accounting; the court petition requests as its specific goal the vacating of the judicial decree dated January 6, 1959. Success in this area would prepare them for the larger goal of unseating Bator as Trustee. If all went well it would be a two-stage process.

Although the suit was filed in Ditta Bartók's name, too, because of her nationality the matter was treated as if the main petitioner was Peter Bartók. American courts had shown great reluctance to render judgments that would result in money being transferred to countries behind the Iron Curtain. The suit thus opened as a conflict between Peter and Victor Bator, even though it was transparently clear that the Hungarian government had direct involvement in the case. Bator's main attorney for Estate business, Gustave Rosen, recom-

---

27 Henry Ess III, letter to Victor Bator, June 8, 1961 (Collection of Francis Bator). Here I paraphrase Ess's list, which he distilled from the original petition filed in court.

mended that they bring in a litigator from Sullivan and Cromwell who had specific expertise in the wills and trusts area. Henry N. Ess III was the big gun.[28] By September 1959 the defense team had accelerated into full response mode. They recommended that Bator begin preparing an extensive documentation of his activities as Trustee. The resulting Memorandum, which is liberally featured throughout this book, took him over five months to prepare.

Ditta already felt conflicted about the lawsuit and its allegations. No wonder. She had no conflict so deep with Béla Jr. that she should feel compelled to lay claim to all the royalty income he had received so far within Hungary. Why would she want to steal back from him like this? She had no say in the matter, of course. The government lawyers concocted this allegation as a way to attack Bator in court. She did what she could to protest the grab bag of claims being put forward in her name. As revealed in court documents, she wrote an important letter to Peter on July 2, 1959—right as the suit was being prepared—to underline her support for Victor Bator on all substantial matters. "As far as the past is concerned," she wrote her son,

> I consider payments toward the publication of phonograph records, toward the preservation of Father's manuscripts, and toward the helping of our relatives, as proper. I acknowledge and approve that these payments, together with the monies transferred to me and your grandmother, as well as with the monies used by you, should agree with the total amount of monies transferred to you by V.B. from the income of the estate... For the future it is important that the income of the inheritance should be used also for the previously mentioned purposes to about the same degree and in about the same proportion, according to the possibilities.[29]

These and other comments from Ditta were interpreted by surrogates as showing her "substantial assent" to Bator's actions and decisions.

This letter appears to have been one of Ditta Bartók's last personal comments on the litigation, and should be considered carefully; from this point forward, until her death in 1982, her "voice" in all the litigation over the Bartók

---

28 Ess came from a prominent Kansas City family and attended Princeton University ('42) and Harvard Law School. He later (1973–75) served as president of the New York County Lawyers Association, the bar association for New York City. Like Bator he was a collector of rare objects, in his case historical law books. An appreciation can be found on the Harvard Law School website at http://www.law.harvard.edu/faculty/martin/ess_bio.htm.
29 Ditta Bartók, letter to Peter Bartók, July 2, 1959. As translated and quoted in Milton Goldman's Referee's Report, p. 40.

Chapter 6

Estate would be the voice of her lawyers. To some degree the suppression of her individual thoughts and opinions might be expected: in litigation processes plaintiffs participate through their lawyers and, at times, if needed, through direct testimony. In a police state the dynamics of that relationship differ profoundly. When a plaintiff is "not fully competent," as Bator described Ditta in 1957, those dynamics verge on total control, even more than might otherwise be assumed. Reconstructing Ditta Bartók's positions has not been possible from the documents I have on hand. After 1946 she never returned to the United States. Her presence in these proceedings always took place long distance. What did she really think? All we have to go on is a patchwork of comments that got recorded in court documents over the years. Her directions to Peter in mid-1959 seem to be those of someone who is upset about the actions being carried out against Bator, but unable to remonstrate freely. Bator cites them at greater length in his Memorandum as evidence of her loyalty, as well as her support for the Archives. Where did she stand two years later, post litigation? And after that? In these proceedings Ditta Bartók appears as a name, a cipher, a woman whose personal voice—her worries, her concerns, her attitudes, her positions—had been stifled. She always "spoke" through lawyers.

Suchoff told me many years later that, in his opinion, neither Victor Bator nor Peter Bartók were people you'd want to cross. "Victor's response was to hire Sullivan and Cromwell as the Estate's attorneys," he reminded me.

> The biggest and the best. They supplied secretaries of state and cabinet ministers to the government. Extremely prestigious. I met these attorneys and they were marvellous people. They were sympathetic people, but they were *sticklers* to the law. And they weren't going to allow any Hungarian People's Republic to come in and strip an American citizen of the Estate, even if he was a former Hungarian![30]

The Memorandum Bator gave them to work with was an extraordinary document—a lawyer's dream. They cannot have had many clients who gave them such fine preparatory material. As a lawyer himself, he knew what was needed of him. He devoted extraordinary care to preparing his written defense. With its exhaustive detail and sometimes week-by-week narrative, backed up by hard evidence from over a decade's worth of correspondence, the Memorandum forcefully rebuts each allegation, offering substantial analysis of his many decisions as Trustee. When he handed it over to his attorneys he attached over 300 original letters from his files to serve as primary evidence. With a document of

---

30 Suchoff, interview with the author, June 20, 2002.

this size and scope, the lawyers had all the ammunition they needed to mount a vigorous defense.

Bator charged the costs of defending his actions to the Estate. One of the sad ironies of the Bartók Estate litigation is that it was sustained from within by royalty income from the sale and performance of Béla Bartók's music. From 1959 on, all the way through 1985, legal expenses related to the American Bartók Estate litigation were paid out of the Estate's income. Licensing income was pouring in from all the performances worldwide of the Concerto for Orchestra and the Third Piano Concerto, and from all the sales of Books I, II, and III of *Mikrokosmos*, not to mention the six quartets and many other works, even the less familiar ones, that during these years approached the apogee of their popular appeal. Suchoff told me that during his Trusteeship ASCAP royalties for the Concerto for Orchestra alone topped $100,000 in some years. And that was just for ASCAP. A lot of that money went right back out the door to attorney's fees.

Calmer minds recognized the necessity of this practice, though it pleased no one. Bator wasn't being sued personally. He was being sued in his role as Trustee. Legal and accounting fees had been routine business expenses all along for the Bartók Trust; prosecuting the copyright encroachments of Hungarian publishers required attorney involvement in London and Vienna since the early 1950s. The costs of suing Boosey & Hawkes and Columbia Records in 1948–49 were likewise borne by the Estate, again, as a business expense. That attorney fees now ballooned in volume didn't fundamentally change the legitimacy of the practice. He certainly wasn't going to foot the bill himself for hiring Sullivan and Cromwell. Nor would, later, Suchoff, for exactly the same reason. These were Estate expenses. And the Estate could well afford it. This situation, as it became known to the plaintiffs in the years ahead, came under heavy fire from Peter Bartók and the Hungarian communist propaganda machine. Perversely, their own actions were causing waste of the Estate's assets. Rather than shoulder that blame, though, they chose to see it as additional proof of the Trustee's corrupt behavior. They plowed ahead.

With the flows of money suddenly called into question like this, his attorney recommended that Bator stop making payments to the heirs until the litigation could get sorted: no point increasing his liability. Bator announced to Peter that effective August 1, 1959, no further Trust income would be paid to him. He cut Peter off. There would be no more support for Bartók Records for the time being. His attorney recommended the same treatment for Ditta, but Bator, characteristically, refused to go that far. "The poor woman in Hungary has to live," he argued with Rosen, "and I don't think Peter is sending her any money unless I give money to him. Therefore I would like to send her $500 [monthly]. If I failed to do so, inimical feelings may arise in her and her brother toward me."³¹ Peter Bartók would not receive any income from the Trust again until May 1962.

In their conversations together in Budapest, Peter and his mother realized that they held an important piece of information in their hands. From the mists of memory they recalled a legal document, another Will, that they'd seen briefly in September 1945. What had happened with that Last Will and Testament Béla Bartók had almost signed in the hospital in his dying days? They no longer knew. Neither of them had ever been given a copy. All they could be certain of is that it had once existed. Perhaps somebody in New York had saved the document? The Hungarian attorneys urged Peter to investigate. When he returned to New York, Peter mentioned this Will to his attorney, Barbara Zinsser, who naturally felt compelled to investigate, too. Bator's staff had only recently been cataloguing and preserving the Bartók family papers for the Estate; they pointed Bator to the missing document. In June 1959, from its long slumber, the deathbed Will resurfaced in New York City. Zinsser received a copy and saw immediately that it had no potential to materially reshape the litigation. To the heirs, though, its terms and provisions seemed to speak from beyond the grave to their current situation.

As we saw in Chapter 3, this revised American Last Will and Testament preserved the Trust feature but directed that royalty income be shared between Peter and Ditta, with Peter to receive 2/3 of the Trust income. Its allocation plan seemed eerily predictive, in fact, to the general contours of what had evolved organically over the last 14 years in response to natural and historical events. Even Béla Jr.'s revised bequest seems to prefigure the Interpretive Declaration by assigning him all property in Hungary and five other countries, one of which was Russia.

Although it would never be admissible in court, we know from letters and various statements by the plaintiffs and their attorneys that this deathbed Will carried outsize significance to the Bartók heirs when it resurfaced in 1959. Particularly for the two sons, their own father's last thoughts on the disposition of his estate gave them permission to see their current situation in new light. From beyond the grave their father appeared as if summoned in time of need; his dying wishes, they saw, had endorsed a different solution than the one they felt saddled with now. For Peter, who really was left with nothing from the Estate unless his mother (or Bator) chose to give it to him, the rediscovered Will proved to him beyond any doubt that his father had intended to leave him with a substantial share of his material legacy. Timing accentuated the discovery's significance: two months later he found himself cut off completely from any Estate income. From

---

31 Bator, letter to Gustave Rosen, September 8, 1959 (Collection of Francis Bator).

this point on the deathbed Will runs like a slender thread through the entire Bartók Estate litigation. Peter never could forget it. It shows up in his book *My Father* and, again, in his late-in-life retrospective review of the Estate's history on deposit at the Sacher Stiftung. It was the great "what if" of his life.

In August 1959 Zinsser filed her petition in Surrogate's Court to begin litigation. Suchoff remembered the event. "I was there. And I was involved in all of it." Between Bator, Rosen, the attorneys from Sullivan and Cromwell, and a man who now surfaced for the first time, Surrogate S. Samuel DiFalco, an almost unbreachable wall of defense was erected. DiFalco was known in legal circles as a conservative judge and a stern opponent of communism.[32] "I mean, think of McCarthy," Suchoff told me. "My impression is that he was that kind of a guy." The Hungarians and Peter never had a chance. The contorted logic of their allegations worked against them. Then there was the matter of who they were going up against. Suchoff chuckled at the memory. "They had no more way of unseating Victor in the New York Surrogate's Court than they had of counting the grains of sand on the beach!"

Surrogate DiFalco had first become involved in Bartók Estate matters when he judicially settled the First Intermediate Accounting in January. For the next two years he presided over the lawsuit from the bench. (He would remain in charge of Bartók Estate litigation in Surrogate's Court until the early 1970s.) After reviewing initial filings on both sides, he issued an intermediate ruling that the only real question before the court was whether Bator's conduct constituted "fraud and misrepresentation." Attorneys were instructed to confine their arguments to helping him determine whether the January 6, 1959, accounting should be vacated. He himself had already approved that earlier document, so the challenge from Peter would have to be rigorous and well-argued to meet the "sufficient cause" threshold needed to re-open a settled accounting. A trial ensued in the spring of 1961. DiFalco handed down his Opinion re Estate of Béla Bartók on May 3, 1961, in Surrogate's Court.[33]

Every one of the plaintiff's claims was repudiated by the court. <u>DiFalco found no fraud or misrepresentation anywhere in Bator's management of the Estate.</u> Bator was exonerated. "The petitioner [Peter Bartók] has failed to establish any ground for vacating the decree on accounting," he pronounced. The First Intermediate Accounting would stand. On page after page of the written opinion he reviewed the plaintiff's complaints and dismissed each of them in

---

32 Suchoff, interview with the author, June 20, 2002. Judges' personalities are widely known to litigators in their home jurisdictions; it can be assumed that Rosen and Ess shaped their defense in subtle ways to appeal to DiFalco's aversion to communism, and that Zinsser carefully positioned her arguments for similar reasons.

33 His opinion can be found online at https://www.leagle.com/decision/196135228misc2d3241248.

impressively reasoned, concise terms, backed up by precedent where appropriate. Peter had claimed, among other things, that Bator had failed to acquaint him with the basic legal documents defining his rights and his mother's, including the Will and powers-of-attorney. Nonsense, responded DiFalco after hearing testimony and reviewing the evidence before him. A sample from his judgment shows how he dismantled such allegations:

> The petitioner testified that he first saw a copy of the general power of attorney in January, 1959, although he admits being in the room when his mother signed it, and he admits seeing "about a corner of it" at that time. The petitioner could not say that he was wholly unaware of the existence of a power of attorney, because in January, 1958, and again in September of that year, he executed instruments as attorney-in-fact for his mother. Nor does the petitioner say that he never saw a copy of the will. It would be incredible that between 1945 and 1958, the petitioner never saw a copy of his father's will. What he complains of is that the respondent never did "sit down with him and discuss the terms of his father's will." (Minutes, p. 19) With respect to the assignment of income to himself, the petitioner was asked whether he had been told that an assignment of income was invalid, and he said: "Nobody told me it was invalid. Nobody even told me it existed." (Id., p. 100) Yet the petitioner had received money from the estate for his own use. It is inconceivable that he was totally unaware that he was an assignee of his mother's interest in income. The failure of the respondent to read these instruments to a man of the age and business experience of the petitioner, cannot fairly be said to constitute fraud.

The plaintiffs had also mounted numerous challenges to the accuracy of the accounting for the Estate. They particularly objected to the appearance that, in some years, Bator had spent Estate income on Archive development, when, in fact—as all parties conceded—the Archive was Bator's own private, personal collection and thus should not have been supported financially by the Estate. Bator conceded the point; he had done just that. But in the early years he had personally supported Ditta and Peter when the Estate was generating little income. He hadn't said anything at the time. The amounts should more or less balance out, he explained. DiFalco heard testimony, reviewed the evidence, and ruled again in Bator's favor. "It is clear, therefore, that there was no fraud or misrepresentation on the part of the respondent with respect to the Archive collection." And so it went. Point after point.

Bator's attorneys viewed the Surrogate's decision as complete vindication for their client. Bator had been "shamefully attacked" by Peter Bartók in these proceedings, Rosen believed. In the end, he was happy to report, justice prevailed.[34] Francis kept a copy of DiFalco's opinion in his home for over fifty years. He pointed to it as one of his father's key early victories in the Bartók Estate litigation.

Post-trial Developments in Budapest and New York

And there it could have ended. DiFalco's repudiation of the charges against Bator left no doubt where the American justice system stood. At the very least Peter and Ditta [recte: Hungarian government] could say they had had their day in court. They had lost, and lost badly, but their complaints had been heard. Turmoil kicked up by the litigation process, however, severely strained the relationship between Victor Bator and Peter Bartók. The months and years of Affidavits, Memoranda, and hearings, of strategy sessions with lawyers, and, finally, the painful experience of a bench trial in court, permanently estranged them. Their relationship never recovered. Bator kept the door open to reconciliation; he tried periodically to hand over to Peter some direct agency in the Estate's management. Peter always balked. The Estate's business, meanwhile, continued on, unaffected by the court proceedings. The underlying legal contests over copyright control had not gone away. Physically, too, the Estate and Archives remained right where it was, in New York City—now with a vindicated Victor Bator at the helm. The Hungarian lawyers and bureaucrats at the Office for Protection of Authors' Rights and the Ministry of Finance merely regrouped, made some changes in strategy, and started in again. They were like crocodiles: they never let go of their prey.

Back in Budapest Ditta Bartók's personal attorney got replaced. Her new lawyer was a Communist Party member and prominent bureaucratic head in the law profession of Hungary, Dr. Ernő Vajda. From 1961 on Vajda represented Ditta Bartók in the Estate litigation. This placed her more firmly under the control of the communist bureaucracy. Vajda had no concerns over her compliance; when he asked her to grant him complete authority to act on her behalf, she felt unable to resist.[35] She signed the power of attorney that effectively made him the Estate's chief antagonist in years ahead, even though the legal maneuvers were always carried out in her name.

---

34 Gustave Rosen, letter to Victor Bator, May 5, 1961 (Collection of Francis Bator).
35 Peter Bartók, "The Fight Over the Bartók Estate, 1945-1985" (BBC-PSS Basel). Vajda's name shows up repeatedly after 1963 in Estate litigation matters; he evidently served as Ditta's attorney from 1961 into the late 1970s.

Chapter 6

In a separate but not unrelated action, frustrated attorneys lobbed over the Atlantic an answering lawsuit on less technical grounds, using different tactics, this time demanding action in a Hungarian jurisdiction. In August 1961 the Office of Government Notaries in Budapest prepared a petition to force the return of the Estate to Hungary. These Hungarian government lawyers declared Bator's trusteeship "terminated." His response, if he should choose to file one, was to be delivered to Budapest directly. Having failed to advance its cause in New York, the Hungarian government now wanted to get the matter into court in Budapest. (An English-language translation of the original decree, dated August 26, 1961, can be found in the correspondence preceding this chapter.) Papers were served on Bator at his building on E. 72nd Street on October 21, 1961, well past the deadline indicated for his response. The doorman signed for the registered letter; technically, it hadn't been properly served. Unconcerned, Bator shrugged off these procedural irregularities. He refused to acknowledge the threat, which had been couched in a bizarre mishmash of ominously worded, arbitrary declarations. "I am sure nobody expects in Budapest that the New York Courts or I will abide by their decision," he wrote to Viennese attorney Eric Habernal several days later. "It is my guess that this whole procedure was instituted for one purpose only, that is to present the Court in Vienna with a legal-looking document according to which Béla Bartók Jr. has been recognized by a Court as the owner of all Bartók rights in the seven countries which have often been mentioned in the papers, which include Austria and Germany." The decree also named Peter Bartók, who, like Bator, was asked to turn over to his mother all the Estate income he had received. Simultaneously—the right hand apparently not knowing what the left hand was doing—it declared Peter the new owner of all copyrights owned by the Estate.

In this same letter to Habernal Bator explains how these new developments affected his relationship with the Bartók heirs, as well as their relationships to each other:

> The essence of all this is that there is a kind of conspiracy between the Hungarian Government and Béla Bartók Jr., not helped, but neither prevented or contradicted by the two other members of the Bartók family. **In fact, Peter Bartók told me in July of this year, between two journeys to Hungary, that neither his Mother nor he is in control of what is happening in Hungary, that the Hungarian Government is actively directing every step**, and because of the presence of his Mother, Mrs. Bartók, in Hungary,—he and his Mother—simply could not take the risk of contradiction or opposition.

The bold highlighting here is my own. In the correspondence preceding this chapter I include the full text of this remarkable letter to Habernal, an attorney who had represented Bator for many years in his dealings with Universal Edition. It confirms Bator's belief that since late 1958 the Hungarian government had been actively scheming through the three heirs "to acquire the control over the entire property" of the Bartók Estate. They use Béla Jr. "as their dummy or agent for the purposes they want to realize." Concern for his mother's security kept Peter in line.

That blustering lawsuit by Hungarian government lawyers went nowhere. But, as with the rest of the litigation of 1959-61, its effects lingered. In one instance, in 1981—twenty years later—Peter Bartók cited the Hungarian decree in a threatening cease and desist letter he wrote to Dover Publishing. He cited it as proof that he was "proprietor" of all the Bartók copyrights, and that he viewed any Dover Edition of Bartók's piano works as unauthorized. Suchoff, responding to Peter on behalf of the publisher, patiently reminded him that the old Hungarian decree had no effect in the United States, and that he, Suchoff, was the Successor Trustee, in charge of copyright decisions, not Peter.[36]

Victor Bator and His Attorneys Sue Béla Jr. for $135,000

One of the stranger features of this early lawsuit was its insistence that the royalties collected by Béla Jr. throughout the 1950s should be reimbursed to Ditta Bartók. On this openly absurd claim the plaintiffs helpfully placed a figure of 1,500,000 forints, or $130,000 at the official rate of exchange. Transparently a legal maneuver designed to extract additional American dollars for the Hungarian state, it drew forceful resistance from the defense, who rightfully saw its larger purpose as a beachhead for claims still to come against the American Will's legitimacy. They decided to open another front in the battle. In January 1960 Victor Bator devised a countersuit against Béla Jr., demanding repayment to the Estate of that same amount, 1,500,000 forints, now $135,000 at the updated official rate of exchange.

A petition was served on Béla Jr. in New York City that month. The Hungarian heir was then on his first American visit. He had arrived in New York around Christmas 1959. He planned to visit with Peter for four weeks, then travel around, ostensibly to conduct research on North American railway sys-

---

36 Peter Bartók, letter to Hayward Cirker, February 9, 1981. Suchoff, letter to Peter Bartók, April 11, 1981. Both BSCB Tampa. A large amount of miscellaneous Suchoff/Peter Bartók correspondence from 1954-85 can be found in BCSB Tampa.

Chapter 6

tems. He stayed with Peter at his apartment on W. 57th Street. The suit demanded payment to the Estate of all monies Béla Jr. had earned from any income-generating source in the disputed territories of the Interpretive Declaration. (A copy of the entire letter is included in the correspondence published above.) The plaintiffs had put the figure of $130,000 on the table. Bator's attorneys chose a comparable figure in their countersuit.[37] An eye for an eye.

What a welcome to America for Béla Jr.! In the country for the first time and what happens? He gets served a lawsuit.

When viewed in the context of the larger litigation already underway in Surrogate's Court, this aggressive counterpunch by Bator and his attorneys shows its real purpose as a tool to achieve advantage in the current dispute. Its motivation was strategic, not punitive. Bator didn't expect Béla Jr. to actually refund the Estate this money. No one did. It still says something about Bator's impatience with Béla Bartók's oldest son that he was willing to countenance a legal action so baldly aimed at a man he had been trying to help for the past decade. My own sense is that Bator—who always thought two steps ahead on legal matters—was trying to open up a wedge between Béla Jr. and Palágyi with this action. He was frustrated with Béla Jr.'s continued fealty to Palágyi and the complicity with communism that allegiance made possible. For years Bator had been trying to get the Office for the Protection of Authors' Rights to acknowledge the priority of his claims as Trustee to the rights to manage all of Bartók's copyrights. They hadn't budged. Now maybe they would. It was worth a try.

Sometime later in 1960 or early 1961 his attorneys withdrew the suit. It had shaken things up, but having failed to achieve its immediate goal it became a distraction they no longer needed. They trained their attention on the larger litigation then progressing to its final stages in Surrogate's Court.

The Creation of the Béla Bartók Archives in 1963

Victor Bator always planned to leave his collection of Bartók "mementos"—a term he preferred early on—to an institution in the United States. As far back as 1951 he had mentioned to Otto Gombosi the idea of an eventual institutional home. By 1953 he had hired employees to begin the process of organizing, cataloging, and preserving the growing collection: Clifford Wooldrich, Nike Varga, and then, in December 1953, Benjamin Suchoff. Later, Iván Waldbauer and John Vinton joined them, as would Elma Laurvik and others. All worked part-time, paid

---

37   My research has not yet turned up an actual copy of this lawsuit. Its terms may differ from the suggestions Bator put forward in his letter to Rosen.

by the hour. Bator's home office housed the growing collection and its associated work spaces. The collection grew bigger through acquisitions. "Anything by and about Béla Bartók" was its goal.[38] Peter, happy to help, used his name to open doors that Bator might not be able to go through as easily. Already in 1949 Koussevitzky donated his personal Bartók holdings. From there the collection grew, establishing momentum with each new addition. In many cases—not all, certainly—the objects' owners were happy to part with a treasured letter or two to show their support for the project. Béla Bartók meant a lot to many people. Most material came trickling in a few items at a time, the result of letters of inquiry sent around the globe. The famous Róbert Berény oil portrait of Béla Bartók (1913) was acquired for the Archives in 1957. Bartók's publishers handed over their complete holdings of correspondence between 1955 and 1958, minus a few items which came in later.[39] They were intrigued by Bator's vision, and not insensitive to the value of maintaining a good working relationship with him. By 1961 most of the letters and remaining scores at Boosey & Hawkes and Universal Edition firms had been "repossessed" or successfully deposited at the Archive.

Correspondents from around the world sent envelopes to Bator stuffed with clippings, concert programs, articles, and leads. By 1959 the Archive held an estimated 1,900 letters, 1,000 scores and other examples of printed music, 300 books, 700 photographs, 200 pamphlets, and 1,600 newspaper clippings, plus several thousand other items, according to a report prepared by Laurvik. "The material is increasing daily," she commented.[40] Organizing all these materials was a priority for Bator; a study collection dramatically increased the value of the overall Archives to students and scholars. Safeguarding the priceless autograph manuscripts was a higher priority. "I would consider myself a great failure," he confessed to Sándor Veress, "if, by the time I finished my trusteeship, at least all manuscripts of Bartók are not well catalogued and physically safe, and further, if whatever unpublished folk music work exists, it were not published. I hope I shall succeed."[41]

---

38 Suchoff, in my interviews with him, indicated that he had used this phrase in conversation with Bator in the early days, and that Bator seized on it as a useful expression of his goals in building the Archive (Suchoff, interviews with the author, June 19 and 20, 2002).
39 Boosey & Hawkes and Universal Edition employees voluntarily kept an eye out in London and Vienna for new Bartók materials to add to Bator's archives in the early 1950s. Both firms deposited with him in 1955 all of their Bartók correspondence files. They did not relinquish ownership; these materials came to him with strings attached. Universal Edition specifically made as a condition of their deposit the requirement that a permanent home for the new Bartók Archive be secured. Universal Edition London added more materials in 1958, again with a strong expression of the need for Bator to establish the archive as a separate institution, or place it in a museum or other appropriate institution (Bator, Memorandum, Chapter J, p. 29-30).
40 Elma Laurvik, typed note to Victor Bator, March 1959 (BSCB Tampa).
41 Bator, letter to Sándor Veress, January 28, 1958 (Collection of Francis Bator).

Chapter 6

He and Suchoff consulted with staff at the Library of Congress and New York Public Library on best practices for conservation of autograph materials. Based on those conversations the decision was made to physically separate the folios of Bartók's autograph manuscripts to allow each page to be photographed, paginated, and stamped with an Archives indicium. Nested bifolios for many manuscripts were separated down the middle, and an effort was made to place any inserted pages in their proper locations to fix in place a complete manuscript for each piece. Any drafts or copyist manuscripts were treated similarly. Each page got placed in a clear plastic sleeve for protection. This decision to physically pull apart some of Bartók's autograph scores and reassemble them in binders for viewing has struck many later musicologists as misguided, tantamount to desecration. It is the one decision Victor Bator made that I wish could be undone. It drew less criticism at the time. Bator may have approved this controversial action for the best of reasons—he wanted scholars to have open access to all the autograph materials, and this way each page could be photographed separately to create a reference collection. But in separating the bifolios all manner of information got lost, including the relationship of side sketches that may have ended up in another binder, or the relationship of folios to one another within autograph score aggregations for works such as the *Mikrokosmos*. Ben Suchoff had been present at the Archive when this task was carried out. He personally supervised. I asked him why they'd done it.

> Why did I separate the pages? On the advice of the Library of Congress. The best way to protect those pages was to take the individual pages—number them all—and to put them all into inert plastic envelopes. And that's what we did. Bator had a plastics company, and he'd gone to the Library of Congress. They told him that's the only way you can protect it and let individual scholars examine each page without destroying it, with the sweat and so on. That was why we did it. We put it all into ring binders. Photographed. You understand it now. So you can look at any manuscript page: it was beautiful. Turn over the page, you could see it. Everything was labelled. Nobody could steal it because the estate stamp was on it. And the code number, too.[42]

Librarians will recognize this as yet another example of the familiar tensions between preservation and access. To our modern eyes the idea of plastic sleeves as protection for paper materials appears dubious. We know the risks. In the mid-1950s that solution was still new and forward looking. (Suchoff used the

---

42 Suchoff, interview with the author, June 20, 2002.

A Thorn in the Rosebush

Fig. 6.3. Tri-fold pamphlet for the Béla Bartók Archives, produced in late 1966 for distribution in brochure racks around New York City. The other side of this pamphlet is included as **Fig. 1.2** in the Introduction to this book. Source: BCSB Tampa.

term "beautiful" to describe the result.) The page protectors were not manufactured by Bator's company, it should be pointed out. They were purchased from an independent vendor. Because he knew more about plastics than most people of the time, though, he did take pains to make sure the sleeves held no potential for damage. In 1956 he asked a scientist at Natvar to deliver a verdict on them. He sent a sample to be examined. Would paper stored in these be safe? The word came back: yes.[43]

In 1958 Victor Bator heard news of a proposed Museum and Library of the Performing Arts to be located at the Lincoln Center development in midtown

---

43 Bator, letter to E.T. Severs of Natvar Corp., October 23, 1956. Severs's response is dated October 29, 1956. Both in BSCB Tampa. Severs, Technical Director at Natvar, identified the sample he'd been given as "cellose acetate" [=cellulose acetate]. This type of clear plastic sleeve, he indicated, is commonly used to protect printed material. He vouched for its stability. He volunteered, moreover, that he would be visiting the Mellon Institute soon, and would confirm with their staff, too. Many of these original plastic sleeves from the mid-1950s still can be found in the binders remaining in CPB Homosassa. They indeed have held up well over time. The exception is the photographs, whose chemical content has caused the sleeves to suffer weeping damage that in some cases has compromised the original images.

281

Chapter 6

Manhattan. Intrigued, he wrote to John D. Rockefeller. "Perhaps," he suggested, "the new addition to the Lincoln Center Project may be the suitable accommodation for the Béla Bartók Archives as part of the Museum of Performing Arts." He sought to encourage "scholarly use" and "public use" of the specialized collection. (See correspondence above.) Those conversations did not yield fruit. He broached the idea with New York Public Library at some point, too, and also the Library of Congress. In the 1960s Bator approached Columbia University to gauge their level of interest. After his death both NYU and SUNY Stonybrook received serious consideration by Victor Bator's sons, the Archives trustees, and Suchoff. None of these prospects moved past the formal proposal stage. Some, not even that far. The NYU proposal (1967–68) gathered the most momentum. It was supported by Bator and all of the Archives trustees. Peter Bartók's opposition to the idea, unfortunately, was absolute. He actively worked to sabotage it.

In 1963 the Béla Bartók Archives formally opened to the public. Described as a "library-museum" in some early materials, it was housed initially in an annex to 30 E. 72nd Street in a small office suite that offered some exhibit cases and work tables. By 1966 it had moved to larger quarters at 333 E. 79th St. At both locations, massive safes held immaculately ordered binders full of original documents and study materials. Tribute artwork celebrating the great Hungarian musician hung on the walls. Bartók's autograph manuscript collection—the vital heart of the Archives—was stored separately in the safe deposit vault of Hanover Trust bank a short walk away. High quality photographic copies of every manuscript had been prepared, and would be available for inspection by interested scholars, students, and musicians. Staff were on hand to host visitors. Bator and Suchoff prepared the handsomely produced catalogue, which opened with an extended philosophical rumination on the value of archives to human society, written by Bator. A board of trustees had been appointed to comply with the requirements of New York State law for charitable trusts. Further publications were planned to highlight the Archives and draw attention to its holdings. Waldbauer and Vinton had been working for several years on a Bartók Thematic Catalog. Preparations were well underway, too, for the publication of Bartók's *Rumanian Folk Song* study.

Most specialists today are loosely aware of the Archives' early history. What interests us here, for our story, are the factors that led to its demise, which have long been harder to discern. The Archives was clearly a good thing for Bartók studies: ambitious, well funded, with an almost dazzling array of materials that had at its center the massive collection of autograph scores Bartók himself had assembled as a record of his life's work. It was headed by a man of exceptional administrative talent. Yet five years after it opened the lights started to flicker, then went out. The Archives effectively closed down after 1969. What went wrong?

As far back as 1954 Victor Bator had taken pains to lay his thoughts about an Archive before Peter Bartók for consideration. It was to be an independent collection, separate from the Estate. Peter was confused at first. He thought it would be part of the Estate. In a follow-up letter, later much quoted in the litigation, Bator stressed that, in his words, the "idea of an Archive as a cultural institution, independent from the Estate… was so dear and so important to me that his refusal to agree to its independent existence—outside of and separated from his own dominion, the Estate—might prompt me to consider resigning the Trusteeship rather than to sacrifice the Archive."[44] Peter, engrossed with his own expanding vision for Bartók Records at the time, gave his assent to Bator's plans. He continued to actively scout for new materials to help it grow. Then came the events of 1958. He found himself drifting away from his earlier supportive position, and willing, as he hadn't been before, to countenance the disapproving voices he heard while in Hungary. One year later came the lawsuit, in which he and Ditta claimed that Bator had wasted Estate assets building up what was essentially a private collection.

Bator was astonished. Disgusted, too, at Peter's mutiny. How could Peter have missed the point of all their conversations?

> There can be no doubt that… Peter knew with such certainty as could be produced in his mind that the Archive was not and had never been part of the Estate and would never become his own private property. He might not have understood that although the Archive was not his, that did not mean that it was mine. This point may have surpassed his legal and philosophical level of understanding, but the disassociation and segregation of the Archive from the Estate could not have been made more positive, clear-cut, and complete."[45]

Here stood the problem in its starkest terms. Victor Bator could perceive the bright, clear line separating the Archives from the Estate. Peter couldn't. And he never could. It's hard enough for non-lawyers to grasp the distinction between a Trust and an Estate, much less an Estate and an Archive, when to both belong autograph manuscripts that appear to form a single, unified collection. Legal abstractions can frustrate even other lawyers. In letters written after 1958 Peter expressed worries about where his father's manuscripts really

---

44   Bator, Memorandum on the History of the Bartók Estate, Chapter J, p. 19–19a.
45   Bator, Memorandum on the History of the Bartók Estate, Chapter J, p. 19b–20.

belonged, legally speaking. Was the Stefi Geyer concerto manuscript a part of the Estate? Or did it belong to the Archives? (Sacher gave it to the Archives.) Where did the main collection of Béla Bartók's autograph manuscripts belong? Or the new troves of Bartok's own correspondence that had just come in? The latter had been placed on deposit with Bator with the proviso that he create a separate institutional home for them.

Adding to the potential confusion, materials housed in Bator's archives showed one of two separate ownership marks. Most of the more recent materials coming in were getting stamped "Bartók Archives" on their pages. The original autograph collection belonging to the Estate had been stamped "Estate / Béla Bartók" during processing. Why the difference? Did all the new autographs and correspondence arriving from Universal Edition and Boosey & Hawkes *not* belong to the Estate? Could one Bartók autograph belong to Estate while the autograph right next to it belonged to the Archive? Evidently so. This matter of indicia came up in the litigation. Bator's explanation made sense to the judge, if not to Peter and his attorney. The Archives stamp was "a practical matter," he indicated, because the manuscripts are all held physically on the premises. The stamps were for routine security purposes only, to prevent embezzlement or theft. They were "without any relevance or influence on the legal title."[46]

With his long years of business experience Victor Bator saw clearly the organic connections linking these two entities in a mutual vitality. In his Memorandum he invoked metaphors from advertising and real estate to illustrate how an investment in one side of a business, or in an adjacent piece of property, can raise the value of something touching it that happens to be owned separately. An attractive housed, comprehensive, and well organized Bartók Archive enhanced the value of the Bartók Estate. (Similar thinking had helped him justify the expenditure of Trust monies to support Peter's Bartók Records business.) Because Bartók's music, he explains, is written "in a new, specific musical language, its acceptance by the world of music needs to be helped and enhanced by its knowledge among the teachers of music appreciation and musicologists." Inspired by this opportunity to explain the thinking behind his vision, he continues with ardor in his Memorandum:

> Interest among such teachers, writers of music, scholars of musical theory, and authors of musical literature introduces Bartók's music in the courses of music conservatories, colleges, and probably soon of high schools also. More Ph.D. degrees written on Bartok's works means more teachers understanding and spreading its knowledge and appreci-

---

46 Bator, Memorandum on the History of the Bartók Estate, Chapter J, p. 7a.

ation. With the increase in numbers and in quality of those who understand that new musical language, who can sing it while it is being played, the interest in the performances will grow. More performances bring about greater understanding; greater understanding creates more performances, more sales, more mechanical reproductions [LPs]. The existence of the Béla Bartók Archive makes musical and musicological research and understanding easier, bringing the music itself closer to the music loving public. By its mere existence it creates curiosity.[47]

In building the Archives Bator openly planned for a future where musicologists, students, and musicians of all skill levels could use its holdings to foster greater public appreciation for Bartók's music. It is useful to remember that Bator had known Paul Henry Lang since the early 1940s and considered him a friend and ally, a feeling that was returned by the eminent scholar. At the time of this writing he had two Ph.D. musicologists on his staff, Suchoff and Waldbauer. And of course he had witnessed Bartók himself at work on his folk song research. More than most businessmen, then and now, Bator enjoyed the company of academics and valued their work.

When challenged in court to explain his decision to use Estate income to defray the costs of "creation, enlargement and maintenance of the Béla Bartók Archive that does not belong to the Estate," Victor Bator patiently explained his reasoning. He offered to reimburse the Estate the entire amount if that would help. He didn't see the need for this to become a major issue. The plaintiffs weren't reassured. DiFalco, as we have seen, came down strongly on Bator's side. Had even the slightest whiff of actual mismanagement been discovered, he would have flagged it during trial—the whole point of which was to determine whether any type of fraud or misrepresentation actually took place. His exoneration of Bator tells us all we need to know about the validity of the allegations: they held no substance. But blood had been drawn. Quite probably there was little Bator could have done to convince Palágyi and other bureaucrats in Hungary who were pulling the strings in this whole trial that *any* expenditures of income towards an American-based Archive might be legitimate. The proceedings confirmed that Bator still viewed the Archive as his private property, held in custody for future institutional placement. His longterm vision did not interest the Hungarians in the least.

Again, we need to remember that Ditta Bartók in all likelihood held less malignant views of Bator's activities. It's not out of the question that she may even have supported his archives ambitions; she had been intimately acquainted

---

47 Bator, Memorandum on the History of the Bartók Estate, Chapter J, p. 9.

Chapter 6

with her husband's goals for his manuscripts. Unfortunately, teasing out her individual views from those of the lawyers representing her appears to be unachievable—at least from the trail of records preserved on the American side.

After 1963 the new Archives was subjected to numerous legal claims and objections by Hungarian lawyers acting in Ditta's name, and by Peter Bartók, spawning a mountain of litigation that seemed to sprout new complications just as soon as any progress had been made towards resolution. Those closest to the Estate and dependent on it financially had failed, for reasons of their own, to appreciate the Archives' benefit to them. The Second Intermediate Accounting, rather than quashing the impulse for further rebellion among the heirs, only inflamed it. Annual revenues for the Bartók Estate now topped six figures a year, it showed. Where was all that money going? (Measured in today's U.S. dollars, the total income for the American Bartók Estate in 1961 alone was equivalent to $976,067.) Following Bator's death in December 1967, questions proliferated about the flows of money. Had Bator directed the right amounts to Ditta over the years? To Peter? To Bartók Records? To the growing Archives? Each party held divergent views. Questions arose, too, over which specific manuscripts or items belonged to the Estate, and which were instead the property of the Archives. Bator had been building his private Archive of mementos since 1948. Now that he was gone, to whom did all these materials belong?

Bartók's two publishers in the West had grown used to seeing legal conflicts materialize. With dispiriting regularity they found themselves pulled into copyright and licensing disputes, caught in the crossfire between Hungarian state publishers and Victor Bator. Because they generated most of the Estate's income, they could not escape the family litigation dramas. They also had a vested interest in the fate of the rich collections of original Bartók materials they had deposited with Victor Bator. Those gifts had been provisional, not absolute. If the Archives ship went down, they would withdraw their property before they saw it turned over to contentious heirs, two of whom resided in communist Hungary. Their interests lay in seeing the materials comfortably settled in an institutional home. Until 1985 both Boosey & Hawkes and Universal Edition would be parties to the Bartók Estate litigation. They would send observers to sit in at hearings or court proceedings. Events still to come would draw them into periods of more active involvement as reluctant hostages to the growing acrimony.

An agitated Peter Bartók disputed the inventories that had been prepared. In a letter to Suchoff in 1968 Peter reminded the Successor Trustee of his persistent reservations about the "variety of expenses" Bator had been incurring for the Trust. The justification for those expenses was "unclear," which is why the matter was under review yet again at Surrogate's Court. He objected to using

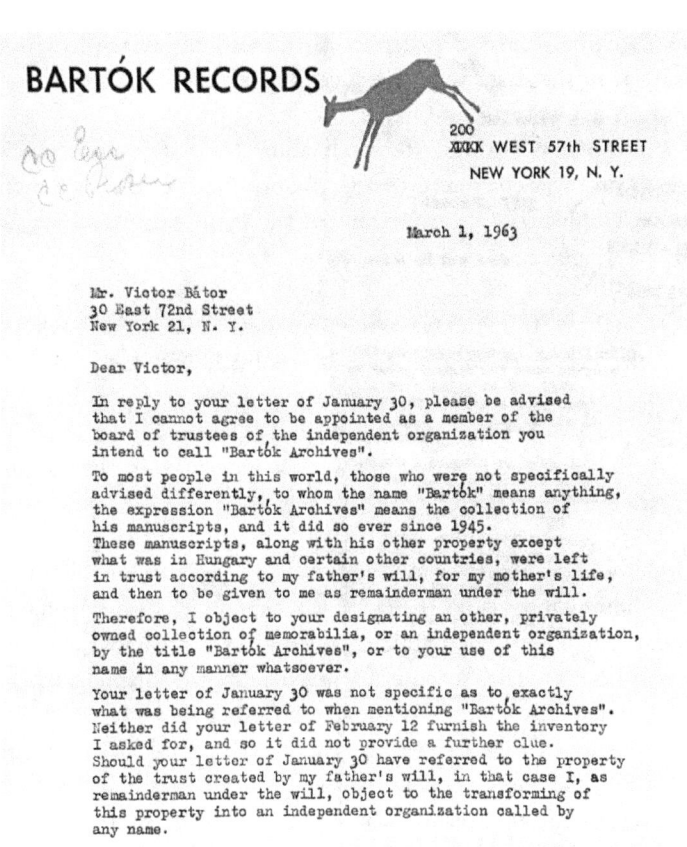

Fig. 6.4. Letter written by Peter Bartók to Victor Bator in response to receiving an invitation to join the board of trustees for the new Béla Bartók Archives in early 1963. Source: BSCB Tampa.

Estate income for "the 'promotion' of Béla Bartók's works."[48] As some people feel called to the ministry, or to a life as a poet, Peter responded to tug of higher calling and became a full-time antagonist. He grew militant in his opposition to the Archives that honored his father's life and career. Litigating against the Bartók Estate consumed his thoughts, preventing him, as he often said later, from continuing with his Bartók Records business or any other form of career. In separate actions, by way of example, he sued the three Bator sons on Decem-

---

48   Peter Bartok, letter to Benjamin Suchoff, July 25, 1968 (BSCB Tampa).

Chapter 6

ber 3, 1968, seeking return of 52 letters his father had written to him during World War II; in the early 1970s he sued Boosey & Hawkes over copyright ownership for the Concerto for Orchestra.[49]

Suchoff, who spoke to me extensively about the Estate's history, both on and off the record, was convinced that this confusion over the legal ownership status of the Archive collection was one of the main reasons for its ultimate downfall.

> Victor thought of the Archive as his, not Peter's. And that's what did him in. He was forced to give it up. It was his hobby. He loved it. He enjoyed it. Only certain kinds of men can afford to set up archives. You know how people save things? Collect things? Stamps and all that nonsense? Well, Victor thought that this was a wonderful thing he was doing for posterity.

The litigation wore on Bator, especially in the last years of his life. He unburdened to Suchoff on long walks they took together on Madison Avenue. When he observed the heirs and their attorneys still locked in combat over minutiae in the Second Intermediate Accounting, i.e., persistently misunderstanding his intentions, he gradually came to the realization that the only way to stop the fight—the right path forward—was to give in. "All right," he said finally, "I'll agree that it all belongs to the Bartók Estate."[50] He was encouraged in this direction by a ruling from DiFalco, whose principled support for Bator's actions had started to waver in response to ongoing complaints from Peter and the Hungarian plaintiffs. Sometime in 1966 or 1967—I have not been able to determine the exact time—he transferred ownership of the entire Archives collection to the Estate. Everything, literally everything, now belonged to the Estate.

Few people noticed. Even though this action completely redrew the ownership structure of the Béla Bartók Archives holdings, it took place behind the scenes. Seven years earlier his plans for all those materials had been quite different. "I have never had any intention to incorporate the Béla Bartók Archive

---

49 Two important decisions were handed down in U.S. District Court (Southern District of New York) and U.S. Court of Appeals, Second Circuit, in 1974 and 1975, respectively, on the legal question of whether the Concerto for Orchestra qualified as a posthumous work for copyright renewal purposes. In each case Peter Bartók brought suit against Boosey & Hawkes and Benjamin Suchoff. He won the case on appeal. See Bartok v. Boosey & Hawkes, Inc., 382 F.Supp. 880 (1974) and Bartok v. Boosey & Hawkes, Inc., 523 F.2d 941 (1975). Both judicial opinions are available online at https://www.leagle.com/decision/19741262382fsupp88011142 and https://www.leagle.com/decision/19751464523f2d94111302.

50 As quoted by Suchoff, who remembered Bator using these words, or words very similar to them, in 1967.

in the Estate," he declared in his Memorandum, reiterating his longstanding position. The collection was "his" only for the near term, until he could find the right home for it. He was its custodian, its assembler, its guardian. "[Peter] might not have understood that although the Archive was not his," he wrote, "that did not mean that it was mine."

The court judgment of 1961, in addition to clearing Bator's name, also revealed to the plaintiffs how much power had been vested in him as Trustee by Béla Bartók's Will. If they didn't grasp that truth before, they did now. They began to discern a more ominous threat that loomed behind Bator's obvious displeasure at finding himself in court.

The Nuclear Option

After the Béla Bartók Archives had been successfully launched in 1963, and the collection assembled there for public use, Victor Bator updated his own Last Will and Testament to give specific direction to his heirs. In that document he bequeaths his personal collection of Bartókiana—"all manuscripts, letters, documents, books, copyrights, and materials of every kind and description written by or relating to the late Bela Bartok or his works"—to the new Archives. His Will further directs that Trustees of the Béla Bartók Archives shall hold these materials "and make them available to scholars, musicians and the public." He includes in that bequest the "autographs and manuscripts of the 51 works entrusted to me by Béla Bartók before his death upon the understanding that such autographs and manuscripts would ultimately become part of a collection of Bartók materials which would be available to scholars, musicians and the public."[51]

Here stands revealed the "atomic bomb" that he mentioned in an earlier letter to his son Paul in late 1959. Under the terms of Bartók's Will the Trustees had been granted exceptional latitude to act independently with regard to Trust property. Specifically, Bartók authorized Bator and Báron "to take any and all steps… to protect such rights [and] <u>to do any and all acts with respect to musical or literary properties which I may own at the time of my death which I could do if I were living</u>." This was an exceptionally broad charge. Bator knew in his heart that Béla Bartók would have refused outright the claims of a Hungarian

---

51 A copy of this Will, showing just the first two pages with the Bartók bequest, is preserved in BSCB Tampa. Lacking a signature page, its exact date cannot be established; internal information allows it to be dated August 1963 or later. Whether he later revised this Will in 1966 or 1967 I have not been able to determine; probably a later version reflecting the revised bequest to the Estate must exist.

Chapter 6

communist regime on his autograph manuscripts, and, for that matter, for the copyrights. He was in the habit, we know, of acting as he thought Bartók would have wanted him to do with respect to family and property. As one of the composer's few close friends in his last years, Bator arguably knew more of his heart in these matters than most; he and Bartók talked politics fairly often, as we've seen above in Chapter 2. He and Báron, too, were perhaps the only people outside immediate family with whom the composer had openly discussed his plans for his manuscripts and the overall legacy he hoped to establish. In short, Bator was privy to all manner of confidential information Bartók had shared with him. In letters to Béla Jr. and Peter he reminded them of his many-layered conversations with their father about the fate of the manuscripts, in a way that makes it clear he always tried to frame his actions honestly, as an extension of how Bartók himself would have wanted him to act. "When I write that your father did not know whether members of the family would be in a position to handle the artistic value of the estate in the 'best' possible way," he wrote to Béla Jr. in 1957, "I refer to the legal, financial, and artistic significance altogether."

He knew, in other words, that if he really needed to—if either the heirs or the communist regime threatened the manuscripts with dissolution—he had the legal authority to take the entire collection of Béla Bartók's autograph manuscripts and donate them to an institutional home. He had been given the power to do this in the Will, <u>as long as it was an action Bartók himself would have done if he were living</u>. The U.S. court system would probably back him up. Like the atomic bomb, though, this was a solution of last resort. "I don't dare or even want to use [my bomb]," he told Paul. For the time being, the manuscripts belonged to the Estate. His 1963 Will makes it apparent, however, that if he were to die, those same manuscripts would become the legal property of the Béla Bartók Archives, their ownership vested in the charitable trust, and governed by an independent board of trustees. He had no intention of letting the manuscripts go to the People's Republic of Hungary.

Peter Bartók's pointed refusal to join that board of trustees guaranteed, therefore, his non-involvement with these manuscripts after Bator's death. (See Fig. 6.4.) Here we see the origin of his claim that Victor Bator tried to "steal" the manuscripts from him. Here, too, the inspiration behind another of his cherished allegations, in which Bator tried to sell him on the idea by reminding him of the potential tax advantage should the manuscripts be donated to the Archives. Bator may well have advised Peter of the tax advantages of placing the manuscripts in a charitable trust; he had always discussed with Peter his thinking about the Archives. Writing to Peter in 1963, Bator chided him for his resistance to facts. "All of your letters overlook certain fundamental facts which have been brought to your attention before, but which I am bringing to your attention again in the hope that you at length understand the considerations under which the trust under your father's will must operate." (See correspondence above.) Again, for Peter after 1961 this battle was always personal. He no longer had any interest in buying into Victor Bator's larger vision, or in legal castles built in the air above their heads. He just wanted Victor Bator out of his life.

Orlando Sentinel reporter Stephen Wigler interviewed Peter Bartók about the history of the Estate in 1983. With recent developments still churning in courts in New York and Budapest, Peter unburdened himself to the reporter. Already in 1957, he explained, Victor Bator began to suggest, in various ways, that the manuscripts belonged to him, and not to the heirs. For nefarious reasons the trustee tried to establish "ownership" of the manuscripts. When he subsequently tried to gift them to the New York Public Library, he tried to buy Peter off with the promise of a tax deduction. "Bator said I was to have $1 million if I agreed to let the library have them. I refused, and then in 1963 Bator began claiming that the manuscripts were not the estate's property."

Now that the manuscripts would be coming to Peter as his inheritance, he knew what he wanted to do with them. He would donate the materials to a public institution. "I want them to use the money they would pay me to hire scholars to edit the manuscripts." Wigler, listening carefully, observed that Peter's plans for the Archive materials in the 1980s more or less exactly matched what Bator had been planning to do twenty years earlier. So he put a direct question to his fellow Floridian. Was it worth more than twenty years of his life to simply carry out what Victor Bator had been planning to do all along? Peter bristled at the question. "But I had no say in the matter!" he cried. "Look, it was *my* inheritance from *my* father. Then someone says, I'm going to save you the trouble of disposing of your inheritance by stealing it from you. Instead of giving them [the manuscripts] to you when you're entitled, I'll put them in an institution of my own making."[52]

Bator, of course, at no point tried to make the manuscripts his own property. He *housed* them in his apartment for many years, and created an archives to hold them, but he never claimed personal ownership. He saw himself merely as their steward. Peter willfully misremembers this established fact. What I find completely honest and authentic in the *Orlando Sentinel* account, though, is Peter's outburst at the end, where he identifies his chief complaint: <u>he had no say in the matter</u>. That's a serious and legitimate charge. To which Bator might have responded, "yes, exactly—but I tried." Between 1958 and 1963, and again in 1967, he extended Peter Bartók multiple offers to get involved in managing the Estate. He would bring him on board, teach him what he knew, give him

---

52 Wigler, "Composer Bela Bartok's Legacy of Litigation," 4. Copy preserved in BSCB Tampa.

Chapter 6

Fig. 6.5. Zoltán Kodály visits the Béla Bartók Archives in September 1966 during his North American tour. On site at the Archives, with Benjamin Suchoff (left) and Victor Bator (center). Photographer: G.D. Hackett. Source: CPB Homosassa.

use of a knowledgeable secretary. Peter always refused. We don't know why, really. At least I haven't yet discovered the reasons why. I would suggest that it may have had something to do with their relationship itself: here, too, was another area where Peter knew he could not measure up to the man his father had appointed Trustee. Peter had staked out a career as recording engineer. He observed firsthand how much work it took Bator to manage copyrights around the globe. Perhaps his spirits did not lift at the prospect of fielding numerous inquiries about licensing arrangements. Perhaps, to get to the heart of matters, the business side of the Estate held little appeal for Béla Bartók's youngest son.

So he did have some say in the matter. He simply chose other paths.

Lost amid the wounded tropes in the 1983 *Orlando Sentinel* article is the fact that Bator never intended to gain personally by his actions, other than, understandably, to enjoy the reflected glow of association with a noteworthy cultural institution he had created. "My father was motivated by zero self-interest," Francis Bator is quoted as saying in the same article. "My father had a vision of

Fig. 6.6. Zoltán Kodály adds his signature to an Archives book, with the Robert Berény Bartók painting behind him. Photographer: G.D. Hackett. Source: CPB Homosassa.

a public institution where Bartók scholars from all over the world could come to do research on Bartók."

Outwardly, in terms of daily operations, nothing changed for the Béla Bartók Archives. It kept its doors open. Bator hosted Zoltán Kodály at the Archives in September 1966 (Fig. 6.5, 6.6). Kodály was evidently pleased with what he found. He approved of the Archives set-up, and privately vouched the opinion that there should be two Archives like this, one in Budapest, one in New York, so that scholars from all parts of the world would have access to materials.[53] Suchoff worked diligently towards the publication of Bartók's *Rumanian Folk Song* study. Bator's preface to that publication records the entire saga of how this magnum opus finally came to be published 22 years after Bartók's death. He appointed Suchoff his Successor Trustee. In what physical location the Béla Bartók Archives would continue after his death he left its board of trustees to determine.

---

53 Suchoff, letter to Peter Bartók, November 14, 1967 (BSCB Tampa).

Chapter 6

Milton Goldman's Referee's Report, May 14, 1971

During my meetings with Francis Bator, the legal document he pulled out most often to tell me about his family's involvement with the Bartók Estate was a marked up copy of the 57-page Referee's Report from New York Surrogate's Court in 1971. Litigation had grown so messy and complicated by the late 1960s that Surrogate DiFalco, who was still supervising the dispute from the bench, directed Milton Goldman to serve as referee for one important piece of the puzzle, the ongoing litigation over the Second Intermediate Accounting. Goldman's report, when finished, would go to Surrogate's Court to help them move forward with other parts of the litigation. Hearings before Goldman lasted from 1967 to 1969, resulting in 1,450 pages of testimony and over 300 exhibits entered as documentary evidence. Peter Bartok represented himself throughout. In the midst of the many hearings Victor Bator died; his place in the litigation was taken by Peter, Paul, and Francis Bator, his executors, all of whom were represented by the same attorneys who had been with Bator on this case since 1959, Gustave Rosen and Henry Ess. Francis had just left the Lyndon Johnson administration to accept an appointment at Harvard University to start their public policy program. Peter was working in the corporate law practice at Davis, Polk in Manhattan. Paul, an expert in federal law, had been serving since 1959 on the faculty at Harvard Law School.

In an earlier judicial opinion (1966) DiFalco had gotten right to the heart of the Archives/Estate issue when he determined that Victor Bator had been "unable to differentiate between his duty as an estate fiduciary and his desire to enhance his own reputation as the owner and keeper of the Bartók Archives." Bator's duty as estate fiduciary "supersedes and must take precedence" over any actions he may take on behalf of the Béla Bartók Archives. (Quotations in this and the next paragraphs are all from the Referee's Report of 1971.) Because of this, he had ruled that the Stefi Geyer concerto belonged to the Estate, not the Archive, giving the plaintiffs an important victory.

Bator was not immune from the public perception that he had tried to burnish his own reputation by establishing the Béla Bartók Archives. There was almost no way to avoid such comments. Benjamin Suchoff had seen Bator get attacked from numerous directions, and grew to feel some compassion for his embattled mentor. Bator, he told me, was "very cautious" about people "riding on Bartók's back to glory."[54] Iván Waldbauer perceived a deeper motivation behind the Trustee's actions. "Victor Bator used Béla Bartók as an entree into the world of intellectuals," he explained. "He was an ambitious man. He made the Béla Bartók

---

54 Suchoff, interviews with the author, June 19 and 20, 2002.

Archives as a self-serving gesture."55 Bator tried to ignore whispers like these, but they could not be shaken off completely. At a trustees meeting in November 1967, one month before he died, he urged all trustees to vote in favor of the NYU proposal then under consideration. He supported attaching the Archives to the university in a formal agreement. He didn't want his name anywhere near the Archives going forward. "It would be a gross error, and offensive to those who were closest to Bartók"—a reference to the trustees sitting around the table (see listing above in Fig. 6.3)—"if the Archives in New York would not become what it was intended to be: The Bartók Archives without any reference to Bator."56

Peter remained joined to his mother [recte: Vajda] throughout the 1960s in ongoing litigation over the Trust's finances. Eventually they, too, fell out with each other. (By then the Hungarian attorneys held the legal reins on now much income got distributed to Peter Bartók. They chose a noncharitable path.) Goldman noted their perennial objections to many aspects of the account under review, the Second Intermediate Accounting. The principal thrust of their opposition, he observed, was to present "a total challenge to the acts and activities of Victor Bator," which, among other matters, include the charge that Bator had "wrongfully commingled trust assets with other materials and properties, in particular those materials which he had identified as those comprising the Archive and to which he at one time laid claim." The plaintiffs also claimed that Bator had "expended large sums of money for activities which were either totally unauthorized by the decedent's will or . . . unnecessary and excessive." And, as could be expected, they charged that Bator had "wrongfully incurred and paid from trust funds certain fees for legal and accounting services."

Goldman bought none of it. His extraordinarily detailed report goes back to Bartók's 1943 Will to frame his findings; he reviewed the history of the Estate litigation across the 1960s to bring it into the present before turning to the current claims. <u>Again, an American judge with all facts at his disposal, and having heard extensive testimony, exonerated Bator</u>. Goldman evidently felt that far too many people had been running Bator down in these proceedings. In his report he goes out of the way to validate Bator's work, placing on the record his considered opinion that Bator had been an extraordinary Trustee (the bold highlighting is my own):

> Just as it is undisputed that the decedent died a poor man, so also it is an uncontrovertible fact that the products of his musical endeavors were brought to economic fruition after his demise while in the stewardship of

---

55 Iván Waldbauer, interview with the author, January 5, 2011.
56 Bator, draft Memorandum dated November 12, 1967, with red pencil corrections (BSCB Tampa).

Chapter 6

his good friend and trustee, Victor Bator, whose efforts have come under such severe criticism by the beneficiaries. . . . Based on all of the proof, **I find as fact that Victor Bator was a man of integrity, free of any corrupt motivation in the performance of his trust, and faithful to his fiduciary duties and responsibilities.** To the extent he may have erred, as I shall find he did in certain limited areas, his error was not born of malice or dishonesty.

It is abundantly clear upon the record before me that Victor Bator was dedicated, as only a trusted and good friend can be, to the enhancement of the renown of Bela Bartok, and to the appreciation of his genius as a composer and musicologist by scholars, artists, and the public at large. To that end he devoted his efforts and organized and enlisted the expertise, skills, and assistance of others. **This commitment led him to an excellence in the performance of his trust duties, well above what might have been accomplished by another fiduciary equally faithful to his trust but lacking the inspiration which moved Victor Bator.**

Goldman reminded both Peter and Ditta that they had each assented to Bator's collecting activities for the Archive. With regard to the Second Accounting, he rejects their claims outright:

I further find and report that Victor Bator's activities during the period covered by this Second Accounting were and will be of substantial value, benefit, and advantage to this trust. Having examined all of the expenses incurred and paid by Victor Bator relative to those activities, I reject all objections attacking those expenses as unnecessary and excessive, and I find and report that all of those expenses were reasonable, necessary, and proper and were properly charged against the income of this trust in the account filed herein.

To close his report Goldman takes up the related issues of Bator's compensation and estate taxation. In each, his review of evidence turned up minor discrepancies and willful distortion of the record by Peter Bartok, who consistently refused to remember his earlier agreements made with Bator. The amount and quality of work Bator put in as Trustee drew high praise from Goldman.

Nothing could be clearer in this case than the fact that Victor Bator rendered services to this trust well beyond his ordinary responsibility as trustee. This was true during the period of the First Intermediate

Accounting, and it was equally true during the period now under review. ... All his combined activities on behalf of the trust were such that they may be described as tantamount to a full-time job. Peter Bartok and his mother, at times when their estimate of Victor Bator's worth and extraordinary devotion of time, energy and talent could be more objective, recognized the extraordinary nature and quality of his service in their behalf.

The report concludes with Goldman taking all parties through the justification for recommending "reasonable compensation" for Bator [deceased, now referring to his personal estate] of "10 percent of gross" income.

Ditta Bartók's Trust Distributions

One of the charges later laid at Bator's door is that he deliberately withheld monies that should have been paid to Ditta Bartók, allowing her to live in poverty in Hungary. Many variations of this he-let-my-mother-starve charge were recorded in Peter Bartók's later letters and writings. It became for Peter a type of original sin, something he could not forgive. His own mother! Palágyi's office seized on this slander in 1959, making it the emotional centerpiece of its larger campaign to unseat Bator as Trustee. From there the Hungarian propaganda machine picked it up. Scholars will recognize this charge as a close cousin of the hoary, communist-era view that held the United States responsible for mistreating Béla Bartók during his final years. (On which, see Bator's lecture on "Bartók and 'Dollar Imperialism'" reproduced as Appendix D in this book, a new source for musicologists to consider.) How the accusations of mistreatment came about, and gained plausibility through excess repetition, warrants closer examination. For here, too, the politics and personalities of the Bartók Estate during the Cold War prevented the growing community of Bartók scholars from knowing what actually took place.

The roots of this charge go back to the misery imposed on so many people in Eastern Europe by their own governments during the Cold War. Communism shattered the standard of living most people had enjoyed, dramatically shrinking the amounts of staples and consumer goods available to purchase, while seizing full control of the means of economic support for its citizens. Ditta suffered doubly under the new system. Her fragile emotional health lowered her resilience to the sudden changes. Her prominent name and foreign income streams assured her extra attention from the new ministries and government offices that were proliferating. Bator, to his credit, quickly recognized the special perils she faced. His response was nuanced, caring, and strategic.

Chapter 6

Like many Hungarians in North America, after the Iron Curtain came down he actively sought information about the changes taking place in Hungary. Reports and tidbits of news reached him piecemeal via the émigré community, while each issue of *Amerikai Magyar Népszava* and other Hungarian-language news sources brought focused coverage of the country's seismic socioeconomic transformation. Unlike most other Hungarians in the United States, though, Victor Bator had longstanding professional connections to State Department circles through old friendships with ambassadors, embassy staff, American Hungarian Federation leaders, and his many friends from Sullivan and Cromwell days. With Allen Dulles, former head of the OSS in Europe, and, after 1951, a senior director of the CIA, he was on first-name basis going to back to their years together working on bond issues in the 1920s; as Dulles ascended to the top ranks of US government he corresponded with Bator on political matters of mutual interest.[57] Bator continued to associate with fellow Hungarians from the country's pre-war economic and political elite. These and other sources of deep-level knowledge left Victor Bator unusually well informed about the changing conditions in Hungary.

Determined to engage in the Cold War struggle against communism, he purchased an ownership stake in one of the more authoritative news sources of its day, Deadline Data on World Affairs, published in New York City. By 1960 he was Chairman of its Board. This well-known but very expensive service offered subscribers an independent source of breaking news from around the globe, augmented by its own proprietary analyses of individual countries. It specialized in deep-level knowledge of the forces driving foreign policy decisions around the globe. An advertisement placed in an American journal of economic affairs in 1965 neatly sums up its ambitions (Fig. 6.x), while also positioning it as a critical source in the struggle against communism. News and information, one might say, was Bator's business. Hungary's unfolding experience with Soviet-led communism—its leadership changes, shifts in foreign policy, economic developments—absorbed his attention. According to Suchoff, Bator "had spies all over the place in Hungary" in the 1950s and 60s, people who would confidentially funnel information to him via secure channels. "Victor had spies—let's call them spies—who knew what was going on in the cultural life with Béla Bartók in Budapest."

Yet Bator always had larger goals in mind. Viewed as a whole, his many business enterprises shared one common purpose: they each, in their ways, were

---

57 As federal records from this era get declassified, miscellaneous correspondence between Bator and Dulles can now be found online through the CIA's open records website, www. https://www.cia.gov/library/readingroom.

A Thorn in the Rosebush

Fig. 6.7. Advertisement for Deadline Data on World Affairs, from the economic affairs magazine *Challenge* 14/2 (Nov.-Dec. 1965).

directed at the global struggle against communism. By its nature this struggle transcended the tragic experience of any one single country. His crowning public achievement came in 1965 with the publication of his book *Vietnam—A Diplomatic Tragedy*. He had grown concerned about American foreign policy in Southeast Asia. In his book he offers a thoughtful analysis of the decisions made—or not made—by American presidents, their Secretaries of State, and other political leaders in the years after 1950 when what had been essentially a French colonial struggle exploded into a global confrontation between the Free

Chapter 6

World and Chinese-Russian communist power. He reviews how a fragile coalition of unwilling Western allies, each headed by humans with varying degrees of commitment to the struggle, maneuvered through NATO and the 1954 Geneva Conference. American leaders, including Allen Dulles and Dwight Eisenhower, as well as Secretary of State John Foster Dulles, debated for too long political solutions to a military conflict, including nonintervention, with the result that they inevitably found themselves drawn into committing the United States to a leadership role the country didn't want. How America and Britain settled into their mutual roles in the spreading Cold War is a central preoccupation of the book:

> The conflict between the two Anglo-Saxon countries was on two levels. At the base there was disagreement on policies. Washington's view stemmed from Eisenhower's falling domino hypothesis. He compared Indochina to the first in a row of dominoes which when knocked over, made the fall of the last one a certainty. Loss of any part of Indochina would result in losing all of it. This, in turn, would render all Southeast Asia indefensible from the offensives of international Communism with its monolithic structure, set upon the conquest of the world; each step forward, each success, no matter how small, would serve as a base for the next move. No genuine settlement could be arrived at, for the Communists would concede nothing unless it advanced their general purpose and made new conquests possible. Washington felt, therefore, that the United States would be in violation of its moral credo if it did not prevent the thrust of Communism into any area where Washington could act. For Eisenhower and Dulles the war in Indochina was part of the global crusade against Communism. Another special feature of American Indochina policy was an emotional frenzy against contact with Communist China. Any contact, it was thought, would somehow be changed, as though by magic, into a step towards recognition and United Nations membership. For the President and Secretary of State this possibility was a nightmare. For fear of Republican Party hostility, they could not relax the rigid stand in which Chinese "terror" held them, no matter how advantageous it might appear to do so in a given situation.[58]

Close analysis of the psychology of decision making behind American foreign policy is a defining feature of Bator's Vietnam book. He plainly admires British Foreign Secretary Anthony Eden for promoting solutions that were "simple,

---

58 Bator, *Vietnam—A Diplomatic Tragedy*, 102.

logical, unemotional, and practical." Wishing for containment of communism and actively engaging in that battle, he cautions, were two quite different options. In England, he writes, "for the containment of Communist imperialism there was almost unanimous British support; for a crusade against it... there was none."[59]

During all the years Victor Bator served as Trustee for the Bartók Trust he passed much of his time in other pursuits. He was writing the Vietnam book at the same time he established the Béla Bartók Archives. Managing the American Bartók Estate had always been an important project for him, even moreso in his later years. But it was only one of his enterprises. He held significant ownership stakes in three large businesses—Natvar, Deadline Data, and *Amerikai Magyar Népszava*. While day-to-day management of those businesses was often left to others, their needs could occasionally claim significant amounts of his time. He mentions in his Memorandum, for example, the pressures of getting Natvar through a worker's strike in the 1950s. His real estate holdings, too, required steady oversight. By the late 1950s, if not earlier, he held an ownership stake in another New York apartment building at 333 E. 79th Street. On a daily basis he remained vigilant for ways he could help Hungarians—individually or generally—in humanitarian ways.

To help manage these many and far-flung interests he employed a personal secretary who worked with him full-time, a practice he brought with him from Budapest; she worked out of his home office, which occupied the other half of the 16th floor of E. 72nd Street. Here was the headquarters for what we might call "Victor Bator, Inc." (These days we would call it his family office.) The growing Bartók Archives were housed in this home office initially, across the hall from his family apartment. Whenever Hungarian-language correspondence was needed he brought in additional secretaries who could take dictation and type in Hungarian. His main secretary was fluent in German. The latest in 1950s office technology, a dictaphone, helped him keep up with the brisk pace required of business correspondence. A photograph he took of his home office around 1955 shows us where he managed the Bartók Estate (Fig. 6.7).

As we saw in Chapter 3, from 1945 to 1948 Ditta Bartók had received critical financial support from Bator himself, using a mixture of his own dollar-denominated funds and, later, his unused pension at the bank in Hungary. (For part of this time she may also have had access to the widow's benefit from Béla Bartók's pension.) Once the communist regime took over, Hungary's banking

---

59 Bator, *Vietnam—A Diplomatic Tragedy*, 105. In a personal touch he dedicates his book to "three true friends, my sons Francis, Peter and Paul, and to the memory of Franci, an unforgettable woman." His new expertise led him to pen several letters to the editor of *The New York Times*, in 1965 and 1966, to clarify errors or misstatements made by public news figures.

Chapter 6

Fig. 6.8. The desk where it all happened. Victor Bator's home office for the Bartók Estate and Archives, ca. 1955. At left can be seen a copy of the Halsey Stevens Bartók biography. At right, the dictaphone he used to dictate business correspondence. Here originated most of the letters and documents found in this book. Photographer: Victor Bator.
Source: personal collection of Francis Bator.

system got reorganized along Soviet lines as a single central bank under close political supervision. The task of getting money to her became much harder. Exact figures are no longer possible to reconstruct, but it appears that in the early 1950s she generally received a monthly stipend of between $100–300 from the Estate in New York. By 1958 and 59 the amount had increased to $400–500.[60] To these amounts would be added whatever income Hungarian state agencies chose to pay her.

To our eye these figures look quite low. Yet they had been carefully calibrated with Ditta's welfare in mind. They're anything but arbitrary or punitive. Economic conditions in communist Hungary were so depressed that even a

---

60 See Bator's Memorandum. Peter Bartók, in a memorandum he prepared for Paul Sacher's review, dated April 20, 1961, writes that his mother recently has been receiving "very nice remittances" from Bator, "often with the accompaniment of letters promising more if only she would cause me to stop the suit against Bator" (Paul Sacher correspondence, PSS Basel). Elsewhere he indicates that from 1945–57 both he and his mother received "monthly allowances" from either Bator himself (early on) or from the Estate (Bator, Memorandum). Bator also sent modest remittances to Ditta's mother, at her request.

few hundred dollars per month went a long way. "The limits of rational spending were quite low" in the country, he explained. Furthermore, he remembered what Ditta was like with money. "Mrs. Bartók is not an entirely rational being when it comes to finances, spending, and way of life." If she had extra money "she would spend it in a way that might have damaged her health." Her disinclination for handling financial matters responsibly had been noted by friends. The Kecskemétis worried in New York over her indifference towards learning how to manage wartime ration books. She had developed along the road, moreover, some form of alcohol dependency that concerned her family, including Peter. This sensitive private matter they all managed, survived, and covered up as best they could. Bator apparently had direct personal experience with Ditta's fondness for drink during her American years. He kept quiet about it, the way people will do. But he remembered. And it played a role in his care for her later on. "There are certain temptations offered by life to which she easily succumbs. I trust that Peter B. will know what I am referring to" (these quotations all from the Memorandum). It was to protect her from situations like these—to a large extent, from herself—that he had her sign the power-of-attorney in 1946 that allowed him to control the distributions and, if necessary, to give that money to Peter instead.

From the start of his Trusteeship, then, Victor Bator knew he would have to play the role of paterfamilias. He thought carefully about how he could support Ditta and Peter, opening his own wallet to help them through the early years after Béla's death. As time went on and the Estate began bringing in substantial revenues, he took steps to minimize the downside risk of seeing their inheritance squandered or stolen from them. He adopted a generous, open checkbook approach to supporting Peter Bartók's career in the 1950s. With Ditta, meanwhile, he carefully gauged the amounts she could actually use in a communist state without imperiling her health or drawing too much unwanted attention.

Evidently his care extended even to the methods used to get money to her overseas. Instead of relying on the notoriously unfavorable official rates for foreign currency exchange in communist countries, he learned to route money through back-door channels, further safeguarding Bartók's widow from prying eyes. It worked like this, apparently: someone from his network of family and close friends in Hungary would regularly deliver Ditta Bartók bundles of Hungarian banknotes. Back in New York he would write himself a check from the Estate to cover the transaction.[61]

***

---

61 Peter Bartók, memorandum on recent events in the Bartók Estate, April 20, 1961 (PSS Basel).

Chapter 6

Exerting pressure on those payments from another direction was US foreign policy. Even sending a few hundred dollars a month to Hungary became difficult after 1954. Longstanding trade agreements with Eastern Bloc countries had been suspended by Congress in the Trade Agreements Act of 1951, signed into law by President Truman on June 12, 1951.[62] In the wake of that legislation the US Treasury Department suspended official governmental banking relations with Hungary and other Iron Curtain countries. On July 5, 1952, Congress formally ended *all* trade agreements with Hungary, angered by an international incident in which four U.S. airmen who were shot down over Hungary were imprisoned and held hostage while the communist regime demanded $30,000 each for their release, a series of events Senator Hubert Humphrey of Minnesota condemned as "an act of aggression against the United States and its people." NATO strategic trade controls added further international pressure. The new Treasury ruling was quickly interpreted by U.S. courts as applying to individuals, too. By 1954, if not earlier, it became exceedingly difficult to transfer dollar denominated assets to any of the countries behind the Iron Curtain.[63]

Against a sea change of this magnitude the Estate of Béla Bartók had little choice but to bob along in the prevailing currents. During the Cold War, American foreign policy began to affect individual inheritance rights. Across the United States in the early 1950s probate judges blocked bequests from estates to beneficiaries in Eastern Europe. They reasoned that if the wishes of the deceased were to provide an inheritance to family members in the "old country," the rise of communism meant that those funds, if remitted, would in many cases never make it to the beneficiary. Particular concern was expressed over exchange rates which subjected bequests to state sanctioned theft. Between new statutes and judicial precedent in probate courts, a wariness for Eastern European and Russian matters descended upon American court systems. Judges began to impound assets, temporarily depositing them in city treasury or court accounts, or even settling a bequest on completely unassociated organizations. In one prominent case a judge in New York Surrogate's Court awarded a bequest to the Brooklyn Institute of Arts and Sciences, and NYU, rather than allow the money to go as directed to the Soviet Union. In 1953 *The New York Times* reported that a Hungarian expatriate's estate in New York had been ordered to deposit funds with the New York City treasurer instead of sending a bequest totaling $4,000 to Hungary. The Surrogate ruled

---

62 https://history.state.gov/historicaldocuments/frus1951v04p2/d169
63 See Martin Domke, "Assets of East Europeans Impounded in the United States," *American Slavic and East European Review* 18/3 (October 1959). The quotation from Hubert Humphrey in this paragraph comes from a news article, "U.S. Debates Ways to Free 4 Airmen Jailed in Hungary," published in *The New York Times* on Dec. 25, 1951.

that "even if the funds had been transmitted to Hungary, the legatee would not have received them."[64] During those proceedings the Hungarian legation offered to set up a bank account here in the United States to hold the bequest. The Surrogate forbade that compromise, too, for the same reason: the money would never get to the recipient.

Another New York Court in 1951 ruled that "since Hungary is a member of this block of Communist captive countries, this Court would consider sending money out of this country and into Hungary tantamount to putting funds within the grasp of the Communists." The Supreme Court of New Jersey in 1950 ruled that if a bequest were honored to send funds to a Catholic orphanage in Hungary, "a large part" of the payment "would be confiscated and diverted to the use of the Hungarian government." The Supreme Court of Alabama in 1955 denied the distribution of proceeds from a realty sale to next of kin in Hungary. Treasury regulations during this period didn't specifically forbid remittances to Eastern European countries by private parties. In practice, however, probate courts soon took into account the federal determination. Larger bequests, in particular, were subject to indefinite impoundment because of courts' skepticism that a beneficiary behind the Iron Curtain would actually receive those funds and be able to use them. Judges were well aware of the property rights conflict that resulted when they in effect disinherited a beneficiary by diverting bequests to escrow accounts for longterm retention. A patchwork of solutions emerged.

Attracted to the intrinsic tensions these decisions exposed, legal scholars began to address the serious philosophical issues that arise when private laws of succession come into conflict with federal law. Martin Domke, writing in 1959, argued that developments in Cold War foreign policy after 1958 warranted "a relaxation of the prevailing prohibition against the use of funds from American estates for the benefit of residents of Communist-controlled countries."[65] Situations with regard to Poland and Yugoslavia differed during these years, he noted. But still, he writes, courts were "inclined" to follow federal policy.

In New York Surrogate's Court, fifty-one lawsuits were decided between 1939 and 1963 involving estates that had left bequests to residents in totalitarian countries; one of these was the 1961 Bartók decision. Fewer than 10% of these cases resulted in funds being released to beneficiaries domiciled in communist countries. Bernard Freeman, writing in 1963 for the *Buffalo Law*

---

64 "Iron Curtain Barrier to Bequest is Upheld," *The New York Times*, March 6, 1953.
65 Domke, "Assets of East Europeans Impounded in the United States," 355. The other legal decisions mentioned in these paragraphs are taken from Domke's review of cases in this article. See also Bernard Freeman, "Distribution of Estates to Beneficiaries Behind the Iron Curtain," *Buffalo Law Review* 12/3 (June 1, 1963): 630-39. Surrogate's Court relied on its Statute 269, passed in 1939, to guide decisions in this area.

Chapter 6

Review, took the position that Surrogates in New York were "actually deciding these cases based on foreign policy" rather than the wishes of the deceased.

Even had he wanted to, then, Victor Bator would not have been allowed to send large distributions to Ditta Bartók over in Hungary. Any substantial transfers of American dollars from the United States to Hungary could expect to be blocked, either by the U.S. Treasury Department or by American courts. Bator's solution? He distributed more money to Peter (Bartók Records and other expenses), and he devised work-arounds that allowed him to get lifeline levels of money to Ditta. He allocated funds to the Archive for processing and conservation. He also let the bank balance build up. In 1958 he finally consented to let the Estate pay him a routine fee for managing its copyrights, which also tapped some of the pressure.[66] Uncommonly skilled in navigating international banking systems, Victor Bator somehow kept a portion of the Estate income flowing to Ditta Bartók in spite of these headwinds. Her letters confirm receipt of money from him in 1954 and 1955. I have not been able to figure out how he did it. Cloak and dagger contacts in London or Vienna? Promises of repayment to his sisters in Budapest? It's one of the mysteries of the Bartók Estate. One letter even refers to an individual in Peru who may have helped as an intermediary or cut-out.[67] Peter Bartók remembered the secrecy that surrounded these "unofficial" transfers to Ditta during the 1950s. That same secrecy, he later claimed, left him in the dark about how much money was actually getting to her.[68] At no point in the 1950s did he or Bator know with absolute certainty that Ditta was getting full benefit of the money coming to her. They suspected the opposite at all times.

* * *

The domino theory in American foreign policy held that communist victories anywhere in the world strengthened the radical ideology's power, making it more likely that further countries would succumb. Often associated with Dwight Eisenhower, who used the term in an early speech about Vietnam, it

---

66 By early 1958, under guidance from his lawyer, Bator worked with Peter Bartók to standardize the Trustee compensation system. In March Peter paid a sum of $32,000 to Victor Bator to cover back pay for all the work he had done for the Estate during the period of the First Intermediate Accounting (12 years since 1946 at $200/month). In a letter to Bator Peter confirmed that this remuneration was made "in recognition of the valuable services which you rendered the estate. These payments were entirely voluntary, and made with the consent of my Mother." (As quoted in the 1971 report of Milton Goldman).
67 Peter Bartók, letter to Victor Bator, Aug. 31, 1957 (BSCB Tampa). His uncle János knew someone in Peru who might help with the transfers.
68 Peter Bartók, memorandum on recent events in the Bartók Estate, April 20, 1961 (PSS Basel).

became a useful tool to justify American intervention abroad during the Cold War. One of its corollaries is that *any* action that strengthens a communist state contributes to the spread of communism around the globe. By extension, any action that weakens a communist state strikes a blow for democratic ideals. Every small victory counted, as did every battle engaged, no matter how trivial they might seem on a global political scale. His own words in the Vietnam book, where he writes about Washington's irritation over Britain's desire for reconciliation in the growing Vietnam conflict, reveal as if by accident the policy of containment Victor Bator had been forcefully prosecuting against Hungarian publishers and their representatives since the early 1950s:

> International Communism with its monolithic structure [is] set upon the conquest of the world; **each step forward, each success, no matter how small, would serve as a base for the next move. No genuine settlement could be arrived at, for the Communists would concede nothing** unless it advanced their general purpose and made new conquests possible.[69]

The bold emphasis here is my own. Wherever he could, Bator opposed copyright infringements by Hungarian publishers. "Having discovered their devious acts," he wrote in his Affidavit, "I blocked them, not completely, but sufficiently to become first a nuisance, then a real roadblock." Doing so was a matter of principle for a man who viewed himself with no small pride as a thorn in the rosebush for Hungary's communist regime. The Uniform Trust Code empowered him with rights and responsibilities as a Trustee that gave him the authority to push back. Additional motivation for his zeal in policing the globe for copyright infringements came from his certainty that in doing so he was living into the antitotalitarian stance taken by his friend Béla Bartók, in whose name he now acted.

He had seen already, with the Interpretive Declaration of 1951, what could happen when he offered a concession on copyright control and people like Palágyi learned of it. In the 1950s Zeneműkiadó Vállalat began going forward with plans to publish some of the student works whose manuscript scores Bartók had left behind in Hungary. Bator could do nothing to prevent their publication behind the Iron Curtain. But when the publisher made efforts to license those publications in the West, he immediately blocked them. His action made the newspapers in London and New York. A short article in *The New York Sun* in July 1958 reported on the standoff under the headline "Bars Hungary Release of New Bartok Works." Explaining his actions to the reporter, Bator invoked Béla Bartók's political views:

---

69 Bator, *Vietnam—A Diplomatic Tragedy*, 102.

Chapter 6

> There is nothing that Bartok hated as much as a dictatorship and the idea of exploitation of his name and art for the propaganda purposes of a dictatorship. All licenses and permits will be withheld from the Hungarian government until that government acknowledges the legal rights of the estate and the trustee.[70]

All of Victor Bator's other enterprises were safely located in North America; they would rise or fall based on their success in a free market economy. The Bartók Estate, though, touched Hungary directly. He was quick to appreciate its potential as a weapon in the fight against communism.

For similar principles he refused to send money to Hungary that would not get to Ditta. He thoughtfully calibrated the amounts. Through his network of contacts he kept tabs on her living conditions. He cared too much for her family legacy to have it stolen from her by any of the opaque methods used in communist countries to seize foreign income. Instead, he kept as much of the money as he could at home, safe in the United States, deploying it on Peter's spiraling ambitions and on the growing Archives project. So as to not seem too unilateral, or *too* paternalistic, he regularly consulted with Peter about the amounts he was sending over to his mother. On July 16, 1959, in one such instance, he wrote to Peter asking his advice on how much to send his mother. Peter should also tell him what he'd like him to do with the net income from the Trust. "I want to abide by the practice not to ask directly... your mother for instructions. As long as instructions come from you datelined outside of Hungary, I know that they represent the free will of the beneficiary."[71]

Peter's later allegations of mistreatment characteristically overlook this political dimension, focusing instead on the images burned into his mind after seeing his mother again in 1956 for the first time in many years. The US State Department forbade travel by American citizens to Hungary for all of the early 1950s. That prohibition was lifted in early 1956. For a week in the spring of 1956 Peter was able to spend time with his family in Budapest. He made plans to return again, but travel restrictions descended again that summer.[72] During the chaotic aftermath of the Hungarian Revolution he managed to spend several months with his mother, this time in Rimaszombat, Slovakia, where she had fled with her brother to find temporary refuge in their childhood home town.

---

70 As preserved on a general paste-up of newspaper clippings from 1958 in CPB Homosassa.
71 Victor Bator, letter to Peter Bartók, July 16, 1959 (Collection of Francis Bator).
72 Peter Bartók, letter to Denis Dille, August 14, 1956 (BSCB Tampa). Prevented from meeting them in Hungary by State Department restrictions on travel, Peter was able to get a visa to enter Slovakia, and it was there that he reunited with his mother and extended family on the Pasztory side. He stayed there from late October 1956 into January 1957—a three-month visit.

Peter again felt appalled at her poor health. He recognized injustice when he saw it. (And certainly we have no business passing later judgment on the authenticity of his emotional response.) She appeared listless, and couldn't sustain conversation. Her family lamented that she wasn't getting good medical care in Budapest. Afterwards, back in New York, he discharged his worries on Bator, imploring him to do something—anything—to help. Bator was jolted by the first-hand news. He consulted with New York physicians about latest treatments for schizophrenia, and in a long letter to Andor Chatel (see correspondence above) he deployed his trusted childhood friend, now an eminent Budapest physician, to look into improving her mental health care.

Peter's later animus for Bator appears to have left him unwilling to attribute his mother's straitened circumstances to the hard realities of life under a repressive political regime: far simpler, and more wounding, to lay this charge, too, at the Trustee's door. Here he was influenced by the Hungarian attorneys. Plaintiff's positions in the upcoming litigation attempted to paint Bator as a scapegoat for Ditta's poor health. The he-let-my-mother-starve charge first surfaced in 1959. It became a point of attack for plaintiffs' attorneys, one of the many trumped up allegations they introduced in those proceedings to fluster opposing counsel and gain advantage before the court. DiFalco heard testimony on this sensitive issue directly from Peter Bartók and Victor Bator. After reviewing the evidence before him, he found no wrongdoing. This judicial finding alone should push any remaining doubts from our mind. (Highlights here are my own.)

> The refusal of the respondent [Bator] to disburse all of the receipts cannot be said at this time to contravene the will. **Moreover, the executors and trustees would not be justified in transmitting income to a resident of a foreign country, without some assurance that the beneficiary would have the benefit, use and control of the property sent to her (Surrogate Court Act, sec. 269-a). Permission to transmit estate funds to Hungary has been refused** [lists citations]. The executors and trustees were undoubtedly aware of such complications and of the possibilities of personal liability, but they were apparently willing to help the decedent's family, and may have regarded themselves as protected by the consent of the petitioner, both as assignee and attorney-in-fact of the income beneficiary and also in his own right as the remainderman. . . . It is clear that, in the absence of a judicial construction of the will or judicial instructions, they were not obliged to send all of the income receipts to the income beneficiary or to distribute them to the petitioner.

Chapter 6

Only if he felt Ditta Bartók was actually able to benefit from the money sent to her would Bator be supported by the court. Anything in excess, and he might have been held personally liable. He had to walk a narrow path.

* * *

There is a happy ending to this story. Almost. Beginning in the late 1950s, Bator's attorneys instructed him to start holding back significant portions of Trust income each year, pending resolution of claims against the Estate. He let this money build up separately so it could be verified. For similar reasons ASCAP, GEMA, and Bartók's publishers began to escrow portions of Bartók-related income they collected. This practice continued throughout the 1960s. All that frozen income accumulated, year after year, in interest-bearing accounts, awaiting judicial instruction. (Ditta continued to receive regular payments from the Trust during this time.) When Suchoff became Successor Trustee, one of the first big decisions in the ongoing litigation he witnessed was Milton Goldman's Referee's Report, which had ended with the direction that "all the net income of this estate on hand as of the closing date of the account… be paid to the income beneficiary." Narrowly speaking, Goldman's directive covered escrowed funds up to and including Dec. 31, 1961, that had been tied up for over ten years awaiting a court ruling. Even so, a lot of money got suddenly released. A *very* large amount of money. His ruling set a precedent. In years ahead the legal situation would develop some clarity in this area, freeing Suchoff to send Ditta Bartók large checks. Which he did. No Treasury regulations constrained his actions as they had Bator's. "I began to send them *huge* amounts of money," he recalled. "And they loved me."

But did she receive it? Notice Suchoff's choice of pronoun. After the publication of *Rumanian Folk Music* Suchoff was invited to come to Hungary to meet the Hungarian heirs. The invitation came through Ditta's lawyer, he recalled.[73] With his wife Eleanor he attended an outdoor performance of *Madame Butterfly* on Margit Island in the company of Béla Jr., whose behavior puzzled them the entire evening. "I guess he didn't want to be there? He was noncommittal… indifferent." What the Suchoffs remembered most about that evening was the feeling of being abandoned after the performance by Béla

---

73 Suchoff's own lawyer, Shirley Thau, worked at Wolf, Popper, Ross, a well-known firm in New York that offered specialized legal work for clients who had business internationally, including Russia, China, and the communist-controlled countries in Europe. According to the firm's website she was its first female associate, a distinction for which she is honored and remembered today; she became a partner in 1962 (www.wolfpopper.com). From Suchoff I gathered that Vajda was somehow known to her firm from previous work they had done in Hungary.

Jr., who seemed eager to get away from them. Left on their own in downtown Pest, with no taxis in sight, they had to walk back on their own at night across the river and up the steep streets to the Hilton Hotel, an experience that left a deep impression on them.

When he met with Ditta Bartók her living circumstances shocked him—as an American beholding the effects of communist government for the first time, but also because he knew the Estate had been sending her substantial income for years. He met her lawyer, too: an intimidating man. "I thought he was a Svengali. Wow. He scared me." Though he could no longer remember Vajda's name, his impressions of the Hungarian lawyer and Ditta remained vivid.

> She lived off what is called Moscow Tér. She lived in one of those streets, in an apartment building, on the ground floor, with the trash cans in the front. I thought, Ditta, my God, with the money that we're sending? I went in to see her with her lawyer. He was the old-time lawyer who liked my lawyer. He was a *tough* character. I forget his name. Very difficult. And I went into the apartment and we sat down, and he was just talking with me a little bit. Out comes Ditta. She was holding the first three volumes of the *Rumanian Folk Music*. Let me do this right [imitates her voice in a cooing, childlike way] "Look! Dr. Suchoff!" Can you imagine? And that was my introduction to Ditta. Then she went back in her apartment and was making refreshments for us. No maid. A bird-like, shadowy-like woman.

In our interviews Benjamin Suchoff defended the amounts that Ditta Bartók received from Victor Bator. They were appropriate, he felt. Anyone who felt otherwise simply didn't understand the situation. "By 1959 Victor's policy had been to send Ditta the money he thought she needed and could spend. Because he knew that she couldn't spend any more."[74] Ditta, too, to the extent she felt able to write freely to the United States, appears to have expressed contentment. She wrote to Bator in 1955, "I thank you very much for your financial dispositions. This is very satisfactory, and all right with me." In another letter dated October 2, 1954, she requested a slight increase to $300.

After 1958, however, when the amounts Bator *could* be sending to Ditta became known in Hungary, in Communist Party controlled government offices and agencies, the gathering legal storm over Béla Bartók's legacy could no longer be held back. The battle for control of the American Bartók Estate began.

---

74 Suchoff, interview with the author, June 19, 2002.

Chapter 7

Per Finire

In the fall of 1941, around the time he became involved with the Movement for Independent Hungary, Béla Bartók began to work on a two-piano transcription of his Second Suite for Orchestra, a work he had written some 35 years earlier, near the outset of his career. Now that he had relocated to the United States, his publisher sought his help preparing new American editions of the suite and two other works whose copyrights needed renewal, the Four Orchestral Pieces and the Three Rondos for piano. The Suite's more Romantic style gave it the potential, he recognized, to appeal to American audiences. He and Ditta had several upcoming concerts scheduled as duo pianists. If they could learn the new transcription in time, they might be able to program it on those events. They did. The new work received its premiere in Chicago on January 6, 1942. They programmed it three times that winter. Then, their hopes for future concert performances dimming as the war set in, they shelved it. The Suite for Two Pianos, Op. 4b, would lay dormant till long after his death; it was published for the first time by Boosey & Hawkes in 1960.

In the course of transcribing the music, Bartók, his creative impulse irresistibly engaged, found himself making surface changes of all sorts as he went along, resculpting its sound for the new medium. Most noticeably, he added programmatic or descriptive titles to each of the four movements: 1. Serenade, 2. Allegro diabolico, 3. Scena della Puszta, 4. Per Finire. László Somfai drew attention to these movement titles in one of his earliest published articles; scholars ever since have found the title for the finale intriguing.[1] "Per finire" draws attention to itself. A close cousin to the familiar "finale," it pulls away from the connotations of that term even as it relies on the cognate for meaning. As a designation for a last movement in the western classical music tradition, it's quite unusual, actually. Bartók, ever alert to the most minute shades of linguistic subtlety, may have intended to suggest a different way of looking

---

[1] László Somfai, "Per Finire: Some Aspects of the Finale in Bartók's Cyclic Form," *Studia Musicologica* 11 (1969): 391–408. See also Leafstedt, "The Source Materials for Bartók's Suite for Two Pianos, Op. 4b (1941)," *Contemporary Music Review* 38/3–4 (2019): 366–88.

Chapter 7

at the suite's last movement; it was not to be just a "closing movement," but more of a process, or possibly even a rhetorical gesture—literally, "by way of wrapping up."

His aggregation of scores for the Second Suite eventually came to rest in the Béla Bartók Archives, allowing us to appreciate anew, through this example, the variegated history of its collections. Any materials he had in his possession for the Suite at his home in Budapest in 1938 he gathered into the large manuscript collection he sent out of Hungary for safekeeping. (They can be seen on the packing list as "II. Suite" in Fig. 1.1 in Chapter 1 of this book.) His original autograph may have been one of those retained by Universal Edition in Vienna; if so, it came to New York long after Bartók's death as part of the materials the publisher handed over to Victor Bator (1955-61) for preservation in the Archives. To make his transcription in 1941 Bartók worked from his already brittle Handexemplar of the 1921 orchestral score, an item he had deposited—at that specific point in time—in Boosey & Hawkes's offices in downtown Manhattan. The autograph tissue master of the transcription and its two coil-bound copies—the performing scores he and Ditta used on stage in Chicago for the premiere—he gave to Bator for safekeeping while he was still alive.

These scores and their geographical movements tell the story of the Béla Bartók Archives. Between 1943 and 1961 they all found their way to an apartment on the 16th floor of E. 72nd Street in New York City, where, together, they embodied Bartók's complete thoughts on the Second Suite. Later, stamped and paginated, each page laboriously microfilmed, these scores helped inspire the creation of one of largest collections devoted to a single artistic figure anywhere in the world. Out of reverence for his deceased friend, Victor Bator built a living monument to the great Hungarian musician's life and works in downtown New York City.

He also made sure the Suite for Two Pianos got published.

He had been instructed to keep manuscripts like these together. Béla Bartók repeatedly spoke to Bator about what he should and should not do with the manuscripts now in his care. In letters to the heirs, several examples of which are published in this book, Bator reminded them about their father's wishes for the manuscripts. In his preface to the 1963 Béla Bartók Archives catalog he waxes philosophical, situating the Archives project more broadly in western intellectual history. He emphasizes the composer's expressed intention that the manuscripts remain intact and together, free from political intrusion or dissipation.

> Their special deposit with me during Bartók's life plainly indicates his understanding that they should be treated as a collection, an indivisi-

ble whole, not to be dispersed but eventually to become part of a larger collection of Bartók papers at a suitable public institution where they would be available to scholars, musicians and the public... The manuscripts were, to Bartók, a monument of his life and works.[2]

Notice here the word "indivisible," which to Americans carries strong associations with the country's Pledge of Allegiance, an allusion that would not have gone unnoticed by readers during the Cold War. The pledge was newly topical in the 1950s.[3] Even if accidental, the allusion is telling in the context of the rest of his preface, which speaks in exalted tones of personal freedoms and just governance.

Since we are so unaccustomed to hearing Victor Bator's voice as a first-hand observer to the last years of Bartók's life, some further quotations from his Archives catalog bear mention:

> Life in a country under a dictatorship, controlling all intellectual and creative activity, was in conflict with his adamant insistence on freedom and independence.

> [He moved to the US so that] the sole aim of his life—creating, composing and writing—could be carried out without interference by dictatorial, political or any other kind of outside control.

> Bartók's concern for dictatorial rule and Nazi power, on the one hand, and the overwhelming importance he attached to the safety of his manuscripts, on the other hand, are demonstrated with such moving emphasis in his letter written to Ms. Muller Widman.

> The conscious recognition of my obligation to create a Bartók Archive was brought about not only by my obligation as a fiduciary owner, trustee of the estate, to preserve and develop every facet and source of value entrusted to me, but also by the knowledge of the incessant care given by Bartok to the safeguarding of his manuscripts. The Bartok Archives is the offspring of these two parents.

---

2 Bator, *Béla Bartók Archives*, 14. This and the following quotations all may be found on pages 14–16 of his preface.
3 Visceral public reaction against communism led conservative social groups in the United States to begin adding the phrase "under God" to the words of the pledge, a practice that spread rapidly through the country. With Dwight Eisenhower's encouragement Congress passed a law in 1954 that made the amended Pledge official.

Chapter 7

> Priceless papers are now in a "forted residence 'gainst the tooth of time and the razure of oblivion."

His preface as a whole is suffused with references, some of them oblique, to Bartók's well-known aversion to dictatorships.

In his earlier Memorandum, after some 290 typed pages devoted to answering the charges laid at his door by Peter Bartók and Hungarian lawyers acting in the name of Ditta Bartók, he finally turns to the Archives project. The methods by which he accumulated its holdings, and his many efforts to keep Peter Bartók informed of his collecting work, constitute the bulk of this chapter titled, simply, "The Béla Bartók Archives." When he works his way at last to his final thoughts he eases onto a loftier plane, like a lawyer in open court delivering his closing statement.

> Summing up, I consider the Béla Bartók Archive as an institution of culture. I hope and trust that the beneficiaries of the inheritance of Béla Bartók will share my enthusiasm and will willingly contribute those manuscripts, papers, other memorabilia which—being part of the inheritance are today on temporary deposit from the Estate in the Archive and make the Archive thereby near-complete, enveloping almost the entire treasure of Bartók memorabilia and mementos. While my administration as Trustee of the Estate may end at any moment by chance events of nature, and while I may come to the conclusion that disagreements like the one now *sub judice* make my Trusteeship much too burdensome for me, and may of my own volition resign, abandoning the office of Trusteeship, I shall defend with everything I have the Archive from becoming—insofar the depositor's will does not exclude it anyway—private unrestricted property of whosoever with the risk of destruction and dissipation.

> This, the future of the Archive, is the only genuine conflict between the Trustee and the beneficiaries. Every other line of complaint is imaginary and played up from misrepresented trifles into an issue. The Archive is a real issue. If the beneficiaries of the Estate are willing to recognize the Archive as a cultural institution, there is no disagreement. If they want it as their private dominion and use it as a financial asset, then I feel that I defend a cultural institution against vanishment, and it is my duty not to budge. They will not pass.

> The Béla Bartók Archive is too dear for my or Peter Bartók's possessing. I hope that Peter Bartok will join my complete disclaim of possessiveness

and will match my 12 years' work for the creation of the Archive by adding his own Bartók-mementoes to the Archive collection and participate thereby at erecting a monument to Béla Bartókhis father, and my friend.

These are, quite literally, the final words of his Memorandum.

By way of closing, then, some open-ended reflections on the politics that shaped the creation of the Bartók Archives. Within the Hungarian émigré world in New York City, Victor Bator kept himself apart from those whose entire life still seemed to remain in Hungary. He had little patience for Hungarians who cherished a storybook Hungary and passed their time indulging in lament. His son Francis spoke to me at length about this distinction, because he felt it had distorted the image of his father that had been handed down within the Bartók studies world.

> My father very much disliked, and was never willing to play, this sort of inner New York émigré politics. He thought it was trivial: it was a lot of silly people who hoped the world would change, and they could ride back on a white horse and take over their estates and get all their money back. It was a *fantasy life*, what they lived. One of the remarkable psychological aspects of my father—you know, he was at the height of his career, a major figure, and in the United States suddenly he found himself in a very strange and different world—is that he didn't spend an ounce of energy looking back and wanting the past. He was enormously curious and interested in this new world and doing something in it: he set up a manufacturing firm, and did lots of things, including the Bartók Archives. The Vietnam book, too. He was enormously smart, enormously energetic, and basically forward looking. And that means he didn't want to engage in the cocktail party politics of the New York refugee community. A lot of people in that community thought that he snubbed them. Which intellectually he did. And that he was an aloof and separate figure, and very oriented to American life and making something of American life. It didn't mean that he cut his emotional connections. A lot of the motivation behind the Bartók thing was really his sense of Hungarian-ness. That was very deep and strong in him. But he wasn't up to spending Saturday afternoons going to cocktail parties with any of them in particular.[4]

---

4   Francis Bator spoke freely with me on this topic on multiple occasions, wanting me to understand the world his father inhabited. Speaking of his parents and their friends, he said, "Their cultural and social sustenance didn't come from midtown Manhattan. On the other hand, there were conflicts about who accepted and was curious about American life, and those people whose

Chapter 7

When he arrived in the United States Iván Waldbauer found equally refreshing Bator's disinclination for the internal politics of New York émigré circles. The Hollós shared that point of view, too, which may explain why photographs document the Hollós and Bators socializing well into the mid-1950s. Gyula Holló in fact warned the young Waldbauer to steer clear of the complainers and "rabid America haters" in the émigré community, advice Ivan took too heart.[5]

The Laxes, also Hungarian, became friends with the Bators in New York City. Dr. Henry Lax was one of Béla Bartók's doctors in New York—the doctor to whom Bartók spoke his famous last words in the hospital in September 1945 about "leaving with his suitcase still full," referring to all the ethnographic work and composing he had left to do. Contacted in preparations for this book, Peter Lax, the son of Henry Lax, remembered Victor Bator fondly. "I loved and admired him," he wrote to me, "and enjoyed being in his company." Bator was "an interesting, benevolent figure of the Hungarian immigrant community." Unlike most immigrants, Lax explained, "Bator had money; he used his money to support immigrants who were less well off. Most prominent among them was Bartók."[6]

The image of a benevolent Victor Bator who kept some distance between himself and large portions of the New York émigré community arose in part, of course, from the natural insulating quality of wealth. He had prospered in prewar Hungary. He continued to prosper in America. He deployed his resources generously to help fellow Hungarians, as we've seen, especially those who were trying to escape. He was a life raft for many. Nonquitt, Massachusetts, was a site many of his closer acquaintances enjoyed visiting. A photograph taken at Nonquitt around 1957–58 shows Peter Bartók socializing casually with the Bator family (Fig. 7.1) and some of their friends, including Iván Waldbauer.

---

whole life was in Hungary, particularly with their tens of millions of dollars. Bartók never really connected, as you know, with American life." Interview with the author, September 24, 2010.

5 Iván Waldbauer, letter to the author, July 12, 2004. The soft-spoken Holló gave Waldbauer additional advice: "When I arrived in the U.S. in '47, he struck me as the voice of reason and sanity. All the older Hungarians asked me questions about the old country, but he was the only one who didn't tell me that he knew better. The others drove me to distraction; I thought they were crypto-fascists. But Gyula Holló was also the one who explained to me in a long (3-minute) soliloquy that my hopes for Henry Wallace were misplaced. I lived in the Boston area those days, where I tried to develop a balanced view of my new country by reading *The Christian Science Monitor* and *The Daily Worker*. Just two weeks into this regimen was enough for me to see old Gyula vindicated. *The Daily Worker* was dropped." Waldbauer recollected to me his growing dislike for the "U.S. bashing" he encountered in émigré circles, especially from those "who had never been west of the Hudson River, but knew everything about this country." [Author's note: Henry Wallace was the Bernie Sanders of his day, a Democrat with long service in Washington, D.C., whose politics sat sharply left of mainstream after the war, leading him to campaign as a progressive in the 1948 presidential election.]

6 Peter Lax, Email to the author, Oct. 11, 2012.

Per Finire

Fig. 7.1. A winter gathering at the Bator family vacation home, Nonquitt, Massachusetts, ca. 1957–58. From left, Iván Waldbauer, Peter Bator, Peter Bartók, Franci Bator, Paul Bator, Christopher Bator (child), Yolanda Martin, Jean Martin. Photographer: Francis or Victor Bator. Source: personal collection of Francis Bator.

This is, as far as I know, the only photograph we have of Peter Bartók among the Bator family. He had already begun to separate himself from them, emotionally and psychologically, at the time this photograph was taken.[7] The way he holds Mrs. Bator's arm in this photograph, with Paul Bator taking her other arm, suggests some lingering emotional warmth for the woman who came closer than anyone else to fulfilling the role of surrogate mother for him in the 1940s and 50s.

Tied up in these observations about Victor Bator's position within the complex, charged environment of New York City's post-war Hungarian émigré community is the underlying topic of his personal political views. Lax described him to me as "conservative." Francis Bator also described his father as "conservative." Shades of meaning in that term should be distinguished, he was careful to add. "Relative to the communists, he was a *strong* conservative," he clarified. A better characterization overall, he felt, might be "Edmund Burkean

---

7 At right in the photo, Jean Martin was a French chemist who worked at Coty. A very fine musician himself, he frequently visited the Bators in Nonquitt as part of their extended family. His daughter Micheline Martin (Radcliffe '49) had married Francis Bator in New Orleans in June 1949. The Martins lived on E. 89th Street in New York City.

conservative," i.e., not rigid in his views, marked by eclecticism—"like Harold Macmillan in England." I spoke with his grandson Christopher Bator in preparations for this book. He remembered his grandfather as a mixture of political inclinations: conservative with regard to international affairs, more liberal on domestic issues. Let us pause to consider these distinctions. The English conservative mind identifies Edmund Burke (1729–97) as a forerunner for moderate conservatism, or what Edmund Fawcett, in a recent magisterial survey of conservatism's intellectual tradition, describes as a conservatism marked by "a tone of balance, openness to facts, and all-around moderation that stood out in contrast to the blind zeal of conservatism in France and Germany."[8] As Fawcett notes, respect for custom, and the rules that emerged from custom, further distinguishes this strain of conservative thought. Adam Gopnik puzzles over the many faces of Burkean conservativism in an essay published in *The New Yorker* that teasingly identifies the species as "the kind liberals pretend to want" as opponents, before moving on to this description of the underlying type: "Someone who has great respect for traditional order as a guarantor of social peace but not, on the whole, as a guarantor of liberty."[9] A desire for maintaining constitutional order further marks the Burkean mindset, as does, for many adherents, in one way or another, a respect for the institutions governing civil society. Traditionalist conservatism of this sort does not shirk progressive demands. Its defining feature, Mark C. Henrie notes, is a sense of loss, and of *nostalgia*, from which it gathers its moral force.[10]

In the highly charged political environment of the early Cold War, attitudes like these placed Victor Bator in the expansive middle bands of the political spectrum, away from the zealous ideologues whose loud voices dominated national conversation in the McCarthy years. There, in that reasonable space, he was joined by other prominent émigrés such as Tibor Eckhardt and John Pelényi, the distinguished Hungarian ambassador to the United States (1933–40). Pelényi had resigned his ambassadorship in December 1940 in public protest of Hungary's precipitous drift to the right. He sought asylum in the United States—his wife Sue was American—and soon joined Bator and Eckhardt in the leadership circles of the Movement for Independent Hungary. They had been friendly since the 1930s. After the war they remained in contact as they each built new lives. (Francis Bator once referred to them as a hyphenated unity,

---

[8] Edmund Fawcett, *Conservatism: The Fight for Tradition* (Princeton, NJ: Princeton University Press, 2020), 3.
[9] Adam Gopnik, "The Right Man," *The New Yorker* (July 29, 2013), available online at https://www.newyorker.com/magazine/2013/07/29/the-right-man.
[10] Mark C. Henrie, "Understanding Traditionalist Conservatism," available online from the Hoover Institution at https://www.hoover.org/sites/default/files/uploads/documents/0817945725_3.pdf.

the "Eckhardt-Pelényi-Victor Bator grouping" in Hungarian émigré politics.) Men like these loathed communism. In their adopted country that attitude was mainstream, shared by the overwhelming majority of U.S. citizens.

Inclined to lead, over time they came to the reluctant conclusion that what was left of Hungarian culture must be rebuilt abroad, where it could be honored and preserved in its new environment. Pelényi in 1955 became one of the founders of the American Hungarian Library and Historical Society, an institution that would soon be joined by the American Foundation for Hungarian Literature and Education (Magyarház on E. 82nd Street, est. 1963), the American Hungarian Foundation (New Brunswick, New Jersey, est. 1955), and the Béla Bartók Archives (est. 1963) as institutions dedicated to preserving Hungarian culture in the greater New York area.[11] Together these organizations shared an attitude that was specifically anti-communist in orientation. Its founders envisioned the American Hungarian Library, for example, as "a home for Hungarian culture in the free world," echoing the reasons the Bartók Archives came into being.[12] Several of these new organizations were launched by friends of Bator's, including Eckhardt, Pelényi, and Ferenc Chorin—men whose pragmatic natures and proximity to power in pre-war Hungary left them disinclined to reflexively villify Regent Horthy, even as they abhorred the spread of Nazism.

During World War II Béla Bartók found himself drawn into the political world these men inhabited. He actively participated in the Movement for Independent Hungary, as we've seen. An extraordinary new archival discovery places Bartók at a meeting of the Movement's Executive Committee held in New York City on March 1, 1945, long after the Movement had seen its last sunset. The Yalta conference had just taken place, and in January Hungary had signed an armistice with the Allies in Moscow. These developments prompted Pelényi to convene the Executive Committee for the first time since June 1942. At that meeting Bartók joined Bator, Pelényi, and Tibor Eckhardt to consider

---

[11] Most of these organizations were nonprofits chartered according to the Revenue Act of 1954, which established Section 501 of the Internal Revenue Code and its various subclassifications. The Béla Bartók Archives was granted IRS status as a 501(c)(3) charitable trust. To establish and maintain this IRS classification, a board of trustees was required, and certain standards needed to be met annually to demonstrate adherence to regulations. The IRS carefully monitors organizations like these for evidence of improper financial benefit for their founders. (*Very* carefully, I might add.) Victor Bator may have still kept his name on the trustee list, but by establishing the Archives as an independent institution he insulated it from perception that he stood to gain personally (somehow) from its operations. Annual IRS filings would have demonstrated this financial independence in subsequent court proceedings.

[12] The brief online history of the American Hungarian Library and Historical Society indicates that its founders were motivated by this goal in 1955. See https://www.hungarianlibrary.org/about.

post-war outcomes for their country.¹³ Plainly, there is more we have to learn about Béla Bartók's wartime political engagement. His willingness to fraternize on occasion with deeply political men like Eckhardt and Pelényi suggests, at the very least, that he found their company stimulating. (Francis Bator: "Pelényi was a very distinguished human being.") More intriguing still, in a possibility we mustn't discount, is that he had developed somewhat overlapping political views himself. To Iván Waldbauer, Bartók was "somewhat left of center," a characterization Francis Bator agreed with ("I would say he was probably on the left somewhere. All that work on folk music.") Manifest interest in patriotism, and patriotic initiatives, tugged the famed Hungarian musician late in his life into territory traditionally identified more closely with conservative thought. These scattered observations don't in any way amount to a rounded or cohesive picture. I mention them here because they seem significant, as if they're pointing towards some elusive, long buried realization that resists easy discovery, requiring further pondering to reveal. I don't have a ready answer.

His persistently hard-line stance against communism contributed to Victor Bator's estrangement from Peter Bartók in the late 1950s. Peter's political convictions are difficult to discern from the historical record. For a while in the late 1950s, however, under the influence of Béla Jr., he tilted sufficiently far to the left that he appears to have entered fellow traveller territory. Bator chided him for it. When Zeneműkiadó began publishing Bartók juvenilia in Hungary, Peter found himself enlisted by his half-brother and Palágyi to convince Bator to allow these publications in the West, too. From Vienna he cabled Bator in November 1957. Bator, suspicious, responded as diplomatically as he could:

> Although it is difficult to believe that Zeneműkiadó, an agency wholly owned by the Hungarian Government, could be independent and have no underground or above ground connection with any other agency of the same Government, since you are inclined to trust and accept Béla's and Palágyi's statement to that effect, I am giving you my reaction to your cable as if I accepted and fully believed what Béla and Palágyi seem to have said.¹⁴

Bator resented the publisher's efforts to use Peter Bartók to influence copyright decisions abroad. "It is none of Zeneműkiadó's business to be consulted and

---

13 See Katalin Kádár Lynn's forthcoming book on Tibor Eckhardt, which draws on archival research in Hungary to establish a more detailed understanding of the Movement for Independent Hungary. I am grateful to Kádár Lynn for sharing some of her archival findings with me in advance of publication.
14 Bator, letter to Peter Bartók, November 13, 1957 (Collection of Francis Bator).

influence the internal relationship between the beneficiaries and the administration of the Estate."

For complex emotional reasons tied to his mother's presence in Hungary, after 1958 Peter Bartók dabbled in the unlikely role—for him—of self-appointed cultural attaché. He actively tried to sustain and repair historic relationships across the Iron Curtain. In the process he allowed himself to be lulled into complicity. After seeing his mother and grandmother and uncle for the first time in many years in late 1956, he responded very emotionally to learning of their poor quality of life. All of his immediate family remained in Hungary and Slovakia. He returned to the US determined to help. To what extent his subsequent actions resulted from active manipulation by communist bureaucrats, who held his mother's welfare in their hands, cannot be established with certainty. His turn away from Bator happened gradually at first, then precipitously after the First Piano Concerto recording incident.

Coleridge felt that the Industrial Revolution elevated men to positions of power who valued "an overbalance of the commercial spirit." Peter, too, seems to have yearned for an Estate less fixated on the business of copyright protection—a kinder, gentler Estate willing to support without question an old friend and prominent advocate such as Sacher, or willing to allow his father's early unpublished works to be printed in the West even if the Hungarian State claimed those copyrights by fiat.

How far Peter had drifted to the Hungarian side by mid-1958 can be seen in the comments he directed to the editor of *The New York Sun* after reading that paper's coverage of Bator's successful blocking of Zeneműkiadó editions in the West:

> You attribute to Mr. Victor Bator a quotation about the exploitation of Bartok's name and art for propaganda purposes. May I ask, since when is music publishing and music performance considered propaganda of any kind? And since Bartok disapproved of politics in the arts, why make a political issue of that which is only a legal dispute?"[15]

Good questions. Depending on your perspective, comments like these either ooze naiveté or show admirable idealism. Perhaps both: Peter had an idealistic streak that drove many of his decisions throughout his life. That impulse could leave him unguarded in the worlds of politics and law, where the rules of engagement were set by others. Anthony Trollope in his younger days felt no aptitude for the commercial world of London, and even less interest in it.

---

15   Peter Bartok, letter to the editor, *The New York Post*, July 28, 1958 (BSCB Tampa).

Chapter 7

"Uncanny documents," he writes in his *Autobiography*, "of which I never understood anything, were common attendants on me." So, too, with Peter. Peter Bartók in the 1940s and 50s showed an active indifference to the legal documents that defined his family's relationship to the Estate. If we are to believe the comments that surfaced in court during the litigation of 1959–61, Peter never read these documents closely. This nonchalance left him looking foolish and shockingly ill-informed before the court. Surrogate DiFalco was the first to remark on Peter's dual nature in court. On the witness stand Peter, 34, often appeared bewildered, claiming to have hardly known a thing about the Will or any powers-of-attorney. (Pleading ignorance of legal documents and their exact contents is a venerable plaintiff's strategy in litigation proceedings.) DiFalco saw right through it. In his opinion he astutely observed, "the witness was neither so naive nor witless as the present argument of his counsel would make him appear."[16] Indeed. The new Peter Bartók was about to emerge from his chrysalis.

To his credit, by the mid-1960s Peter developed a considerably sharper legal mind, not only from necessity, but also from genuine inclination and talent, as he would soon discover. Details he once ignored he ignored no longer. His crusade forced him to think like a lawyer in terms of state law and court practices. He became good at it. Year by year he learned to speak the language. His letters grew pointed and detailed. Unlike a practicing lawyer, he sometimes let his penchant for conflict inflame his actions—behavior that was completely consistent with, and made possible by, his insistence on representing himself. He didn't always know where legal boundaries lay. He didn't have the training. Nor did he seem to care. As an example we can point to his early 1980s quest in Surrogate's Court to have the Estate reimburse him $1.3 million for his own legal fees and expenses, on many levels a preposterous claim.[17] On the other hand, his lawsuit over the Concerto for Orchestra's copyright renewal, which was reversed on appeal, shows him at his best, smartly navigating copyright law and legal precedent to argue against the work's posthumous status, and then sticking to his guns after the first judge ruled against him, forcing the case to an appeals court. He was helped in that instance by an attorney in New York.

All this lay in his future. By 1959, after repeat trips to Hungary to prepare for the first lawsuit, he came as close as he ever would to aligning his interests

---

16   S. Samuel DiFalco, Opinion re Estate of Bela Bartok (1961).
17   In her decision Lambert felt obliged to walk him through law-school fundamentals before she rejected his claim. "It should be pointed out that even if the court were disposed to compensate petitioner for legal services performed, it would be hardpressed to find a rationale or power under which it might do so." Opinion of Surrogate Marie Lambert in re: Estate of Bela Bartok (March 1981). Copy preserved in the Collection of Elliott Antokoletz.

with those of the Hungarian communist government. Only in his case he didn't see it that way: he saw instead, or must have seen, a new and powerful ally in his quest to gain some measure of control over the Estate.

* * *

Litigation over the American Bartók Estate began its last lap with the death of Ditta Bartók in 1982. Her own Will had left a portion of her estate to the Liszt Academy. The mechanics of unwinding her estate from the ongoing litigation took several additional years. Bartók's publishers in the West were still party to the litigation. So was Sacher, who had stayed involved all these years just to make sure he had a say in the fate of the Stefi Geyer Concerto autographs. By the terms of Béla Bartók's 1943 Will, the American Estate—which since 1967 had also legally included the complete contents of Victor Bator's Archives collection, as per his direction—would now come to Peter as the remainderman. Peter couldn't wait. Literally. Suchoff told me the following story:

> When she died in 1982, Peter *immediately* came to see me. And I immediately took the Slovak materials and manuscripts—I was working on them at home—to the bank. This is the bank on 72nd Street and Madison Avenue. And the bank said I no longer had authority to go into the bank vault. I said, "Who told you that?!" It turned out that I had to have my attorney call their attorneys, and they rescinded it. Peter had tried to put a block on my re-entering it! He intimated I might want to go in to steal something, I guess. And I wanted to put stuff back.[18]

This modest little story encapsulates the Bartók Estate's disfunction. Peter was so mistrustful of Suchoff by that time, and so eager to push him aside, that he barrelled ahead and asserted legal ownership to the safe deposit box holding the autographs, disregarding due process, probate, and the thicket of litigation that surrounded the Estate. Calmer minds had to intervene. Peter wanted no one's hands on his father's materials but his own. In pursuit of this goal, against the Estate, and against Suchoff, for over two decades he carried out what Francis Bator described as "guerrilla warfare."

Of special concern to him, as the years dragged on, were the Estate's several inventories of assets, prepared under court direction. Simply spectacular amounts of time were wasted in hearings and court in the 1970s and early 80s to settle his worries about the location of two poems he remembered seeing in

---

18 Suchoff, interview with the author, June 19, 2002.

Chapter 7

his apartment in the early 1950s, which he claimed he had subsequently turned over in a manila envelope to Bator. Those poems—possibly of folk origin—had not been separately itemized on the 170-page inventory prepared in 1968. Perhaps Suchoff had stolen them, Peter wondered? His mind turning darkly on the possibilities, he decided to sue, an action that dragged numerous people through dense inventories in pursuit of a chimera, all at great cost to the Estate.[19]

During these years the relationship between Peter Bartók and his mother broke down completely. Disheartening tales of their family strain dot the landscape of Bartók studies, etched in our collective memory. Of them I will say nothing more here. Iván Waldbauer, who knew Peter fairly well, heard more than his share of these family woes over the years. He had this to say: "Peter once told me that there is no one in the world he hates more than his mother. Yes, can you believe it?"[20]

* * *

Whether or not the Budapest Bartók archive would have come into existence in 1961 without the legal dramas taking place overseas is a question that should probably be reopened. We've always accepted the obvious chronology. Both institutions, unsurprisingly, were preceded by years of planning and preparation. Victor Bator's Archives project had developed into a major collection by the mid-1950s, and was already supporting work on its holdings as early as ca. 1950–52, with Otto Gombosi and Halsey Stevens; it produced its first Ph.D. dissertation in 1956 with the work of Benjamin Suchoff. The scope of Victor Bator's ambitions stood plainly before Hungarian attorneys by 1958. In response, as we've seen, the Hungarian government took the precaution of reasserting jurisdiction over Bartók's Estate by formally declaring, through its Office of Government Public Notaries, the composer's Hungarian Will to be the valid legal instrument. By the summer of 1959 lawyers led by Palágyi were pursuing a proxy lawsuit against Victor Bator in New York City. Their purpose was plain: to unseat Bator

---

19 See Surrogate Marie Lambert, Opinion re Estate of Bela Bartok, *New York Law Journal*, October 25, 1983. Also among the contested items in the Estate was the Róbert Berény oil painting. In hearings it was adduced that Victor Bator as Trustee had first used Trust funds to purchase the painting in 1957, then later reimbursed the Trust for those costs when concerns were raised by plaintiff's attorneys in the first litigation, which allowed him to legally claim the painting for the Archives. Whether the Estate or Archives owned the painting hovered in the background of the Bartók Estate litigation for the next two decades, only to be resolved in 1983, when Surrogate Lambert ruled that it should belong to the Archives as Trust property, and that the original cost ($12,000) be transferred to the Estate of Victor Bator as reimbursement. As Archives property it therefore went to Peter Bartók in 1985.

20 Waldbauer, interview with the author, January 5, 2011. Many other people who knew Peter or Ditta Bartók will have their own stories.

as Trustee, installing one or more of the heirs as his successors, and to secure for Hungarian use the Estate's hard currency earnings going forward.

While these legal actions may have remained wholly unknown to some of the musicologists in Budapest then engaged in establishing the Hungarian Bartók studies field, we cannot say the same for the Hungarian ministries of finance and education, the Office for the Protection of Authors' Rights, or for Béla Jr., whose collections were used to start the Hungarian archives, or for Ditta Bartók, who, feeble though she may be, and reclusive, still commanded great respect in a country that venerated her husband. A letter Peter Bartók wrote to József Újfallusy at the Ministry of Public Education in 1955 got handed off to Robert Palágyi for response. Peter had been inquiring about the regular shipments of Hungarian-language articles to Victor Bator? Those would continue, Palágyi assured him. A "museum" was being planned for Béla Bartók. Would Peter consider visiting Budapest in 1956 to observe the festivities planned for the 75th anniversary of his father's birth?[21] Béla Jr. himself spent three months in the United States starting in December 1959, a rare privilege in those days for a Hungarian outside diplomatic circles. Much of that time was spent with Peter in New York City. He had close personal knowledge of the ongoing litigation, and of everything that Peter Bartók had been involved with to date. He'd even, as a special reward for his involvement, had a personal lawsuit served on him while in New York. Can it be coincidence that one year later he helped launch Hungary's own archival collection? In August 1961 the Hungarian government initiated legal action to force the return of the American Estate to Hungary.

How interwoven all these threads had already become in the Bartók world is neatly illustrated by a letter Peter Bartók wrote to Dille in 1956, years before the Belgian musicologist would be appointed to helm the new Bartók institute in Budapest.

Dear Professor Dille:

As you know I am helping whenever he needs it the Trustee of the Bartók Estate, Victor Bator, to complete, enlarge and enrich as far as possible the Béla Bartók Archives about which you know. Just in case you are not entirely in the picture I want to mention that he, sometime in 1948, had the bright idea to begin collecting the Bartók mementoes and save them,

---

21 Robert Palágyi, letter to Peter Bartók, September 17, 1955. English translation prepared by staff at Victor Bator's archives, ca. 1958. Marked "Enclosure I$_6$" for inclusion in Bator's Memorandum (BSCB Tampa).

Chapter 7

> index them, catalogue them, building thereby something that deserves the name BELA BARTOK ARCHIVES. It is far from being complete, but he continues his efforts and work relentlessly to achieve the desirable result. He has told me many times that he does not know yet where ultimately the Archives will be housed. Should the political situation in this troubled world become more peaceful, and the Iron and all other Curtains disappear, he may send it to Hungary. But we are not that far yet.[22]

Peter goes on in this letter to invite Dille's help in helping them assemble a list of his father's early works.

Looking back over the institution's history in 1981, László Somfai explained to attendees at an international conference in Budapest that "pure idealism" had motivated the Budapest Bartók Archívum's founding:

> At that time (1961) there was no thought in building up a Hungarian Bartók institute and research centre but pure idealism: to rescue Bartók's manuscripts, to buy and collect documents—at the Hungarian state's expense. Neither financial nor political considerations motivated the creation of this institute: as a matter of fact the founders were not yet aware that the Budapest archives would soon become the rival, the counter-institution, of an American one.[23]

The contents of this book suggest a different narrative. For those creating the Bartók studies field in Hungary political considerations may well have been peripheral to their work; many of them may have actively wished to be freed of those constraints. But their actions took place in a state that was unavoidably politicized, profoundly so when it came to official decisions involving figures as well known as Béla Bartók. Victor Bator's inexhaustible energy as Trustee had already put him on a path to becoming, as his son would later put it, a "hate figure for communist Hungary." In other areas of the Hungarian Bartók world, the economic and legal areas, tensions had been running high for several years. 1961 brought them to a boil. It became apparent that making Bartók their own, materially, at least, was not going to happen easily for the Hungarians. The battles would have to continue. It's impossible to disentangle the Budapest institution from the geopolitical environment which gave it birth. We can say the same of the American Archives. At the height of the Cold War these two insti-

---

22 Peter Bartók, letter to Denis Dille, August 14, 1956 (BSCB Tampa).
23 László Somfai, "The Budapest Bartók Archive," in the report of the International Association of Music Librarians Annual Conference in Budapest, *Fontes Artis Musicae* 29/1–2 (January–June 1982): 60.

tutions arose in opposition to each other, like twin stars spinning in each other's gravitational orbit, each depending on the other—remotely, invisibly—for motion and energy.

When Victor Bator opened the doors to The Béla Bartók Archives in 1963, informed observers could be excused for seeing it as a reaction to the parallel action in Budapest two years earlier. In fact, as we've seen, awareness of Bator's Archives plans was circulating already in Budapest by 1958, and in certain areas of the bureaucracy as early as 1955. This was the age of the Space Race, of Sputnik, Yuri Gagarin, and Alan Shepard. The Hungarians, here, got to the starting gate first. What Victor Bator thought of this development has not been preserved. Events on the ground in New York were claiming his attention. He had an Estate to manage, and one deeply unhappy heir plotting revenge. After the DiFalco judgment in May 1961, the Hungarian government unilaterally declaring Bator's trusteeship terminated. All copyrights, government attorneys directed, now belonged to Peter Bartók, they claimed. "All annuities, profit, income and gain realized" from those assets should be paid to Ditta Bartók. In pursuit of this dream the Hungarian government lawyers, including Ditta's new lawyer Ernő Vajda, settled in to strategize, and to plan. They had little idea, at that point in time, how long the road would stretch ahead of them.

* * *

Peter Bartók died on December 7, 2020, as this book was being written. He was 96. The priceless collection of his father's autograph manuscripts had been hand delivered to Basel over a decade earlier, where they remain to this day, excellently cared for and securely housed by Felix Meyer and his staff. Peter had always liked Switzerland. In the 1960s he even considered moving there. A strong sense of historical justice led him to return his father's autographs to Europe, and to Switzerland in particular, one of his father's favorite countries. His executor, Peter Hennings, now supervises the administration of copyrights in conjunction with the longstanding publishers of Béla Bartók's music, as well as any residual sales of Bartók Records albums and the revised score editions they printed in Florida. What happens to the remaining copyrights, which now belong to the Estate of Peter Bartók, is up to him to decide. So, too, the fate of the remaining Archives holdings that are kept on the premises in Homosassa. The long arc of history has come full circle. Where this remarkable collection comes to rest in coming years is a matter of great interest for all who love Bartók's music. From its holdings many tales remain to be told.

Acknowledgements

Content for this book was amassed over several decades. A long trail of individual contributions made it possible. To Francis Bator I offer my deepest gratitude. His crisp memories brought the subject to life for me in dozens of interviews and literally hundreds of email conversations, as well as two memorable weekend-long conversations at his home outside of Boston. Had he not decided to save a small stack of copies of his father's business papers as a souvenir of his family's involvement in the lives of Béla Bartók and his family, this book would not exist. For his personal encouragement in expanding this project to book-length form I am deeply grateful. I wish that he were alive to see it in print. His son Christopher Bator—the grandson of Victor Bator—generously endorsed his father's desire to see Victor Bator's writings and letters published. For Christopher Bator's permission to reproduce all of the Bator family writings, photographs, and interviews found in this book I am deeply grateful.

To Benjamin Suchoff the world of Bartók studies owes a debt it still has not fully paid. Suchoff kept the Archive and Estate going during a difficult time when litigation drained these entities of the vitality they once promised. Ben was an inspiring figure for me when I got into the Bartók studies field in the 1990s. During my two-day conversation with him at his office in Florida I didn't always ask the right questions, not knowing then what I knew later about the Estate. But I did manage to get on tape many of his memories about the Estate's history, as well as his personal experiences as Successor Trustee. He had much to say. His presence, like Francis's, hovers gently over most of this book, for some of the same reasons: he saved valuable documentary materials, hoping that those pages might someday tell their tales. They both believed that the history of the Bartók Estate needed to be told.

Institutional support for this research was provided by Trinity University. I am fortunate to work for a university that supports its faculty so generously. David Heller, Chair of the Music Department, has been particularly supportive of my many travel requests in recent years in connection with this project. Additional support early on was provided by a National Endowment for the Humanities

Acknowledgements

Summer Stipend that made possible my 2002 interviews with Suchoff and older musicians with personal stories to tell about Béla Bartók.

The staff at the Sacher Stiftung in Basel, Switzerland, and the Special Collections staff at the University of South Florida in Tampa both offered courteous, patient help of the sort that makes all on-site researchers grateful. To Felix Meyer, director of the Sacher Stiftung, I remain especially thankful for his willingness to share his institution's history with the Bartók materials, and for the many personal courtesies he extended to me during and after my month-long residency at the Stiftung in the summer of 2018. He leads a remarkable institution with skill and grace.

Portions of Chapter 1 were published previously in *Studia Musicologica*. Péter Bozó, Editor-in-Chief of the journal, generously approved their re-publication in expanded form in this book. László Vikárius, head of the Budapest Bartók Archive, is a remarkable resource for all of us in the field. I am grateful for his help locating materials or background information that went into this book.

After a lecture I gave on this topic at the University of Alberta in 2017 I met a graduate student there, Etelka Nyilasi, who in short order became a helpful translator for Hungarian language documents from the Bator family. Soon we were sharing digital files back and forth between Texas and Alberta, polishing the translations she kindly prepared at my request. I am grateful for her enthusiastic work. Earlier in the project's history David Nagy, a student of Peter Laki's, provided the initial translations of Victor Bator's lectures that now stand at the back of this book.

During the recent coronavirus pandemic, institutions that might normally be open to visitors were suddenly closed. For their long-distance help obtaining archival materials and, in some cases, illustrations for this book, I am grateful to: Tomaro Taylor (University of South Florida), and Adrienne Pruitt and Pamela S.M. Hopkins (Tufts University). Sarah Lucas (Texas A&M University, Kingsville) shared copies of her research files from the University of Iowa Library's Philip Greeley Clapp Collection.

A special debt of gratitude is owed to Peter Hennings, Executor for Peter Bartók, who generously helped me with my research during several on-site visits. He granted me a level of access to Peter Bartók's holdings in Homosassa, Florida, that I never dreamed possible. For decades a closed fortress inaccessible to most Bartók scholars, Homosassa has in its twilight years become a welcoming place. He generously granted me permission to include in my book many illustrations from the collection, as well as factual content and quotations from unpublished archival materials. Peter: thank you.

I never met Peter Bartók. After a brief window of time in the late 1980s and early 1990s when he attended occasional academic conferences as an honored guest, enjoying the acclaim of being Béla Bartók's son, Peter Bartók retreated from sight in the musicological world. By nature a quieter man, comfortable with his solitude, he preferred to handle inquiries by mail. For the sunlight of fame he felt some discomfort. He was, in this regard, truly his father's son. He had other tasks, too, which claimed his time. I interacted with him only by mail. In the 1990s and early 2000s he patiently helped me with many inquiries for materials, aided by Hope Kellman and other staff members. I made several efforts to interview him. On-site visits, I learned, he did not encourage. He rebuffed me each time, clearly not eager to talk. Eventually he grew tired of my inquiries. "I wish you'd confine your questions to the music, and leave these personal questions aside," he grumbled to me in a letter. (I had been asking about his father's fleeting diagnosis of recurrent tuberculosis during World War II.) He was at his best when fielding hopeful inquiries from graduate students, many of whom were thrilled to get communications from Béla Bartók's son. I felt that way myself when started corresponding with him in 1991 about *Bluebeard's Castle*. For preserving *all* of the Victor Bator Archives essentially intact he deserves our collective gratitude. He recognized and honored his place in the long arc of history.

To Rich Miller in New York: thank you. Your encouragement meant more than you know. My own three B's in San Antonio—Bondari, Boyle, Burnett—kept me from overworking during the last few years. My wife Ann, a superb attorney, helped me articulate my thinking more carefully and precisely in the chapter on Bartók's wills. She has been with me on this entire journey since the name "Béla Bartók" started surfacing among my doctoral dissertation ideas. Over the years she came to know Ben Suchoff and Elliott Antokoletz. In so many quiet ways she helped me surmount the extra work this project involved. My son Kent, an avid golfer, tore me away from my computer many times for a round of golf, which proved restorative and helpful to my writing. My son Wendell, a violinist, composer, and experienced copy editor, read through draft chapters for this book with a careful eye, helping me develop my ideas. I am grateful to them both.

Acknowledgements

Helena History Press has been a joy to work with at all stages. From acquisition through publication, Katalin Kádár Lynn and her staff, including Krisztina Kós in Budapest, have guided this book through to completion with a refreshingly professional, efficient, and personable style.

Finally, I would like to thank those who read portions of this book prior to its publication: Peter Laki (Bard College), Claudia MacDonald (Oberlin College), Wendell, and my editor, Katalin Kádár Lynn. Their careful reading helped me catch errors, add new information, and refine the book's content. The book is better for their advice.

Works Cited

Archival and Unpublished Materials

Source materials for this study are preserved in the following archival or private collections.

Collection of Peter Bartók, Homosassa, Florida (CPB Homosassa)

Béla Bartók Collection, Paul Sacher Stiftung, Basel, Switzerland (BBC-PSS Basel)

Budapest Bartók Archívum, Budapest, Hungary (BBA Budapest)

Benjamin Suchoff Collection of Bartókiana, The University of South Florida, Tampa, Florida (BSCB Tampa). A finding aid for this collection is available online at: https://digital.lib.usf.edu/SFS0032063/00001.

This book is made possible by the generous sharing of family documents held privately by the descendants of Victor Bator, especially by Francis Bator when he was still alive (Collection of Francis Bator). In preparations for this book I conducted extensive interviews with Francis Bator, Iván Waldbauer, and Benjamin Suchoff over a span of years from 2002 to 2018. Those interviews are transcribed and preserved in the collection of the author. Elliott Antokoletz was involved at arm's length with the Estate from the 1980s onward. He generously shared his historical correspondence files with me, some of which found their way into this book. Legal documents pertaining to the Bartók family, the American Bartók Estate, and the years of litigation are cited as they arise in earlier pages of this book; they are not shown separately below.

***

Anon. "Composer's Son Devotes Bartok Records to Furthering Father's Music." *The Presto Recorder* 5/8 (August 1953).

———. "Bartók's Music Lives Again." *Audio Record* 10/1 (Jan/Feb. 1954).

Antokoletz, Elliott. "The New York Bartók Archives: Genesis and History." *Studia Musicologica* 53/1–3 (2012): 341–48.

Applebaum, Anne. *Iron Curtain: The Crushing of Eastern Europe, 1944–1956*. New York: Doubleday, 2012.

Árokszállási, Éva. "Peter Bartók in Budapest." Transl. Peter Laki. n.d. Unpublished photocopy preserved in the papers of Elliott Antokoletz.

Baron, Julius G., et al. "Reviews of Internal Medicine: A Primer on Radiation Hazards for Physicians." *Archives of Internal Medicine* 103/2 (Feb. 1959): 308–28.

Baron, Julius G. "Medical Radiation." *Public Health Reports* 74/1 (Jan. 1959): 36–38.

Báron, Julius, and Julius Holló. "Kann die Klangfarbe des Klaviers durch die Art des Anschlages beeinflusst werden." *Zeitschrift für Sinnesphysiologie* 66/1–2 (1935): 23–32.

Báron, Julius G. "Physical Basis of Piano Touch." *Journal of the Acoustical Society of America* 30/2 (1958): 151–2.

Bartók, Ditta. "26. September 1945: Zum 20. Todestag von Béla Bartók." *Oesterreichische Musikzeitschrift* 20 (1965): 446-49. Translated. In Malcolm Gillies, ed., *Bartók Remembered*. New York: W.W. Norton, 1990.

Bartók, Peter. "Bartók Records & Publications." Homosassa, FL: Bartók Records. Privately printed catalog (October 1, 2012).

———. "Béla Bartók's Estate: Its Administration." Coil-bound typescript, n.d. [ca. 2005?]. Unpublished. BBC-PSS Basel.

———. "In the Groove . . . ." *The Nation* (Dec. 4, 1954).

———. Memorandum in Reference to the Bartók Estate. Unpublished (1961). Paul Sacher Correspondence Files. PSS Basel.

———. *My Father*. Homosassa, FL: Bartók Records, 2002.

———. "The Fight Over the Bartók Estate, 1945–85." Coil-bound typescript, 2004. Unpublished. BBC-PSS Basel.

———. "Up to Now." Unpublished press release (1953). BSCB Tampa.

Bator, Paul M. *The International Trade in Art*. Chicago: University of Chicago Press, 1983.

Bator, Victor. Memorandum on the History of the Bartók Estate. 1959–60. Unpublished. Benjamin Suchoff Collection of Bartókiana, The University of South Florida, Tampa, FL.

———. *The Béla Bartók Archives: History and Catalogue*. New York: Bartók Archives Publication, 1963.

———. "Tibor Eckhardt: Portrait of a Statesman." *Amerikai Magyar Népszava* (January 28, 1945).

———. *Vietnam: A Diplomatic Tragedy. Origins of U.S. Involvement*. Dobbs Ferry, NY: Oceana, 1965. Reprint. London: Faber & Faber, 1967.

Berman, Harold. *Justice in the U.S.S.R: An Interpretation of Soviet Law*. Rev. Ed. Cambridge, MA: Harvard University Press, 1963.

Bodek, Richard, and Simon Lewis, eds. *The Fruits of Exile: Central European Intellectual Immigration to American in the Age of Fascism*. Columbia, SC: The University of South Carolina Press, 2010.

Botos, János. "The Hungarian Banking System from the Trauma of Trianon to Nationalization." Online at http://bankszovetseg.hu/Public/gep/2017/175-194%20Botos%20Janos.pdf.

———. "The Stages of Victor Bator's Career." Unpublished report sent to Francis Bator (1994–95). Transl. Etelka Nyilasi.

Boxx, Karen E. "Of Punctilios and Paybacks: The Duty of Loyalty Under the Uniform Trust Code." *Missouri Law Review* 67/2 (Spring 2002).

Brinkmann, Reinhold, and Christoph Wolff, eds. *Driven into Paradise: The Musical Migration from Nazi Germany to the United States*. Berkeley and Los Angeles: University of California Press, 1999.

Büky, Virág. "Bartók's Heiress." *Studia Musicologica* 53/1-3 (March 2012): 187-97.

Cornelius, Deborah H. *Hungary in World War II: Caught in the Cauldron*. New York: Fordham University Press, 2011.

Csehi, Zoltán. "The Law of Succession in Hungary." In Miriam Anderson and Esther Arroyo i Amayuelas, ed., *The Law of Succession: Testamentary Freedom*. European Perspectives, 177–84. Groningen: Europa Law Publishing, 2011.

Deák, Francis, and Dezső Ujváry, ed. *Papers and Documents Relating to the Foreign Relations of Hungary*, Vol. 1, 1919–20. Budapest: Royal Hungarian Ministry for Foreign Affairs. New York: Columbia University Press, 1939.

Demény, János, ed. *Bartók Béla levelei*. Budapest: Művelt Nép Könyvkiadó, 1951.

Domke, Martin. "Assets of East Europeans Impounded in the United States." *American Slavic and East European Review* 18/3 (October 1959): 351-60.

Dreisziger, Nándor F. "A Hungarian Patriot in American Exile: Béla Bartók and Émigré Politics." *Journal of the Royal Musical Association* 130/2 (2005): 283-301.

———. "Spying on 'Mr. Bartók' in Wartime America." *The Hungarian Quarterly* 46, No. 179 (Autumn 2005). Online at www.hungarianquarterly.com/no179/17.shtml.

Fassett, Agatha. *The Naked Face of Genius: Béla Bartók's American Years*. Boston and New York: Houghton Mifflin, 1958.

Fawcett, Edmund. *Conservatism: The Fight for Tradition*. Princeton, NJ: Princeton University Press, 2020.

Fenyő, Miksa. *A Nation Adrift: The 1944–45 Wartime Diaries of Miksa Fenyő*. Transl. Mario D. Fenyő. Reno, NV: Helena History Press, 2018.

Ferkai, András. *Buda építészete a két világháború között: muvészeti emlékek*. Budapest: Magyar Tudományos Akadémiai Muvészettörténeti Kutató Intézet, 1995.

Fleming, Donald, and Bernard Bailyn, eds. *The Intellectual Migration: Europe and America, 1930-1960*. Cambridge, MA: Harvard University Press, 1969.

Fosler-Lussier, Danielle. *Music Divided: Bartók's Legacy in Cold War Culture*. Berkeley, CA: University of California Press, 2007.

Frank, Tibor. *Double Exile: The Migration of Jewish-Hungarian Professionals Through Germany to the United States, 1919–1945*. Exile Studies 7. Oxford and Bern: Peter Lang, 2008.

———. "Budapest-Berlin-New York: Stepmigration from Hungary to the United States, 1919–1945." In Bodek and Lewis, eds., *The Fruits of Exile: Central European Intellectual Immigration to American in the Age of Fascism*, 197–221. Columbia, SC: The University of South Carolina Press, 2010.

Freeman, Bernard. "Distribution of Estates to Beneficiaries Behind the Iron Curtain." *Buffalo Law Review* 12/3 (June 1, 1963): 630–39.

Gillies, "Bartók in America." In Amanda Bayley, ed., *The Cambridge Companion to Bartók*, 190–201. Cambridge and New York: Cambridge University Press, 2001.

Gopnik, Adam. "The Right Man." *The New Yorker* (July 29, 2013). Available online at https://www.newyorker.com/magazine/2013/07/29/the-right-man.

Grzybowski, Kazimierz. *Soviet Private International Law*. Law in Eastern Europe, ed. Z. Szirmai, vol. 10. Leyden: A.W. Sijthoff, 1965.

Hazard, John H., William E. Butler, and Peter B. Maggs. "Inheritance and Socialism." In *The Soviet Legal System*. Parker School Studies in Foreign and Comparative Law. Dobbs Ferry, NY: Oceana, 1977.

Henrie, Mark C. "Understanding Traditionalist Conservatism." The Hoover Institution. Available online at https://www.hoover.org/sites/default/files/uploads/documents/0817945725_3.pdf.

Holzman, Jac, and Gavan Daws. *Follow the Music: The Life and High Times of Elektra Records in the Great Years of American Pop Culture*. Santa Monica, CA: FirstMedia Books, 1998.

Jaconelli, Joseph. "Wills As Public Documents—Privacy and Property Rights." *The Cambridge Law Journal* 71/1 (March 2012): 147–171.

Kádár Lynn, Katalin. *Tibor Eckhardt: His American Years, 1941-1972*. Boulder, CO: East European Monographs, distr. Columbia University Press, 2007.

Kuttner, Fritz. "Der Katalog des Bartók-Archives in New York City." *Die Musikforschung* 21/1 (Jan-March 1968): 61–63.

Laszlo, Ervin. *The Communist Ideology in Hungary: Handbook for Basic Research*. Dordrecht, Holland: D. Reidel, 1966.

Leafstedt, Carl. "Rediscovering Victor Bator, Founder of the New York Bartók Archives." *Studia Musicologica* 53/1–3 (September 2012): 349–72.

———. "The Source Materials for Bartók's Suite for Two Pianos, Op. 4b (1941)," *Contemporary Music Review* 38/3–4 (2019): 366–88.

Lampert, Vera. "Bartók at Harvard University as Witnessed in Unpublished Archival Documents." *Studia Musicologica Academiae Scientiarum Hungaricae* 35/1–3 (1993-94): 113–54.

Lenoir, Yves. *Folklore et transcendance dans l'oeuvre Américaine de Béla Bartók (1940–45). Contributions à l'étude de l'activité scientifique et créatrice du compositeur*. Louvain-la-Neuve: Institut Supérieur d'Archéologie et d'Histoire de l'Art, Collège Érasme, 1986.

Lisigor, Nancy, and Frank Lipsius. *A Law Unto Itself: The Untold Story of the Law Firm Sullivan and Cromwell*. New York: William Morrow, 1988.

Marmorstein, Gary. *A Ship Without a Sail: The Life of Lorenz Hart*. New York: Simon & Schuster, 2012.

Maurice, Donald. *Bartók's Viola Concerto: The Remarkable Story of His Swansong*. New York: Oxford University Press, 2004.

Mihály, András. "Előszó." In Demény, ed., *Bartók Béla levelei*. Budapest: Művelt Nép Könyvkiadó, 1951.

Molnár, Hella. "The Position of the Surviving Spouse in the Hungarian Law of Succession," *ELTE Law Journal* (Budapest) 2014(2): 89–105.

Móricz, Klára. Introduction. Béla Bartók, Concerto for Orchestra. Complete Critical Edition. Budapest: Editio Musica Budapest, 2017.

Nadányi, Paul. *Hungary at the Crossroads of Invasions*. New York: The Amerikai Magyar Népszava, 1942.

———. *The Free Hungary Movement*. New York: The Amerikai Magyar Népszava, 1942.

Nass, Herbert E. *Wills of the Rich & Famous: A Fascinating Look at the Rich, Often Surprising Legacies of Yesterday's Celebrities*. New York: Warner Books, 1991.

Nettl, Bruno. "Displaced Musics and Immigrant Musicologists: Ethnomusicological and Biographical Perspectives." In Reinhold Brinkmann and Christoph Wolff, eds., *Driven into Paradise: The Musical Migration from Nazi Germany to the United States*, 54–65. Berkeley and Los Angeles: University of California Press, 1999.

Pelényi, John. "The Secret Plan for a Hungarian Government in the West at the Outbreak of World War II." *The Journal of Modern History* 36/2 (June 1964): 170–77.

Pesti Magyar Kereskedelmi Bank. *A Pesti Magyar Kereskedelmi Bank: Százéves Története, 1841–1941*. Budapest: Pesti Magar Kereskedelmi Bank, 1941.

Puskás, Julianna. *Ties That Bind, Ties That Divide: 100 Years of Hungarian Experience in the United State*. New York and London: Holmes & Meier, 2000.

Ránki, György. "The Hungarian Economy in the Interwar Years." In Peter Sugar, Péter Hanák, Tibor Frank, eds., *A History of Hungary*, 356–67. Bloomington, IN: Indiana University Press, 1990.

Ruffy, Péter. "How I Found Béla Bartók's Will." *Magyar Hírek* 23/19 (Sept. 19, 1970). Unpublished translation. BSCB Tampa.

———. "The Dispute Over Bartók's Will." *The New Hungarian Quarterly* 7/22 (1966): 206–9. Reprint. Todd Crow, ed., *Bartók Studies*, 141-46. Detroit: Information Coordinators, 1976.

Somfai, László. *Béla Bartók: Composition, Concepts, and Autograph Sources*. Berkeley, CA: University of California Press, 1996.

———. "Per Finire: Some Aspects of the Finale in Bartók's Cyclic Form," *Studia Musicologica* 11 (1969): 391–408.

———. "The Budapest Bartók Archives." Proceedings of the IAML Annual Conference in Budapest. *Fontes Artis Musicae* 29/1–2 (Jan.-June 1982): 59–65.

Stevens, Halsey. *The Life and Music of Béla Bartók*. New York: Oxford University Press, 1953. Rev. Ed. New York: Oxford University Press, 1964.

Suchoff, Benjamin. "Bartók in America." *The Musical Times* (February 1976): 123–24.

———. *Béla Bartók: Life and Work*. Lanham, MD: Scarecrow Press, 2001.

———. "The New York Bartók Archive." *The Musical Times*, 122/1657 (March 1981): 156–9. Reprint, in expanded form. "The New York Bartók Archive: History and Sources," 250–57. In Suchoff, *Béla Bartók: A Celebration*. Lanham, MD: Scarecrow Press, 2004.

Szentkiralyi, Endre. *Being Hungarian in Cleveland*. Reno, NV: Helena History Press, 2019.

Tallián, Tibor. *Béla Bartók: The Man and His Work*. Budapest: Corvina, 1981.

Ullein-Revitczky, Antal. *German War, Russian Peace: The Hungarian Tragedy*. Transl. Lovice Mária Ullein-Revitczky. Reno, NV: Helena History Press, 2014.

Várdy, Stephen Béla. "Hungarian Americans During World War II: Their Role in Defending Hungary's Interests." In M.B.B. Biskupski, ed., *Ideology, Politics and Diplomacy in East Central Europe*, 120–46. Rochester, NY: Rochester University Press, 2003.

Wallace, Ed. "Bartók's Son Dedicates Life to Recording Father's Music." *New York World-Telegram* (June 25, 1953).

Watson, John. "Monument of Music." *New York Journal-American* (April 7, 1955).

Wigler, Stephen. "Composer Bela Bartok's Legacy of Litigation." *Orlando Sentinel* (Nov. 27, 1983).

Appendix A. Victor Bator: Memorial Speech On the 15th Anniversary of Bartók's Death (1960)

This speech was found in the papers of Francis Bator. The original typescript, in Hungarian, bears a handful of autograph corrections and emphases in pen, indicating that the surviving copy was the one his father used at the actual lecture. (No other copy has been found.) Here it has been translated for publication by David Nagy and Etelka Nyilasi. Its title, typed at the head of the document's opening page, suggests that Victor Bator gave it to a general Hungarian audience in New York City, possibly organized by the American Hungarian Foundation, around the same time as the 1960 Bartók memorial celebration at Columbia University. I have not been able to identify the exact occasion.

In this deeply political speech Bator defends Bartók's reputation against falsehoods he perceives gaining currency as a result of the communist Hungarian government's propaganda. He takes on "the cult of Bartók in Budapest" and systematically dismantles several of the lies about Bartók's time in the United States that he has encountered recently. Particularly interesting here are his reflections about the Hungarian émigré experience in World War II, and his strong denunciation of any claims that Bartók had been sympathetic to communism.

Around the world, wherever music is the treasure of the body and soul, the mind and the heart, Béla Bartók is known as a great 20th century musician. This is his title, his rank: <u>Great Musician</u>. Performers and piano interpreters like him have been a rare breed over the centuries. Without a desire to reach technical virtuosity, and without even committing his life, or any considerable amount of time or attention to his playing, he managed to become a great virtuoso. He had wide and thorough knowledge of music history. He knew everything about music, he remembered every piece, and he published critical editions of many great composers. Bartók was one of the world's most recognized folk music scholars, and had extensive knowledge of folk culture. Finally, he was, if not the greatest, among the 4 or 5 greatest composers of the 20th century. In addition to enriching the repertoire with new works, he also created a

Appendix A

new musical dialect that is now an essential part of the classical music realm; contemporary composers have adapted this Bartókian musical language to express their own thoughts and feelings.

Outside the Hungarian circle, the mental image of Béla Bartók is built upon this title, rank, and role. But for us Hungarians, regardless of our actual citizenship, the location of the place we call home, Bartók means something more today: he is a legendary, great Hungarian who created and later led the movement that helped the Hungarian spirit escape from the unproductive floundering of the latter half of the 19th century, returned with it back to the foundations of folk culture (national psyche) and from there brought it back in a vivid, lively, and creative fashion. Quoting Zoltán Kodály: "During the latter half of the 19th century academics abandoned the Hungarian language and became alienated from Hungarian music. In a chance encounter they would feel unfamiliar with it, regardless of them being assimilated or natives of Hungary. These intellectuals are not a direct continuation of the nation; the culture will not live on in them like the child does in the adult; they do not understand the folk's speech, music, problems, and joy." I am not suggesting that ethnologists, the new spirit of *The Hungarian Review* [Magyar Szemle], Ady, Zsigmond Móricz, Dezső Szabó, Attila József, and all the others would not have existed without Bartók, but it was his unconditional love of Hungarian folklore that inspired the collective return to our own, tiny, rich, and original heritage from the mimicking, mostly German-spirited, infertile culture. "A nation lives in its language," but among the words, music is also a language and thus it was Bartók who created the enriched revelation that, in addition to their language, the Hungarians live in their music, "he sings / dances / celebrates / that / his / heart / can / hardly / keep up."[1] "Language has something of a magical influence on a nation," wrote Széchenyi. Bartók revived the already half-buried magical influence of folk music, and thus he became the legendary magician in the eye of 20th-century Hungarians. It happened by chance that today another musician, Zoltán Kodály, is the greatest living Hungarian, and in his magic lives the same linguistic and musical past that also inspired Bartók. Thus, the Hungarian imagination sees in him its own image, along with Bartók's image as well.

Sadly, as Bartók started to gain recognition as a legendary figure, history had his fate sealed. Small-minded successors are trying to take advantage of him and his name today, filling their own pockets with his coins. It is only appropriate that on the 15th anniversary on Bartók's death I start the process of

---

[1] A quotation from Arany's poem "Dal" [song] (1856).

refuting a few forged facts. Soon enough a well-documented publication will execute this task fully, but for now a little teaser will do.[2]

The main source of forged historic fact is the cult of Bartók in Budapest. It is certainly not from the growing appreciation of Bartók's music, which is not bigger in Hungary than almost anywhere else in the Western world. Certainly, in Hungary it does not even reach the level it reached, for instance, in Germany, the United States and The Netherlands, according to trustworthy witnesses. Bartók's music is an emotional and intellectual treasure of the highest order, it cannot be reached, understood and felt without thinking and elaboration; it will never be the music of marching bands. Therefore, only people unfamiliar with his music would organize a stormy protest after a Bartók concert. But, as I said, now I shall not be talking about Bartók, the creator musician. There are four different lines of this historical falsification.

First is Bartók's connection to pre-1945 Hungary. According to the propagandists in Budapest, while the "people's democracy" recognized Bartók as a great composer, the old Hungary ignored, disdained, persecuted, and diminished him. The truth, of course, is only that Hungarian audiences were slow to understand and appreciate Bartók's music. Bartók would not be the first artist who did not earn the recognition he deserved during his lifetime, simply because it took a longer time to form and grow than a 30-year-long generation lasts. The propaganda in Budapest however says something different: they proclaim that Hungarian workers, Hungarian audiences liked, adored, and recognized Bartók, but Hungarian officials blocked him from emerging and purposefully obstructed his work with folk culture. There are a few facts that disprove this fiction. Out of 400 concerts between 1904 and 1943 that The Philharmonic Association played, 80 of them (in other words, every fifth one), had at least one Bartók piece on the program. However, since he only had a few orchestra pieces written before 1918, it would be more appropriate to look at this year as a start date for this data. Between 1918 and 1943, then, every third concert had a Bartók piece on its program. How could it be true that the rumored fascist and Horthy-ist official circles disapproved of Bartók's folk song collecting work? In 1907 (at the age of 26) he was offered a teaching position at the Liszt Academy. Also in 1907, as his attention turned toward folk music collection, he was given a 1600 gold kroner government scholarship towards his studies of Székely folk music. The Ethnographic Association, an organization strongly supported by the government, supported, recognized,

---

2 This may be a reference to further plans Bator was contemplating for his Memorandum on the History of the Bartók Estate, which he had recently prepared in connection with the litigation underway in New York Surrogate's Court.

and advanced his studies of Romanian and Slovakian folk music. In 1928, at the Prague congress of Folk Music Collectors,[3] Bartók said the following during a presentation:

"Pre-war Hungary was one of the most interesting and diversified regions in terms of musical folklore. It made perfect sense to start our work here, as the regions inhabited by Hungarians were closest to Hungarian scientists not only locally but linguistically as well. However, to make the comparative musical folklore research possible, which is one of the most important goals of the study of musical folklore, we expanded the area of our research to regions inhabited by minorities. Official circles, namely the Folklore Department of the National Museum, fully perceived our endeavors and our work continued with their moral and financial support."

Difficulties only occurred in connection with the performance of one work. Performances of *The Miraculous Mandarin* were cancelled twice at the Opera House. When a few years after that the N.Y. City Ballet performed the *Mandarin* in New York, its press release claimed (God knows who wrote it) that Hungarian authorities banned the performance of the work twice; always after the dress rehearsal but before the premiere. This is simply not the truth.

The first time Bartók cancelled the performance was because he did not find it good enough. A living witness of this is Menyhért Lengyel, the librettist, who was present at the time, and even tried to appease Bartók without success. The second time *The Miraculous Mandarin* was cancelled was in the 30s, and because of the Catholic Church's objection to having the story of a prostitute performed on the stage at the Opera. Obviously it was not a protest against Bartók's music, but the text, which was not written at his initiative, but was published as Menyhért Lengyel's completely independent pantomime text in *Nyugat* in 1917. Besides, The Philharmonic Association performed the music of *The Miraculous Mandarin* 5 times between 1928 and 36, so the Opera's hostile attitude towards the piece could not have been the result of official action against Bartók.

The second lie [legenda-hamasítás] is that Bartók was treated so badly in the uncultured, capitalist America that he almost perished of hunger. I even read things that claimed that he literally died of hunger. It is true that Bartók certainly was not the center of attention in America from 1941 to 1944. But whoever claims that this was the result of unworthy, rough, capitalist crudeness, or even worse, of fascist repugnance towards the folk-minded Bartók, is influenced only by selfish falsification of the past, instead of by true facts.

---

3   Congrès International des Arts Populaires. Held in Prague from Oct. 7–13, 1928, this conference brought together representatives from 31 nations for conversations about the popular arts and society. It was sponsored by the League of Nations through its International Committee for Intellectual Cooperation, a committee Bartók would later be invited to join.

Bartók emigrated in order to escape from German-Italian fascism. To support him in this situation, Columbia University offered him a scientific grant from the Ditmar Fund to work there on a subject of his choice.[4] This fund helped Bartók write his important work on Serbian heroic-epic poetry. When his funds dried up, America was in the middle of that Sisyphean, stressful period when it needed to quickly assemble an army of 10 million, a navy, an air force and an armaments industry that would not only supply the demands of the military and allied nations, but also build the atomic bomb and other missiles, and build hospitals for the wounded. Between 1942 and 1945, it was not only Bartók, the alien, unsociable musician of a nation that got pushed into the enemy side, who was neglected, but all the arts and artists. The world's most renowned performers played almost exclusively in front of soldiers. The worried parents of 10 million soldiers, civilians accustomed to owning a car but deprived of their car-based lifestyle, mothers and children without their husbands and fathers away in the military, certainly did not provide fertile soil for the abstract and lonesome Bartókian foreignness [a magaslatokban magányos bartóki idegenségnek]. There was no concert life, no artistic atmosphere, in music or in any of the other arts. Inter arma silent musae. But we cannot talk of starvation or absolute neglect. Columbia University found a way to extend Bartók's scientific position without the Ditmar Fund. Harvard University also offered Bartók a visiting position. The University of Washington also signed an agreement with Bartók for a well-paid position, the start of which was left completely to his discretion. The American Composer's Association [ASCAP] decided to pay for all of the already sick Bartók's medical expenses: the rest house in the mountains, his travel fares, doctors, hospital bills and medications. The Boston orchestra commissioned an orchestral work for which they paid a $1,000 honorarium in advance; thus resulting in the birth of the highly successful *Concerto for Orchestra*. There were 3 or 4 others who offered similar commissions, two of which Bartók even accepted. Furthermore, we must remember that America did not neglect Bartók financially. Because of the war, he did not receive royalties for his compositions from anywhere. Therefore, if we should call this America's neglect, we must also call it England's, France's, Germany's, Switzerland's, Italy's, The Netherlands's, etc. neglect, too. His great Swiss friends, Dr. Sacher, Frau Müller-Widmann, did nothing to help him. Why? Because the war severed artists, including Bartók, from the world. Compared to them, America did a great deal simply because Bartók was in view there, therefore he was not cut off as completely.

---

4 Bator misremembers the exact name of the fund here. He means to refer to the Alice M. Ditson Fund.

Appendix A

Let us allow the numbers to speak, instead of simply sounding out words. It perhaps is appropriate now to state that Bartók's actual income was never less than $4,000–5,000 a year, which would be about $8,000–10,000 today, or 20–30,000 forints. This is little, very little, but still very far from starvation standards. And of course this does not include medical expenses, which came in addition.

The third falsehood is that Bartók was a people's democrat—in his heart and soul—and not in the sense I described earlier, but let's call a spade a spade, saying that he actually sympathized with the communists. This is also false. In his letters from 1945 to his son, Peter, and to me, he writes in horror about the Soviet communist burglars marching into Budapest and their destructions. In a letter of March 5th, 1945, he writes: "For that matter, bad news is leaking from the Moscow Radio and also from the neutral countries about the conditions at home; also about the organization of an anti-fascist military (the name of which sounds good but in reality these are terrorist groups), and about the deportation of Hungarian democrats (the Russians do not want whoever is a friend of England or America) etc. So the situation—apart from the devastation and misery—<u>seems to be an out of the frying pan, into the fire kind of deal</u>."

A letter dated April 2nd, 1945: "One of the (new Hungarian) papers claims itself to be democratic. It is a communist paper. It saddens me that F. D. Roosevelt did not live till the end of it all, but who knows, the future might have had disappointed him. He was a great man. He appealed to me the most when he replied to Molotov simply: "it is up to you" (in Hungarian: tedd, ami jól esik), when the latter wanted to extort a second front line from him with a peace treaty (sometime in 1942 or 43)."

He did not accept the seat in Hungarian parliament with which they wanted to honor him. He wrote about this on May 4th, 1945: "Why of course it is a nice gesture, but let's hold our horses with the exaltation until we find out who gets elected and how, and what the significance of it all is." And then on May 23rd, 1945: "I feel rather dejected because of the Hungarian and the general situation… Waiting, waiting, waiting and weeping, weeping, weeping—this is all we can do as the news starts to slowly reach us here, ever alarming and staggering."

To prove the degree of Bartók's disapproval of Russia-friendly, Benešian, half-Bolshevik Hungarians, there is a piece of evidence that is beyond mere feelings. In 1941 he accepted a position on the National Committee (Nemzeti Bizottmány) led by president Tibor Eckhardt, and in 1943 he took over its presidency.[5] The Benešian, Russia-oriented immigrants also had an immigrant organization led by Rustem Vámbéry. Every month Vámbéry attempted to talk

---

[5] See Chapter 2 for a detailed chronology of this part of Bartók's American experience.

Bartók into leaving the Eckhardt Committee, condemned by him as a fascist organization. But the answer was always no.

It must be noted regarding this connection that the same false propaganda that claimed America's ignorance of Bartók of course also uses double talk, and claims that fascist America tried to expropriate and vindicate Bartók for itself. Ferenc Szabó, the Bolshevik-minded director of the Music Academy, wrote the following in an editorial published in *Új Zenei Szemle*:

"You reactionary Americans and other dollar-imperialists dishonorably vindicated Bartók to your own advantage. In order to reach your selfish goals of becoming a super power and to start a war that would shed more blood and be more destructive than any before, you want to mobilize the peaceful crowds to enroll them, shamelessly fooled into supporting the new, American-style fascism."

He goes on:

"It follows that Bartók is on *our* side and belongs to the peaceful crowds. He has nothing to do with arsonists of war... activists of a new world war... dollar-imperialists. To Göbbels' successors: the foul comedy bearing his name must stop! Bartók does not compromise!"

In the same *Új Zenei Szemle* we also can read that "Bartók is led by the intent of endless hate and rebellion... his operation is filled with conscious political content... his interest in folksong is nothing more than the sound of a shrill plebeian's political ambitions ... his artistic and scientific work played the earnest and most crucial part of his standing up for the demands of the democratic revolution." Propaganda papers, however tolerant, must blush seeing this filth, this forgery. In America, of course, Bartók is not the legendary Hungarian, but "the great musician," as we said earlier, and so no one is vindicating him or has any interest in his political views. This whole notion is just provincial, and silly idiotic,[6] however, it is disconcerting that over there, where Bartók is the great, legendary Hungarian, perhaps some might even believe this pretentious claim.

Finally, the fourth falsehood is the image of the poor, neglected, starving Bartók who was deeply depressed by homesickness. This fiction was based on a sentence, quoted to exhaustion in articles, talks, memoirs of every single Hungarian Bartók scholar, from a letter to a Hungarian living in California. Here is the last paragraph of the letter:

"As I see things now, even a thought of going home is impossible. I have neither a way of transport, nor the necessary authorizations. Even if there were a way to do it, it would be wiser to just wait and see how things develop. God knows how long it will take for the country to pull itself together (if it will be able to at all). Still, though, I too would like to move back, permanently..."

---

6   Word crossed out by hand in Bator's typescript.

Appendix A

To date I have not met any immigrants, Hungarian or other, who have not felt a longing for their families, friends, lost memories, the food and drinks they're accustomed to, all in all, for their "home," regardless of the sort of persecution that chased them away from there. Bartók, too, me, my neighbor, and all the Hungarians around the globe have had tearful hours, days, or minutes, all of which feel the same whether life is treating us well or during times of suffering. My family and I spent more private time with Bartók than anyone between 1941 and 1945 and I bear witness to the fact that his homesickness was likely less acute than most others', and definitely less acute than mine, as he preferred to live in the high-up regions of clouds, sunshine, sense and sensibility, unlike us little people.

It is only appropriate and respectful to have a few positive thoughts in this memorial speech after all the negativity. A few words about Bartók, the man, toil their way to my lips. He was only happy when surrounded by common folk. He was passionate not only about their music, but about all their habits, their ways of speech, their art and he also found that, regardless of all discomforts, men can be live happier their own way than when living amid the comforts of urban civilization. He had predecessors in these views, including Horatio, however in Bartók's case it influenced not only his lifestyle, but his work as well: this influence was part of the sustaining foundation of his work of collecting folk songs.

His simplicity went so far that, throughout his life, he did not accept and apply to himself the formalities of urban societies. Very many of those claiming publicly to have been his friends he never called anything more than "acquaintances." Only when he really meant it did he say "thank you," as he never used even formalities like this without true conviction. He also avoided clichés in any form.

In his modesty he never anticipated or required any distinctive attention, but if someone acted disrespectfully, his pride would keep him from ever saying a word to that person again. I know of two people who took the liberty of speaking to him in a patronizing manner in times of difficulty; they never had a chance to do so again in the future. They got a quick glance, a goodbye, and were never able to establish contact with him again. A Hungarian musician, whom he actually liked, happened to start lecturing Bartók once—somewhat patronizingly—on how he should be more practical, more conformist, ordered him to follow the practicality that he is presenting and thus gain popularity. Bartók did not talk to this person for over a year after this conversation. He did not gain popularity in Hungary, nor in America, because he would never compromise his truthfulness, unadorned character, or ideals, for popularity, success, applause, or money.

Appendix B. Victor Bator: "The Hungarian Problem," from Memorandum on the History of the Bartók Estate (1959–60)

In the chapter reproduced here Victor Bator reviews his relationship with the Bartók heirs and with communist government functionaries in Hungary. The title of the chapter alone suggests his frame of mind at the time of writing.

Although lengthy, I have chosen to reproduce the entire chapter here for its rare insights into methods used by the Hungarian communist government to manipulate Béla Jr. in the early 1950s, and for its informed commentary on how the communist takeover affected the lives of the two heirs in Hungary. Bator chronicles with an observant eye the evolution in Béla Jr.'s position from victim to co-conspirator. Almost Shakespearean is his narration of how Béla Jr.'s character allowed him to slowly turn away from a family legacy of principled stances against totalitarian ideology towards an equivocal position as fellow traveller or front for the communist regime. Throughout, Bator's comments about currency restrictions, world politics, and the Hungarian economy in the communist era show quite clearly the reasoning behind some of his early actions as Trustee.

A learned man, Bator habitually expressed himself in luxuriously long sentences. His fondness for elaborate sentence structures and itemized lists came naturally to him as an attorney: these traits reflect decades of experience drafting and reading legal documents. His métier further developed in him the habit of orderly reasoning. These features of his prose style are abundantly evident in the document below. Over the course of his life he developed expertise in topics as varied as the financial implications of the Versailles treaty after World War I, international copyright law, and the geopolitical foundations of the Vietnam War. Below we find one further example of his intellectual proclivity for topics commingling international politics and finance.

At times his expansive trains of thought—in the later New York years expressed verbally, using the Dictaphone in his office—overtax the conventions of written English. His secretaries, when typing, did their best to capture the correct formatting, syntax, and punctuation in his sentences. Sometimes, clearly, they just punted. In the Memorandum's typed pages Bator let stand these occasional imprecisions or syntactical knots. He intended it to be a working document. The document as a whole doesn't even bear a title. (Each chapter is titled, however.) To transcribe it

349

with an eye to publication, as I've done here, required me to make silent corrections, chiefly in the areas of punctuation, verb agreement, and sentence division. The text is otherwise unaltered.

The Hungarian Problem

The Estate would have had a "Hungarian problem" even if no member of the Bartók family had lived in Hungary. Béla Bartók became sometime in the 1920s a great figure of the international world of music. In fact, successively in the 1920s he shed his exclusive Hungarianness and transferred intellectually his creative world from Hungary into the wide world of creation without end. He dissociated himself from the provincial type of Hungarian music publishers who never had any other composers in their catalogue but Hungarians, and joined Universal Edition A.G. Vienna, that belonged into the Western European music-publishing community, who in the past had been the publishers of Mozart, Beethoven, Schubert, Schumann and all other great composers of Western civilization. In the 1920s he resigned from the Hungarian Performing Rights Society (MARS) and joined the Austrian society. Even that wasn't the final step. Whenever opportunity presented itself he knocked at the door of the wider regions of the Western world, and by the end of the 1930s he transferred himself in the catalog of the English publishing firm Boosey & Hawkes, and became the member of the British Performing Right Society. He loved his Hungary that connected him with his beloved mother, family, friends of youth, but these were the roots connecting him with the good earth while the high and wide branches of his genius reached out in every direction and were seeking the sunshine coming from above and from every direction.

Thus, though most of his compositions were independent, not in their emotional and intellectual roots, but in their legal and material existence from Hungary, the 21 works published by Hungarian publishers earlier in his youth would have connected the Estate and the Trustees' activities with Hungary under any circumstance.

Yet, this "Hungarian" chapter of my trusteeship is loaded with heavier content than the 21 works. My life as Trustee had to be quite substantially devoted to the events and ingredients of the Hungarian globe, because out of the three members of the Bartók family two have been and are living in Hungary, and the third one, Peter Bartók, though a naturalized American citizen, has never ceased to belong in his soul, in many ways to his native land. And this connection of at least two members of the family hasn't been and isn't accidental.

While Béla Bartók several times during his life considered emigration, transfer of his physical abode outside of Hungary where psychological and material surroundings would favor or give more freedom of action to his creative spirit, I do not think that Béla Jr. would ever consider to separate himself from the Hungarian globe. The same is true for other reasons in regard to Mrs. Béla Bartók. In fact, though she had lived before her husband's death five years in the United States, she never had any other friends but Hungarians or Hungarian born Americans, she never learned to speak fluently and with ease the English language, and felt here lonely and rootless. After her husband's death very soon she and I jointly and in agreement came to the conclusion that the only wise thing for her to do was to return to Hungary where her mother, her brother and many other Hungarian relatives and friends would make her feel at home again.

The Hungarian problem of the Estate being thus intertwined with the presence in Hungary of two members of the Bartók family, and a special respect, devotion toward that country by the third Bartók, it is rational, in fact, the only possible approach to the description of the Hungarian field of the Trustees' activities, to devote this chapter to and put it within the frame of the relationship of Mrs. Béla Bartók and Béla Jr to the Estate.

The relationship to Mrs. Béla Bartók.

Béla Bartók during the last five years of his life in the United States developed intimate personal relationship, friendship, with two persons only, with me and Dr. Paul Kecskeméti. He had many "friends." Still more people would have showered on him attention, would have surrounded him with feelings and acts of friendship, had he not been in his social contacts as retiring as he was. It sounds perhaps immodest to restrict in this story his friendship to two people only, with me one of them, had he not shown many ways that I was one of his trusted friends, and I do not know anybody else equaling, maybe even surpassing, our relationship but Dr. Paul Kecskeméti, a philosopher and aesthete with a good musician and pianist as wife. But both of them were not a "man of the world," and not experienced in business or law, publishing, or many other aspects of the American way of life.

This being so during Bartók's lifetime already, Mrs. Béla Bartók also turned to me with many of her worldly and emotional problems for advice. She had such problems aplenty. To be the wife of a genius who happens to be 25 years older, with an ascetic nature, the life of a much younger, beautiful, blonde musician woman could not possibly be easy and without difficulties. It was therefore natural that after Bartók's death, surrounded by the big city of New York, whose language she did not understand well, with a son of young age with

Appendix B

whom she did not develop—despite her ardent affection for him—an intimate or undisturbed living partnership. Dr. Kecskeméti and I were the only persons who took care of her life. Her health broke down. I took care of her hospitalization, of her financial problems. I succeeded to help her through the financial difficulties by letting her have income of the first performances of the Third Piano Concerto, by advances by Boosey & Hawkes, and by many other ways. And nobody else would have done this for her and to nobody else would she have turned for such help, even if I had not been appointed as Trustee of the Estate by her husband. The decision that she should return to Hungary was mine. I solved all the technical problems of traveling to Hungary that immediately after the war was not so easy. She flew to Vienna. I arranged that the Hungarian Consul General in Vienna, who was a friend of mine, met her at the airport and took care of her while she was in Vienna before she started on the last leg of the journey to Budapest. Naturally I was assisted by quite many people, among them Peter B. But these friends and Peter B. did what I told them to do.

This introduction serves only one purpose, i.e., to explain the fact that Mrs. Béla Bartók after her husband's death considered me as her main support, advisor, and mentor. She assigned her income from this side of the Iron Curtain, more especially those of the United States, to her son. She did it upon my advice. She executed documents appointing her son, Peter B., as her attorney in fact. She did it upon my advice. But I am sure that she felt much safer that a similar power of attorney was executed in my favor also, and she trusted too that her son's activities will be supervised, helped, and guarded by me.

Correspondence between her and me in the turbulent years after the war following her return to Hungary couldn't be more scarce and fragmentary. But she didn't write many letters to her son or anybody else, either. In fact I don't think she wrote one single letter to the Kecskemétis, with whom she had lived before her departure in the same house, and who had been in daily contact with her, more than I. But nevertheless she wrote whenever she felt that a direct letter was helpful or necessary. To characterize the warmth of the personal relationship there is enclosed (Enclosure I_1) an English translation of my letter to her dated October 20, 1955. That was an answer to her letter of October 4, 1955, in the first paragraph of which she wrote:

"I thank you very much for your financial dispositions. This is very satisfactory, and all right with me."

Enclosure I_2 is the English translation of her answer, dated December 5, 1955.

But references to such letters serve only the demonstration of the warmth of the personal relationship and its continued existence between her and myself and my family in spite of the many years and many thousand miles separating me from her relatively narrow, restricted mental and psychological state of life. Thus, the important connection between her and the Estate and myself as Trustee, was based on the practically limitless power of attorney given by her to me before her return to Hungary, and indirectly by my undisturbed relationship to her son and attorney in fact. Yet it needs be mentioned, that though Peter B. held a power of attorney from her giving him equal rights to those given and conferred upon me, every letter, every sign of life shows that she wanted me to be the decisive factor and be in control when it came to decisions on her interests. On October 2, 1954, in a letter (photocopy of Hungarian original is Enclosure I_3) she wrote to me (translated in English):

> "Dear Victor, I mentioned in my recent letter that I would write to you again and ask you to do certain things for me:
> "Under the present circumstances I would like to receive a monthly remittance of $300.00. Would you please Victor do this for me?
> "It was a surprise for me to receive since June $100.00 per month.
> "This is my other request: I would like to be sure Peter has easy access to the income from musical royalties and that he can use any part thereof that he may require. Please Victor let me know about this.
> "Many thanks and affectionate greetings, Ditta."

This is perhaps the proper occasion to explain the consideration controlling the amount of remittances to Mrs. Bartók. First of all, her wishes and the amounts communicated by her like the one mentioning $300.00 here above were taken into consideration. The figures were reviewed at regular recurring sessions between Peter B. and myself. Again in recurring intervals I made inquiries through members of the Bartók family and independently about the income and spending factors of life in Hungary. It wouldn't have served any useful purpose to send Mrs. Bartók more than what she could spend. Since the end of the war there has never been limitless or even fair-sized possibility of spending and levelling upwards of living conditions in Hungary. News published generally and those reaching U.S.A. from friends and relatives living in Hungary have never ceased to confirm that the limits of rational spending were quite low. There was always another consideration that was on my and on Peter B.'s mind when we discussed and reviewed this question. Mrs. Bartók is not an entirely rational being when it comes to finances, spending, and way of life. It seemed very important and in her interest not to send her more income than what she could rationally spend, because had we exceeded that amount she would spend it in a way that might have damaged her health. There are certain temptations

Appendix B

offered by life to which she easily succumbs. I trust that Peter B. will know what I am referring to. It was always carefully considered and with some difficulty ascertained how much she should receive to secure her comfortable living without giving more or substantially more that would have been damaging her health and well-being.

Outside of this direct and personal link and channels of communication with Mrs. Bartók, I had two indirect connections with her. First I had my indirect link to her through her son, Peter B. Second, and this is of equal legal and material importance and relevance, that from 1954 I had another channel that connected the Estate and my activities as Trustee with her. In October 1954 accompanied by the letter quoted in English translation here-above (Enclosure I_3), I received a letter from an attorney in Budapest, Dr. Béla Keresztes; a photostatic copy and English translation is enclosed. Dr. Béla Keresztes, who will be mentioned in this chapter of my statement quite many times, was judge on the Appellate Division of one of the Courts of Hungary, and after the purge by the Communist Government became member of the Bar. His daughter married János Bartók, a cousin and friend of Béla Jr. and Peter B. Thus Dr. Keresztes was not only, as the letter testifies, attorney of Mrs. Bartók, but a trusted friend and "in-law" relative. From October 1954 until the end of 1956, that is for more than two years, I was in frequent and continuous correspondence with Dr. Keresztes. That correspondence was interrupted by the Hungarian revolution of October 1956 and was not resumed for quite a while, because after the revolution and the return to power of the Communist regime, most people who had relatives and friends in Hungary avoided direct correspondence with friends in the United States for quite a long time, because the Kádár regime and the newly reinstated police state suspected and smelled American spying, encouragement of revolutionary resistance everywhere, and thus correspondence or any other contact might have created risk and dangers to Dr. Keresztes.

A collection of this most important letters exchanged (in Hungarian language) between myself and Dr. Keresztes is enclosed to this statement (Enclosures I_{5a-}). Its voluminousness, its confidential character, harmony with my views and agreement on practically every point affecting the relationship of the Estate and the Trustee to the Hungarian problem, to Mrs. Béla Bartók, her interests, make it necessary and useful to include them by reference into this statement to be evidence of the fact, that between Mrs. Bartók, the life beneficiary, and myself, as Trustees, there existed not only agreement, harmony, good understanding directly, but as the letters show, the same agreement, harmony, and understanding was expressed through her attorney in regard to the period preceding 1954 and continuing up to the end of 1957.

Appendix B

The essence of the opinions, views, and decisions of Mrs. Bartók expressed through her attorney directly and stated in the letters of Dr. Keresztes, who was and is an intimate of Mrs. Bartók, may be summarized as follows:

1. The Last Will and Testament of Béla Bartók distinguishes strongly between the corpus (the copyrights themselves) and the income of the Estate. This is clear not only out of the text and wording of the Last Will and Testament, but had been expressed by Béla Bartók in his previous Testament made before he left Hungary and signed by him in 1940. In that Testament he asserted the necessity and desirability of holding the corpus of the copyrights as one unit regardless of the distribution of the income. The Trusteeship is in the final realization of that intention of Béla Bartók (see letters by Dr. Keresztes to the attorney of the publishing agencies of the Hungarian Government and Dr. Robert Palágyi, friend and legal advisor of Béla Jr., dated April 15, 1955, enclosure I_{5b}.

2. All income no matter which country, which publisher, whatever other source it may come [from], should be collected by the Trustee and should be reported by all users, exploiters of the Bartók music and works too him. Only that system can enable the Trustee, acting for all three members of the family, to control the use and exploitation of the Bartók works and to check on the completeness and satisfactoriness of the payments due to the Estate. The Trustee may direct for practical reason one or other user, exploiter of Bartók works, to pay directly to one or other of the beneficiaries, but such instructions would be given only on account of special circumstances and should be revocable any time.

3. Since the distribution of the income between the life beneficiary, Béla Jr. and Peter B., was done not according to some kind of arithmetical fractional figure allocating shares from whatever source the income might have come, but by an artificial system, and this was done because members of the family, their residence in different continents, under different political systems and the political and international difficulties connected therewith were anticipated and envisaged it should be the duty and the right of the Trustee to seek and find ways and means how to keep in balance and make fair the actual distribution of the income insofar [as] the difficulties anticipated and envisaged by the Testator do not prevent such result.

Appendix B

4. The fact that the balance of the income of the Estate was used after the requirements of Mrs. Bartók and Peter B. were taken care of for the maintenance and improvements of the manuscripts (the physical embodiments of the works), and for the maintenance and increase in value of the copyrights themselves, for the preparation for publication of the unpublished works,—was communicated to Dr. Keresztes, attorney and intimate of Mrs. Bartók, and was consented to and approved by him on her behalf.

5. Condemnation and repudiation of the stand taken by the Hungarian agencies in regard to the control of the copyrights, the distribution of the income, and, after Béla Jr. allied himself with them, of their joint stand, was expressed in unmistakable terms by Mrs. Béla Bartók through her attorney, Dr. Keresztes.

6. It has to be assumed that the stand taken now by Peter B., who allied himself now with Béla Jr. and with the Hungarian Government agencies conspiring jointly against the interest of the Estate, the Trusteeship, and the Trustee, has not been approved, consented to, by Mrs. Béla Bartók. There is no reason to assume that since 1957 she would have changed her opinion about the wisdom of the Last Will and Testament of her deceased husband, about the theoretical and practical value of the handling of the inheritance by the Trustee. On account of her continued residence in Hungary, and being under the control and censorship of the Hungarian authorities, there is no possibility to prove by direct evidence this assumption, but certainly the statements made on her behalf by both conspirators should not be accepted as satisfactory proof of her views and will.

The relationship to Béla Bartók, Jr., Budapest

This relationship appears in three different configurations, seemingly in conflict with each other. Corresponding to the changing design and silhouette of that picture, Béla Jr. appears in the proceedings before the Court as if he came from three different avenues. At one of the gates of the Court he is standing without being beneficiary of the Estate as one of the beneficiaries of "inheritance." In that stance he is interested in the Estate financially and, being one of the sons of Béla Bartók, in its artistic future. At the other entrance gate he is standing as the brother of the remainderman, Peter B., in very close personal relationship to him. They are in continuous consultation with each other, they synchronize their decisions and acts, yet they pretend to be at cross purposes. Finally, at the third gate Béla Jr. fronts for the Hungarian Music Publishing arm of the Hungarian government, which asserts a political and financial stake in the Bartók Estate.

Summarizing this multiple personality at the end of this chapter, I shall attempt to give it a composite synthesis, but one cannot make this relationship understandable without separating it in these three component parts. Thus, first I shall describe all three facets of Béla Jr.'s appearances separately as if the other two did not exist.

A. *The Direct relationship of Béla Jr. to the Estate*

After 1941 no attempt was made either by Béla Bartók, the deceased, or by his eldest son, who lived in Hungary, to establish any kind of contact with each other, though some indirect correspondence or messages between most residents and citizens of this country and their relatives over there in Hungary were successfully established. Béla Jr. did not know about the Last Will and Testament. An institution like a Trusteeship does not exist and is foreign to Hungarian law, and as some later statements indicate, Béla Jr. assumed that outside of some life interest of Mrs. Béla Bartók, he would share the inheritance half and half with his younger brother, Peter B. At the time of the death of Béla Bartók everything that he left behind in Hungary, that is, furniture, personal possessions, some cash, etc., was under the control and in the possession of Béla Jr., and insofar as they were not disposed of, still are. A letter dated March 12, 1951, written by Béla Jr. informed me that there had taken place some kind of proceedings before a Hungarian Court (corresponding to our Surrogate Court), that some inheritance tax was paid by him and that a Hungarian Government agency having expropriated and nationalized music publishers and performing rights societies, paid him until 1951 such royalties which were due and payable under a compulsory system. According to the same letter, between August 1946 and the end of 1950, Béla Jr. collected from the Hungarian Government-owned publishing companies about $5,000 worth of Hungarian currency; that must have amounted at that time to about 50,000 forints, and in purchasing power, much more. During the same four years' period Peter B. once visited Hungary, established contact with his brother in the course of which he told his half-brother that much about the Last Will and Testament that the Hungarian income was his—Béla Jr.'s—and that under the Will he was not beneficiary of the income coming from the West European countries and from America.

In evaluating and describing the situation until the end of 1950 one has to take in consideration that Hungary was overrun both by the Germans and the

Appendix B

Russians, that the last bitter battles between them were fought on the ruins of Budapest, that the Russian army was in full control of the country, that for all practical purposes an Inter-Allied Commission under Russian predominance governed the country, that the Hungarian Communist Party was in the process of taking over the power from a combination of leftist and socialist elements, that the city of Budapest was more or less destroyed, that people were struggling with establishing and rebuilding a modest frame of existence in which normal life could be lived again, and that therefore problems like what should be the relationship in regard to copyrights, authors rights, how to share a more or less nominal income, how to get hold of income from abroad that wasn't coming anyway, played a very secondary role in the thinking of Hungarians. The Hungarian Communists succeeded to take over the Government sometime between 1947 and 1949 by successive stages of Putsch, and until about 1950 or 1951 not even what is called "socialist legality" existed. Government was exercised completely arbitrarily, the new Communist bureaucracy, untrained in administrative procedures, ran every part of the political, economic, social machinery by arbitrary decisions. No individual rights were respected, and nobody had the courage to assert even the slightest measure of independence. Between Hungarians who lived in Budapest and their relatives, friends, who were abroad the relationship was based on principles of charity. Every Hungarian abroad spent half of his life and time in attempts to send to his Hungarian relatives and friends some kind of material support, mostly by charity packages. The former currency of Hungary disappeared. The inflation erased and eliminated its value 100%, and until the new currency could assert itself and acquired the minimum confidence of the populace, remittances in money were not important and had very little purchasing power.

All this description serves only one purpose: to explain why the entire relationship until 1951 cannot be given a well confined and definite description. Everything was informal about it. The idea behind every step taken by me or Peter B. was to have the Hungarian income collected wherever it could be collected, and to use it for the benefit of the two members of the family living over there, none of them getting anyway more than something not much above the minimum. It should be remembered that the income in the United States did not amount at the time to much, either. Whatever small amounts were incoming from Boosey & Hawkes were used for remittance to Mrs. Bartók in Hungary and modest payments to Peter B, and nobody could have objected that the Hungarian income was used by Béla Jr., all the more because remittance abroad from Hungary were impossible anyway. Yet, out of the scarce remnants of correspondence and instructions disclosing the intention of Peter B., it is clear that he wanted his half-brother, Béla Jr., to receive the Hungarian income, that is,

Appendix B

whatever income could be scraped up in Hungary out of sales, performances, royalties. On November 10, 1949, in a letter to his brother, a copy of which he sent to me, he instructed Béla Jr. how to arrange the first Hungarian performance of the Viola Concerto:

> "We ask for the Budapest first performance 30,000 Forints (at the official rate of exchange, $3,000) and it should be paid in the proportion of 50:50 to you and my mother."

I find in my files a copy of a letter written by Peter B. to Béla Jr. dated December 22, 1950, the last paragraph of which in English translation is the following:

> "I use this opportunity to request you [Béla Jr.] to send me or to the Executor of the Will a yearly report how much is your income out of the inheritance. The idea is that we want to examine whether you receive everything that you should, but it has another purpose, also. We want to know whether or not you are getting into a disadvantaged or <u>unequal situation compared to me</u>."

In spite of that request I have never received from Béla Jr.—or from anyone else—information, factual and numerical, about what happened in Hungary, except a few occasional scraps of facts. This was due obviously not only to the scarcity of correspondence caused by the fear of writing or receiving correspondence to and from abroad. It seems that both Béla Jr. and Peter B. are not prolific correspondents or bookkeepers. The situation was aggravated by the fact that Government and the Communist Party group surrounding it has always been equally feared and disrespected by everyone in Hungary. People hide and conceal every facet of their life because as soon as anybody not belonging to the inner circle of the Communist Party shows independent (including income not paid by the Government) suspicions, restrictive methods and arbitrary expropriations may, and mostly do, happen. Letters going and coming from abroad are censored and therefore are not used for disclosure of facts and figures which may be used for such interferences, arbitrary taxation, confiscation, or any other purpose.

This period of informality, absence of regular contact and a state of purposeless drifting began to change in January 1951. Sometime in the first days of January Peter B. received a letter from his brother Béla Jr., and on January 14th he wrote me the following (English translation from Hungarian, first paragraph of the letter):

Appendix B

> "The enclosed letter came from my brother Béla. Please peruse the whole letter. <u>Important matters are being discussed in it</u>."

Unfortunately the letter itself is not in my files; obviously it was returned to Peter B. But I remember well the essence of what Béla Jr. wrote in that letter. He complained in the letter that he was almost completely ignored by the Hungarian bureaucratic machinery handling copyrights, authors-rights, royalties, that he wasn't even invited to festivities commemorating his father's life and works, that while at the beginning he had received payments which—compared to the general level of income in Hungary—were more or less satisfactory, recently, that is just before the letter was written, he was not given either financially or morally the position and standing that—he thought—would be due to him as the son of Béla Bartók. He referred in vague language to certain intrigues against him.

My memory is reinforced by a letter that I wrote to Béla Jr. on February 7, 1951. English translation of the first two paragraphs is the following (Enclosure I_6):

> "Peter handed over to me your letter of January 7th requesting me to do whatever needs be done. I cannot understand and it is unclear to me what may cause the intrigues. I do not see why anybody could be interested in objecting to the system now practiced. Everything that <u>you</u> do not collect is being paid in its entirety to Peter on the basis of an agreement between Ditta and Peter, who takes care out of these collections of his mother. With other words, I do not understand "<u>cui prodest</u>", who could possibly be interested in that relationship in order to make inquiries or investigate. In my opinion nobody. Yet, if there is smoke, there must be somewhere fire.
>
> <u>I shall prepare today the declaration</u>. I shall send it to the other Executor for signature, and as soon as it will be returned by him, after Peter will put his signature on it, I shall send it for notarization and it will be mailed to you."

Out of my recollection and this letter of February 7, 1951, and the letter of transmittal by Peter B., dated January 14, 1951, advising me to take care of Béla Jr.'s request, the facts and the factors instrumental in the bringing about of the 1951 "Interpretive Declaration" in favor of Béla Jr. can be easily woven into the following picture: Béla Jr. reported to his brother Peter B. that official, bureaucratic inquiries are being made aimed at questioning his legal position and right to receive the payments whether arbitrary or not, that actually were made and were to be made to him by the Hungarian Government agencies in charge of authors-rights. Béla Jr. became worried, wrote to his brother and requested an "Interpretive Declaration" that would build him up into someone who is not only a son expecting arbitrary favors, but an heir and beneficiary who has rights of his own. My approach to the problem was that the Estate could not possible expect as a practical matter at that time any collections, payments from Hungary, and not even from Germany and Austria. Foreign currency regulations in force at that time in all those countries made it impossible to hope or expect that any payments, even if recognized by the local authorities and available in local currencies and approved by the international or purely Russian commissaries hold the reins of the Government, would be permitted in "scarce Dollars." The free market rate of conversion of local currencies—Hungarian Forints, Austrian Schillings, and German marks—demonstrated the impossibility of such conversion by the several hundred percent premium paid for hard currencies, or to express it in another way, by the depreciation-percentages beyond reason. Could anybody in that position be less eager than I was to let the son of Béla Bartók handle toward the Hungarian authorities both the financial and the non-financial problems of the inheritance? I had no reason to assume or be afraid of going overboard and giving "too much" to Béla Jr., because there had been <u>undisturbed harmony within the family, also between the family</u> and me and the problem had one facet only, that deserved attention, i.e., to protect the inheritance <u>as a unit</u> from interference, plunder, infringement. As it was stated in my letter of February 7, 1951, to Béla Jr., the relationship within the family and their relation to the Trustees, to me being as harmonious as it was, only the outsiders' intrigue was taken care of, to be warded off, i.e., interference by party-bosses and their fellow-travelers. The motives were made clear by the last paragraph of my letter to Béla Jr. dated February 27, 1951:

> "I have obtained yesterday the consent of ASCAP, the American Association of Composers. They will instruct their correspondents in Hungary, Germany, Czechoslovakia, Austria, and Roumania to pay the performance fees directly to you. I hope that I shall be able to achieve that unpaid arrears from the past which have not been remitted here on account of foreign currency restrictions should retroactively be paid to you also."

The number one task I wanted him to handle was <u>first</u> to force the Hungarian Government Agencies (handling authors-rights, copyrights, royalties) into recognizing the Bartók copyrights, their duty to respect them, and their liability

Appendix B

to pay; and, <u>second</u>, to remit to Béla Jr., who was over there, whatever they were willing to pay. Whether he received more or less than his share determined by the Will, or not, had to be a secondary consideration. More especially, in view of the intrigues and the suspected preparations to deprive Béla Jr. of the payments made until the end of 1950, even if arbitrarily, prompted me to make an attempt to build him up into the strongest possible position to be able to put pressure on in both directions.

The presentiments or suspicion of Béla Jr. about the oncoming attacks against him were not mistaken. On the day when he received the "Interpretive Declaration" signed by the Executors and Peter B., transferring to him the right to act on behalf of the Estate, the beneficiaries, and the entire Bartók group toward the powers to be in Hungary, he received a notification from the Ministerium of Education and Culture, numbered 1732/51 (copy of which was sent to Peter B. also) by which he was informed that all payments to be made by the Hungarian Folk-Democracy will from that time be divided between him, Peter B. and Mrs. Bartók in the proportion of ¼ and ¼ to the two sons and 50% to Mrs. Bartók. His letter reporting all events in that connection is dated March 12, 1951 (Enclosure I_7). The second paragraph of the letter of Béla Jr. that is relevance in this connection says the following:

> "Against the disposition that is quite arbitrary, I put in a protest and filed the Interpretive Declaration sent by you. On the basis of that declaration they promised reconsideration of the entire problem."

How much I was at that time influenced by the weak position of Béla Jr., by his insistent request that my support should be such that would overcome his situation's inherent weakness and his inability to negotiate as equal from strength, is attested to by another part of the same letter. In the third paragraph he wrote:

> "I am certainly not in the situation to negotiate with the Music Publishing National Company as an independent party of the same rank or <u>someone who is of their equal</u>."

And how much he considered that the Declaration of 1951 sent to him was not a genuine statement of interpretation, but was the result of care and concern for him, is shown by the last few lines of the letter, written by a laconic, uncommunicative person that he is, who disliked and dislikes mostly everybody but especially attorneys (which sentiments were strongly expressed and voiced in his first few letters to his brother, Peter B., which were show to me by Peter B.):

"I use this opportunity to send you [Victor Bator] my thanks for all the different acts and things you have done and for the care with which you handle all our affairs, among them those of the inheritance."

It should be noted that everything that was in this letter was of course known to Peter B. The postscript of the letter advised me to show this letter to Peter B., though he intended to write to Peter B. in the same sense, and as I remembered distinctly, he did.

The contact between Peter B. and his brother was continuous all the time in 1951. In a letter dated December 31, 1951, Peter B. wrote to me:

"I send you enclosed the letter from my brother Béla, which informs me more or less about the situation at home."

After that Peter B. asked me to remit money to an aunt of his and supports his request in spite of the spare resources of the Estate by writing:

"I believe both my mother and my brother Béla would be pleased if the Estate helped Aunt Elsa."

The basic idea behind the Interpretive Declaration was to let Béla Jr. get hold, collect, and take possession of everything that could not be gotten out of Hungary anyway, and unless collected by him would be lost, while whatever was accruing outside of Hungary be collected for the Estate in non-Hungarian currency. A letter written by the head of Boosey & Hawkes, New York, to the head of their London office, dated February 28, 1951 (Enclosure I_8), <u>the very same day when the Interpretive Declaration was dated</u>, points out and spells out the ideas behind the Interpretive Declaration:

"The Bartók Estate should not be required to give up any of their normal royalties, no matter who printed this work . . .

"Mr. Bator would prefer to have the Bartók royalties payable in Hungary to Béla Bartók Jr., and the publisher's royalty to be paid in London in pounds. Evidently this question has arisen between the Bartók heirs and the Hungarian State Edition in the past over works not controlled or owned by Boosey & Hawkes and as Mr. Bator was in the process of writing to Béla Bartók Jr, he has today written him of our present discussion . . . .

Appendix B

> "He is also stipulating to Béla Bartók Jr. that providing such an agreement is reached between Boosey and Hawkes and the Hungarian State Edition, no copies are to be distributed outside of Hungary, and that the Mikrokosmos be published in a limited edition only . . . Mr. Bator further indicated that should this State Edition not adhere to the arrangement which he is outlining to Béla Bartók Jr., that Béla Bartók Jr. is in a position to bring the matter to the Hungarian courts and, as the son of a composer who is constantly being held up as a nation figure in present day Hungary, there is little likelihood that the State Edition could go very far with an unauthorized edition."

After the receipt of the "Interpretive Declaration" (signed by the two Trustees and Peter B. and sent to Béla Jr.) according to information which, through Peter B., reached the Trustees, Béla Jr. succeeded to assert and to acquire himself the dominant position in regard to exploitation of the Bartók works (music compositions and writings) toward the Hungarian Government Agencies in charge of intellectual productions. But while before 1951 Béla Jr. was kind of a weak sister who badly needed being propped up, who had begged me directly and through his brother Peter B. to give him stilts, rope and underpinning, soon forgot how did he get in that position. Between 1951 and 1954 he developed the conviction that that position was due to him not toward the Hungarian Government, but rather toward the Estate. It is psychologically not surprising that this happened. The shrewd Communist bureaucrats seem to have known how to handle him. In a letter written to me by Dr. Keresztes, attorney of Mrs. Bartók, dated March 16, 1955, he wrote to me:

> "The Government is giving to Béla [Jr.] tremendous influence and material advantages."

Summarizing the events which appeared to me and the outside world in small mosaic squares, which can be put together to present an understandable picture, this is what happened between 1951 and 1954: The Communist authorities developed an ever increasing interest in the exploitation of Béla Bartók's name, political, and popular appeal, and foreign currency earning possibility of his works. They seem to have discovered also that the inheritance being controlled and administered by Trustees who were American citizens and resided in the United States, the fact that the older son with the same name as the father was Hungarian and within their jurisdiction could and might be used as their own prop to swing that exploitation in the direction in which they wanted it to go. The surrendering of Béla Jr. and accepting the allocated role did not happen from one day to another. For quite a long time after 1951 Béla Jr. continued to associate himself with Mrs. Béla Bartók and Peter B. and the Trustees of the Estate, and was willing to form a unified front against the different Hungarian Government Agencies engaged in the exploitation of Bartók's person and works. A letter by the same Dr. Keresztes to the Hungarian Music Publishing Agency dated September 8, 1954, still asserts that:

> "the Bartók heirs agreed on September 3, 1954, unanimously to refuse to agree to the publication of certain Bartók letters that the Music Publishing Company wanted to print and publish without license from them."

On September 25, 1954, Dr. Keresztes was still authorized by Mrs. Bartók, Béla Jr., and Peter B. to demand the payment of royalties for a publication printed and distributed though without licence in 1951 (Enclosure I10). With other word, for two to three years the front against the arbitrary and confiscatory Hungarian Communist authorities was not broken by Béla Jr. Hesitatingly, but he lent his name and supported the struggle that seems to have carried on against the Communist authorities as far as it could by the attorney retained by Mrs. Bartók, Dr. Keresztes.

The correspondence related to me by Dr. Keresztes in September and October 1954, though revealing, was however only the last straw that broke the camel's back. The disquieting signs of encroachments, arbitrary using of Bartók's works, had reached me before that time already. The disturbing facts which had come to my attention earlier were:

a. That Bartók works (especially non-musical writings) were published and attempts were made to have them distributed everywhere in the whole world;

b. That no accounting was ever given to Béla Jr. and by him to the Estate about the payments made by the Hungarian Government Agencies in charge of publishing, recording, performing musical works and printing and editing writings generally, and that on account of an assignment executed by Mrs. Bartók in favor of Peter B. in New York before her return to Hungary, they stopped all and any payments to Mrs. Béla Bartók, made all payments whatever they decided, arbitrarily as should be paid to Béla Jr. only. (This brought Mrs. Béla Bartók into an embarrassing financial situation that had to be solved by payments from the income of the Estate, which at that time, in 1951-52, after payments of taxes, and expenses to Peter B., were not overly ample.

Appendix B

[Not enough funds were on hand] to step in and take care with sufficiently high amounts of Mrs. Béla Bartók's requirements.)

c. That they concluded sub-publishing contracts in Italy, Germany, Switzerland, the United Kingdom, and collected payments, royalties on the basis of 21 Bartók works originally published in Hungary, mostly works composed prior to 1923, to divert foreign currency royalties in hard currencies to Hungary.

In regard to points a) and b) my information was fragmentary. But as to point c) no secrecy or reticence was shown. The Hungarian publishing companies, that is, the music-using and publishing arms of the Government, claimed the right to own 21 Bartók works, to do with them what they wanted. They were fully engaged in exercising the ownership of all rights pertinent and incidental to the copyrights under the laws of all countries of the world in regard to those 21 musical compositions, some of them of great prominence. In a letter dated March 21, 1955, written by Dr. Robert Palágyi of the stationery of the Office for the Protection of Rights of Authors, but obviously on behalf of all the Government Agencies for whom he acted as a modern Janus, having not two but a handful of faces, he put on record their and Béla Jr.'s claim to complete control of the copyrights of all Bartók works originally published by Hungarian publishers, in the whole world (Enclosure I11—English translation of letter in toto).

In spite of my growing dissatisfaction about the infringement and encroachment of the Hungarians—until October 1954—I did not do much in order to counteract them. My hands were full between 1951 and 1954 by renegotiating the publishing contracts with Boosey & Hawkes and Universal Edition. After all, the beneficiary of the Hungarian income, Béla Jr., showed in his correspondence signs of satisfaction about the situation that was brought about by the Interpretive Declaration of 1951. His brother, Peter B., showed every sign of assent and satisfaction of the situation brought about by the Interpretive Declaration, and Mrs. Béla Bartók seems to have consented (even if she whispered inaudibly, "I will ne'er consent.") The Zenemükiadó Vállalat" (Music Publishing Agency) in a letter dated June 26 (quoted in a Boosey & Hawkes letter of September 24, 1952):

"In accordance with the agreement made mutually between Bartók's heirs:
    Béla Bartók's widow, Budapest
    Béla Bartók, Jr.
    Peter Bartók, New York,
we render most accurate accounts for royalties due for Béla Bartók's

Appendix B

works published by our firm. Mr. Victor Bator should know of the agreement mutually concluded between Béla Bartók's heirs."

Thus, I chose to devote my time and energy to the relatively more important and pressing problem of the relationship to Boosey & Hawkes and Universal Edition. This was all the more unavoidable as my knowledge and information about the relationship of the Estate to the three Hungarian publishers, or after the nationalization, to their "would-be" successor, was far from complete. I was not even in the possession of the basic publishing contracts between Bartók and the Hungarian publishers.

Yet, I was not entirely inactive. On February 25, 1952, I wrote to the New York office of Boosey & Hawkes (Enclosure I_{12}) requesting it to get for me information about a certain Mr. Sugar, who according to rumors that had reached me, was engaged in selling, printing Bartók works in Italy. I tried to interrupt payments from Germany (my letter to Boosey & Hawkes, London, April 15, 1953, Enclosure I_{13}). On September 30, 1953, in a letter written to Boosey & Hawkes, London, I wrote the following:

> "As to the copyrights, especially the mechanical rights for the Iron Curtain countries, I will consult a lawyer and revert to this matter soon. I am sure that the Hungarian society is in error regarding Western Germany. But before I form my final opinion I want to consider the situation from every viewpoint.
>
> "I appreciate the fact that you are waiting with your answer until I make up my mind."

On September 29, 1953, I requested Counsel (Charles Seton) to give me opinion on the construction of the Testament. On November 17, 1953, I instructed by cable Boosey & Hawkes, London:

> "To refrain from accounting to Zenemükiadó (the Hungarian music publishing agency) the royalties for "For Children" and agreed to defend and indemnify them should Zenemükiadó sue you in England. I consulted an attorney in London who advised me that we should appear in the proceeding should Boosey & Hawkes deposit in court the royalties which they upon my request and insistence would not pay to the Hungarians."

Finally, on the basis of a legal opinion given to me by counsels in England in New York I wrote the following to Universal Edition, London, on March 30, 1954:

Appendix B

> "As of today I give you specific instructions not to remit anything to Béla Bartók Jr. Under the will, every payment has to be made to the Trustee, the legal owner of the Estate. Whether I might want to make direct payments to Béla Bartók Jr. or not, I am considering now together with the entire legal construction of the will and the situation of the Estate."

> "It is very probably that I am not going to make any decision until I have the contracts with you and with Boosey & Hawkes all signed, sealed and delivered. The two questions have very little to do with each other legally, yet as a practical point I want to cross one bridge at a time and tackle the second problem after the first one has been put in satisfactory shape."

Another letter written by me on June 22, 1954, to Universal Edition discloses my increased dissatisfaction with the situation:

> "For your private information, I want you to know that For Children has not been picked and chosen by me in order to tackle thereby the general question of the Hungarian publications. As it happens, the Hungarian publishing company was threatening Boosey & Hawkes with legal suit and other coercive measures if they would not pay without delay the license fees due to them or expected by them. Under such circumstances I had to act without delay and right away, and took the steps about which you are informed.

> "Yet I am perfectly willing to follow your idea and concentrate myself rather on the Sonatina, and I shall now consult a German lawyer in West Germany who is well acquainted with copyright situations generally. Have you any suggestion to make to me regarding the person of the lawyer?"

The same growing determination to stop remittances to Hungary is shown by a letter to Universal Edition on June 28, 1954. On October 14, 1954, again to Universal Edition I spelled out my opinions and intentions to prevent the Hungarians from publishing and exploiting the Bartók works outside of Hungary:

> "I am answering your second letter of October 4th regarding the works originally published by Rozsavölgyi and Rozsnyai . . . .

> "It is not my fault that I have not begun the legal steps which will eliminate this situation very soon. Yet it will not be much longer before they will be instituted. In fact, the Hungarians requested Dr. Roth to relay to

me the message that they would like to make a general settlement and they would approach me through an American lawyer. I am not going to wait long for this, but this will show to you that I have my ways and means not only to prevent the present infringement from continuing, but to remedy the situation regarding the past also.

"Regarding Schott you are right. I shall now give them the final warning to eliminate from their catalogue the Bartók works."

Counsel of the Estate, Mr. Charles Seton, on October 15, 1954, delivered his "Legal Opinion and Recommendation" advising me to

"repudiate expressly and without qualification the Interpretive Declaration of February 28, 1951, and to inform ASCAP of the repudiation of the letter of April 25, 1951, to ASCAP confirming the Interpretive Declaration both to be signed by Peter Bartók."

Finally, on October 19, 1954, answering the informative letters of Dr. Keresztes I spelled out and explained fully my opinion and intentions how to handle that situation:

"I have received your letter dated October 6.

The late Bela Bartok left his entire estate to a legal entity created by his will, called the Estate of Bela Bartok. He appointed Dr. Julius Baron of Chicago, Illinois, and myself as Trustees who under American law, own the estate in law with the obligation to use the income and any other proceeds according to the will.

The income of the estate, according to the will, would have been paid by Mrs. Bela Bartok and the two sons of the testator. However, by notarized documents signed by Mrs. Bela Bartok, she assigned everything that was due to her to Peter Bartok. Thus as far as I am concerned, there is only one beneficiary of the trust and that is Mr. Peter Bartok.

One part of the income of the estate has been spent in the past and will be spent in the future for improvement, development, and maintenance of the inheritance of Bela Bartok, that is, for the preservation of the copyrights, the publication of his non-musical works, and other related activities. All other income of the trust has been spent and will

Appendix B

be spent according to instructions of Peter Bartok. If Peter Bartok wants me to pay him every cent of the income in excess of sums required for the purposes set forth above, the entire balance will be paid to him. What amounts not sent to Mrs. Bartok were sent according to Peter Bartok's instructions. I have no power to do anything else.

"In other words, it is my duty and right to maintain, develop, increase in value the principal and the income of the Estate of Bela Bartok. On the other hand, it is not my right and not my duty to determine what should be done with the net proceeds. I follow the instructions of the only beneficiary, that is, Peter Bartok. The only qualification I have to make to the above is that certain payments have to be made by me directly to Bela Bartok Jr. Peter Bartok cannot and would not interfere with that part of the income. This is my direct responsibility. Regarding everything else, you have to write to Peter.

"I hope you don't mind that I am answering your Hungarian letter in English, but I have no secretarial service and it would be quite difficult to express in Hungarian legal language the legal situation of the Estate that is very different from the way all this might have happened in Hungary, where corresponding or similar legal institutions do not exist. I am afraid you will have to think in terms of the law of the United States, where the will was drawn and the transfer of the Estate was and had to be effected."

This letter deserves special attention not only because of the Hungarian situation, but it specified very clearly other aspects of my intentions how to handle the Estate. Part of the income was being spent and would be spent in the future for the improvement, development, and maintenance of the inheritance of Bela Bartok, that is, for the preservation of the copyrights, the publication of his non-musical works, and other related activities. Continuing, I emphasized and pointed out that the net income was spent according to the instructions of Peter B., and that I had no power to do anything else. I pointed out that it was my duty and right to maintain, develop, and increase in value the principal and the income, but that it was Peter B.'s business to determine what should be done with the balance, with the exception of the income that according to the Will was to be paid out to Béla Jr. It should be noted and remembered that I wrote this in October 1954 to the attorney of Mrs. Béla Bartók, and that copy of this letter was sent to the Counsel of the Estate and Peter Bartók.

Yet, by that time, in October 1954 the impediments to devote my time and the necessary attention to the Hungarian problem were more or less out of the

Appendix B

way. The contracts with Boosey & Hawkes and Universal Edition were under cover. Thus the time was ripe for general and overall action. This and the legal opinion of Counsel dated October 15, 1954, discharged the trigger. The withdrawal and repudiation of the Interpretive Declaration was carried out by the letter written to ASCAP on October 27, 1954, with the signature of both Trustees and Peter Bartok.

Lacking regular and routine correspondence with the Hungarian authorities, with Mrs. Béla Bartók and Béla Jr, and in the absence of a systematic description of the arbitrariness and the ever changing policy of the Hungarians in the handling of the Bartók copyrights, it may serve a useful purpose for the understanding of the problem facing the Trustees to put on record at least one case characterizing the situation. I choose the incident of the publication in Hungary of Bartók letters and non-musical writings in three volumes. No license had been asked from the Trustees or from the members of the Bartók family for such publication. The attorney of Mrs. Bartók, authorized to take action on behalf of Béla Jr. and Peter B., also, took action:

a. To protest against the publication of the third volume that had not been published at the time when this correspondence took place,

b. To demand royalties for the publication of the previous two volumes, even though they were unlicensed. (Enclosure I_{14}, letter of Dr. Keresztes dated September 8, 1954; Enclosure I_{15}, letter of Dr. Keresztes of September 25, 1954; Enclosure I_{16}, letter of Dr. Keresztes dated October 22, 1954, give the whole story how the three members of the Bartók family represented by Dr. Keresztes took stand against the publications. Enclosure I_{17}, letter written by the publishing company dated October 15; Enclosure I_{18}, letter written to Dr. Keresztes on October 28, and finally an inter-office correspondence between the Counsel Dr. Palágyi, Enclosure I_{19}, written to the writer of Enclosure I_{18}, give the record of the official reaction to the stand and protest of the Bartók family.)

The essence of the reaction of the different Government agencies acting under different names was simply this: "The publication of letter or writings of Béla Bartók is none of your business; we publish it whether you agree or not. Though the law in all countries which adopted the Bern Union protects the letters, we construe Hungarian law differently. In regard to royalties, again nobody but we control and decide what royalties to pay. We classify works according to our whim and pleasure and pay what we want." The inter-office letter of Dr. Palágyi

Appendix B

made an attempt to persuade the other government officials to change the interpretation of their own arbitrary rules, but not as of law or not, because the Bartók family would have control over what royalties they ought to be paid, but because of the importance and greatness of Béla Bartók they should be given special favor and consideration.

What was the stand taken by Béla Jr. in regard to the encroachments, infringements, or to call a spade a spade: control over the Bartók copyrights in Hungary? We know that he started out with non-recognition and complete disregard by them until 1951. After the Interpretive Declaration of 1951 he became slowly the person to be consulted, to be given standing and recognition. At the time between 1951 and 1953 during which time the arbitrariness and whimsical and high-handed despotism of the Hungarian regime gave place step by step to socialist legality, Béla Jr. did not dissociate himself yet entirely from the unified family group acting in harmony attempting to assert the rights of the Bartók family against the different Hungarian publishing agencies. It is true that that was not too much of an effort. In a letter written by Dr. Keresztes on December 31, 1954, to me I read:

> "The publishers (agencies of the Government) made Mrs. Bartók and Béla Jr. sign all kinds of publishing contracts on the basis of which publications were brought to the market."

In other words, Béla Jr. could maintain the unified front without braving or resisting the Government agencies. Yet, his hesitancy to be allied with Mrs. Bartók and Peter B. and with me grew continuously. Letters written by Dr. Keresztes on March 16, 1955, March 23, 1955, describe the then prevailing state of mind of Béla Jr. not yet dissociating himself from Mrs. Bartók, Peter B. and myself, yet showing detachment, refraining from joining firmly the protests by the other members of the family. A letter written by one of the Hungarian government agencies to Peter B. dated September 17, 1955, and a postscript thereon by the hand of Béla Jr. (Enclosure I[20]) shows the slow transformation of Béla Jr.'s stand from hesitant neutrality into open changed side and going over into the other campus. I quoted already from the letter of March 16, 1955, of Dr. Keresztes the passage that the Hungarian government had given "tremendous influence and material advantages to Béla Jr." Another letter of Dr. Keresztes dated August 21, 1955, reported that he could not possibly use it or spend it (in Hungary like in many other Communist countries where houses, land, cannot be purchased by private individuals, there is little or no possibility of private saving.)

The last phase of the development of the relationship between Béla Jr. and the Hungarian publishing agencies seems to have been brought about by the personal alliance and perhaps friendship between Béla Jr. and Dr. Robert Palágyi. Dr. Palágyi before World War II and the coming into power of Communism was one of the few specialists of copyright law in Hungary. It isn't surprising therefore that in spite of his non-political and non-Communist past, he succeeded to build up a controlling position as legal advisor of all government agencies handling publications of books, music, and copyright matters generally. How central and overwhelming was his position and role in all matters affecting this field was described in a letter he wrote to me on September 27, 1955. According to that letter (Enclosure I_{21}) he was at that time simultaneously attorney and legal advisor of a) Béla Jr., b) Office for the Protection of Author's Rights, c) Performing Rights Society, d) Office for the Publication of Music, e) Corvina, company for the publication of foreign language works, f) Association of Hungarian Musicians, g) other companies or agencies engaged in exploitation of copyrights (not mentioned by name in paragraph VII of the letter), h) company for the production of films. It is not surprising therefore that Béla Jr. joined the group and had himself be led by the hand of Dr. Palágyi who not only flattered his ego, but engineered for him an income that was beyond that of most other people in Hungary. This development became formal and complete when, accompanied by Dr. Palágyi, Béla Jr. was given the possibility to go to Vienna and retain attorneys there to sue as a front for the government agencies Universal Edition for the payment of all income due and paid in the past to the Estate from Austria and Germany.

The question may be properly asked why would it be surprising and not the most natural and human experience to see Béla Jr. disengaging himself from the Estate, the Trustees, his brother and Mrs. Béla Bartók? How could Béla Jr., living in Hungary, strewn by government favors, be expected to resist the temptation to ally himself with the Hungarian authorities?

Béla Jr. has not inherited his father's genius and brilliancy. His standing in society as a higher-echelon engineer of the State Railways, and more recently his honorary professorship at the Hungarian State Institute of Technology, was attained by him because he was the son of the great man, Béla Bartók. Thus cooperation, harmony with the other members of the family, and recognition of the Trustees appointed by his father for the administration of the Estate would not have been unnatural. One could have expected him not to ally himself with the deep game and maneuvers of the Hungarian Communist agencies. Let us describe two instances which were known to him.

In order to form an opinion about the assets of the inheritance (out of which some income was to go to Béla Jr.) in 1949 I began to ask for the Bartók contracts with the Hungarian publishers. In a letter written by Peter B. to Béla Jr. on February 14, 1949, he (at my request) asked Béla Jr. to make an attempt to

Appendix B

purchase the publishing rights in Western Europe and U.S.A. to make the dissemination and use of those 21 works more efficient (Enclosures I_{22} and I_{23}, Peter B.'s letter to Béla Jr. and my letter to Peter B., both of the same date). The answer of Béla Jr. dated March 20, 1949, was this:

> "The contracts in regard to the compositions enumerated by you (21 works) are mostly in my possession. I shall collect them, have them copied and sent to you (both) to enable you to negotiate with the publishers."

Nothing happened. The contracts were not sent, not received. Peter B. on my behalf mentioned to Béla Jr. in his several letters. No response.

On June 6, 1956, I turned to Dr. Keresztes, Mrs. Bartók's attorney:

> "Just now I have one urgent request. Please get for me the copies of the Bartók contracts with Rózsavölgyi, Rozsnyai, Bard. And please find out for me what happened to these three publishers. Are these firms stricken from the register of business-firms and in what form, by what kind of transaction, did their business devolve and come into possession of the State Music Publishing Agency."

Again, on September 2, 1955, when the contracts were still not forthcoming, I wrote to Dr. Keresztes:

> "I have just received your letter written in Budapest. It is regrettable that there is no news yet about the Rózsavölgyi, Rozsnyai, Bard contracts. They do not seem to trust their contractual rights, otherwise they would not show such reluctance about them."

Finally, the copies of the contracts arrived in November 1955. But the accompanying circumstances are worth being noted. Dr. Keresztes's letter of January 29 (Enclosure I24) relates his innumerable attempts to get hold of them, to obtain them from Béla Jr ("He kept on temporizing, dodging.") and Dr. Palágyi who flatly refused to hand them over. A letter written by a Bartók cousin (son in law of Dr. Keresztes) on March 1, 1956, to Dr. Palágyi is most revealing:

> "I have just learned from a letter of the trustee dated February 22, 1956, that you were kind enough to mail him the copies of the contracts. I appreciate this; otherwise I should have done the job of mailing. This

Appendix B

changed attitude is all the more appreciated because it was not long ago when your statement—answering the request of Dr. Keresztes for the delivery of the contracts to the Trustee—consisted of this sentence: 'It is none of his business.'"

It should be noted also that the delivery of the contracts did not happen as a gesture of fairness or minimum cooperation. Far from it. It was connected with the application for license by Dr. Palágyi and his innumerable clients from me for distribution of a Hungarian publication of a Bartók book on this side of the Iron Curtain. When I refused even to consider the request unless copies of the contracts would be sent, then—under this pressure—obliged. And, when I refused the license anyway, Dr. Palágyi complained that the quid pro quo, the license as consideration for letting me have the contracts, was not forthcoming.

Needless to say, the data about the alleged succession of the Hungarian government agencies into the rights of the confiscated Hungarian private publishers have never been disclosed. The letter of Dr. Keresztes (Enclosure I_{25}) of January 29, 1956, relates his futile attempts. The sabotage was maintained and has never been given up.

This scheming against me obtaining information was carried on more or less openly. The intrigue against any kind of attempt to reach a reasonable settlement was not declared. My knowledge is based on letters written to me by members of the Bartók family.

From a letter written to Peter B. dated March 20, 1955:

"We have heard about a journey planned by Dr. Robert Palágyi or Tibor Vasvari to meet the Trustee in Europe. We recommend extreme caution. These gentlemen have deceived, broken faith, with the Bartók heirs all the time, and are doing everything to bring them into conflict with each other. Also, they did everything to gyp the income of the inheritance. They violate the law of copyright, the international conventions, conceal facts and figures."

The postscript of a letter written by the same gentleman to me of March 23, 1955:

"The Office for the Protection of Authors' Rights (?) does everything to avoid a meeting with the Trustee in Vienna or in Switzerland that could bring about the clarification of the situation. Keresztes is doing his utmost to persuade the Ministry of Education and Culture that the pro-

Appendix B

> posals of the Trustee are constructive, and that an orderly system should be aimed at that which would serve the best interests of the Bartók heirs. The present situation is impossible. One illegal Bartók publication follows another. The Office – on the basis of the premium system – harms and short changes the heirs by many hundred thousand forints."

Despite the lure and bribes, I believe that it could have been expected from the son of Béla Bartók not to join the Communist bureaucrats engaged in these intrigues, scheming, and practices.

Yet, human weaknesses being what they are, this does not answer the questions satisfactorily. Béla Jr.'s relationship to his family and to the Estate may be separated into two different problems: a) finances, b) control over the copyrights, granting prestige, and moral position.

A. Béla Jr. has never had any reason to come into conflict with his family and with the Estate for reasons of income and financial benefits. From time to time in the late 1940s when the American and Western European income was quite small, and compared thereto on account of the wide popularity and acceptance of Bartók's music in Hungary, the Hungarian income was more substantial. The Estate and Peter B. did everything to let him have all or almost all of the Hungarian income. The Interpretive Declaration sent to him in 1951 served that purpose, and it did achieve to force the Hungarian government agencies in charge of this field to withdraw and cancel their decision to give him only ¼ of the Hungarian income, even though for a while until 1954 he was given only half of the income, with the other half going to Mrs. Bartók. Since he was employed by the Government in a relatively well paid job, he was well off anyway. In fact, between 1951 and 1954 he did never complain about the insufficiency of the income. Letters written to him by his brother and me never ceased to carry assurances that we not only wanted him to get the Hungarian income, but bring him up to the level of 1/3 of the income realized abroad of the whole income of the inheritance. Béla Jr. just have been of the opinion during all that time that his income was more than 1/3, because besides occasional glimpses and tidbits of information he never answered any of the inquiries—how much was his income regularly, yearly, and in recurring periods. Each and every time it was emphasized by us that the purpose of the inquiry is not to take away anything from him, but to watch out that he shouldn't be disadvantaged.

Yet, there is one point where the financial and income interest of Béla Jr. were not and possibly could not be satisfied by payments made to him by the Hungarian government agencies. Béla Jr. is not an intellectual in the sense in which this word is used in the United States. He is neither well read, nor is he mainly interested in intellect and products of intellect. But he has an inquisitive mind, a curiosity about the world, and therefore the restriction imposed upon him politically (lack of passport possibility to go abroad and travel) and financially (lack of foreign currency income to pay expense of such travelling abroad) was felt by him as a discrimination compared to the situation of his brother or the big wide world. He might have conceived the idea that the blocking by the Trustees of the income from abroad might be an obstacle to, or harm, his moral right to claim from the Hungarian Government allocations of foreign currency for travel abroad. This claim couldn't rest on a strong moral basis. Even though the city of Basel invited him just as well as Mrs. Bartók to the two-week-long Bartók Festival in May 1958, and volunteered to pay his lodging and board expenses, Béla Jr.'s request for a passport and permission to go to Basel with his wife was rejected and ignored. It was only at the last minute, two days before the Festival began, that upon strong representations by him and some others who wanted Béla Jr. to be there for Hungarian prestige reasons, the passport was acquired for him. Yet not a cent of foreign currency was allotted to him for expenses. In fact, solely a remittance—a payment of $1,000—to him by the Estate ordered by Peter B. made it possible for him to have funds available for doing anything else but stay in the hotel and eat the meals paid for by the city of Basel. On the other hand, Peter B. and I agreed with him in May 1958 that the Estate would always be willing to remit the entire income coming from Austria and Germany to an agent of his choice in foreign hard currency, to be deposited in a confidential account in Switzerland. These funds would be his, regardless of any doubt or question about income from Austrian and German copyrights. In fact, I informed the attorney of Béla Jr. in Vienna that I was willing to enter into such agreement with him as agent and alter-ego of Béla Jr. in case he would be denied the right to collect from Universal Edition the income from Austria and Germany.

Thus, it is very improbable that his alliance with the Hungarian government agencies was motivated by financial considerations.

B. Outside of regard to political and personal safety reasons, there remains as the only motive for his dissociation from the Estate, the Trustees, and Mrs. Béla Bartók the prestige consideration to acquire for himself a standing lent by the complete control of the Bartók copyrights. He claimed the right in regard to the seven countries mentioned in the Interpretive Declaration of 1951—that is, Germany, Austria, Hungary, Czechoslovakia, Poland, Yugoslavia, and Rumania—to be the only person to decide any and all questions in regard to publication, distribution, sale, performances, recordings, of Bartók works, whether musical or of other nature.

Appendix B

I, as the Trustee, had many reasons not to agree to this.

a. The Last Will and Testament allocated certain income to Béla Jr. but put under the administration of a Trustee all copyrights. Thus, without giving up rights which under the Will and Testament were put in my hands and for which I was responsible, I could not let Béla Jr. take them over either generally or for a given territory, specifically. A Trustee cannot delegate his authority to other persons. It is true that the 1951 Interpretive Declaration could be construed as if I had given over to Béla Jr. rights in regard to the control of and decision over the copyrights in the seven countries. The excuse for that may be found in the approval of the other two beneficiaries, by the signature of Peter B. Another excuse may be found in the fact that at any time, in 1951, as a practical matter I was not and could not expect to control the copyrights in those seven countries, and therefore entrusting this task to a member of the Testator's family was not to be construed as a complete and definitive delegation of my rights.

b. As soon as the emergency situation created by the complete lawlessness in Hungary was slowly receding, I withdrew the Interpretive Declaration, again approved and co-signed by Peter B. This withdrawal was based on and supported by the opinion of Counsel.

c. It was explicitly expressed to me by the Testator that one of the main considerations to entrust the administration of the Estate, his inheritance—not the income, but the management of the copyrights overseeing the publications, performances, recordings and the artistic quality of the work done by the publishers—was to secure unified, unsplit control. Without violating this behest of the Testator I could not let slip this central control into anybody's hand. This idea of the Testator was not something new that was conceived by him at the time when his Last Will was made. I have not in my possession the Last Will and Testament of Béla Bartók Sr. made and signed on October 4, 1940, in Budapest, Hungary, but three letters written by Dr. Keresztes, the attorney of Mrs. Bartók, to me reference this will, and the desire of Béla Bartók Sr. are strongly emphasized. Letter of December 31, 1954:

> "I have studied the Last Will and Testament written in Hungarian language signed by Béla Bartók on October 4, 1940. This Testament is not valid. Yet this Will and Testament helps and gives a clear-cut picture about the final dispositions which were in the mind of Béla Bartók and therefore may be used for the construction of the Last Will and Testament now valid and in force."

Appendix B

That Will and Testament divided the assets among the wife and the two sons in three equal 1/3 parts, but—and that's what I want to point out specifically now—it distinguishes very sharply between the corpus of the copyrights and their income. According to that Will any assignment or disposition about the corpus of the copyright must have the unanimous decision of the three heirs in order to "prevent the splitting of the author's rights (copyrights)."

Letter of March 16, 1955:

"It is my main and most important task to make the heirs or rather the beneficiaries to understand the Last Will and Testament. I referred to the Testament of 1940 though it is no more valid because in that Testament Béla Bartók distinguishes sharply between the corpus and the income of the copyrights. This will be one of the important points and subjects in my conference with Béla Jr."

Letter of March 23, 1955:

"Last Saturday Béla Jr. appeared in my office and I had a four-hour-long conference in regard to all important questions. The primary purpose of the conference was to explain and make him understand what a Trusteeship is and what a Trustee is . . .

"After having explained to him these concepts (Testator, Estate, Trustee, beneficiaries) I turned over to the construction and interpretation of the Last Will and Testament. In that regard it was most important for me to explain and emphasize that under the Last Will and Testament the authors' right (copyrights), the title to them was transferred without division, split up, as a unit, in the ownership of the Trustee, and that nobody but the Trustee can make dispositions regarding them. I explained that, under the Will, Béla was not allocated or given any part of the authors' rights (copyrights), or any portion or part thereof. The Trustee is the owner of the copyrights. He may entrust somebody else to exercise all or parts of the rights included in the copyrights, but whoever he is, he will be his delegate and agent and the Trustee remains the principal. Also, the Trustee must have the right to withdraw that transfer at his will should he find this necessary or practical. While the Trustee had the right to authorize Béla temporarily to control and dispose of the copyrights in the territory of Hungary, he must have legally the right to change that disposition and withdraw it. In consequence of that legal situation and of

Appendix B

the withdrawal of the authority of Béla, I informed him that he had no right to make publishing or any other contracts with the State publishing agencies regarding the Bartók copyrights. I have informed you already that the Government agencies, and more especially Dr. Zakár, legal advisor of the Ministry of Public Education and Culture, and Dr. Palágyi, the counsel of the Office for the Protection of Authors' Rights, hold opinions entirely different from this. They believe that authors' rights can be parceled up, allocating some in regard to the territory of the United States to someone, and allocating some others in regard to the territory of Hungary to somebody else . . . .

"I pointed out to Béla Jr. in the course of our conference that I have written to you already that his father attributed great importance and laid stress upon his will and desire to exclude the cutting up and the dividing of the authors' rights."

d. I might have considered with certain limitations the transfer to Béla Jr. of the practical exercising of the Trustee's right in regard to copyrights, if Béla Jr. did not live in Hungary under the thumb of Communist-minded and entirely politically oriented bureaucrats whose entire thinking is influenced by arbitrariness, complete lack of feeling for freedom of thought, private rights even under the ramshackle semblance of socialist legality. I was disposed to transfer to Béla Jr. the practical and everyday handling of the copyright problem in Hungary and other countries behind the Iron Curtain if in principle he would recognize that he would do this as my agent and should he be unable to use his own judgment and act as a free agent, that I be authorized to withdraw that authority. I explained to him that that will help him and that he can use this construction to his own advantage because whenever he doesn't want to do something that the Government would want him to do, he could bottom his refusal upon the threatened or expected withdrawal of his authority and my resistance. During our negotiations in Basel, Switzerland, in May 1958 Peter Bartók strongly supported that argument and tried to impress upon Béla Jr. that this was in his own interest. It seems that in 1958 and ever since his Ego problem was already beyond rational thinking. He wanted unconditional surrender of the Trustee's rights in the countries behind the Iron Curtain and in Austria and Germany. It is difficult to decide how much and how far this is at the same time a "fronting" for the Hungarian Government. His acting is in unison and synchronized with the Hungarian government agencies. It serves not only what I called his Ego, but serves at the same time the aims and purposes of the Communist bureaucracy. The entire controversy is summarized in two letters that I wrote to Dr. Palágyi on December 21st,[1] and to Béla Jr. on the same day; and the answers given by Béla Jr. relayed to me by Dr. Palágyi himself dated January 13, 1958 (Enclosures I_{25}, I_{26}, I_{27}, and I_{28} in English translation). Three more letters written to me on the same day, January 23, 1958 (Enclosures I_{29}, I_{30}, I_{31}), by Dr. Palágyi on February 5, 1958 (Enclosure I_{32}), and by me again on February 10, 1958 (Enclosure I_{33}) complete the picture of the possibilities and impediments of an agreement. The distribution of the income did not play any part in the disagreement. On that score I had never wavered. Exactly the way as I explained it in my first letter to Dr. Keresztes on October 19, 1954, the net income of the Trust

> "has been spent and will be spent according to instructions of Peter B. (and/or Mrs. Béla Bartók). If Peter B. wants me to pay him (Béla Jr.) every cent of the income in excess of the sums required for the purposes set forth above, the entire balance will be paid to him. If he wants it to be spent differently, that's what will be done. Whatever amounts were sent to Mrs. Bartók were sent according to Peter B.'s instructions. I have no power to do anything else."

III

Peter B. on page 7 of his Affidavit charges me with misadministration of the Estate because by the Interpretive Declaration signed by the two Trustees and by himself, his brother

> "has received and is still receiving substantial sums of Trust income in Hungary. Since the decree was entered herein, I have learned that the income so received by my brother has amounted to some 1,500,000 Hungarian forints, or approximately $130,000 at the official rate of exchange. I am now informed by my attorney that such income that is nowhere reported in the accounts filed herein, should have been collected and accounted for to this Court by Bator, as Trustee, and should have been paid over to my mother."

The essence of this charge is that I imposed upon Peter B. a declaration consenting to and approving of payments to his brother an amount he appraises now to be $130,000—and that I am responsible for the fact that that amount was not collected by me as Trustee and was not paid over to Mrs. Béla Bartók.

---

[1] This letter has survived. See correspondence elsewhere in this volume.

Appendix B

No objection has ever been raised, until this affidavit reached me, by Peter Bartók or by Mrs. Béla Bartók or by anyone else, against Béla Jr. collecting in Hungary whatever he succeeds to collect. No objection has ever been raised by anybody to the payment to Béla Jr. income from certain territories from which according to Paragraph 2 of the Will, income was due and payable to him. While my contact with Béla Jr. was scattered and spotty, Peter B. was practically in continuous contact by correspondence with his brother. It can easily be proven also that the payments made to Béla Jr. were known to Mrs. Béla Bartók. The attorney of Mrs. Béla Bartók was officially informed by the Hungarian government of the payments to Béla Jr.

Out of those letters written by Béla Jr. to Peter B. we know that before the Interpretive Declaration of 1951 the Hungarian government agencies in charge of copyrights had paid amounts which at that time—and compared to the income of the Bartók copyrights—were quite considerable.

Peter B. knows that in 1954 I consulted Counsel about the construction of the Will, and based upon this opinion of Counsel I withdrew the Declaration of 1951, instructing all agencies engaged in the exploitation and exercising of the Bartók copyrights to stop payments to anybody in Hungary, including Béla Jr. That document of withdrawal was signed as co-signator by Peter B.

Correspondence, statements verbal and written, are in our possession proving that Peter Bartók at each and every occasion pressured me, persuaded me, and expressed opinion to the effect that payment of 1/3 of the Estate income be made to Béla Jr., his half-brother.

Letters, informations, are in our possession proving that the harmony, cooperation and synchronization of all acts and activities of the two brothers have always been complete, and recently, in the last two years, and especially since the visit of Peter B. to Hungary in 1959, were strengthened, reinforced, and made complete.

Finally, Béla Jr. arrived in the United States sometime before Christmas 1959, and lived in the apartment of his half-brother Peter B.; they traveled together in the United States for about four weeks, and since Béla Jr. doesn't speak English, whatever he did, wherever he went, he was accompanied by his brother Peter B.

In regard to the renewal rights of the Bartók works, Boosey & Hawkes, New York, was officially informed by Peter B. and Béla Jr. (Peter B. acting on his own behalf and on behalf of his mother), that there is complete agreement between the widow and the two sons of Béla Bartók that the renewal right copyright income be divided between them equally, that is, 1/3 going to each.

IV.

Béla Jr. as front of the Hungarian authorities.

Béla Jr.'s connection and alliance with the Hungarian publishing agencies and all other Hungarian organizations engaged in the exploitation of the Bartók copyrights has been fully described and exposed in the part A) of this chapter of my statement. The assumption of the explanations given in A) was that on account of the payments of all sums collectable, due and payable by the Hungarian agencies out of the exploitation of the Bartók copyrights in Hungary and in the Iron Curtain countries generally, there was no conflict between the Hungarian government agencies and organizations and Béla Jr.'s interests as long as everything was paid to him. Yet, there is a further field where such conflict of interest outside of the exploitation mentioned above ought to exist. Yet, Béla Jr. in regard to that field where his interests are in conflict with those of the Hungarian government organizations fronts for them, and supports their stand. This concerns the use and the exploitation (publication, sale, performance, mechanical, reproduction, use on films and television) of 21 works originally published by Hungarian publishers insofar as they are being exploited, used in any way outside of Hungary and the 7 countries where Béla Jr. claims specific rights on the basis of Paragraph 2 of the Last Will and Testament.

The controversy is simple.

a. The three Hungarian publishers who originally had their publishing contracts with Béla Bartók ceased to exist and disappeared. They never transferred their rights to any other Hungarian publishing company. The alleged transfer and claim to hold those rights is based on Hungarian confiscatory legislation. Supported by legal opinion of internationally recognized experts, I maintain that the confiscatory legislation of the Hungarian government has no effect and validity outside of Hungary, and therefore those rights do not belong to the Hungarian government or to its publishing organizations. To whom do they belong? The publishers who had their contract with Béla Bartók are not in existence. They disappeared. The copyright law does not know "abandoned copyrights," that is, copyrights without proprietors, owners. Copyright is a summarizing conception, expressing the right of the author or his assignee for protection against those who have no rights whatsoever. Thus, it is my stand and thesis that Béla Bartók and on his behalf, the Estate of Béla Bartók, in the moment of the disappearance of publishing firms, reacquired all rights which by the old publishing contracts passed to those publishers that passed out of existence.

Appendix B

b. Since the Last Will and Testament of Béla Bartók restricts the rights of Béla Jr. to income from certain territories among which neither the Western European countries, nor the United States, nor the British Commonwealth, or Asia, Africa, and all other countries of the world do not belong, Béla Jr. is not entitled to the income out of those territories even if his rights are valid in regard to those seven countries, in which, according to him, the rights belong to him. Yet, the Hungarian government (insofar I have not succeeded yet to block the income from such countries and insofar such countries by their legislation did not terminate yet the publishers' rights based on contracts concluded with Béla Bartók in regard to those works—countries of the British Commonwealth —) has no right to income from those 21 works. Yet the Hungarian government pays to Béla Jr. voluntarily and without legal obligation, out of the income collected from the exploitation of these 21 works outside of the territories where Béla Bartók has or may have rights to the income, substantial sums. Béla Jr. owes the repayment of such amounts, sums of which are unknown to me, to the Estate. Until now I could not possibly demand repayment and collect anything from Béla Jr., all the more because the amounts were entirely unknown to me. Out of the affidavit of Peter B. I have learned now that that income amounts to 1,500,000 forints, equal, according to him, to $130,000. I assume that that amount represents the income out of the exploitation of these 21 works outside of the seven countries where Béla Jr. has or may have official rights, because I do not believe that insofar that income has originated in the territories of those seven countries, Peter B. and his attorney would demand from me to deprive Béla Jr. of such income.

It is obvious that Béla Jr.—who in statements published in Hungarian government-controlled publications reproached and attacked me for preventing the Hungarian government from collecting income from countries on this side of the Iron Curtain for the 21 works—did so because the Hungarian government pays him—even though it is called arbitrary and voluntary—considerable amounts. Whether this fronting for the Hungarian government is caused entirely by his financial benefit, or whether he does it because living in Hungary he cannot avoid subscribing to the thesis of the Hungarian government agencies that claim ownership of those 21 works for the entire world, I do not know.

Appendix C. Victor Bator: Affidavit in the Litigation Proceedings of 1959–61 (1960)

This typewritten document, 27 pages long, bears numerous handwritten additions and corrections by Bator. At the top of the first page appears a handwritten annotation: "To be written up on D.D. plate and recopied in 10 copies!" It bears no title. Its content makes plain its intention to be entered into the litigation as an Affidavit for the defense. At one time stapled, it shows annotations in several colors of ink and other signs of editing. A single copy survives in the Benjamin Suchoff Collection of Bartókiana in Tampa, Florida, the source for this transcription. The original is in English.

Here he describes how the communist government in Hungary asserted control over the material and spiritual legacy of Béla Bartók after 1950. The government's "Master-Servant" relationship with Béla Bartók Jr. is of material importance to understand, he feels. So, too, is the "co-conspiracy" between Béla Jr. and his half-brother Peter, who joined together after 1958 to advance the litigation currently awaiting trial. Róbert Palágyi's role as "mouthpiece of the Hungarian Government" elicits extended commentary. The level of specific detail in this account is extraordinary. The inner machinery of communist decision making rarely comes alive as well as it does here.

Victor Bator's expressed intent in this document is to counter the arguments of fraud and misrepresentation currently placed before the court by Peter Bartók. Surrogate DiFalco took into account the information in this Affidavit and its attached Exhibits during the trial. It can be presumed that the Affidavit was written largely for his benefit.

My answering affidavit represented that this motion is the first step aimed at seizing the control of the Bartók inheritance by Hungarian Communist Government. Peter Bartók calls this idea a product of groundless imagination and a representation by me without evidence. I shall now provide the evidence and proof of the scheme that hides behind the motion of Peter Bartók. Needless to say such schemes are hardly ever provable by producing a notarized,

Appendix C

signed document. The evidence must be put together out of pieces which are found separated, but in this particular case the fact that they are meshes of a net that was planned and schemed will be obvious as soon as one sees the separated meshes piece together.

For the understanding of the scheme it is absolutely necessary to know the relationship of the Government in a Communist country like Hungary to the products of mind, to the authors, composers, writers, artists and their creations, both the law and the administrative procedures through which—even though the basic copyright statute has been hardly changed—the Hungarian Communist Government has complete and absolute control over the literary, musical, and scientific life, the use and exploitation of Hungarian and non-Hungarian literary, scientific, and artistic creations within and outside the country. The general common-sense assumption that of course the Communist Government controls everything does not give sufficient justice to the completeness, the absoluteness of the net that harnesses the Hungarian intellectual world of mind and makes it a servant of the political regime. In this respect the lack of freedom, elbowroom, is zero, while otherwise in other areas of social life slight sectors of slackness may exist.

Three decrees (known by numbering and dates), i.e. 106/1952 (December 31, 1952); 24/1954 (April 4th, 1954); and 1/1955 (March 12, 1955) were enacted by the Hungarian Government with aim to bring about complete control. The political aim of such control is obvious. It serves the internal safety of the Communist regime. It makes possible the exploitation of the creative mind and soul for the prestige build-up of the regime within the country and abroad. Finally, it is used, since Hungary is—in regard to literature and music, art and science—an export country, for the acquisition of badly needed foreign exchange, which is used again in its turn for acquisition of foreign raw materials, machinery, and external propaganda.

The power and control of the Government would be almost complete anyway on account of the fact that publishing, printing, all other industries serving multiplication, duplication of manuscripts or art-objects, dissemination by sale, distribution to the public, disposition over paper and ink produced in Government-owned factories, means of transport are all and sundry Government-owned, Government-run. Yet writers, composers, and artists, using their moral authority and recognition, may get around this and may use moral and financial support from foreign lands to establish a limited independence and response abroad. They may build, by bargaining with those Government-owned businesses, certain kinds of privileges. Thus, the Government Decrees listed above created a Government agency, called loftily and highfalutingly: "Office For The Protection of Authors Rights," not for the protection of authors' rights but for

Appendix C

their complete domination by the Government. According to those decrees—to begin with the negative side of the picture—the Office is headed by a directorium of five. All five members are appointees of the Government. All financial and administrative matters are in the hand of a Director appointed by the Minister of Folk-Education. All other employees are appointed by the Director (Paragraph 2 of 24/1954). In other words, writers, composers, artists have no say: they are objects not participants. There is no autonomy whatsoever. The Office has the power to represent the writers, etc., toward the publishers. Of course, the publishers, concert agencies, broadcasters, etc. are all Government agencies themselves. But the game is played as if they were independent. The Office determines in which category of 4 Government-ordered classifications a writer or a work belongs. Once this tagging is done, the above-mentioned decrees determine how much will be the royalty per page, per word, per copy, etc. No nonsense, no interference. All is printed, tabulated in the decrees.

Outside and in addition to all of the above, there are special rules in regard to every and all channels connecting the intellectual life of the authors, writers, artists with the world outside Hungary. Nobody, but nobody, is allowed to enter into any contract with anybody abroad in regard to "literary, artistic creations, scientific and technical works, textbooks and all other works, writings, creations protected by copyright in regard to every and all fields of exploitation" unless a special permit is granted by the Hungarian National Bank (Paragraph 5 of 24/1954). No claims or demands can be made before a foreign Court without the special permit of the Minister of Finance (Paragraph 5 of 24/1954). Should the Office want to enforce or assert a claim on the basis of a copyright-protected work "the author or his heirs and successors are obliged to put at the disposal of the Office Power of Attorney and any other required documents necessary for the institution of proceedings" (Paragraph 10 of 106/1952).

Summing up: the complete control of the Government is assured three-fold: a) the publishing and distributing agencies are all Government-owned; b) there is a Government Office that is appointed as the obligatory attorney-in-fact of the authors, etc., whether they like it or not, and even if they get approach to the agencies of publication this Office decides their rights; c) in regard to links and connections with foreign countries, authors, composers, scientists are under 100% tutelage.

This picture would not be complete if I did not add that performances, concertising, lecturing abroad is subject to the same tight control. Passports are of course a matter of exceptional privilege. Beyond this, the authors, concertizing artists must use a Government outfit to negotiate contracts for performances, concerts, and lectures abroad. The fee is determined by the Government outfit. It must be turned over to the Government. The amount they may spend on liv-

Appendix C

ing expenses abroad is fixed: so much per day. What they receive as fee is determined by the Government outfit. All doors are closed. The only path open goes through the strictly controlled, barbed wire fence.

Before I go over to the specific points affecting the Bartók Estate, I insert here the presentation of Dr. Robert Palágyi, who until recently was the mouthpiece of the Hungarian Government and the mover, promoter, and leading spirit of their anti-Bartók-scheme.

Dr. Róbert Palágyi first appeared as the mouthpiece of the Government in a letter addressed to Dr. Keresztes, attorney of Mrs. Bartók, dated March 21, 1955. That is the first letter where the claim that <u>Béla Bartók Jr.</u> be granted by me as Trustee exclusive title to and control over the Bartók copyrights in the territory of Austria, Germany, Hungary, Czechoslovakia, Yougoslavia, Roumania, and Poland <u>was asserted not as a private claim of Béla Bartók Jr., but as the demand of the Hungarian Government.</u> But, in a letter dated September 27, 1955, that will be referred to presently, Palágyi claimed that from 1952 it was he who was in charge of the Bartók affairs behind the anonymity of office procedure. Ever since that date it was Dr. Robert Palágyi who put forward, maintained, and asserted that claim on behalf of the Government organizations of which he was General Counsel. Why is it that the concern of the Government has never been explained, but the Office for the Protection of Authors' Rights, which was described hereabove, the Government outfit for the overall control of all authors' rights and on its behalf Dr. Róbert Palágyi was the leader of the campaign to acquire for Béla Bartók Jr. and, through him as their puppet, the material and moral essence of the Bartók rights.

The description of Dr. Palágyi's role as the champion in the front rank was given by himself repeatedly. In the letter written to me on September 27, 1955, just mentioned he pointed out that in the three years preceding that letter he had the leading role in regard to the protection of the Béla Bartók copyrights. The same letter underlines what the Government decrees say that "the exploitation of authors' creations in foreign (non-Hungarian) lands and the use of foreign works in Hungary is the exclusive domain of the Office" of which he was General Counsel. He sets forth, however, that his role does not end at that point. "All publishers" (all of them, of course, Government outfits) "come to me for advice or legal work." Thus, "in Bartók matters I have been consulted by the National Music Publishing Company and the Corvina Company of Publications in Foreign Language." That is not all. "I am General Counsel of the Association of Hungarian Musicians, also," says Dr. Palágyi in the same letter. But, to make sure that the close Government character of his official capacity be not forgotten, he adds: "Our Office is under the control of the Ministry of Folk-Education." He also pointed out in the same letter that he was the mouthpiece "of the united will of the Hungarian Government Agencies engaged in the exploitation of intellectual and artistic creations."

This assertion of Dr. Palágyi's role as commander of the Government task force against the Bartók Estate was restated by him in a letter written on April 19, 1956, to my Co-Trustee Dr. Julius Baron. "I am the General Counsel of the Government Office of the Protection of Authors' Rights; our Office is in charge of the defense in Hungary of all rights for all and every author. All other Government Agencies, even though they have their own General Counsel, turn to me in matters connected with this special field."

Reverting now to the description of the complete control of the products of mind, represented toward the Bartók rights by Dr. Palágyi, it needs to be pointed out that a system of power over everybody and everything creates the state of mind in those at the steering wheel that everything depends from them. Whatever falls under the concept "Hungarian"—men, land, chattel, all the living and inanimate objects under and above the surface—are supposed by them to be their tools, parts, meshes of the net holding the system together. If somebody or something was left out of consideration they issue a new decree or do what they want with the help of their police, their censorship, and the scare that their existing or suspected whips instill in everybody—until an eruption discloses how shallow that power is. Meanwhile every voice we hear is the "Master's Voice."

Yet, there are always thorns in rosebushes. One such thorn, ever since the establishment of the Hungarian Communist regime, has been the existence of the Bartók Estate. This sounds ridiculously disproportionate. It would be if Béla Bartók were but a composer of music, no matter how great or important as such. But a legend surrounding his name made out of Béla Bartók, the scholar and composer, the "greatest Hungarian" of the past generation, as just now, in our contemporary period, the name of the "greatest living Hungarian" would no doubt be voted by all Hungarians to be another musician, composer, and scholar, Zoltán Kodály. Thus, the subjection of the Estate of Béla Bartók to the complete control of the Government is not a problem of rule over a few dozen musical works, not even over the use of the substantial foreign exchange income, but the possibility to exploit the name, reputation, and fame of Bartók—the Bartók legend—for the political, propaganda, soul- and mind-control scheme of the Government. Had Béla Bartók not protected his name, reputation, work, and legend, surrounding himself by giving over his estate to independent trustees who are not under the thumb of the Communist Government (through Mrs. Bartók and Béla Jr., who *are* under their thumb), by the strength of the system, by playing on the "Magyar" heart of Peter Bartók, by stick and carrot, they would be free to do what they see fit for using the Bartók name, works,

Appendix C

reputation, legend for their political purposes. Of course, it does not occur to them to attempt the capture of the Estates of Puccini, Richard Strauss, or Bernard Shaw, or any other foreign author's works. They are not bothered by such ideas. But Bartók having been Hungarian and a great national figure, they consider it unnatural, irrational, and an outrageous restriction of their dictatorial power that their tentacles cannot reach it.

In fact, spoiled and corrupted by their habitual thinking, they began treating (between 1946 and 1954) the Bartók field exactly the same way they deal with all other Hungarians. But, suddenly they ran into difficulties. Having discovered their devious acts I blocked them, not completely, but sufficiently to become first a nuisance, then a real roadblock.

With this in mind I have to admit that strictly speaking I greatly exaggerated when I said previously that a "conspiracy" exists between Béla Jr. and the Hungarian Government. Béla Jr. is not only a Hungarian citizen who speaks one language only, the Magyar language, tied to his native country by habits, friendships, family ties, etc., but he is a Government employee himself. If that did not hold him to toeing the mark, the "stick and carrot" that we shall describe presently does. Therefore, instead of talking of conspiracy we should think of the relationship between tamer and collaborator, master and performer, or simply ventriloquist and puppet. The Government decrees oblige him to collaborate. They prevent him from doing anything of his own volition. But in order to get "enthusiastic" collaboration he is granted privileges, money, and external recognition as the son of the great Hungarian.

[Pages 10–23 omitted here. They concern Béla Jr.'s actions in the 1950s, and substantially duplicate the information found in Chapter I, "The Hungarian Problem," of the 1960 Memorandum, printed above. The affidavit concludes with the following summary remarks]

So far this memorandum has covered the conspiracy or the Master-Servant relationship between the Hungarian Communist Government and Béla Jr. But, in form, Peter Bartók being the sole petitioner we shall complete the circle by presenting the relationship in regard to this procedure between Béla Jr., co-conspirator with, servant to, the Communist Government on the one hand and Peter Bartók on the other.

Until 1958 Peter Bartók neither as remainderman or as attorney-in-fact was in conspiracy with Béla. On the contrary, he was firmly of the opinion that the Trustee as independent administrator of the Estate must be supported by him and his mother. He carried on a lively series of conversations and correspondence disagreeing, arguing, and finally compromising in regard to some matters (remittances to Mrs. Bartók, title to Archive, manuscripts, expenses on manuscripts and Archive, etc.), but always with the understanding that these conversations concerned details, procedures, not the basic principle.

Yet, there were warning signals.

a) A letter from Dr. Alfred Kalmus, Director of Universal Edition, publishers of Bartók works, dated November 4, 1958:

" . . . I should like to mention that it has been repeatedly reported that Peter and Béla Bartók Jr. have come to an agreement between themselves to the effect that both <u>shall receive 50% of the income of the inheritance, with proper provisions for the mother's support</u>. Incidentally, the two brothers, who were in Vienna a year ago, confirmed privately this 50/50 sharing arrangement to my colleague Schlee . . . "

b) Another letter from the same Dr. Kalmus dated March 27, 1959 (Exhibit D of Respondent Affidavit, p. 15) stated:

"Referring to your letter of the 19th inst. I am informing you that Mr. Béla Bartók Jr. is not aware of the details of the negotiations which are being carried out by his brother in New York. <u>Even so, the brothers are absolutely in accordance with each other in every respect</u> . . ."

c) A letter from a Swiss publisher, dated June 6, 1959, requesting license to publish certain Bartók works:

"We have also been informed that the two sons of Bartók are about to take over the entire Administration of the Estate within foreseeable time."

Yet, these warning signs were not conclusive. The Trustee now has in his possession written statements as to the conspiracy, both written in 1960. ~~The signatures on these statements will be withheld but should the facts be denied, the original papers will be submitted. Here the text follows:~~

In April 1959 in Budapest Peter Bartók stated to his mother and Béla Bartók Jr. that in regard to the administration of the Estate he is unable (unwilling) to cooperate with Victor Bator. He stated that he wanted to

Appendix C

change the administration of the matter. At the same time Béla Bartók Jr. set forth his demand that the participation in the inheritance as determined by the American Testament of 1943 be changed, and that the principles expressed by the Will of 1940 made in Budapest be abided by. He also believed it impossible to administer the Estate together with Victor Bator.

The changes wanted by the two brothers were not in conflict with the opinion of the widow, Mrs. Béla Bartók. This is all the moreso because the intention of the testator, Béla Bartók, is expressed truest in the Testament of Budapest and the last American Testament written in 1945 that was not signed. It should be added that Mrs. Bartók as early as 1947 proposed to Béla Bartók Jr. to eliminate the American Last Will and Testament by an agreement in regard to the administration of the Estate and the sharing of the assets according to a system realizing the intentions of the testator. At that time, in 1947, Béla Jr. refused to accede to that proposal. In 1948 Peter Bartók was in Budapest and he was not willing to change the participation in the Estate. At that time he set forth also that Victor Bator did not object to the collection of the Hungarian income by Béla Bartók Jr. Further, at that time he informed the others that Victor Bator would be willing at any time to let the heirs take over the estate. Similar statements had been made by Victor Bator many times during the years, the last time in 1957 to Béla Bartók Jr.

Mrs. Béla Bartók took note that the two brothers cannot cooperate with Victor Bator. Emphasizing this she consented that the two brothers take over the Estate from Victor Bator, all the more because Victor Bator repeatedly expressed his readiness to give over the administration. The practical execution would happen in that form that Victor Bator resigns without a successor. In this case, according to the paragraph of the Testament relating to this problem, the right to designate the new Trustee would belong to Mrs. Bartók. Hence, in that case, Mrs. Bartók would be in the position to transform administration of the Estate in a way expressing the real will of the testator.

After all these antecedents and considerations, Mrs. Bartók authorized her son Peter to arrange with Victor Bator the turning over of the Estate. (The writer of this memorandum believes that Mrs. Bartók expected in regard to the rearrangement of the administration of the Estate support and friendly help from Victor Bator, and not resistance.)

Appendix C

Thus Peter acts with the authorization of his mother. Yet, it depends on Victor Bator only whether this procedure be executed amicably or against his will. No member of the Bartók family desires controversy with Victor Bator. They would not avoid it, though they do not understand why animosity should enter the picture.

It should be known that the purpose of Mrs. Béla Bartók is to realize in every respect the maximum of real intentions of her husband. It is certain that she is the person to know best what was the essential intention. She has the sturdy moral power for its realization. For that reason it would be desirable that Victor Bator, who enjoyed the trust and the appreciation of a friend by Béla Bartók and his wife, should not aggravate the situation and should support the realization of the purposes stated above. April 1960. Budapest. ~~Signature.~~

[*Handwritten note by Bator at bottom of the page*: "This statement, record of the conspiracy-agreement, was prepared, signed, and sent to me by Jenő Pásztory, brother of Mrs. Bartók, uncle of Peter Bartók, as a document putting on record the scheme of Peter and Béla Bartók Jr. and the limited consent of Mrs. Bartók. Jenő Pásztory was the fourth person present at the conference, as advisor and support for Mrs. Bartók."]

The English translation of the second statement:

After the valid Testament of 1943 (Trustee), the testator had the intention to make a testament in 1945 (distribution to three). D. (Mrs. Bartók) wants an agreement along the lines of the 1945 testament, in other words taking over the inheritance (Estate) by the heirs. According to the writer of the statement they would retain and commission someone with the administration of the Estate (it would be a good idea to retain for this purpose V.) but that person would not be a Trustee; he would be an agent of the heirs.

D. (Mrs. Bartók) did not agree to the partition of the inheritance between the two brothers.

[*Handwritten annotation by Bator in the margin*: "this statement was made by János Bartók, first cousin of Peter and Béla Bartok"]

The complete agreement between Peter and Béla Jr. is not only proven, but admitted and confessed to by Béla in the supporting affidavit joining Peter in

Appendix C

this proceeding. Without taking into consideration Béla's conspiracy with the Hungarian Communist Government, this would amount to the confessing of a lie only affecting the private relationship of Peter to Béla—the lie about his opposition to the pocketing of Hungarian income by Béla and my guilt over not preventing this. But Béla being a conspirator, servant and fellow traveller, the concerted one voice of Peter and Béla is the wirepuller behind them, the Communist Government.

The Affidavit of Béla Jr. admits that he came to New York "to render what assistance I could do to my brother (Peter) and my step-mother." ~~This statement contradicts first of all his statement given to the American Consulate according to which he would come to the U.S.A. to study the railway system and railway administration. But~~ This admittance should be considered in the light of the Government decrees which do not permit any action in a foreign court, or any step in regard to rights, claims, concerning copyrights, royalties, etc., without Government approval. Béla Jr. must have been given a Hungarian passport, a rare document issued as a rule to fellow travellers only, must have received scarce dollars, never given to any Hungarian by the Communists unless someone travels on official mission. Béla Jr. himself who, as reported above, did get a passport, arrived in 1958 in Bâle to the Bartók-Festival without money; the Trustee upon Peter's request gave him $1,000 to have cash over and above the hotel and food expenses, which were paid by the City of Bâle, because otherwise Béla could not have accounted for the fact that he was able to live for 14 days with his wife in Bâle. Yet, for this journey to New York he did not get dollars. Why? Because he was on official mission. Seemingly to help his brother, he was in fact here to aid and abet the scheme for the capture of the Bartók Estate—its moral and material value—for the Communists.

Appendix D. Victor Bator: Bartók, Politics, and "Dollar Imperialism" (ca. 1952–53)

This lecture by Bator was given before a Hungarian émigré audience in North America, most likely in New York City, in the early Cold War years. The exact occasion is not identified. Originally in Hungarian, the 14-page typescript is unfinished. It has been translated here by Etelka Nyilasi and David Nagy. Towards the end the lecture becomes looser and more fragmented, making clear the text's purpose as a working draft, an impression further encouraged by the numerous typewritten corrections and crossed out words ["xxxx" etc.] found on each page. Given the history of the Béla Bartók Archives, and the limited chances for survival of documents like this, it is unlikely that a polished or more complete draft of the speech will ever be found. It survives in a single copy in the Collection of Francis Bator.

In the speech Bator vigorously defends Béla Bartók from political propaganda emanating from Hungary. A recent pamphlet on Bartók made available by the Hungarian Consulate in Washington, D.C., provides him with many specific examples of how Bartók is being presented "as a Bolshevik, a friend of communism." It's important that Hungarians living abroad, he writes, "know the truth."

I.

First and foremost I wish to talk about Béla Bartók, the composer, but I feel that it would not be right to limit myself only to his compositions. In today's world, the performing artist is appreciated considerably more than the creating artist. I should therefore mention that the reason why Béla Bartók is not recognized more for his interpretive and performance work is that it took third place on the list of his interests. He only performed when he had to, when he needed money for survival. When he emigrated to the United States, where performances take place in front of "great" audiences (large audiences of questionable quality that bring in a lot of money from ticket sales), he was cast in the role of "composer," just as some actors get cast in the role of a "villain" and never get to play anything else. And he was not willing to start fresh, as a newcomer piano

Appendix D

virtuoso to be discovered in America. Now when I tell you who Béla Bartók was, I have to mention that as long as he practiced the profession, he was one of the greatest performing artists of his generation. If you want to measure greatness by money, he received honorariums equal to what the great piano virtuosos like Busoni and Schnabel got paid. This period did not last long, because he was not really interested in it and wanted to move on. Neither the cheering, clapping nor the money (and the performing artist receives much more of these than the composer, folk music collector or scientist) interested him. Later on in life he only performed when he could play his own compositions.

In the words of Constant Lambert, as a composer Bartók "is one of the dominating figures of our time." Lambert is one of the greatest authorities and connoisseurs of today's musicians (I recommend, to those interested, the Pelican Library edition of his book).

However, there is no need for me to discover all this for you. Everyone knows this much. I think that we Hungarians know that Bartók's greatness as a composer comes from the fact that he Hungarianized modern music, and that he gathered and discovered Hungarian folksongs and incorporated them into his compositional style. This much is definitely true. For those people in the audience who did not know this much about Bartók, I will say it again: Bartók's music is highly ethnic, Hungarian in style, incorporating many Hungarian themes. For those that already knew this much I am going to get to the important thing: This is not the essence of Bartók's greatness. He is not great or different from other composers because of this, but because he is one of the few composers who, despite using folk musical influences in his work, his music does not sound provincial or even exotic, but instead catches the interest of a highly educated individual with its so-called "Citizen of the World" characteristics.

Since I wish to correct any misconceptions, I am going to focus on the negative aspects of that previous phrase. It is not true that he is a pioneer of incorporating folk music, national elements, into his musical works. Compared to the universal classical music language of the 18th century, in the 19th century all over Europe we saw the rise of romantic, nationalist, proletarian (and thus not aristocratic) music. I want to mention a few of the real pioneers of this trend: In England we had Vaughan Williams, in Russia, Glinka and Mussorgsky. They used ethnic and folk elements in their music long before Bartók. The music of the 19th-century composers included folk elements not only because a folk song is the easiest and most available expression of ethnic feelings, but also because folk elements capture characteristics of the social and ideological aspects of a nation that can easily be incorporated into music. Even in Hungary as well, Bartók was preceded by Kodály's use of folk music, not as a craze, but as an essential element incorporated into his compositions. In fact, Kodály is really a more strictly Hungarian composer (as emphasized by Bartók in one of his articles) since he only used Hungarian folk music. Meanwhile, Bartók also incorporates Romanian, Slovakian and even North-African influences in his music.

So far I have only addressed Bartók's Hungarianness as a composer. When I talk about Bartók as a man I will also emphasize that Kodály was more exclusively Hungarian than Bartók. But getting back to music, Bartók's greatness comes from the fact that even though he borrows melodic and rhythmic elements from folk music, he transforms them into original music, giving them an individual characteristic. And even though folk music is traditionally short in length he builds it up into a large-scale composition. Most of the music based on ethnic themes and folk influences sticks to being short (as folk music is), even if it is not provincial. Those who enjoy listening to music and get to love Bartók's work do not have to face the same impediment as with other music that incorporates ethnic themes and folk music: that to really enjoy it you had to be Hungarian, or Czech or Russian. And some of his work is so architecturally grand that it can be only compared to the universal music written by the international classical composers of the 18th and 19th century.

Now I am glad to move on to the next part of my speech. I really do not know much about music and I just relayed you a lot of second hand information that I gathered by talking to excellent musicians. If I managed to do this eloquently, then that is a big achievement for me. I would not have mentioned much about Bartók as a composer had I not decided to help out the few people in the audience who do not know much about his work.

However, since success is also measured in terms of money, you might be interested to find out that in Bartók's case we have an occurrence that is common in cultural history: that it is not the artist/composer, but only his or her descendants who get to enjoy the fruit of the artists' work. Bartók's recognition did not wait until after his death. The fact that in Europe he was greatly recognized and appreciated, and despite not exerting too much effort, he could make a good living from his work. I'll get back to this subject when I talk about how Hungary and Hungarians have treated him. But when he arrived to the United States, his compositions were not yet successful here. However, today ASCAP—the organization that collects composer royalties from radios, concerts, and any public performance—reports that since 1948 in the category of "artistic" composers Bartók is the top-ranking composer. He receives the most royalties. Of course, this is only compared to those composers whose works are still subject to royalties, not Beethoven or Mozart, whose works are part of the public domain.

~~I have already talked about why Bartók rises above other composers, why he's a great composer; one of the greatest composers of our generation. Of course, one cannot determine with a vote who is the greatest among them. But there is a reason to declare that Bartók stands out among other modern composers who use folk material.~~[1]

Bartók's significance and magnitude in music culture is not only based on the prominent position he occupies as a composer in the world of music literature. He was, no doubt, Europe's and America's most recognized expert in the field of folk music. To prevent any misunderstanding when I am talking about Hungarian folk music, I do not mean the 100 or 200 songs that have been adapted by the gypsy orchestras and using their Oriental creativity have been changed sometimes beyond recognition. Also many of these "gypsy" songs are not even of Hungarian origin, but of Slavic origin (for example the song "Azt mondják nem adnak engem galambomnak" ("They say they're not giving me to my honey"). Thus I am not talking about pseudo folk-influenced musical works, including those with gypsy influences, or the ones that only have a couple of verses and are composed by dilettante composers like Szentirmay, Simonffy, Dankó and Frater.

I am talking about peasant music that expresses the feelings of the peasant class; with a multitude of melodies that have similar characteristics and melodic structures across regions. These melodies were created by people uninfluenced, or only marginally influenced, by urban culture, separated from the mud with its ancient, ideal simplicity.[2] This is the folk music that influences composers not only in Hungary but also worldwide.

Between 1905 and 1909 Bartók, Kodály, László Lajtha, Antal Molnár and others gathered in the old Hungarian territory approximately 8,000 Hungarian, 2,800 Slovak, 3,500 Romanian and 150 other ethnic origin (Ruthenian, Serbian, Bulgarian, gypsy) melodies. Most of these melodies had been recorded with a phonogram.

When it became evident in 1918 that there were no further opportunities to continue the gathering of songs, Bartók and his collaborators turned towards scientific analysis of the gathered material. When it comes to Hungarian folk music Bartók and Kodály are at the same level, but Bartók surpassed all the others when it comes to the folk music of the neighboring countries. He also

---

1   These lines are crossed out by hand in the draft.
2   In the margin Bator adds a handwritten note, in Hungarian, that reads, "Acquisition from a village, where no one knows how to read or write."

stands out because of his scientific analysis and categorization of the material. To make a comparison for those that have no knowledge of this field, his activities in the field of folk music analysis can be compared with what, for example, Linnaeus achieved in botany. He created a structure, with categories, for folk music that made it possible to analyze and compare folk music from different countries and regions. Before Bartók, folk music collections were like Erk's and Boehme's *Deutscher Liederhort*, where they were grouped based on the words on the song, and the publisher left out everything that he considered inappropriate. Just think about editing the Bible, because we consider parts of it inappropriate!

The importance of studying folk music reaches far beyond musical interests. Comparative folk music study can shed light on the cultural connections of ancient tribes that were separated at one point, the relationship between neighboring ethnic groups, and their similarities or differences. All of this analysis is still in its infancy. Bartók's uniqueness and greatness can also be proven with the following facts: 1) in 1937 he gathered folk music in Turkey and in 1913 in North Africa he collected Arabic music in the Biskra region; 2) he published his collection of Hungarian folk songs in three languages (Hungarian, German and English); 3) he wrote a book about Romanian, Slovakian, and Turkish folk music that has been published jointly by Columbia and Harvard; 4) he analyzed a uniquely rich collection of Serbian folk music. (Nevertheless, he was not Serbian, nor American, but there was no expert that he could be compared to in this field in any of those regions.) That being said, within the boundaries of this lecture, I believe I have sufficiently characterized his uniqueness.

For a minute let's get back to the fact that he was the 20th century's greatest composer, or at least one of the three major composers. We also have to consider that you can't really enter the world of folk music just by reading about it. To quote Bartók: "Those who want to get beyond the dead surface of the melodies, those who want to truly experience the lively life of this folk music, have to experience it first hand, and that is only possible through direct contact with peasants. In order to fully get under the influence of this music—which is necessary if it is to influence our compositions—it is not enough to learn the melodies. It is equally important to see and experience the environment in which these melodies are alive. I have to emphasize that when we collected this music our goal was not only to incorporate them in their entirety or partially into our own work and to modify it using traditional techniques. This would have been the work of a craftsman. Our task was to get to know the essence of this so far unknown music and then starting from this essence to create a new musical style. This is why we had to personally do the collection of the songs on location."

Appendix D

For Bartók to create the music he did, three things had to come together: great composing genius, lengthy collection of folk music from different countries, and detailed knowledge of the collections made by him and others. His music is unique, original at the national and universal level. He was truly a unique figure in music history.

II

Under ordinary circumstances a presentation about the life of a composer would end right here. The exception to this rule might of course be Paderewski, who also played a political role. Bartók is an exception in this regard, too. Although he did not play an active political role, his name and figure has and had political meaning during the last six years of his life. He was such an important figure in Hungary that his political orientation was also important. His greatness as a musician is for eternity, but the interest in his political orientation is temporary. 10–20 years from now nobody will care about his political affiliation. But today, when the Hungarian government (if we can call it a government) tries to use Bartók's name and his figure for propaganda purposes, they try to present him as the friend of Hungarian "popular democracy," basically as a Bolshevik, a friend of communism. It is important that we—Hungarians living abroad—know the truth.

For those that are not aware of this propaganda I am going to tell you the form that it takes here in the United States.

If you request it by mail, the Hungarian Consulate in Washington DC will send you a printed pamphlet. They've sent it to me too although they don't like me too much. This pamphlet includes 4 contributions and 4 letters written by Bartók. The first contribution is from Kodály. There is not a word that is political in his 5-page essay. Nobody can coerce Kodály, even today. He only writes the truth; maybe there is half a sentence in which he makes a little concession to those in power. It is hardly noticeable. The second contributor is Bence Szabolcsi. Szabolcsi is a professional musician and musicologist, and his article "Bartók and Folk Music" is not political or filled with propaganda. That's it for Captatio benevolentiae. This is the extent of objectivity in this pamphlet. In the next article we find out that "our Bartók is an example to the young composers in the West who are looking for new roads to explore, who have had enough of bourgeois music and its misery. This desire has inspired more and more of them to join the Society of Progressive Composers (Haladó Zeneszerzők Szövetsége). As a result of this, more and more composers are leaving the ISCM musical conglomerate. Under this influence more composers rely on help and inspiration from the top musical culture: the music of the Socialist Soviet Union. It is of great meaning to us Hungarians that Bartók has been a role model for these young composers." Of course the writer, András Mihály, has no evidence in order to back up his statements. The only evidence he has is a statement in a French journal, "Les Temps Modernes," the official mouthpiece of Sartre's existentialism, in which the author—Leibovitz—criticizes Bartók because he did not become or remain a supporter of the music theories developed by the Austrian composer Schönberg. He does not substantiate that there are more and more communist composers, or that these communist composers would be followers of Bartók. But those who do not read the article carefully might not notice this and might find this kind of András Mihály-style "wishful thinking" believable.

Finally comes the pièce de résistance written by Ferenc Szabó, professor at the music academy, with his article entitled "Hands Off Bartók." Professor Szabó is one of those independent figures that, while living under a communist government, decided to write a symphony about our father Stalin. I notice in the journal *Opera*, already in fall 1945, that Mr. Szabó Ferenc was writing a cantata with the title "Stalin's Rule." So with simple deductions, this Mr. Szabó brings forth the following "facts."[3] He tries to convince the innocent readers: "You, reactionary Americans and other dollar imperialists, claim Bartók as your own and in order to achieve world dominance and to start a new bloody world war you want to enlist him as a supporter of new American fascism." All of this is included in the pamphlet that can be requested free of charge by anybody. This pamphlet has been translated beautifully into English from Hungarian. Now, here comes the proof. Bartók was against the Habsburg Empire, and in his youth he was inspired by Kossuth and the 1848 revolution, so much so that he dedicated his first symphony to Kossuth. It is true, says Szabó, that in this Bartók only sees the fight for Hungarian independence but the truth is that "the 1848–1849 revolution had as its main goal the elimination of feudalism. The revolution for independence was only a side consequence." Now I am going to quote Prof. Szabó word for word: "The young Bartók could not know this, since the Marxist-Leninist characteristic of the 1848–1849 revolution only became known later." However "the reinstatement of the Habsburg Empire is one of the most detailed achievements in imperialistic America's plan for worldwide dominance." It is evident to everybody that this new enslavement would mean exploitation and suffering to our nation, brought about by the Habsburgs. Since the Habsburgs only stayed in power

---

3 The typescript here includes four extra lines tightly squeezed in the bottom margin, with some handwritten corrections. From the context it is unclear whether they were intended to continue the previous sentence. The lines read: "but he also writes sentences such as "Bartók, with typical 1908 Hungarian nationalist slogans, is also beginning his Romanian, Slovakian and Russian folk collections," forgetting that Kodály was 3 pages ahead of the game, and that this was a 1500-crown Hungarian state scholarship."

because of American imperialist benevolence, they would follow the beck and call of Americans. And since Bartók was anti-Habsburg, which is indeed true, he was therefore on 100% on the same side as the Szabó communists.

The second conclusion that helps him enlist Bartók as a comrade goes like this: "Bartók did not only gather Hungarian folk music, but Hungarian, Romanian, Slovak and Bulgarian folk music all came together in a unified style. Bartók had understood Kossuth's teachings stemming from the 48–49 revolution and from his years of exile: that the nations on the Danube cannot be really free and independent without brotherly collaboration." … "From the activities of Titoish-American-English spies in Southeastern Europe it became evident that their major goal was to sabotage the good relations between various Southeastern European nations." … "Based on the teachings of the great leader of the Soviet Union, Stalin, the nations of Czechoslovakia, Hungary, Romania, and Bulgaria do not understand that their independence and happiness hinges on reciprocal goodwill and understanding." … "Bartók's life work has no relation with the dollar imperialism that allows the politics of the Habsburgs, Mussolinis, and Hitlers to continue." Here now I am going to interrupt the quoting in order to emphasize that even if there was such a thing as dollar imperialism, Bartók's work can have no relation to it. How could it? But professor Szabó does not say this. Instead he writes that "Kossuth's revolutionary tradition and the musical voice that Bartók brings to it, is boldly materialistic and free-thinking, and emphasizes the friendship and brotherhood of the nations living along the Danube, while turning against the inhumanity of fascism. Bartók is an integral and inseparable part of us, even if we do not agree with some of Bartók's views."

After all this, you would think that they, over there, truly love Bartók's music, truly recognize him, or at least that everyone is free to love Bartók, his music, all his work, or as much as they choose to. Of course, this is not the case. Ferenc Szabó's article justifies such naive thinking. "Bartók's art, though, is so great and brilliant, as he has left it behind with us, in its entirety and all its integrity, that it cannot continue … We have to shake off the foreign influences of Bartók's folk-rooted music and all that is unsuitable for expressing the spirit and spirituality of our time. The enormous artistic value of his music cleansed from slag…" pay attention to this, "cleansed from the <u>mud</u>" etc. etc. "In Hungary, we primarily play the works in which the new Plebeian voice, the folk music base and the classical traditions of the past, clearly unfold" (Oh, and don't anyone dare not to follow this advice, especially since the English phrase "we play" is expressed in Hungarian as "játsszunk" with 2 sz's, which is not in the indicative mood, but the imperative mood.)[4]

---

4   Parenthetical insertion as found in the original text.

Following all this, Szabó continues, "Bartók is with us and belongs to the camp of peace. He has nothing to do with the dollar imperialists and warriors for war instigators and for those preparing for the New World War." "Descendants of Göbbels: You have to put an end to the stupid comedy with his name. Bartók is non-negotiable."

Before I turn to the fact that this propaganda is actually effective, it is impossible to resist the temptation to talk about another Bartók article. These four articles, which are distributed here by the Embassy in Washington, are good, and I must again mention the excellent and faithful translations of the 4 articles, published in the Hungarian Composer's and Author's Association's *Új Zenei Szemle* [New Music Review] in September 1950 in a separate issue published on the anniversary of Bartók's death. In this issue, apart from these four articles, however, there is a fifth, which was not included in the Washington issue. Of course the order is different in the Hungarian journal. Over there, Szabó's article is the headline, and is the first one, and Kodály's is obscured at the end. However, the longest article is a second treatise not published in English. "Bartók is Ours" from Sándor Asztalos. In this article, Bartók is "led by an upright congregation, the intent of rebellion," his work is full of "conscious political content"; "the turning point of the folk song is the sharp voice of plebeian's political aspirations," his artistic and scientific work is the most decisive, with democratic aspirations. "At the 1928 Prague International Folklorist Congress, as a political protest, wherever Bartók sat, he sat next to the god-like Russian folklorist Bjelarev"… [words missing] save a Russian intellect as well, who might have wanted to escape, but due to a small incident that also has to do with me; but if someone doesn't believe the lies that this sort of Soviet aesthetic is capable of, I will offer a partial explanation.

Page L8[5]

It is of course essential to bear in mind, as it is in all other respects, that from the premise that someone who in this case was an enemy of the Nazis, fascists, and the Arrow Cross, it does not necessarily follow that this person is communist; he might just as easily be against the communists for the same reasons. The fact that this was the case with Bartók, I will prove shortly; but first I want to point out that this anti-Bartók propaganda here in America was not entirely ineffective.

Bartók Memorial Celebration. See Times.

Or take the WABF radio station's broadcast from May 1951. This is the radio station that only delivers good artistic music to its listeners, and on Sundays, it broadcasts listeners' suggestions, without any advertising.

---

5 This notation, which seems to point to an insertion on a separate page, is found in the original. It marks a change in the nature of the speech draft. From this point forward Bator's text becomes increasingly loose and fragmented, with references to books and articles he will quote from, but lacking the actual quotations, almost like a first draft of a speech.

Appendix D

Program Magazine, pages 17–18

It is obvious that there is a connection between this article and the propaganda found in the aforementioned brochures. "His incomplete grasp of the baffling problems" is the same as Professor Szabó's suggestion that he did not find the way to Stalinist truth. Or that his works have been censored and officially denounced due to the expression of the aspirations of a people suffering a slave-like fate, and so on.

At this point, we can now deal with the accusation of condemnation and censorship.

Let's begin with the concerts. The Philharmonic Society presented 10 concerts a year. Bartók's Kossuth Symphony from his youth was his first performed work in 1904. During the following 40 years until 1943, the Philharmonic had Bartók works 80 times, that is, every 5th concert. However, if I leave out the years before 1908, Bartók's younger years, when there were not many works to be performed, they performed 78 works in 35 years, that is, every fourth concert. And if I take January 1, 1918, as a starting point, that is, 25 years, there were 250 concerts, during this time 73 Bartók works were performed by the Philharmonic, that is, 3 a year. From 1928 onwards, in 15 years, 55 Bartók works were performed, alternating 3–4. Of course, there are no statistics about other philharmonic orchestra concerts, but at first Bartók's most notable compositions were not for orchestra, but were rather chamber music, played by all Hungarian musicians and even many foreigners. Yet, as the Philharmonic Society's Orchestra was the same as the State Opera Orchestra, the statistics presented are quite typical; my statistics showed a total of 20 Bartók compositions.

What's the truth about the fact that official circles disapproved of his folk song collecting activity? In 1907, at the age of 26, he became a professor at the Academy of Music. Also in 1907, as he became interested in collecting folk songs, he won a 1,600 gold crown scholarship to study Székely folk music. He regularly presented his Romanian and Slovakian research at the Ethnographic Society's meetings. True, he often complained that the research was difficult among Hungarians, that it was much easier to gather among the Romanians, and the Slovaks. However, as a result of attacks after the war, even from Hubay, because of his reports on Romanian folk songs and folk culture, he wrote the following in defense, or rather as a counterattack: *[quotation missing]*

And to refute "the rumour of the official disapproval," I quote the Hungarian Folk Society's Bartók statement on the day of publication and the publication of another statement two days later: "There is nothing in Bartók's essay that would undermine the national feeling or be deemed foolish to our enemies, in fact, it is more likely to refute the accusation of suppressing nationalities. The panel members do not identify themselves, with their attack (against Bartók) which has no substantive basis, and their protests against the freedom of scientific work."

There were problems with the performance of only one of his works, the Miraculous Mandarin, which was delayed twice before its debut. First, after the dress rehearsal, Bartók refused to allow the performance to go ahead, as he did not believe it was good enough. The second time Mandarin was cancelled was in the 30s. I do not know the facts precisely—I am currently researching them—allegedly the Catholic Church protested due to the telling the story of a street girl in an opera. For the sake of simplicity, let us accept this. They were not against Bartók's music, but against Melchior Lengyel's pantomime tale, which was not the result of Bartók's initiative, but completely independent of him. The story was published in Nyugat in 1917 before Bartók's music was ever written. On the other hand, Mandarin was also performed by the Philharmonic between 1928 and 1936 a total of 5 times. Not that many times, in fact it was not enough at all, but nevertheless there was neither censorship nor prohibition.

Returning back to Bartók's folk song collecting activity; in 1928 Bartók was at the Prague International Congress, where, as we recall, according to professor Mr. Asztalos, he constantly sat next to the Russian ethnographer in protest. This story is probably just as true as the "suburban school singer, with working-class children, where, as I have said, my son also sang." So Bartók presented the following there:

Page 28, Bartók's writings on music

Of course, Bartók talked about this issue in a different way as well. Especially from his position in the Academy, he stood strongly against the behavior of Hungarian rural gentlemen who were against Gypsy musicians and Hungarian peasant music. And this was also true. Not just one rural Hungarian man but he encountered many, of one type or another. However, during the First World War, Bartók collected Hungarian soldiers' songs with the support of the Minister of Defense, which they published in Pécs, and also, with the permission of the Minister of Public Education, he was granted full pay in 1934 from the Academy of Music for the time he put into his arrangements of the material from his folk song collection.

After the rebuttal of the Communist liars, it is now time to illustrate that the Bolsheviks are absolutely right that Bartók was very anti-Nazi, anti-royal, and hated all the manifestations of fascism, even Japanese fascism, of which he could not have known very much about. I'll read some excerpts from his letters.

[the lecture breaks off here]

Index

(numbers in italics refer to illustration captions)

Alice M. Ditson Fund, 345n4
American Foundation for Hungarian Literature and Education, 321
American Hungarian Foundation, 321, 341
American Hungarian Library and Historical Society, 321
Amerikai Magyar Népszava, 39, 60, 72, 298, 301
András, Ernő, 127, 128, 250n4
Anschluss, 17, 18, 62
Antokoletz, Elliott, 10–13, 55, 85n71, 213, 217, 333, 335
Applebaum, Anne, 134n27
Artists and Writers Relief Fund, 50
Asbury, Edith Evans, 209
ASCAP, 49, 52, 77, 94, 96, 230, 251n5, 256, 271, 310, 345, 361, 369, 371, 397

Backhaus, Wilhelm, 3, 179
Balázs, Béla, 169
Banhálmi, George, 155–57
Báron, Alexander, 178
Báron, Gyula (Julius), 6, 52, *56*, 67, 68n30, 76, *86*, 87, 88, 118, 120, 121, 128, 157, 174–84, *185*, *186*, 188, 189, 190, 192, 193, 219, 231, 240, 250, 261, 289, 290, 369, 389
Báron, Jónás, 177
Bartók, Béla
    American Last Will and Testament (1943), 7, 22, 48, 111, 117, 118, 121, 128, 130, 137, 139, 141, 230, 250, 251, 272, 277, 392
    and moderate patriotism, 71–72, 321–22
    Bluebeard's Castle, 9–11, 13, 101, 107, 108, 226, 228, 333
    Cantata Profana, 66
    Contrasts, 20
    deathbed Will (1945), 7, 112, 116, 123–26, 128, 230, 272, 283
    distaste for communism, 43, 71, 307, 308, 341, 400
    First Violin Concerto, 19, 21, 83, 260, 263
    Five Songs, Op. 15, 182, 190
    friendship with Victor Bator, 24, 25, 43, 46, 51, 58, 88, 176
    funeral in New York, 89
    Hungarian Last Will and Testament (1940), 7, 22, 125–29, 138–40, 146–48, 233, 238, 249, 250, 266, 326
    involvement with Movement for Independent Hungary, 61, 62, 68, 70–74, 88, 313, 321
    leukemia and final illness, 6, 49, 74, 76, 77, 81, 82, 111, 136
    Mikrokosmos, 1, 19, 21, 83, 105–8, 222, 271, 280, 364
    Music for Strings Percussion and Celesta, 12, 13, 77
    political orientation during World War II, 71, 400
    Rumanian folk music study, 4, 5, 9, 21, 30, 99, 282, 293, 310, 311, 344, 397, 398, 401n3, 402
    Serbo-Croatian folk music study, 4, 78, 99
    Slovak folk music study, 21, 167, 169n7, 344, 397, 398, 399, 401n3, 402
    Solo Sonata for violin, 223
    Sonata for Two Pianos and Percussion, 20
    Suite for Two Pianos, Op. 4b, 313–14

Index

Suite, Op. 14, 155
Third Piano Concerto, 1, 79, 91, 92, 99n4, 104, 105, 108, 109, 111, 231, 256, 271, 352
Trust Agreement of 1940, 21, 22, 51, 127
Turkish folk music study, 4, 167, 399
Viola Concerto, 7, 15n13, 102, 111, 133, 149n55, 212, 227, 249n3, 256, 257m 359
visa and immigration matters, 4, 46, 55–59, 68, 73–75, 85, 87, 88, 173, 178
Bartók Jr, Béla, 6, 21, 58n11, 118, 123, 124, 126–28, 137–45, 154, 201, 202, 218, 223, 233, 234, 236–44, 246, 247, 249–54, 261, 262, 265–69, 272, 276–78, 290, 310, 311, 322, 327, 349, 351, 354–68, 370–85, 388–94
Bartók, Ditta
  activities in America, 1, 57, 111, 114, 115, 173, 313
  as beneficiary of husband's wills, 6, 117–28
  involvement in litigation (1959 onward), 252, 253, 262, 267–72, 275, 286
  legal documents from 1946, 130, *131*
  mental health care in America, 77, 89, 136, 137
  mental health care in Hungary, 136, 137, 151, 153
  piano lessons with Bator family, 1, 55, *221*
  return to Hungary in 1946, 5, 130, 133, 135, 139, 152, 191, 221
  schizophrenia diagnosis and treatment, 136, 137, 152, 153
Bartók Estate
  21 works, litigation over, 218, 231, 248, 251, 252, 262, 350, 374, 383, 384
  battles with communist Hungary, 115, 148, 218, 246, 248, 249, 255, 286, 311, 328
  first intermediate accounting, 235n1, 255, 263–65, 273, 306n66
  Interpretive Declaration of 1951, 145, 249–52, 266, 272, 278, 307, 360–64, 366, 369, 371, 372, 376–78, 381, 382
  Litigation of 1959–61, 132n35, 147, 148, 212, 214, 233–44, 252, 256, 265–75, 277, 324, 385
  Referee's Report (1971), 294–97, 310
  second intermediate accounting, 265, 286, 288, 294, 295
  two trustees named by Bartók in Will, 6, 14, 21, 22, 76, 88, 90, 118–21, 127, 184, 189, 219, 250, 373, 381

Bartók, János, 253, 306n67
Bartók, Márta, 143
Bartók, Peter
  as named in his father's wills, 7, 124, 126, 143, 239
  Bartók Records, establishment of and early activities, 218, 221, 223, 224, 227, 228, 256, 257
  career as recording engineer, 221–24, 226, 227, 258
  early years in America, 46, 47, 50, 55, 56, 78, 226, 227, 229, 303, 319
  escape from Hungary, 46, 53, 56, 58, 59, 68, 73, 79
  in service for U.S. Navy, 47, 54n1, 218
  involvement in litigation of 1959–61, 45, 214–16, 221, 233, 235, 236n2, 237, 239, 254, 265–68, 271–74, 309, 324, 327, 385, 390
  My Father, 55n1, 56, 58n9, 73, 77, 88, 115
  recording of Bluebeard's Castle, 101, 103, 106, 107, 226, 228, 333
  recording of First Piano Concerto, 151, 164, 226, 257–59, 323
  recording of Folk Songs of Hungary, 225
  recording of Violin Solo Sonata, 223
  relationship with Victor Bator, 8, 88, 90, 93, 95, 97–99, 101, 103, 106, 107, 112, 115, 148, 151, 154–56, 158, 196–99, 203–8, 209, 211, 212, 216, 219–21, 226, 243, 250, 256, 274, 275, 286, 287, 303, 309, 319, 322, 327
Bartók Records, 10, 13, 158, 206–8, 212n5, 218, 222–28, 256, 257, 259, 260, 268, 271, 283, 284, 286, 287, 306, 329
Basel, 13, 18–21, 87n73, 202, 211, 212n5, 257, 260–63, 266, 329, 332, 377, 380, 394
Bator, Christopher, 15n12, 26, 236n2, *319*, 320, 331
Bator, Francis, 1, 4n2, 6, 8, 14, 15, 24, 25n19, 26n21, 30, 31, 34, 54n2, 56, 58n9, 60, 68n30, 69, *86*, 90, 115, 136, 174–76, 178, 181, 182, 184, *186*, *187*, 188, 189, 195, 209–11, 220, 221n18, 229n32, 260, 292, 294, 317n4, *319*, 320, 322, 325, 331, 335, 341, 395
Bator, Franciska, 26, 27, 36, *41*, 180, *185*, *186*
Bator, Paul, 41, 42, *86*, *221*, 235, 319
Bator, Peter, 41, *86*, 302n60, *319*
Bator, Victor
  as guardian of Bartók's manuscripts before 1945, 22, 82–85

Index

career at Pesti Magyar Kereskedelmi Bank, 25n17, 26, 32, 60, 135
creation of Béla Bartók Archives in 1963, 6, 30, 31, 190, 278–91, 314, 321, 329
early career in Budapest, 25–29, 31–35
education, 25
experiences with Béla Bartók, 1940–45, 23, 24, 45–52, 54–60, 67, 68, 71–85, 87–90
home on E. 72nd St., 37, 39, 55, 82, 221, 249n2, 264, 276, 282, 301, 314
home on Somlói utca, 28, 57, 177n12
Hungarian citizenship revoked (1941), 31, 229
Hungarian citizenship revoked (ca. 1948), 229
law publications in Hungary, 29–31
lawsuit against Béla Bartók Jr., 233–44, 277, 278
lawsuit against Columbia Records, 111n1, 231, 271
litigation over Bartók Estate, 2, 8, 9, 14, 41, 45, 79, 92, 112, 123, 132n25, 141, 147, 175n8, 206, 207, 209, 211–16, 221, 228, 229n31, 231, 233–48, 252, 254, 256, 265–77, 283, 284, 286, 288, 294, 324–27, 331, 343n2, 385–94
pension used for Ditta Bartók's benefit, 135, 140, 301
position in Hungarian émigré community in New York City, 37, 72, 174, 179, 181, 189, 220, 317–21
relationship with Béla Bartók Jr., 349–84
relationship with Ditta Bartók, 87, 89, 135–37, 152–54, 191, 219, 230, 254, 270, 274, 283, 285, 303, 306, 308–11, 349–84
relationship with Peter Bartók, 216, 219, 221, 224n23, 256, 275, 292, 349–84
vacation home in Nonquitt, 37, 39, 54n2, 55, 56, 67, 68, 85, 86, 87, 114, 155, 177, 182, 185, 221, 236n2, 318, 319
Vietnam—A Diplomatic Tragedy, 30, 40, 299–301, 307, 317
Bean, Betty, 101, 103
Beneš, Edward, 72, 346n
Berény, Róbert, 4, 279, *293*, 326
Berger, Arthur, 10, 175
Billings Hospital Chicago, 178, 182
Bónis, Ferenc, 126
Boosey & Hawkes, 5, 17, 19, 21n9, 22, 23, 46, 51, 79, 82–84, 91, 94–96, 111n1, 127, 191, 222, 230–32, 234, 246, 248, 253, 256, 263, 271, 279, 284, 286, 288, 313, 314, 350, 352, 358, 363, 366–68, 371, 382
Boosey, Leslie, 6
Börösmény-Nagy, Béla, 159–61
Bosch Co., 35, 36
Botos, János, 25n19, 60n14
Braiolou, Constantin, 163
Brem, Lujza, 46, 57–59
Brinkmann, Reinhold, 12–14
Budapest Bartók Archive, 13, 24, 326, 332
Bull, Storm, 10, 175

Chatel, Andor, 136, 137, 151, 152, 155, 176n10, 187, 197, 198, 309
Chatel, Luigia, 187
Chatel, Marie, 176n10
Chicago Symphony Orchestra, 155n4
Chorin, Ferenc, 60, 61, 65, 187, 188, 321
CIA, 41, 298
Clapp, Phillip, 190, 191
Club, The, 176, 177, 184, 188, 190
Cobb, Candler, 3, 37, 54n1, 66
Columbia Broadcasting, 91, 98, 105, 106, 109
Columbia Records, 82, 101, 104, 106, 111n1, 231, 271
Columbia University, 6, 21, 31, 48–50, 54, 59, 62, 74, 75, 78, 81, 87, 92, 99, 111n1, 171, 172, 190, 210n2, 282, 341, 345
Compulsory Share (in Hungarian estate law), 143
Coolidge, Elizabeth Sprague, 50, 77
Creel, Wilhelmine, 53
Crow, Todd, 125, 126, 149

Darvas, Lili, 40
Deadline Data on World Affairs, 41, 298, *299*, 301
Deák, Ferenc (Francis), 74, 75
Demény, János, 125, 128, 144, 146, 147, 252
Diamond, David, 10, 175
DiFalco, Surrogate Samuel, 132n25, 149, 206, 207, 233, 273–75, 285, 288, 294, 309, 324, 329, 385
Dover Editions, 9
Dreisziger, Nándor, 61, 62, 69, 70, 72, 73
Dulles, Allen, 3, 34, 36, 298, 300
Dulles, John Foster, 34–36, 300

Eckhardt, Ferenc, 176n10
Eckhardt, Tibor, 3, 59, 62–75, 177, 320–22, 346, 347
Eisenhower, Dwight, 300, 306, 315n3

409

Index

Ess, Henry C., 235, 238, 269, 273n32, 294
estate law, Hungarian, 31, 147
estate law, American, 111n1, 118

Fabinyi, Tihamér, 25
Fackenthal, Frank, 49, 78, 80
Fawcett, Edmund, 320
FBI, 213
Fenyő, Miksa, 133
Fosler-Lussier, Danielle, 144, 145
Frank, Tibor, 173

GEMA, 310
Geyer, Stefi, 5, 18, 59, 209, 212, 257, 260, 262, 284, 294, 325
Goldman, Milton, 122, 294–97, 310
Goodman, Benny, 50
Groton Academy, 36, 41

Habernal, Erich, 238, 241, 244, 276, 277
Hajnal, Tibor, 46, 59, 136, 152, 154, 198
Hambro, Leonid, 151, 223, 257, 259n12
Hart, Lorenz, 46, 121, 180
Harvard University, 1, 3, 11, 12, 41, 42, 49, 76–78, 80, 174, 210, 294, 345, 399
Hawkes, Ralph, 21, 22n10, 23, 59, 118, 230, 231
Heinsheimer, Hans, 21, 82, 84, 88, 94
Hennings, Peter, 215n10, 329, 332
Hertzka, Emil, 43
Herz, Otto, 156
Herzog, George, 21–23, 51, 53, 99, 118, 127, 199
Holló, Ágnes, 55, 56n5
Holló, Elsa, 56n5, *121*, 181
Holló, Gyula, 56n5, 76, 77, 115, *121*, 136, 180, 181, 189, 318
Holzman, Jac, 227–29
Homosassa, Florida, 9, 59n12, 127n21, 130n23, 137, 140n39, 211, 258n10, 281n43, 308n70, 329, 333
Horthy, Nikolaus (Miklós), 60, 62, 63, 229n32, 321
Hungarian Commercial Bank (*see* Pesti Magyar Kereskedelmi Bank)

Imrédy, Béla, 3, 25, 37, 60
Independent Smallholders Party, 63, 133

Jászi, Oszkár, 69
Johnson, Lyndon, 3, 42, 294

Kárpáti, János, 126
Kecskeméti, Elizabeth, 89, 218, 222, 303, 352

Kecskeméti, Paul, 71, 89, 218, 303, 351, 352
Kempner, Paul, 3, 35, 38n43, 39
Keresztes, Béla, 226, 233, 253, 354–56, 364, 365, 369, 371, 372, 374, 375, 378, 381, 388
Kiely, Michael, 151, 165
Kirk, Grayson, 171, 172
Kirstein, Lincoln, 102
Klub, The (*see* Club, The)
Kodály, Zoltán, 2, 39, *41*, 48, 144, 254, *292*, 293, 342, 389, 396–98, 400, 401n3, 403
Koussevitzky, Serge, 77, 78, 80, 81, 95, 279
Kroó, György, 313

Lambert, Marie, 211, 324n17, 326n19
Lamotte, Károly, 60
Lang, Paul Henry, 6, 49, 53, 62, 69, 80, 160, 208, 285
Laurvik, Elma, 278, 279
Lax, Henry, 179, 318, 319
Lenoir, Yves, 77
Lieberson, Goddard, 50, 82, 101, 104, 106–8
Lincoln Center for the Performing Arts, 6, 151, 170, 281, 282
Lisbon, *33*, 46, 59
Lucas, Sarah, 191n33, 332
Lynn, Katalin Kádár, 61, 64, 69, 322n13, 334

Mád Vineyard of Sichermann Family, 26, 134, *135*, 230n34
Manheim, Harold, 85, 111–18, 123, 128, 130, 137, 230n33, 231, 251
Mannheimer, Fritz, 35, 36
Martin, Jean and Yolanda, 319
Maull, Baldwin, 3, 35
Maurice, Donald, 15n12, 149n55
McDonald, Harl, 9, 95–97, 108, 109
McNitzky, Mark, 3, 59
Mendelssohn & Co. Bank, 3, 35, 38n43, 39
Mendelssohn, George, 151, 161, 162
Menuhin, Yehudi, 3, 6, 98, 147, 247, 260
Merritt, Tillman, 76, 77, 174
Meyer, Felix, 329, 332
Mihály, András, 144, 146, 401
Moore, Douglas, 49, 50, 80, 88, 224
Moreux, Serge, 151, 158–60, 256
Mount Sinai Hospital, 49
Movement for Independent Hungary, 61, 62, 68–75, 88, 313, 320–22
Müller-Widmann, Anne, 18, 19, 24, 125, 345
Murdock, James Oliver, 59n12

Index

Nabokov, Vladimir, 10
National Institute of Arts and Letters, 52
Natvar, 26n21, 38, 40, 79, 281, 301
Nettl, Bruno, 174, 190
New Music String Quartet, 222
New York Bartók Archive, 2, 9, 11–13, 18n4, 30, 56, 62, *116*, 127n21, 148, 175, 189, 213
New York Surrogate's Court, 8, 117n10, 214, 219, 235n1, 267, 273, 294, 304, 305, 343n2
Nonquitt, Massachusetts, 37, 39, 54n2, 55, *56*, *67*, 68, 85, *86*, 87, 114, 155, 177, 182, *185*, 221, 236n2, 318, *319*
Nyevicsky, Lórant, 25

Office for the Protection of Authors' Rights, Budapest, 275, 278, 327, 375, 380, 386, 388, 389
Oppenheimer, Bernard, 76, 77
Ormandy, Eugene, 6, 13, 93–95, 101, 103, 104, 106, 108, 109, 226, 247
Oxford University Press, 151, 166

Palágyi, Róbert, 143, 201, 233, 252, 253, 260, 262, 266, 278, 285, 307, 322, 326, 327, 355, 366, 371, 373–75, 380, 381, 388, 389
Pelényi, John, 59n13, 61n17, 63–66, 73, 320–22
Pesti Magyar Kereskedelmi Bank, 25n17, 26, 32, *33*, 38, 60, 135
Philadelphia Orchestra, 50, 91, 93–98, 101, 104, 106–9, 226, 231
Puskás, Julianna, 61

Raj, Ferenc, 176, 184
Raj, László, 176, 184
Rákosi, Mátyás, 69, 142
Ránki, György, 33
Reiner, Fritz (Frigyes), 53, 147, 155n4, 157
Rockefeller, John D., 151, 170, 188, 282
Rosen, Gustav, 112, 235, 236, 238, 265, 267, 268, 271, 273, 275, 278n37, 294
Rosenthal, Nathan, 76
Roth, Ernest, 234, 255, 368
Rothko, Mark, 122
Rothman, Stephen, 156, 157, 179
Ruffy, Péter, 125–27, 147–49

Sacher Foundation/Stiftung (Basel), 13, 14, 212n5, 215n10, 263n18, 332
Sacher, Paul, 13, 18, 24, 147n53, 215n9, 246, 256n9, 260, 261, 263, 284, 302n60, 323, 325, 345

Sándor, George, 53, 91, 93–95, 98, 104, 109, 231
Saranac Lake, 52, 54, 87, 111
Schnabel, Arthur, 3, 179, 396
Schneeberger, Hansheinz, 260, 261
Schulhof, Andrew, 21, 53
Schulthess, Walter, 18, 19, 20, 59
Serly, Tibor, 13, 53, 57, 71n40, 72n43, 91–93, 95, 151, 164, 166, 173, 181n24, 209, 210n2, 222, 258, 259, 261n16
Somfai, László, 13, 18n3, 213, 313, 328
Soviet estate law, 142, 144
Stenger, László, 69
Stevens, Halsey, 125, 159, 220, *302*, 326
Stravinsky, Igor, 12, 122, 246
Stravinsky, Vera, 122, 136
Studia Musicologica, 2, 332
Sullivan and Cromwell, 34–38, 54n1, 214, 235, 269–71, 273, 298
Szabó, Ferenc, 144, 347, 401–4
Szabolcsi, Bence, 126, 400
Szigeti, Joseph, 3, 6, 18, 49, 50, 77–79, 81, 82n66, 247
Szladits Jr, Charles, 6, 190, 208
Szladits, Károly, 25, 29–31

Tallián, Tibor, 77, 213
Tallós, György, 30
Teleki, Pál, 62, 63
Thau, Shirley, 216, 317n73
Truman, Harry, 2, 39, *40*, 304
trusteeship (U.S. Law), 6, 90, 99n4, 138, 149, 184, 217, 219, 265, 271, 276, 279, 283, 303, 316, 329, 350, 355–57, 379
Tufts University, 332

Újfallusy, József, 327
Ullein-Reviczky, Antal, 64
Universal Edition, 5, 17, 168, 203, 231, 243, 244, 246, 248, 252, 253, 256, 263, 277, 279, 284, 286, 314, 350, 366–68, 371, 373, 377, 391
University of Iowa, 56, 178, 188, 190, 191, 332

Vajda, Ernő, 143, 253, 275, 295, 310n73, 311, 329
Vámbéry, Rusztem, 69, 70, 72, 346
Várdy, Stephen Béla, 61, 69
Varga, Nike, 264, 278
Vékás, Lajos, 2, 25n18, 30, 31
Veress, Sándor, 279
Vietnam, 3, 30, 40, 299–301, 306, 307, 317, 349

411

Index

Vietorisz, Tamás, 187, 190
Vinton, John, 278, 282
Vox Productions, 162, 222

Waldbauer-Kerpély Quartet, 177
Waldbauer, Imre, 25, 43, 56, 57, 88, 147, 157, 176, 177, 181, 184, *186*, 188–92
Waldbauer, Isabella, 56, 177, 181, *186*, 191, 192
Waldbauer, Iván, 22n11, 56n5, 157, 163, 168, 175–77, 179, 180, 182, 187–92, 278, 282, 285, 294, 318, *319*, 322, 326, 335

Weiss family, 60, 65, 177
Weiss Manfréd Co., 26n21, 33
Weiss, Alphons, 176, 184
Wigler, Stephen, 229n31, 291
Wolff, Christoph, 11

Zathureczky, Ede, 160n6
Zeneműkiadó Vállalat, 251, 307, 322, 323, 366, 367
Zimbler Sinfonietta, 257
Zinsser, Barbara, 214, 267, 268, 272, 273